REVENGE
FOR THE
SIXTIES

SAM ALITO
AND THE **TRIUMPH** OF THE
CONSERVATIVE LEGAL MOVEMENT

PETER S. CANELLOS

Simon & Schuster
New York   Amsterdam/Antwerp   London
Toronto   Sydney/Melbourne   New Delhi

Simon & Schuster
1230 Avenue of the Americas
New York, NY 10020

First Simon & Schuster hardcover edition April 2026

SIMON & SCHUSTER and colophon are registered trademarks of Simon & Schuster, LLC

Simon & Schuster strongly believes in freedom of expression and stands against censorship in all its forms. For more information, visit BooksBelong.com.

For information about special discounts for bulk purchases, please contact Simon & Schuster Special Sales at 1-866-506-1949 or business@simonandschuster.com.

The Simon & Schuster Speakers Bureau can bring authors to your live event. For more information or to book an event, contact the Simon & Schuster Speakers Bureau at 1-866-248-3049 or visit our website at www.simonspeakers.com.

Interior design by Silverglass

Manufactured in the United States of America

10 9 8 7 6 5 4 3 2 1

Library of Congress Cataloging-in-Publication data is available.

ISBN 978-1-6682-0002-5
ISBN 978-1-6682-0004-9 (ebook)

Scan here to get book recommendations, exclusive offers, and more delivered to your inbox.

To Charlie, Luiza, Will, and Peter Savage

Contents

BOOK TWO: THE MOVEMENT

BOOK THREE: THE COURT

REVENGE
FOR THE
SIXTIES

The New World

S ome moments live forever.

For the nine-year-old boy standing on the green between Chestnut Avenue and Division Street in Trenton, New Jersey, this was one of those moments. Sunday, October 25, 1959.[1] Warm with only a few drops of rain.[2] Dressed in his Sunday best.

His impeccable appearance reflected his family's abundant pride. Two years earlier, in a white jacket and tie, he had joined his little sister in her plaid holiday skirt and saddle shoes in handing out presents at the Widows' and Single Women's Home on Spring Street. That act of kindness was memorialized in the *Trenton Sunday Times-Advertiser*.[3] A few weeks afterward, he recited his own original story, "A Squirrel's Christmas," at the Story Lady's hour at Trenton State Museum. A reporter for the *Trenton Evening Times* marveled that the boy "has written over 20 stories."[4]

Now he was part of a bigger event, one that traced the arc of his young life and burnished the legacy that was already so central to it. Just blocks from where his father and grandparents had lived after they emigrated from Italy forty-five years earlier, the Italian-American Civic League was fulfilling its own five-decade-long dream.[5] At a sentinel location facing busy Hamilton Avenue, the community was raising a bronze statue of Christopher Columbus, looking bold and courageous at the prow of his ship, eyes alight for the New World.[6]

The real journey being commemorated, however, was that of Trenton's Italian American community, which now accounted for roughly 25 percent of the city's foreign-born population.[7] For Trenton's Italians, the last century had been a rough passage: their poverty ridiculed, their ethnicity derided. "That the gang of Italians who are quartered in tents . . . are enjoying a pleasant life is evidenced by the amount of food and liquid refreshments they have on hand," quipped the *Daily State Gazette* in 1903.[8] The *Daily True American* was more grimly to the point: "Little Italy Must Keep Place Clean," it headlined, warning that "neighbors have become alarmed lest some epidemic may ensue because of the entire lack of sanitation."[9]

The *Advertiser* followed up the next year, bemoaning "Many Foreign Names on Business Signs," such as "Joseph Cipolla, saloon keeper" and "John Luisi, shoe dealer."[10] That story began: "With the growth of the Roebling wire cable manufacturing industry there has developed in the vicinity of the giant plant a distinctly foreign colony that occupies large solid sections of several streets, although its bounds are becoming less distinct as new accessions of laborers are scattered into adjacent neighborhoods."[11]

That neighborhood was Chambersburg, where both of the boy's parents had grown up in crowded row houses.[12] And the Roebling plant wasn't just any factory of the early twentieth century—with whispered tales of workers' limbs being sliced by wire-making machines and day-long shifts amid deafening noises—it was a leading edge of the industrial revolution. Its wire cables held up suspension bridges that spanned rivers and harbors. The sheer strength of its products was magnificent, revolutionary, game-changing.[13] The boy's grandfather—the lucky one, on his mother's side—was employed there.[14] He was grateful for the job. Working at Roebling made a man feel a part of something bigger than himself. And if that man had been born in the rural Basilicata region of Italy, the move from farming and peasantry to making something that helped connect the world was epochal.[15]

There were, of course, the prejudiced neighbors who cloaked their fear of immigrants in the usual hogwash about the pope and unsanitary conditions and the mob-like padrone system.[16] But those who questioned whether Italians belonged on the streets of Trenton, where George Washington had once marshaled his forces against the British, needed to check their facts. A full 284 years before the Battle of Trenton, an adventurer from Genoa made a journey of discovery from Old World to New. He was Italian, not English; Catholic, not Protestant. And he was every inch the progenitor of the northern Europeans who came later. His face—sunburned and large-featured, under a flowing mane of hair—was as much an icon of North America as John Winthrop's or William Penn's.

For Italian Americans, Columbus was central to their sense of belonging. Just five years earlier, in 1954, the Italian Line had begun transatlantic service along its warm southern route on a sleek white flagship named the *Cristoforo Colombo*. Its maiden voyage traced the path of the *Pinta, Nina*, and *Santa Maria*. Every back and forth across the Atlantic strengthened the ties between Italy and America. "Theme of the décor is the life of Christopher Columbus, one in which a team of the country's architects and artists could co-operate with affection and enthusiasm," crowed *The New York Times*.[17]

Now a nine-year-old Italian American from the Trenton area could gaze up at an image of that very same hero, created by the principal sculptor to the Vatican.[18] The finished work had been transported to New Jersey in thirteen pieces, by way of Boston and an unfortunately timed longshoreman's strike that postponed the dedication beyond Columbus Day.[19]

Once lovingly reassembled, the statue seemed to light up all of Chambersburg. A brimming crowd glowed with pride. The Italian consul gave a speech attesting to the excitement of the government of Italy and its ambassador.[20] City officials scrambled to rename the green Columbus Park in honor of the festivities.[21]

This was the moment, with their hero taking a place of honor alongside those of the Revolutionary War, when Italian Americans really arrived in Trenton. The statue was their flag in the ground. And for the nine-year-old boy and the others in the crowd, it felt good to be home.

Of course by that point, the boy's actual home was not in Chambersburg, with its railroad clatter, belching chimneys, and giant water tower. His parents had scrimped and saved, working odd jobs to pay for teacher's college and then graduate school. Their reward was a suburban tract house ten minutes down the road in Hamilton Township, where the only noise was from lawnmowers.[22] This wasn't a rejection of the old neighborhood. Far from it. It was a natural progression of an immigrant story that began in Chambersburg—or in the mind's eye, on the wooden decking of the *Pinta, Nina,* or *Santa Maria.*

Chambersburg didn't sit still either. Through the restless decades that followed, more children grew up and moved out. They left behind aging parents, but in time, the whole community turned over.[23] The Roebling plant produced its last cable in 1974, its once-thriving industrial campus transformed into a Superfund site of decaying buildings, broken glass, and rusted machinery.[24] Workers fled, their empty houses taken over by newcomers from Guatemala, Costa Rica, and Ecuador.[25]

Suddenly, the Italian Peoples Bakery & Deli on Butler Street—"a tradition since 1936"—became a lonely outpost, as much a remnant of the city's past as the 1719 William Trent House Museum.[26] Around it popped up new businesses bearing Spanish names, like Mi Tierra mini market, Quetzal social services, and Nueva Imagen barber shop.[27]

Nor did perceptions of American history remain as steadfast as in the boy's youth. In 1980, liberal historian Howard Zinn published *A People's History of the United States,* challenging many of the heroic tales that the Baby Boom generation—growing up amid a Cold War celebration of freedom and justice—had been taught in public schools.[28] Columbus was a major target: he brought not civilization but exploitation, in Zinn's estimation, opening the western hemisphere to slavery, colonization, genocide, and human trafficking.[29] Many of the specific allegations raised by Zinn and others have been disputed, but an underlying question remains: Were revisionists using current-day standards to blame Columbus for all the evils and injustices of fifteenth-century Europe?

By the dawn of the 2000s, these shifting perceptions were not lost on the people of Chambersburg, where many immigrants came from places that had been directly impacted by Columbus's actions. The huge statue looming above the park between Chestnut and Division became more of a target than an inspiration.[30] Reactions were crude, visceral, and disrespectful. In 2018, protesters doused the statue in red paint, a stain that proved impossible to erase.[31]

"These are not intended to be harsh words," wrote *Trentonian* columnist L. A. Parker in 2020, "but when Italians fled the Burg [Chambersburg] and Trenton during a white flight precipitated by riots, a deterioration of the city's education system, and the arrival of Spanish speaking neighbors and African Americans, they should have considered taking Columbus with them."[32]

Some Italian Americans defended Columbus, but with dwindling vigor; a GoFundMe campaign to restore the statue raised only $610 out of its $8,000 goal. Others were sympathetic to the idea that the Columbus story was troubling to many of their newer neighbors.

On July 8, 2020, city workers dismantled the statue and hauled the pieces to a warehouse, leaving only the boat-shaped stump surrounded by green-painted plywood. "What we know about Columbus simply makes his image a poor fit for a city as diverse as Trenton," concluded Mayor Reed Gusciora, an Italian American who was also the first openly gay non-incumbent to be elected to the New Jersey legislature.[33]

Maria Richardson, the city's director of recreation, natural resources, and culture, was more emphatic: "I'm Dominican and I'm thrilled he's gone. It's amazing, but we have so many monuments that honor him in the Dominican Republic. It's a shame because educated people know his real story."[34]

Yet there was one person who never forgot that magical October day in 1959. For the nine-year-old boy, the meaning of that event remained deeply ingrained.

The boy was now a man—and quite an old man by the standards of any position, except, perhaps, the one that he attained. He was a justice of the US Supreme Court. Everyone who followed the news knew the name of Samuel A. Alito Jr. A hero to many, he had spent much of his judicial career at the vanguard of the conservative legal movement.

The kind of social revisionism that led to the destruction of the Columbus statue rankled him. It was unfair to people whose hopes, dreams, and even identity were founded on the assumptions of an earlier time.[35]

Extending the arm of justice to those people was a facet of his jurisprudence as well. Specifically, he cited tradition—but only those traditions that were openly acknowledged when the Constitution came into effect—as a means of deciding which practices should be shielded from government interference. Thus, he extended even greater legal protection to social conservatives whose present-day practices might be considered outmoded or even discriminatory by some.

That's because Alito himself had been buffeted by shifting values. His high school years culminated in the deadly Trenton race riots following the murder of Martin Luther King Jr.[36] His college years began as part of the last all-male class to enter Princeton University; social complications arrived along with women in his sophomore year.[37] His time in ROTC rendered him a victim of anti–Vietnam War protesters when his military trainers got booted off campus after a student strike.[38] His law school years coincided with the Supreme Court's granting of abortion rights; some of *Roe v. Wade*'s earliest and most insistent academic critics were teaching at Yale Law School while he was a student there.[39]

To those who knew him in those years, Alito was an enigma: shy and straitlaced, but also kind and polite. He took note of the social tumult around him but wasn't a participant. He was bright and conservative by nature, but also respectful and unthreatening. Friends could see vestiges of the perfectly-turned-out boy in the somewhat stiff and nervous adult.[40]

After joining the Supreme Court in 2006, he seemed to find his voice—and a much rougher version of it than he had shown before. His certitude resonated with tens of millions of Americans. They, like Alito, believed that the rock-solid truths they were raised with had been violated, distorted, and even deliberately misunderstood by people trying to assert their own identities.

On the biggest issues of the day, he laid down his thoughts with admirable clarity and fixity of purpose. And most surprising to those who knew him in his younger years, he rarely hesitated to speak out in public.[41] Unlike some of his Supreme Court colleagues, who confined themselves to their written work, Alito hastened to make his voice heard. This was especially true in the face of perceived slights—whether he was blurting out his disagreement at a State of the Union address or rallying fellow conservatives at a Federalist Society convention.[42]

So when he learned about Trenton's decision to tear down the Columbus statue, he wanted to have his say—to share his anguish and offer a history lesson to those who desecrated the memory of his ancestors. His vehicle was an interview in *We the Italians*, an online publication that aimed to create bonds among people of Italian heritage.[43]

He recounted being present at the dedication of the statue and declared himself to be "very upset" by its fate. "Columbus was seen as a hero because his discovery brought about European settlement in the New World, which was celebrated," Alito said. "Paradoxically, this very accomplishment is why many today see him as a villain."[44]

This statement—a disarmingly simple explanation for conflicts that others might find complex and multifaceted—was typical of Alito. His concern was less for the wrong done to Columbus than the one done to those who'd once embraced him. The great explorer had at one time been a hero to all—"it's why many cities in the United States are named Columbus"—but for Italians, he meant that much more, and that's why they were especially injured in the backlash.[45]

"When Italian immigrants arrived here, they were often scorned. Many thought they were hopelessly backward and could never fit in. Looking for a way to say that they did belong, Italian Americans, exercising a bit of *furbezza* [a Sicilian term for cunning], simply latched onto the Columbus symbol that the general population already knew and valued," he said. "These immigrants, like my grandparents, were overwhelmingly poor and had little formal education. I venture to say that they did not know a lot about the details of Columbus's actions in the New World. What they knew was that he was Italian; he took a great chance in leaving the Old World behind; he suffered hardships during his voyage, but ultimately he 'discovered' America. And knowing these bare facts, they said to themselves: 'That's our story too. We took a big chance, left everything we knew behind, had a difficult time at first in our new home, but now we belong—because after all, our countryman discovered this place.'"[46]

And now Columbus's reputation and their faith in him were crushed, erased by a dawning political correctness. Just like so much of the world of the 1950s and 1960s.

Alito's condemnation drew little notice in Trenton. Except for a sheaf of clippings in the "Trentoniana" section of the public library, the city is largely unmindful of his roots there. But his response to the destruction of the Columbus statue echoed a larger worldview that, filtered through his legal opinions, now resonates in many corners of American life.

In his view, he's fighting to restore the original understanding of the Constitution and protect the people it intended to protect. In practice, his rulings often serve to help those whose lives mirror his own upbringing. The Alito saga is a parable of family, faith, and achievement, set against a series of percussive blows that challenged those beliefs. Many of the most meaningful encounters of his life were touched by conflict—usually initiated by people who saw his values as an affront to their own. At bottom, his story isn't simply a boy-makes-good tale of immigrant striving and achievement: it's an American narrative of struggle between competing interests and players.

It is also emblematic of the great passions behind the movement he helped nurture, one that has grown to ninety thousand lawyers, law students, and scholars.[47] Over four decades, it shifted from the fringes of power—afternoon meetups at a gold-lacquered restaurant in Washington's Chinatown during the 1990s—to dominate the Supreme Court.[48] Alito's own trajectory reflects that of the movement, from his religious, idealistic, and baseball-loving childhood in the suburbs of the 1950s and early 1960s to his increasingly defensive posture in the 1970s and 1980s and hardening of purpose in the decades that followed.

To believers, the conservative legal movement has brought logic and consistency back to the bench. It has banished the judicial revisionism of earlier decades. Its oft-cited mantra has been "A judge must interpret the law, not make the law."

"A judge can't have any agenda," Alito avowed at his 2006 confirmation hearing, in a quote proudly displayed in the presidential library of the man who appointed him, George W. Bush. "The judge's only obligation—and it's a solemn obligation—is to the rule of law. And what that means is that in every single case, the judge has to do what the law requires."[49]

Whether a plan to restore the original meaning of the law is, in fact, an agenda—rather than the absence of an agenda—is the central question of the conservative legal movement. Two decades after Alito's confirmation as a justice of the Supreme Court, the movement's success in remaking the legal landscape calls its early precepts into question. How did an initiative that began as a show of deference become a cause for activism? And whose values are being vindicated: the Founding Fathers' or their self-appointed saviors'?

The sheer force of Alito's feelings—as demonstrated by his fury over the Columbus statue—challenges his claim of judicial neutrality. He and his followers believe they are defending what is, if not a literal truth, then a broadly accepted understanding about the underpinnings of American life. Many of these ideas grew out of religious teachings or some confluence of loyalty to church and country, and thus can be defended as free exercise of faith. It is a sincere and intelligently wrought theory, but one born of intense feelings of anger and betrayal. It seeks to impose what its adherents believe to be right and just from the halcyon memories of their childhoods. And it has rocked the facade of American law in the twenty-first century.

June 24, 2022

The chaos of America in a time of internet-fueled rage filled the Capitol area and spilled down the hill toward giant Union Station. Colorfully dressed protesters, like figures in a French puppet theater, prayed and hugged and cried. They wielded signs like weapons. Sometimes they jostled each other, only to be herded by police. Their slogans betrayed their unyielding beliefs, from "Human Rights Begin in the Womb" to "Pro-Life Is a Lie."[1]

Their stage was the Supreme Court Building in Washington, DC. Its massive staircase and blindfolded Justice statue were blocked by an eight-foot chain-link fence. The "non-scalable" barrier was similar to the one that had cordoned off the Capitol a year and a half earlier, in the wake of the January 6, 2021, riots.[2] The siege-like atmosphere made an effective backdrop to the drama unfolding on the plazas below.

In truth, these types of dueling protests had been occurring across the country for so long that it was fair to wonder if the demonstrators might lay down their placards and break for coffee together. But the vast size of this congregation signaled something unusual and striking in its finality. It was the last Friday of the court's 2021–22 term, and the culmination of a decades-long effort to remake the country's justice system.

Everyone knew what would be coming when the court announced its decisions that day, which added to the uniqueness of the moment. Someone had leaked a draft of the biggest case of the decade: *Dobbs v. Jackson Women's Health Organization*, a withdrawal of abortion rights granted in the 1973 case *Roe v. Wade*.[3] Leaking a judicial decision simply wasn't done; it violated the honor system that had shielded the court's deliberations for more than two centuries. But in recent decades, that honor system had taken a strange turn.

Roe v. Wade came down nineteen years after the court struck down racial segregation in *Brown v. Board of Education.* Those cases bookended two decades of progressive actions. None of the jurists involved in the decisions had been nominated to bring about specific results; rather, the justices—all men and, until 1967, all white—had struggled with their consciences to accommodate the social changes of their era.[4] Old prejudices and gender roles were dying away; the court felt that society's evolution should be reflected in its interpretation of the Constitution. So the removal of legal consent for segregation in 1954 was followed by the granting of new rights to use contraception and enter into interracial marriages. Attention to the plight of racial minorities and the underprivileged also led to enhanced rights to legal representation and freedom from unwarranted searches.[5]

Each of these decisions—hailed as breakthroughs by many progressives—was at least narrowly popular among the general public, as was the granting of abortion rights. But by 1973, opposition was starting to harden. People who disagreed with the court wondered why they had been thwarted by unelected judges rather than allowed to pursue their aims through political channels. The basis for judicial authority was the US Constitution, but how could its umbrella expand so vastly without there being any change in its wording?

Cultural discomfort yielded intellectual critiques of the court's vision of an evolving Constitution. Soon, these critiques had a name, originalism, and a solemn creed: the Constitution is a bulwark—its protections do not stretch just because a judge thinks they should. Times may change, but the document's original meaning does not.

Originalism had the appeal of solidity, continuity, and fidelity to first principles. But it was also radical. Adherents believed that many of the rights granted in recent decades were unconstitutional on their face, even if some, such as the right to contraception, had become deeply ingrained. They were left to ponder which cases deserved to be maintained as legal precedents, simply because so many people relied upon them, and which needed to be overturned. For most of the court's history, it was loath to reopen settled questions, believing that if the justices kept reversing themselves, the public would lose confidence in them—and in justice itself.

Would such fears ever come to pass? What began as law school chatter among conservatives—many of them the children and grandchildren of European immigrants—became a loosely and then somewhat less loosely organized movement. In 1982, three students from Yale and the University of Chicago law schools recruited about two hundred of their peers for a weekend seminar in New Haven, Connecticut, blandly titled "A Symposium on Federalism: Legal and Political Ramifications."

There, the students hobnobbed with giddy members of the nascent Reagan administration, one of whom, Justice Department official Ted Olson, remarked, "I sense that we are at one of those points in history where the pendulum may be beginning to swing in another direction."[6] He was referring to an academic culture that was pushing new frontiers of legal action, animated by visions of a constitutional right to social welfare payments, while critics from even further regions of the left called into question every precedent created by all-male, white-privileged courts.[7] Excited by Olson's prediction of a looming backlash, the students decided to organize themselves into a debating society, dubbed the Federalist Society, to road test new arguments for old themes of limited government and judicial restraint.

The sense that old-is-new-again struck a chord with middle-class strivers of the Baby Boom generation. For many of them, the triumph of American ideals was a living legacy, attested to by mothers and fathers and grandparents. The rightness of the Founding Fathers was an unassailable truth depicted in public school textbooks of the era; it was what made America a beacon to immigrants when fascism and communism ravaged their European homelands. While some people clearly felt that advancing the freedoms of those who were excluded from the mainstream was true to the spirit of the Founding Fathers, young conservatives felt the opposite: the trigger for such decisions was most often a judge, not the Constitution; liberal jurists were replacing the founders' judgments with their own.

This intellectual criticism—a diligent student's desire for logic and consistency in the law—quickly dovetailed with politics. It was easy to forget that Ronald Reagan was just the second Republican president in a century to win the South. His triumph over Georgia native Jimmy Carter had been fueled by the religious right. Its lurch into politics was intended both to block federal actions to desegregate private schools and—notably—to preserve the sanctity of life in the womb. Reagan wanted to satisfy those demands, and that required nominating a different kind of judicial candidate for the federal bench: someone with a proven allegiance to originalist principles.[8]

The result was something unprecedented since the presidency of John Adams: a concerted, multigenerational effort to remake the country's legal system, judgeship by judgeship, case by case, to bring about a specific set of aims.

Intellectual ferment, political demands to end abortion rights, and the credentialing of conservative jurists all exploded over succeeding decades, helped along by lavishly funded think tanks and foundations. The Federalist Society morphed from a handful of students to a ninety-thousand-member behemoth. Soon enough, all the strands of the movement would converge, like train tracks approaching a station, and a powerful new locomotive would be pulling American law to the right.

Still, the overturning of *Roe v. Wade* remained a cherished goal that hovered on the horizon, close enough to glimpse but tantalizingly out of reach. As much as advocates prayed for it, dreamed of it, and even prepared for it, it remained amorphous. Part of the reason was the haze that surrounded the judicial confirmation process: nominees refused to offer views on abortion rights and saw benefit in hinting that they might actually reject their own party's dogma. Conservatives swore their fidelity to precedent, suggesting they might well adhere to *Roe* as a matter of *stare decisis*, the doctrine of applying settled law. Alternatively, the justices could simply peck away at abortion rights, allowing more and more restrictions, without taking the precipitous step of removing a right that had already been granted.

By 2022, a combination of hardball political tactics and fortuitous timing had given conservatives a 6–3 majority on the court. The death of Justice Ruth Bader Ginsburg in the waning days of the first Trump administration and her replacement with Amy Coney Barrett were desperate blows to liberal hopes. Still, it was far from certain that these justices would seize on the first opportunity available—a challenge to a Mississippi law restricting most abortions to the first fifteen weeks of gestation—to overturn forty-nine years of protection for women seeking to terminate their pregnancies. For one thing, they had a potential fallback: simply approving the fifteen-week ban as a reasonable restriction, without declaring that no right to abortion existed at all.

But the scaffolding fell away in early May, when *Politico* published a leaked opinion of *Dobbs v. Jackson Women's Health Organization*, which called *Roe* "egregiously wrong."

The unthinkable had happened. A 7–2 majority for abortion rights had, over forty-nine years of legal and political battle, become a 5–4 vote against.[9] In fact, the overturning of *Roe* was only the most visible of dozens of conservative victories that upended the legal structure of the 1960s through the 2020s, on issues ranging from campaign finance to environmental protection to voting rights.

But on the biggest case of all—the high point of the revolution that began a half-century earlier—the tens of millions of readers who downloaded the draft opinion saw a familiar name. It was that of one of the most dedicated and determined of legal warriors, a child of suburban America of the 1950s, a man whose certitude was masked only by his deadpan logic and somewhat awkward personality.

The name was Samuel Anthony Alito Jr.

. . . .

To THE ABORTION-RIGHTS PROTESTERS holding signs, the *Dobbs* decision was the fruit of bare-knuckle politics and unrestrained spending by religious conservatives. It was a devious hijacking of power by the few against the many.

Portraying *Dobbs* as a tactical victory of single-minded activists over the quiescent masses echoed some of the same depictions, decades earlier, of liberal victories. But it ignored the primary drivers of the conservative legal movement.

From its inception, the movement had been a direct response to the jurisprudence of Chief Justice Earl Warren and his brethren, fused with a cultural backlash against the social changes of the 1960s. According to this unusual alliance, the Warren Court had violated the pure creed of America. It had made itself the primary enforcer of equality, undercutting the notion of pulling yourself up by your own bootstraps and earning your place in society.

Linking the conservative movement to the fight against abortion added a further jolt of action, passion, and organization. Rural evangelicals and urban Catholics who'd never read a legal casebook began rooting for the conservative legal movement.

As it gained steam through the decades, the movement acquired many fathers—and a few mothers as well. There were the students who started the Federalist Society and went on to be leaders for decades; there were presidents and attorneys general, including Reagan's chief lieutenant, Ed Meese; and there were the ideological architects who straddled the worlds of academia and judging.

Samuel Alito was not the first self-described originalist to join the Supreme Court, but he was the one most emblematic of the movement.[10] The earlier generation of conservative jurists—led by Robert Bork and Antonin Scalia—had built the academic foundation of originalism. While teaching at Yale and the University of Chicago, where each cultivated a nest of protégés, Bork and Scalia preached conservatism to overwhelmingly liberal communities of scholars.

Part gadflies and happy warriors, they made a virtue of being outnumbered; it gave them the gravitas and rectitude of principled dissenters. At the same time, they learned how to survive, and even to thrive, as conservatives in a liberal playground; they could lustily disagree with liberal pals in faculty-lounge debates and then repair together to a favorite restaurant or theater. Scalia's love of opera fueled his friendship with liberal antagonist Ruth Bader Ginsburg—she fondly remembered sharing home-cooked meals, shopping for rugs, and watching him belt out an aria at a benefit dinner for the Washington National Opera.[11]

This was law as a priesthood in which well-meaning people exchanged ideas and strove to bring about a constitutionally correct result; each shared the love of digging through common-law tropes and early American texts and obscure Supreme Court rulings. The intellectual combat was real, but the underlying commitment to legal exploration was joyful and communal. "When we sat next to each other on the D.C. Circuit, I occasionally pinched myself hard to avoid uncontrollable laughter in response to one of his quips," Ginsburg recalled of herself and Scalia.[12]

Much of the bonhomie evaporated as the conservative legal movement took hold, provoking an equally resolute liberal response. Everyone in the legal system became intensely aware of which side they were on. Gone were the days when Scalia could be waved onto the Supreme Court by a 98–0 vote, having spent his confirmation hearing jovially introducing senators to his wife and nine children while joking about beating Howard Metzenbaum, the liberal senator of Ohio, in tennis.[13]

By the time Samuel Alito was nominated for the same position almost twenty years later, in late 2005, a press release from liberal pressure groups dubbed him "Scalito," suggesting he was merely a clone of the court's most conservative member.[14] The term was condemned as an ethnic slur, even while some commentators saw truth in it. Alito, however, was no personality match for the flamboyant Scalia; the contrasts between the two illustrated the difference between generations of conservatives, and also between an individualist and a member of a movement.

Alito's career was boosted at almost every juncture by a large infrastructure of conservative supporters. As a young lawyer applying to the Reagan Justice Department, he was asked to put in writing his conservative credentials and quizzed on when and why he identified as conservative.[15] Some in the administration, like his future Supreme Court colleague Clarence Thomas, had their own distinctive and sometimes startling tales of conversion from liberalism to conservatism. But while Thomas was an outlier—a poor Black kid from rural Georgia who came to reject his own progressive ideas—Alito was more typical.

He had been conservative from the start. He could cite many of the same life experiences as other leaders of the movement: a deeply religious upbringing, patriotism rooted in a Cold War sense of American values being challenged from the left, and—most strikingly—a series of direct encounters with liberal protesters during his college years that left him embittered. Yet he had an answer for them: his stated desire to "warm a seat on the Supreme Court," enshrined in his own college yearbook.[16]

After he proved sufficiently right of center to gain entry into Reagan's DOJ, every successive job or nomination was based at least in part on his ability to demonstrate a solidly conservative record. Being conservative was foremost among his professional credentials.

Alito never spent a day in the collegial confines of an academic faculty. Rather, he toiled for fifteen years as a circuit court judge, just a rung below the Supreme Court, writing on hundreds of cases while knowing that every one of them would be scrutinized by both purists on the right and critics ready to pounce on the left. It was a dizzying balancing act.

His chance at the high court finally arrived, at the precipitous age of fifty-five, with the resignation of Sandra Day O'Connor. Alito was on a short list of five potential nominees.[17] It was based on the George W. Bush administration's consultations with dozens of legal conservatives, most of them members of the Federalist Society. In his long years of service on the lower court, while a Federalist Society member in good standing, Alito had passed the high bar demanded by the conservative legal movement.

Bush said he was waiting to be dazzled by one of the candidates, including Alito. He was—by the far less experienced John G. Roberts Jr.[18] But fate handed Alito a reprieve: Chief Justice William Rehnquist died before Roberts could be confirmed. Bush decided to elevate Roberts to the chief's position, reopening the O'Connor seat.

When the president's choice of a new nominee came down, it was a shocker. Bush had bypassed the administration's short list to elevate his chief White House counsel, Harriet Miers. By historic standards, Miers was a qualified nominee. A onetime elected member of the Dallas City Council, she had rung up an impressive string of firsts: first woman managing partner of her law firm, first woman president of the Dallas Bar Association, first woman president of the Texas Bar Association. All that experience, along with her years assessing delicate legal matters in the Bush White House, made her a credible candidate for the court.

But to the conservative legal movement, she was a complete unknown, a cipher. Choosing Miers was an act of "cronyism," in the words of Georgetown law professor and Federalist Society stalwart Randy Barnett, who penned a quick *Wall Street Journal* op-ed raising grave objections. "To be qualified, a Supreme Court justice must have more than credentials; she must have a well-considered 'judicial philosophy,'" he wrote.[19]

Barnett's attack was echoed by dozens of other leading conservative intellectuals who plainly saw danger in Miers's blank slate. This was a sixty-year-old, never-married woman whom conservatives had to trust to overturn *Roe v. Wade*; it seemed like a risky bet, to say the least. The anger of Federalist Society members only grew when it was revealed that Miers had declined to join the group because, as she had explained in an early interview, "it's better to not be involved in organizations that seem to color your view."[20]

After days of siege, Miers withdrew from consideration. Alito—the proven conservative who had earned the unreserved approval of the movement through more years on the bench than any nominee in seven decades—was the obvious successor. His qualifications were the reverse image of hers. He had privately bemoaned the Miers nomination as costing him his best chance to achieve the goal he'd first laid out in college.[21] Now he would be the man to carry the movement forward. Finally, Bush made the call.

On June 24, 2022, when *Roe v. Wade* went down, the full impact of that chain of events would forcefully be felt.

....

THE REASON FOR ALITO'S selection, as author of the decision, became clear when the court officially released its opinion that morning, to the cries and cheers of the thousands gathered outside the building. Normally, the chief justice gets to choose which colleague writes the majority opinion when the chief himself is in the majority, and on such a momentous case, it might have been assumed that Roberts would write it himself. But he wasn't entirely in the majority. He agreed with the decision to uphold the Mississippi law but felt that overturning abortion rights entirely went beyond the requirements of resolving the case—a serious accusation against the other five justices in the majority. Roberts felt the court could have upheld Mississippi's fifteen-week rule without overturning *Roe*, and thus should not have done so.

When the chief is out of sync with the majority, the senior justice among that bloc gets the next shot at assigning the opinion. That was Clarence Thomas. But Thomas, as became clear in his concurring opinion, wanted to go beyond overturning *Roe*: he felt that any right granted under the due process clause of the Fourteenth Amendment that was substantive, as opposed to procedural, should be subject to review.[22] That analysis would imperil the rights to contraception, gay marriage, and many more—a Pandora's box that even his fellow conservatives weren't willing to open.

Thomas passed the baton to Alito, who brought his firm convictions to the task. It was the assignment of a lifetime, the fulfillment of a career shaped in a large part by criticism of all that *Roe* represented. The skills he'd honed through three years as a champion debater at Steinert High in Hamilton Township, New Jersey;[23] as president of the debate panel under the umbrella of Princeton's lavishly named Whig-Cliosophic Society;[24] and as a student at Yale Law School listening to professors bemoan the rationale behind *Roe* all came together in an eighty-page dissertation aimed not so much at overturning *Roe* as stamping it dead.

"Abortion presents a profound moral issue . . ."[25]

The very first words off Alito's pen reflected a precept that guided him as a devout Catholic: abortion is a moral wrong. He'd never discussed his personal views in public, but when he was appointed to the court, his ninety-year-old mother stated definitively, "He is against abortion. We both are."[26] No one doubted it, as he had grown up in a church that preached that life began at conception. Though Alito presented the issue as one that provoked "sharply conflicting views," his decision to frame it from the outset through a moral lens, rather than as an expression of personal liberty, signaled his underlying beliefs.

"Even though the Constitution makes no mention of abortion, the Court held that it confers a broad right to obtain one."[27]

The Supreme Court's willingness to protect rights not specified in the Constitution was a source of fear and motivation for legal conservatives; it meant that liberal jurists could expand social liberties by drawing imprecise analogies and citing open-ended provisions of the Constitution. One such provision, the Ninth Amendment, openly touts the existence of such liberties, stating, "The enumeration in the Constitution, of certain rights, shall not be construed to deny or disparage others retained by the people." But Alito and his conservative brethren held that to have any effect, a right must be based on purely objective standards, not a judge's sense of what the country sees as fair and correct.

"That provision has been held to guarantee some rights that are not mentioned in the Constitution, but any such right must be 'deeply rooted in this Nation's history and tradition' and 'implicit in the concept of ordered liberty.'"[28]

Narrowing the standard for unenumerated rights was a decades-long goal of the conservative movement. Alito's quotations are from an opinion by Chief Justice William Rehnquist—one of two dissenters in *Roe*—in an assisted-suicide case from 1997.[29] By demanding that unenumerated rights be implicit in the nation's history and tradition, jurists can effectively freeze the Constitution at the moment of ratification. Were abortion rights a facet of the nation's early history? If not, they can't possibly gain constitutional protection.

"We do not pretend to know how our political system or society will respond to today's decision overruling Roe *. . . And even if we could foresee what will happen, we would have no authority to let that knowledge influence our decision."*[30]

Alito addressed centuries-long questions about a judge's role with the certitude for which he is famous; from his early years, people marveled at his ability to quickly reduce complicated issues to pithy nubs of right

and wrong. Are judges really barred from worrying about how their decisions will play out? And who denies them that authority? These are
glaringly open questions, but in Alito's words, they sound almost like
eternal truths.

"Roe *was on a collision course with the Constitution from the day it was
decided.*"[31]

Alito laid down a memorable one-sentence condemnation as he con-
signed *Roe* to history. His contempt for the abortion-rights decision bordered on ridicule. *Roe* was not just a mistaken decision but a deliberate
assault on the rule of law: a flagrant foul on the playing field of justice.

Now it was gone, and Alito slipped into his opinion other markers of the
long years of frustration leading up to this moment. He quoted the "famous"
attack on *Roe* made by Yale Law School professor John Hart Ely when he,
Alito, was a student there.[32] He went over old, heavily tilled ground in citing
the unworkability of *Roe*'s successor case, *Planned Parenthood of Southeastern
Pennsylvania v. Casey*, for which he himself was a dissenter during his circuit
court years.[33] His 2022 argument in victory tracked closely with his 1992
dissenting opinion in defeat.[34]

At the moment when the *Dobbs* case moved from draft opinion to law
of the land, however, Alito himself was absent. Pandemic procedures allowed decisions to be released without the justices appearing. After the
draft had leaked, rumors flew that he and his wife, Martha-Ann, had been
forced to flee their Alexandria, Virginia, home. Fox News host Jesse Watters claimed the Alitos had been "moved now to an undisclosed location."
After similar reports flooded conservative media, *Politico* traced the story
back to a legal commentator, who said, "I forget whether I saw the rumor
on Twitter or somebody told me."[35]

Still, Alito had reason to fear for his safety. In the wee hours of
June 8, a California man had been arrested near the home of Justice
Brett Kavanaugh in Chevy Chase, Maryland. The man—who was in
possession of a handgun, ammunition, a crowbar, and pepper spray—
had called 911 and turned himself in, saying he had suicidal thoughts
and planned to kill Kavanaugh.[36]

Like the spectacle outside the court building, the specter of justices holed up in their homes, as if under house arrest, seemed a sad portent: Was the Supreme Court verging on an era when justices would be hounded like politicians, their decisions assailed as partisan missives?

The breakdown in order masked another change: originalism had, in a scant four decades, come to dominate American law. The Supreme Court's 6–3 conservative majority was fortified by billions of dollars funneled from donors to Federalist Society co-chairman Leonard Leo to fertilize a network of think tanks, influencers, professors, and protest groups.[37] This amounted to a closed loop in which activists could create the impetus for a change in the law, theorists could say why the Constitution demands it, practitioners could build a case around it, and all could follow it through to a Supreme Court victory.

Speaking at a Fifth Circuit judicial conference in San Antonio, Texas, in 2023, Alito himself acknowledged the triumph of originalism, even as he suggested, with a hint of foreboding, that its adherents often disagreed about what it entailed. Indeed, the defeat of *Roe* had broken a bond among legal conservatives, who cleaved between those who modeled judicial restraint and those who itched to overturn liberal-leaning decisions. Alito's own *Dobbs* opinion stepped gingerly around a cavalcade of conservative agenda items, from finally burying all substantive due process rights to granting "personhood" protections to unborn fetuses, which could overturn abortion rights even in states where they were legal.

Conservative infighting stirred again when Donald Trump won a second presidential term and began stretching the prerogatives of his office. Suddenly, justices who had voted to rein in Obamacare and block President Joe Biden's student loan forgiveness were scrambling for reasons to approve Trump's gutting of USAID and deportation of non-citizens.

Out of that cloud of dust, Alito emerged once again as a face of the court. A man who had been true to his roots as an observant Catholic in suburban Trenton, New Jersey, was entering uncharted territory. He had felt the pulsation of the movement's beginnings in the 1960s and early 1970s, had brought it to its middle-period apex in *Dobbs*, and now would help craft its endgame.

As Trump pressed for more power, the drumbeat of cases threatened to reveal whether the conservative legal movement was, in fact, devoted to a dispassionate reading of the Constitution or simply clearing a path for conservative politicians. The picture of Samuel Anthony Alito Jr., his hand raised in taking an oath, with his beaming wife, Martha-Ann, and President George W. Bush by his side, once again came into focus.

"A judge can't have any agenda . . ."

Having seized the rudder of the court—sailing past legions of skeptics and altering the lives of millions—Samuel Alito and his fellow members of the conservative legal movement were ready to confront their least forgiving foes: themselves.

BOOK ONE:
THE FAMILY

CHAPTER 1

The Long Journey

The earth erupted at 5:20 a.m.[1] Almost everyone in the cities and villages along the Strait of Messina was in bed. No one had an inkling of warning. Tens of thousands never awoke, crushed under fallen roofs and collapsed floors. Those who could escape fled to the waterfront, the only place free of destruction and debris.[2]

But off the coast, under the swirling seas, the earth's plates shook loose a tidal wave of nearly twenty feet.[3] Everyone on the shoreline drowned—thousands of men, women, and children, their bodies carried inland to blacken and bloat through weeks of halting rescue efforts, punctuated by the screams of the dying. "Thousands are walking about half demented, starving, and suffering from the cold," *The New York Times* reported three days later.[4]

In the village of Saline Joniche, along the jagged southern tip of the Italian peninsula, the decades-old Chiesa del Santissimo Salvatore—Church of the Most Holy Savior—cracked into rubble.[5] Saline Joniche translates to Ionian Salt Pans, a reminder of both the area's connection to ancient Greece and its economic livelihood. For thousands of years, people in southern Italy had dried seawater into salt in low-lying, pond-like "pans" and sold it to customers elsewhere in the region and beyond.

Population growth strained the ability of people in the Calabria region to support themselves through farming and harvesting salt; their simple, elemental approach to life was disrupted.[6] By the time the great Messina earthquake struck, on December 28, 1908, tens of thousands of Calabrians had already spent their last lira to make the fetid steerage-class crossing to North America, hoping to better their chances in the United States.[7]

The quake, wreaking utter devastation just three days after Christmas, marked a significant juncture. For some, the loss of homes made it harder to save enough money to emigrate; for others, it seemed almost a physical jolt to seek a new life somewhere else.[8]

One Calabrian who felt the urge to leave was Antonio Alito—whose name, scribbled by a census taker, translated at first as Alati. In 1913, at the age of thirty-one, he left Saline Joniche for the New World, hoping to collect a few paychecks before sending for his wife, Mary, and baby, Salvatore.[9] He made his way to Trenton, New Jersey, whose location on canals and rail lines between New York and Philadelphia presaged its emergence as an industrial center. Factories provided a steady source of jobs for able-bodied men who didn't speak English. With dreams of good jobs and better wages, Italians had been flowing into the New Jersey capital for more than a decade, turning the Civil War–era borough of Chambersburg into their Little Italy.[10]

Many were disappointed. Life was far from idyllic in the close confines of Chambersburg. People crowded atop each other in multifamily homes. But when the smell of freshly made pastas and pastries emanated from storefronts and blotted out the factory odors, it could feel almost like home.

Hardship and opportunity were two sides of the immigrant coin. For Antonio—now known as Anthony—jobs would come open on the Pennsylvania Railroad but then disappear just as quickly.[11] Work for unskilled laborers was intermittent and poorly paid, not always sufficient to support a family, especially after that family began expanding. Two daughters and another son, Anthony Jr., followed young Salvatore, whose name was soon anglicized to Samuel.[12]

By 1930, the census recorded that Anthony worked as a repairman of city streets. He, Mary, and their four children between the ages of six and seventeen lived in a one-bathroom flat on Pearl Street.[13]

It was a stable family but not a stable home. At times, teenage Samuel would return from school to find his family's furniture on the sidewalk after they had been evicted for non-payment of rent. As the person who spoke the best English, Samuel would be called upon to scour the neighborhood for new lodgings, the fate of the Alitos firmly on his youthful shoulders.[14]

. . . .

LIFE WAS SLIGHTLY BETTER for the family living just seven tenement buildings away, down Pearl Street and left on Hudson. They were the Fraduscos, and their own migrant journey had begun nine years before Anthony Alito's. The parents and three children made the trek from the farming village of Palazzo San Gervasio—about three hundred miles north of Saline Joniche—to the United States in 1904, settling in Chambersburg.[15] They vowed to construct a new life for themselves, step by step, dollar by dollar, after a hailstorm destroyed a year's worth of their crops.[16]

Three more children were born within the next ten years, planting fresh roots in a new land. These new Fraduscos would be 100 percent American.[17] The youngest was named Rose, after her mother, Rosina.[18] She was just a year younger than Samuel Alito but had the advantage of older siblings to bolster the family finances. Her eldest brother, Joseph Jr., toiled in a tailor shop, while his next two sisters, Frances and Mary, had jobs as "forelady" and packer at a candy factory.[19] Their father, Joseph, worked at Chambersburg's largest employer, John A. Roebling's Sons, maker of steel cables.[20]

The Fraduscos' timing was fortuitous. Comfortable in its isolation, the United States had done little to arm itself until the first decade of the twentieth century. Thereafter, factories hummed with the production of war materials. When European nations took up arms against each other in 1914, the US vowed to remain neutral, but demand for the steel cables necessary for shipbuilding soared. It grew further when the US joined the fight in 1917. Employment in the various Roebling plants doubled from five thousand in 1914 to ten thousand in 1918.[21]

It was often brutal work for a paycheck that still left a family of eight on the edge of poverty. But by the standards of the time, it was good enough. The Roebling brothers' pride in their operations went beyond the pursuit of money; the Roebling name was associated with some of the great events in the history of the United States.

The eldest of the four brothers, Washington Roebling—who shared the name of the father of his country—fought with Union forces at Gettysburg and tracked Confederate troop movements through air-balloon reconnaissance at Chancellorsville. Bright and ambitious, he went on to monitor the design of bridges in Europe in preparation for one of the great engineering feats of all time: the epic Brooklyn Bridge project.

Washington succeeded his father as chief engineer on the project in 1868 and, overcoming an astonishing series of life-threatening challenges, witnessed the completion of the bridge in 1883. That accomplishment, and many other bridge-building triumphs of succeeding decades, bore the Roebling stamp. And the company continued to grow in the new century.

At the time of Joseph Fradusco's employment, three of the Roebling brothers, graying men in their fifties and sixties, still commanded attention in Trenton. Their status as civic leaders was confirmed by their proximity to the New Jersey capitol—each brother had a mansion along State Street, steps from the 1792 New Jersey State House. The Roebling homes were Gilded Age showplaces outfitted with elaborate furnishings; the grand staircase in Washington Roebling's estate was lit by an enormous stained-glass window depicting the Brooklyn Bridge. It was designed by the famed Louis Comfort Tiffany and handcrafted by Tiffany & Co. artisans.[22]

The ostentatious wealth of factory owners was offset by the austerity of their workers' lives. They manned the assembly lines in regular shifts, breaking only for meals at assigned seats along rows of tables in institutional cafeterias.[23] Social life centered around ethnic clubs and churches, each defined by the native lands of the clergy and the languages in which services were conducted.

For some people, including Italians, the inequities in this system provoked rage. Immigrant workers' lives were circumscribed. They were excluded from much of mainstream life by dint of language, poverty, and prejudice. Old-world customs didn't always translate. Rosina Fradusco, for one, believed that women shouldn't venture outside their homes alone. Her tentativeness struck relatives as a sign that she missed her old life in Italy; she wasn't really acclimated to Trenton.[24]

Straitened circumstances prompted outbreaks of trade unionism and, in extreme cases, anarchic violence. But the world of John A. Roebling's Sons was mostly placid. The all-enveloping nature of the firm seemed to nurture a sense of loyalty. Not for nothing was an oral history of the company titled, with only a hint of irony, "Now You're Set for Life."

"Roebling was everywhere in Chambersburg," recalled one worker, who was born in 1920 and whose grandfather retired from Roebling in 1924. "It was in your church. It was in your schools. It was in your festivals. Roebling would have a float in the parade, things like that. The Roebling trucks drove by South Clinton Avenue every day . . . Everybody that grew up in the Burg knew about Roebling's. It was part of their life, really."[25]

In this atmosphere, low wages were ineluctable. "You wanted a vacation, you took it on your own time," remembered another worker. "You wanted a sick day, you took it on your own. You didn't get paid for any of this time."[26]

Acceptance of these conditions was a show of faith—in the company and its elevating values, in the amazing growth of the country, in the transformation of families who tore up centuries of roots just to get here. Against these big bets, the fight for a few dollars of sick time could seem piddling and mean, beside the point.

Yes, rewards flowed disproportionately to the Roebling brothers and their relatives, the industrious and lazy alike. But wasn't that in itself a reflection of the company's worth? The mansions on State Street—much like the European palaces on which they were modeled—stood not for the comforts of the few but for the triumphs of the many. And then there were those industrial cathedrals rising out of Chambersburg, smokestacks and water towers reaching like fingers into the sky. They were totems of all that was revolutionary in the United States and utterly missing in the dusty villages of the old country.

No one collected vacation pay or sick time in Saline Joniche either. Most workers seemed to internalize the notion that there's no free lunch in this world, even at your assigned seat in the whitewashed dining hall of the steelworks.

The fact that immigrant life was no nirvana—not for Anthony Alito, with his frequent evictions; not for Rosina Fradusco and her fretful isolation; not for Joseph Jr. and Frances and Mary, toiling in sweatshops—conferred an implicit expectation on the next generation. Immigration was a family project connecting grandparents and parents and children. The young would carry forth the unrealized ambitions of the old.

In later years, there would be no tenements; people wouldn't be living on top of one another. But they would still be together. They would share a common faith and destiny. Wherever children or grandchildren went, their ancestors would be watching, hoping—perhaps even demanding—that their descendants' success give their own hardships a larger purpose.

....

FAMILY STRUGGLES BRED A unique sense of ambition in Samuel Alito and Rose Fradusco. Through child's eyes, they could envision the American economy as a ladder. Their parents' success at grabbing the lower rungs was the starting point for their own climb. And anyone who witnessed the stumbles of adults who'd failed to master English knew that education was the key to advancement.

Sam mastered English so well that he became a stickler for grammar and concision in writing. Expressing oneself clearly and properly, he believed, was the best way to be heard. A declarative sentence, straight and clear as a knock on the forehead, was the essence of communication. And the ability to write cogently unlocked many doors.[27]

Rose felt much the same. She had grown up just a few buildings away from Sam, but each tenement had been packed with multiple families, so she never noticed him.[28] She could not have realized that they were traveling on parallel paths; boys and girls didn't communicate that way. And in truth, personality differences set them apart. Rose, the youngest child, was outgoing and vivacious, accustomed to competing for attention; Sam, the eldest child, was quiet and taciturn, as if the worries of the world were reverberating in his head. Yet they shared a keen desire to improve themselves in the eyes of not only Chambersburg but wider society.

Most girls in Rose's circle married young and bore large families. But she resolved to go to college. Her immediate opportunity was through

Trenton State Teachers College—an acknowledgment that teaching was the highest career an intelligent woman could attain.[29] It was also a shrewd choice in Depression-era America: government jobs were far less likely to fall prey to the vicissitudes of the economy. Family lore has it that her first job offer in a public school was accompanied by a request that she also teach Sunday school in a Protestant church; she refused—unwilling to compromise her Catholic principles—and soon got another offer without any insulting conditions attached.[30]

Unsatisfied with merely a bachelor's degree, she applied for and was accepted to the master's program at Columbia Teachers College in New York City, commuting by train and subway from Trenton. She lived at home but, as her career took off, asserted her independence by buying a car and tooling around Trenton on her own.[31]

Sam was drawn to some of the same opportunities. A stellar student, he was nonetheless too poor to afford any kind of private college. His mother had died young, when he was still in his teens, and his father barely spoke English. That made Sam a de facto caregiver to his three younger siblings, and intensely aware of their deprivations. He got a factory job to cover the bills. Then, armed with a tiny scholarship, he too enrolled at Trenton State Teachers College.[32]

It was a fitful journey. Unable to afford the assigned books, he took to writing out the text of library copies by hand.[33] When he graduated in the teeth of the Depression, no teaching offers were forthcoming, so he worked as a state forest ranger, checking trees for Dutch elm disease.[34] Eventually, friends from his college newspaper vouched for his skills, and he hooked on as a teacher at local schools. Alarmed by the war in Europe, he enlisted in the army a month before the Pearl Harbor attacks. He went on to serve in the Pacific Theater.[35]

After the war, he returned to teaching, this time at Trenton's Junior High School No. 4.[36] America itself was exhaling after more than a decade of economic turmoil and four years of war. People were putting down roots. And Sam, back at home in Chambersburg, was finally ready to join them.

He and Rose Fradusco were roughly the same age and the same religion, and they had been buffeted by the same forces while growing up in working-class families in Chambersburg. They had attended the same college at the same time, though they were seemingly too busy studying to get to know each other.[37] Each had a passion for education. Rose, for her part, was now an assistant professor at their alma mater, Trenton State.[38] Sam, armed with his own master's degree from Rutgers, was on the verge of moving into an administrative position at Trenton Central and later in the state's Office of Legislative Services.[39]

Their marriage at Sacred Heart Church on South Broad Street in 1948 was both a sacrament and a merger of two restless and relentless sensibilities.[40] When, after a year living in Sam's family's apartment, Rose discovered she was expecting a baby, she and Sam made a vow.[41] "I said, 'Sam, our children are going to be the smartest children in Hamilton Township.'"[42]

....

HAMILTON TOWNSHIP WAS WHERE Trentonians tended to move after they reached the middle class. It was virgin territory, a place to put your stake in the ground. Land was quickly filling in with suburban tract houses, part of a building boom driven by returning veterans eager to get out of the city but remain close to family and local landmarks. Between 1950 and 1960, Hamilton's population would increase an astonishing 58 percent, from forty-one to sixty-five thousand.[43]

This wasn't just a Trenton phenomenon. Most cities were growing their own rings of suburbs, as the children of immigrants gained earning power and yearned to stretch their elbows. Coincidentally or not, the urban fabric was changing as well. Companies like Roebling suffered from labor unrest and greater economic competition. Meanwhile, the Great Migration of Black families from the South stirred racial tensions. It wasn't entirely different from the resistance to Italians at the turn of the century, a projection of newcomers as invaders—unsanitary, violent, and defiantly unwilling to fit in.

For Sam and Rose, however, Hamilton Township wasn't a place to retreat to but a place to embrace. It offered a taste of the good life that had been denied to their parents. And it provided, most of all, a gentle atmosphere in which to raise their two namesakes, Sam Jr., who arrived in 1950, and Rosemary, who was born two years later.

There was nothing ostentatious about Hamilton. The single-family homes were modest and usually a single story, with green grass in front, a white ribbon of sidewalk, and bright splotches of flowering trees dotting the roadsides. Fragrant parks and newly constructed schools were often just a walk away.[44]

The Alito home at 137 Fenwood Avenue in Mercerville, the largest of five villages in the township, was typical of those sprouting up all over.[45] It was red brick, with one and a half stories, three bedrooms, and two baths.[46] There were no trees in front, but the backyard was big enough for childhood games of kickball. Most importantly, it was within walking distance of Mercerville Elementary School and Our Lady of Sorrows Catholic church.

Our Lady, just two blocks away, was the centerpiece of the community for the Alitos. Its simple brick construction, strikingly devoid of any architectural flourishes, mirrored that of the new homes in the area and the unadorned nature of suburban life. The church's fast growth also reflected Mercerville's development. It was commissioned in 1939 as a mission of a Trenton church, elevated to its own parish in 1943, and steadily expanded with a separate school building in 1955, two new wings and a renovated "lower church" basement in 1959, and a convent to house twenty-one nuns in 1963.[47]

Sam Alito Jr. wasn't baptized there—his parents chose to have him receive the first sacrament in the Chambersburg parish where they were married—but Our Lady's wooden pews, white walls, marble floors, and altar featuring a cross and effigy of Jesus Christ would be an abiding presence for all his life.[48] So too would be the lesson behind its name. Our Lady of Sorrows refers to the Seven Sorrows of Mary and the horrific pain that she endured in deference to God's plan.[49]

Church attendance was an unbreakable commitment, part of the discipline instilled by Sam Sr. and Rose. In later years, Sam Jr. and Rosemary would recall the weight of expectation from two parents whose pride required nothing short of excellence. Every sheet of homework was scrutinized by both parents, with Sam Sr. enacting a nightly editing exercise, teaching both children to write with the precision he demanded of himself.[50]

"It was unspoken that we get very good grades. We would enter the science fair every year and we would win the science fair every year," Sam Jr. recalled many years later.[51]

On weekends, Sam Sr. would take the two children to the park and teach them the names of trees, a vestige of his Depression-era tenure as a ranger.[52]

Sam Jr. started kindergarten the year that Our Lady opened its new parochial school building, but the Alitos enrolled him in the public school instead. Even seven decades later, leaders of Our Lady professed to be mystified by the decision.[53] But both Sam Sr. and Rose had been public school teachers, and Sam Sr.'s younger brother Anthony also taught in public schools; they had confidence in public education as a melting pot where children of different backgrounds learned civic values and came to see the United States as a great beacon for freedom.[54] Plus, for all the devoutness of their Catholic beliefs and the intensity of their identification as Italian Americans, the Alitos felt a right and a responsibility to be enmeshed in every corner of their community.

In Mercerville, as in many suburbs across the country, children born during the Baby Boom were experiencing a new vision of the good life. Memories of the sheer innocence of their upbringing, from its drive-in burger joints to its schoolyard games to its summer camps and playful fads, would influence American life for decades. So too would the distance between these tribal rituals of the great middle class and the experiences of people growing up in less idyllic settings.

The Alitos had a niche on nearly every limb of the tree of life in Mercerville. Their activities were closely monitored by the thriving local newspapers of the day. Sam Sr. was a member of the American Legion, chief umpire for a baseball league, volunteer adviser to students on high school newspapers, judge of a local spelling bee, fundraiser for the YMCA, and leader of neighborhood opposition to a fast food restaurant whose traffic posed a danger to kids.[55] Rose was on the executive board of the parent-teacher association and a member of the Hamilton Heart Drive, and she organized a painting class in her home.[56]

Young Sam Jr. and Rosemary first appear as immaculately dressed volunteers at the College Club of Trenton Christmas party for the Widows and Single Women's Home; Sam Jr., at age six, recited his own story at the Christmas story hour at the State Museum.[57] The two kids later performed in a play to benefit the YMCA.[58] Rosemary was lauded for helping to protect a fifteen-pound snapping turtle that had waddled into her neighborhood.[59] Fulfilling his father's expectations, Sam Jr. won the science fair three years in a row. He also played in a piano recital.[60]

And then there was baseball, the most pastoral of American sports. It was in its manic heyday in the 1950s and early 1960s. Sam Jr. grew up as an obsessive fan of the Philadelphia Phillies, the major league team closest to Mercerville.[61] When other kids, despairing of the Phillies' chronically losing ways, shifted their sentiments to the New York Yankees, who were in the midst of a historic run of championships, Sam Jr. held firm in his affections. Hometown loyalties weren't to be discarded lightly.[62]

Beginning at age nine, Sam Jr. himself played the infield for the Cubs of the Hamilton YMCA midget league, and when he was fifteen, he moved up to the Harrison Rug team of the Hamilton Township Recreational Baseball Association.[63] The *Trentonian* of July 30, 1965, breathlessly reported, "It was almost a beautiful day for Sam Alito of the Harrison Rug team as the bantam belter slammed three homers to spearhead his team's attack."[64]

Bantam belter? Three homers?

What could ever top that?

CHAPTER 2

The Glorious Suburbs

For the Alitos and most families in Mercerville, the 1950s and early 1960s were a time of gentle healing in the aftermath of the Second World War, a precious idyll like the "normalcy" that followed the First World War. But other legacies of the war rippled the placid surface of American life.

Women like Rose Alito, who worked on the home front, were quite willing to leave the breadwinning to their husbands and happily adapt themselves to raising fine children.[1] But some women resented being forced to give up jobs that they had performed admirably to make room for returning men. It felt like a step backward.

The fight for liberty over tyranny—represented by Nazi Germany, imperialist Japan, and the new threat of Soviet communism—came home in conflicting ways. In the public schools of Mercerville, teachers told the American story as one of freedom versus totalitarianism. Fifth graders learned about Christopher Columbus's discovery of America, George Washington's prescient leadership, and the success of the American Revolution. Eighth graders learned about the Union triumph and the defeat of slavery in the Civil War, while high schoolers studied more recent victories for democracy.[2]

Outside the classroom, the emphasis on freedom gave voice to those who felt the lack of it at home. The NAACP Legal Defense Fund, led by Thurgood Marshall, deliberately avoided challenging racial segregation during the war, wary of disturbing domestic relations when unity was paramount. Afterward, returning Black soldiers wondered why they had fought against discrimination abroad only to accept it at home. A renewed push by Marshall led the Supreme Court to unanimously overrule racially separate public schools, delivering a clear but protracted mandate to dismantle segregation in all forms.

Brown v. Board of Education, the most widely discussed Supreme Court case in generations, was authored by a new chief justice, Earl Warren. He was a former Republican governor of California, a political moderate appointed by President Dwight Eisenhower, but he would oversee an era of progressive reform. It was as if the *Brown* template were being extended to anyone who drew a short stick in life.

In a parade of cases, the court would side with small-time plaintiffs and defendants in ways that tied the hands of local officials. Clarence Gideon, a fifty-one-year-old white drifter accused of stealing from a Florida pool hall, challenged his conviction on the grounds that he had been too poor to afford a lawyer. The Supreme Court ruled that states must provide indigent defendants with counsel, imposing a new obligation on taxpayers.[3]

Dolly Mapp, a thirty-four-year-old Black woman, refused to allow police into her home without a search warrant. When they came in anyway and found some nude pictures, she was tried for possession of pornography. She challenged her conviction on the grounds that the police lacked a warrant. The Supreme Court declared that any illegally obtained evidence must be excluded from trial.[4]

Ernesto Miranda, a twenty-two-year-old Latino man, was accused of rape and interrogated by Arizona police for two hours before signing a confession that stated he was aware of his legal rights. In fact, police had not told him of his right to remain silent or his right to ask for a lawyer. The Supreme Court ruled that the confession was therefore invalid, and that all suspects need to be explicitly informed of their rights.[5]

These decisions provoked varying reactions. Some welcomed the crackdown on abusive police procedures that had been winked at for years; America was finally taking its Cold War talk of freedom from oppression seriously. Others felt that the Supreme Court, with its liberal pretensions, had made them more susceptible to violent crime. Critics claimed the justices had overstepped their bounds by using the Fourteenth Amendment's due process clause to intrude on local matters. And then there were all those orders emanating from the bench: The Constitution may indeed outlaw warrantless searches, but it says nothing about throwing out evidence. The same with rights against self-incrimination. Yes, they exist, but nowhere in the Constitution does it say that police have to spoon-feed them to suspects.

For the bright and thoughtful Sam Alito Jr., just entering his teens, the activist posture of the Supreme Court hit home directly. When he and Rosemary were in junior high, their mother decided it was an appropriate time to resume her teaching career. Hamilton schools were only too happy to have Mrs. Alito, a highly regarded educator, in their classrooms. But there was a catch. Rose, the regular churchgoer, had routinely woven Bible teachings into her lessons, providing a little spiritual uplift for kids.[6] Now the Supreme Court was insisting that public school teachers could no longer do that.

The offending court case, *Abington School District v. Schempp*, originated just across the border in Pennsylvania. For more than twenty years, the Keystone State had required that teachers begin the day with a few lines of inspiration from the Bible. It was not so different from the Founding Fathers, who began their Continental Congress with a prayer. But the Supreme Court declared that circumstances in the country had changed.

As Justice William Brennan, another Republican appointee who turned out to be very progressive, noted in his concurring opinion, "Our religious composition makes us a vastly more diverse people than were our forefathers. They knew differences chiefly among Protestant sects. Today, the Nation is far more heterogeneous religiously, including as it does substantial minorities not only of Catholics and Jews but as well of those who worship according to no version of the Bible and those who worship no God at all. In the face of such profound changes, practices which may have been objectionable to no one in the time of Jefferson and Madison may today be highly offensive to many persons, the deeply devout and the nonbelievers alike."[7]

Brennan then added a rebuke to those who sought to base today's rules on practices in place when the Constitution was written: "Whatever Jefferson or Madison would have thought of Bible reading or the recital of the Lord's Prayer in what few public schools existed in their day, our use of the history of their time must limit itself to broad purposes, not specific practices."[8]

This was consistent with Brennan's view of how each generation should look at the Constitution in light of evolving standards. The document sets out clear precepts, but they need not be interpreted so narrowly as to ignore relevant changes in society: an all-Protestant gathering might not view a recitation from the New Testament as exhibiting a preference for one religion, whereas a classroom of children of different faiths might see it as a preference for a certain form of Christianity.

But to those who resented the heavy hand of the court, Brennan's evolving standards seemed alarmingly subjective—the Warren Court was bending over backward to show its compassion for minorities of all stripes. The plaintiff in the case, the parent of a public school student named Ellery Schempp, was a Unitarian Universalist, a denomination that draws inspiration from many religions but does not share all the precepts of Christianity. His case was combined with one brought by a family of atheists whose matriarch, Madalyn Murray O'Hair, founded an activist group dedicated to removing religion from every corner of public life. It grated many churchgoing Americans to see this grandstanding woman claiming victory over the much larger God-fearing majority: What about their rights?

Trenton newspapers carried stories on the backlash, as religious activists tried to whip up support for a constitutional amendment to overturn the Supreme Court decision and allow school prayer.[9] Years later, Rose Alito could barely hide her disdain for the court's decision, and how it trimmed her sails. "I was teaching then, and it used to irk me," she said. "I read poems that had something to do with the atmosphere and trees when we were not permitted to read the Bible."[10]

....

AT ALMOST THE SAME moment, the court bore down on Sam Sr. as well. When he had gone to work for the New Jersey State Library in 1952, he was a one-man research team, helping state senators and representatives collect information necessary for lawmaking. He was so diligent that legislators quickly learned the value of nonpartisan research. Soon he was heading his own state office, eventually to be known as the Office of Legislative Services, with a staff that would reach into the hundreds.[11]

Sam Sr. was rigorously nonpartisan. He knew that if either side viewed him as an antagonist, they could seek to oust him, so he hid what one politically connected lawyer remembered as the most "brilliant" political mind in the state.[12] Far from shunning electoral politics, he was an intent student of them, drawing on a deep knowledge of New Jersey's clashing constituencies.

In 1964, however, the Supreme Court painted him into a corner. Its decision in a case called *Reynolds v. Sims* prompted his most challenging—and politically freighted—assignment: redrawing the state's legislative districts to accommodate the mandate for "one person, one vote."[13]

Until then, states had maintained their own legislative traditions. Some chose to allot seats in a way that gave urban and rural areas equal power, regardless of population differences. Others simply assigned a fixed number of seats to counties of varying sizes. There was at least an arguable rationale for this: the Constitution grants two Senate seats to each state, despite vast discrepancies in population. Voters who don't live in states, such as those in Washington, DC, have no Senate representation at all. The notion of organizing a legislative chamber around geographical interests rather than population was a facet of the American system, even if it violated the concept of pure representative democracy.

But in the 1960s, suspicion fell upon states whose legislative maps gave much greater influence to some voters than others; while *Reynolds v. Sims* did not involve racial disparities—it was based purely on equal representation—a desire to rid the system of old prejudices and historic inequities hovered in the atmosphere.

A person named M. O. Sims joined a class-action suit on behalf of voters in Jefferson County, Alabama, which included the city of Birmingham. The state assigned each county a single senator, even though Jefferson, the largest county by population, had forty-one times the number of people as the county with the smallest population. These imbalances were not simply a Southern phenomenon. The state of New Hampshire, for instance, gave single seats to a town with three people and another with more than three thousand.[14]

An 8–1 Supreme Court majority led by Chief Justice Warren declared that Alabama had violated the equal protection rights of Sims and other voters. They were entitled to voting power that was roughly equivalent to that of their fellow citizens. One justice, John Marshall Harlan II, issued a forceful dissent, claiming that the framers of the equal protection clause never intended it to be used to balance voters' sway over state legislatures. Nonetheless, states suddenly had to redraw their voting maps.[15]

This was a far tougher task than one might imagine, especially for someone like Sam Sr., whose livelihood depended on nonpartisanship. Entire political structures had been built along legislative boundaries; even small shifts in the composition of districts could cost local kingmakers their power bases. They could be counted on to strike back at anyone who jeopardized their clout.

Years later, Sam Jr. would remember lying in his bed at 137 Fenwood Avenue, listening to the click of an adding machine as his father tried mightily to figure out a fair, minimally disruptive way to construct districts of equal population size. The earnestness with which Sam Sr. devoted himself to this thankless task was proof, in his son's mind, of his total commitment to public service. But it was also clear that the Supreme Court had dropped a red-hot anvil in his lap. And all those clicks? They were like the fingers of the Supreme Court justices monkeying with the gears of New Jersey politics.[16]

Whatever Sam Sr. thought of this unsought assignment remained a secret. But Sam Jr. had an opinion, and it wasn't favorable to the Supreme Court.

His interest in constitutional law, he wrote later, was "motivated in large part by disagreement with Warren Court decisions, particularly in the areas of criminal procedure, the Establishment Clause, and reapportionment."[17]

Those sentiments began at home. The establishment clause was the court's grounds for forbidding Rose Alito from reading the Bible to her students. Reapportionment was what kept Sam Sr. tethered to his adding machine into the wee hours of the night.

. . . .

AS THEY ENTERED THEIR fifties, Sam Sr. and Rose were admired and feared in equal measure. Each was, in the eyes of colleagues, a formidable figure. They had high expectations for their two children, Rose's students, Sam Sr.'s subordinates, and anyone else they encountered.

When, in later years, Rose recalled her vow to produce the smartest kids in Hamilton, she would describe a mission undertaken with a considerable amount of strategic forethought.[18] She had great hopes for the children she taught as well, and Hamilton rewarded her with a string of promotions. At one point, her job was to visit other teachers' classrooms and critique their performance; her very presence inspired trepidation.[19] Later, she was appointed principal of the district's Sunny Brae Elementary School.[20]

"She had very definite ideas about how to teach and administer a school, and she did her job," recalled one former Hamilton teacher who knew Rose and her family. "She was a no-nonsense lady—very firm, very serious. And she raised her kids that way. She was a very dedicated educator. She really was. She never took her job lightly. She was the type who would take kids falling behind in reading and take them into her principal's office and work with them. That's the kind of principal she was."[21]

While Rose freely expressed her approval and disapproval, Sam Sr. was harder to read. Colleagues were left to make their own assumptions about his feelings. He was an inwardly directed man. A trim five foot six, he would arrive at the capitol complex in Trenton in a carefully pressed but blandly institutional suit and tie, his gray hair tightly cropped.[22] Admirers attributed his reticence to both his determination to betray no hint of partisanship—which he demanded of underlings as well—and a deep-seated sense of dignity.

One former colleague, herself of Italian heritage, said he was recognizable as a particular type of upwardly mobile immigrant, "in certain ways a stereotype, you know, first generation of an Italian family from a close-knit Italian community." His sense of belonging was buoyed by strict adherence to the rules and customs of his adopted country, even if his rigidity hinted at "a sense of inferiority."[23]

By the 1960s and 1970s, Italian Americans were no longer outsiders in New Jersey. They numbered more than half a million and made up nearly 10 percent of the population, more than triple the national average and second only to New York.[24] And with numbers came clout. For eighteen years, from 1954 to 1972, Mercer County was represented by State Sen. Sido L. Ridolfi, who served as senate president and acting governor in 1967.[25] The esteem with which Ridolfi was held stemmed partly from the fact that he was among the first Italian Americans from Trenton to attend Princeton University. The twelve-mile trek from Chambersburg to the leafy campus once overseen by Woodrow Wilson covered thousands of miles in psychic space.

Sam Sr. was also a pioneer. He built the Office of Legislative Services from the ground up. "He was truly a beloved figure by political and policy players of both parties," attested one New Jersey lawyer who dealt with him in his heyday.[26]

But as his tenure lengthened, he became less in sync with younger colleagues. They viewed him as a man of an earlier era, stiff to the point of hostility. He let them know that he had no fondness for the social changes of the 1960s and early 1970s. He showed open hostility to "hippies" and Vietnam War protesters. Long hair and beards on men and pantsuits on women were almost beyond his comprehension; he refused to allow anyone to dress informally. By his edict, men wore jackets and ties while women wore dresses.[27]

Other rules prompted skepticism as well. He did not let staffers display their PhDs; they thought it was because he didn't have such a degree himself. There was also his fixation on grammar, which he emphasized by circling errors in red ink. And letters addressed to junior staffers would sometimes appear in their mailboxes with ripples along the seal, as if they had been steamed open; the staffers thought he was monitoring them for any problematic political communications.[28]

Finally, there was the issue of race. Sam Jr. remembered his father telling him how he once stood up for a Black player when both were on the Trenton State basketball team. As they prepared to take on a team from a segregated university, the Trentonians were asked if the Black player could sit out the game.[29] Sam Sr. thought that was wrong. Others who knew Sam Sr. say they never heard him use a derogatory term for people of any race.[30]

One ex-colleague, however, said he at least once engaged in crude racial stereotyping. "I remember standing next to him at a reception, and there was a senator he was talking to," the former colleague recalled. The senator was retiring and the leading candidate to replace him was Black, which was highly unusual at the time. So Sam Sr. "said to the senator, 'Yeah, if he gets it, we'll all be eating hog jowls and chitterlings, you know.'"[31]

Nudge-nudge racial banter was common among white men in that era—almost a bonding exercise—and they could get away with it because racial diversity was virtually nonexistent. For much of Sam Sr.'s tenure in New Jersey government, his office, like many, was entirely white. He eventually hired a Black woman with a law degree, but she was the only person of color on a team of more than seventy people. Two staff members remember feeling embarrassed when Sam Sr. glanced straight at the woman during a staff meeting while explaining that he was willing to hire more Black people, but there weren't any qualified applicants.[32]

One younger ex-staffer of Italian heritage saw this as ironic, because Sam Sr. had sometimes shared stories about anti-Italian and anti-Catholic prejudices. "He talked about it in a way that the Italian people were the only people who were ever discriminated against. And he had suffered this incredible hardship because he was Italian, which I thought was absurd because he was the head of this big office [and had] this incredible reputation."[33]

Both, of course, could be true: Sam Sr. could be a victim of prejudice and a success story. His insistence on only the highest credentials for Black applicants may have betrayed nothing but his desire to judge people, including himself, on what they had achieved rather than suffered. His life was testament to the need to overcome: if someone wants to rise in the world, they must commit themselves to self-improvement and never give their doubters an inch of space. His very creed may be the explanation for the intense, almost painful, repression that some people saw in him.

The next generation was a separate matter. In the immigrant story, life gets freer for the young, thanks to the hard work of their parents. And Sam Sr. and Sam Jr. were bound together in this way. Rose Alito noted that from his earliest days, Sam Jr. took after his father.[34] As the son grew older and became an excellent student, the father's pride began to swell. Sam Sr. didn't usually engage in small talk, but he couldn't resist bragging about his son. Sam Jr. was "the chosen one," one of Sam Sr.'s colleagues said.[35] "It was always Sam, Sam, Sam," complained another, who was upset that the father didn't as often acknowledge his looser, more spontaneous daughter.[36]

SAM ALITO JR. LOOKED at Steinert High as his proving ground. His was the first class of seniors to occupy a brand-new building, built of brick with large, industrial-style windows.[37] It looked like a bigger version of the tract houses in its neighborhood and was instantly recognizable as a suburban high school of its era. Not an extra dime of Hamilton tax money was expended on architectural flourishes, but its fresh paint and polished tiles conveyed a sense of newness. It was a clean canvas on which generations of students could leave their marks.

There were two high schools in Hamilton, one of which was almost exclusively white and the other with a sizable Black population. Students were assigned based on their addresses, and Hamilton High West, near the Trenton border, drew from all the Black neighborhoods. Steinert students came from areas that were almost all white.[38]

A social studies teacher from Sam Jr.'s time described the atmosphere as "very, very conservative" and "very cliquish." The 474 students in Sam Jr.'s class quickly found their niche.[39] There were jocks. There were "carburetors"—kids who "spent their time in the wood shop, metal shop, auto shop." There were also sorority sisters—girls who wore penny loafers and organized themselves in social clubs. Finally, there were students on the "academic track," the ones who aspired to college.[40]

Sam Jr. had a toe in the jock world—running on the cross-country team— but he was also the most serious of students. His academic prowess was so evident that his English teacher, Elaine Tarr, gave him a specially chosen bibliography of extra-credit novels to read: Fitzgerald, Hemingway, Conrad, Orwell, Sinclair Lewis, and more. That august list prompted a handwritten thank-you note from Rose and Sam Sr. The younger Sam read the books but didn't much discuss them or speak up in class; for all his intelligence, he wasn't interested in literary analysis. Tarr described his attitude as "Hey, if it's not printed in black and white, it's not there, then why are you interpreting it?"[41]

He had more relish for political debates. Bill Agress, who was vice president of the Steinert debate team, recalls the coach coming to him and saying, "You're going to need a new debate partner . . . There's this sophomore who everyone says is brilliant and articulate . . . Samuel Alito."[42] Debate was the activity of choice for students interested in current affairs, as New Jersey high schools squared off on topics chosen by the National Speech & Debate Association. It was a bloodless sport: the goal was to be able to argue either side of a contentious issue. It placed a premium on sheer persuasiveness, on the ability to reduce complicated problems to simple choices. Alito excelled. And on at least one debate topic—the Supreme Court's decision to exclude evidence collected through police misconduct—he developed a strong preference for the side that disagreed with the Warren Court's ruling.[43]

He also became fixated on a rival: Jeffrey Laurenti of Trenton Central High School, where Sam Sr. once taught, and whose own father was a gym teacher at Steinert. The two high schoolers were judged by some to be the best debaters in the region; their teams squared off in a memorable match that ended in a tie.[44] Laurenti got under Alito's skin enough that the yearbook staff added a sarcastic quip to his entry: "Jeffrey who?"[45]

Laurenti, who went on to be active in Democratic politics, can't remember why the two feuded: "To be bested by the gym teacher's kid might have been a source of, well, I don't know . . ."[46]

The "I don't know" is typical of most classmates' recollections of Alito. He was an enigma. He was very shy and quiet—a difficult person to figure out.

"I can still picture him when we would get together at debate club meetings: a plaid flannel shirt and corduroy pants," said Agress. "He was not extroverted, but he was a wonderful debater."[47] And yet this sphinxlike figure was also a leader. As a senior, he was the editor of the school newspaper, *The Hy-Liter*.[48]

The newspaper was crisply edited yet concentrated mainly on boilerplate accounts of campus activities. Only by reading the editorials—for which there was no separate editorial-page editor—could a person get a sense of the impact of events occurring outside the school. One editorial, from May 1968, lampooned the stilted and combative language in peace offers from North Vietnam in the form of a mock letter to a faculty member: "To the imperialist and war-mongering swine of a teacher . . ."[49]

Sam Jr. was also president of the student council. And at the awards night for seniors, he almost swept the field, winning prizes for overall academic excellence, American history, outstanding leadership, good citizenship, and journalism.[50] Lest anyone doubt it, he was voted by classmates as the boy most likely to succeed.[51] His mother, Rose, collected his mementoes in a massive scrapbook bursting with dog-eared clippings.

His style of leadership, based on character and discipline, was reminiscent of Sam Sr.'s. While earlier generations might have assigned prestige based on family wealth or social standing, the Alito-era prizes, such as the Danforth Foundation Award for Outstanding Leadership and the Soroptimist Citizenship Award, conferred distinction on kids from the middle class who upheld the ideals of the United States.

And yet, this meritocratic road to success—the level playing field that his immigrant parents and grandparents dreamed of—was already coming under pressure. Causes like civil rights, world peace, nuclear disarmament, and feminism were on the rise. Future campus leaders would prove their mettle through their commitment to social change rather than by embodying *Boys' Life* ideals of patriotism and citizenship. Liberal politics aimed to topple the pillars that Sam Jr. had built his reputation on.

But while the Vietnam War captured the attention of boys who welcomed the chance to fight against communism, the turmoil of the outside world was largely absent at Steinert. "It was Camelot! It was before the hippies, before the drugs; there was no hate, everybody got along," recalled one student of Sam Jr.'s era with a glaze of nostalgia. "It was a very simple place and time."[52]

A *Hy-Liter* survey on the upcoming presidential election, taken in March 1968, didn't attract a huge number of responses, suggesting that most students hadn't developed any serious preferences. But the results pointed to centrism and an inclination toward mainstream politicians. Nelson Rockefeller, the moderate Republican governor of New York, drew fifty-eight votes. Lyndon Johnson and Richard Nixon were second with forty-six votes each. Liberal hopeful Robert Kennedy got only twenty-two, and anti-war candidate Eugene McCarthy had just seven, two fewer than conservative longshot Ronald Reagan. A surprisingly high twenty-six opted for the anti–civil rights candidacy of George Wallace.[53]

Social change was not something to embrace. Despite the growing angst of the outside world, the Steinert yearbook was full of young men with short hair and ties and young women with carefully sprayed and molded hairdos. Even rock music was viewed with a little trepidation, as a potentially destabilizing force.

Among his many other activities, Sam Jr. wrote for "Teen Times," a youth-oriented section of the *Trenton Times*. In one feature, he drew attention to a high school band that had "received the praise of teachers, clergymen, and adult dance supervisors." The leader of the band explained his key to success: "The boys don't have long hair. We don't wear sunglasses, and we don't 'doctor up' our music with devices that produce echoes, false high notes, or vibrating fuzzy sounds."[54]

That, wrote Sam Jr., made the group a rare "hit" among students, parents, and other adults in positions of authority.

. . . .

SMASHING GLASS. SOFAS DARTING up streets as if they had legs. Police bullets and blood.[55] Just a few minutes away from Mercerville, in the city that Sam Sr. and Rose left after their marriage, the lives of teenagers in 1968 were quite different.

Algernon "Algie" Ward Jr.—son of a factory worker and hospital technician—was born just three years after Sam Jr. and a year after Rosemary.[56] He would make his parents proud, graduating from Trenton Central High and Trenton State College, and becoming the first Black research scientist in the New Jersey Department of Health. His strategy for success was similar to that of the Alitos, and at first glance, his dreams were much like theirs too. But something was not the same.

He grew up in the Battle Monument neighborhood of Trenton, a mixture of Black and Italian families in the 1950s. When Algie watched TV, he dreamed of being Dennis the Menace, the spunky white kid growing up in the suburbs. But when white families, including his best friend Ronnie's, decamped for Hamilton, Black families were left to figure out a path forward in a largely segregated city.[57]

Fairness was a big part of their conversations. Older folks remembered the trial of the Trenton Six, Black men who were coerced by police into confessing to the 1948 murder of a white shopkeeper. Four were ultimately set free, after Thurgood Marshall and the NAACP Legal Defense Fund took up the case.[58] Looked at in light of the Trenton Six, the Supreme Court's insistence a decade later that suspects be informed of their rights and that courts exclude evidence obtained by police misconduct seemed a day late and a dollar short. Still, it was comforting that the Supreme Court appeared to have come to the realization that police coercion was not an accidental slip-up but a deliberate strategy for cracking down on Black communities.

From his early teens, Algie recalled, he and his friends debated whether to support Malcolm or Martin—Malcolm X, who promoted Black nationalism, or Martin Luther King Jr., who urged peaceful protest. Either way, something had to change in this country. The only question was how to get it done.[59]

Algie went to Junior High No. 4 in Chambersburg, which in his recollection was far from the sweet-smelling enclave remembered by those of Italian heritage. "You couldn't walk down the streets in Chambersburg, so you had to walk down the railroad tracks to get to school," he recalled. "Chambersburg was a dangerous place if you were Black."[60]

Violence lurked on every corner. White store owners kept their doors locked and wouldn't open them for Black customers.

On April 4, 1968, when Algie was fifteen, an assassin shot and killed Martin Luther King on a Memphis motel balcony. The crime was attributed to a white drifter and career criminal named James Earl Ray. The news had an explosive impact in Black areas of cities across the country. Algie remembered that "rumors were moving like wildfire," and that people were horrified that someone would shoot a minister, a man so close to God. King was the person who preached against violence, who urged followers to "turn the other cheek."[61] Boys in Trenton didn't necessarily buy that, and what greater proof did they need that racism would never be quelled except by violence than that the leader of non-violent protests was gunned down? Images seemed to be swirling together at once—Malcolm vs. Martin, police crackdowns, white store owners locking the doors in the face of Black kids.[62]

On April 9, five days after King's murder, the smell of smoke and the sounds of screaming and breaking glass enveloped most of central Trenton, from the capitol complex to Battle Monument. Algie was among the clusters of young men who gathered outdoors.[63] "Some people felt it was okay to break out the windows of these stores," he said. "And these weren't our stores, these were somebody else's stores, so we felt little ownership of them." Convery's Furniture, Lippman Jewelers, Royal Shoe Store, Phil's Used Appliance Store, and Berrish's Grocery were all broken into and looted, with angry Black men hauling away boxes of merchandise on their backs.[64] When firefighters showed up, protesters pelted them with rocks.[65]

As the night roared on, with fires sprouting throughout the city, Black ministers and civic activists fanned out to try to quell the furor. Instead, they got caught up in it. A Lincoln University sophomore named Harlan Bruce Joseph, who had been active in teen councils, was shot dead by a white police officer outside a looted store.[66]

When morning came, everyone sensed that a Rubicon had been crossed. A total of 108 people, almost all Black men, were behind bars. Tearful merchants bemoaned the loss of their livelihoods.[67] Algie's mother taped the windows and stockpiled food, awaiting the next eruption.[68]

The Trenton Times decried the "orgy of destruction," the "staggering" financial losses, and the whole "insane carnival."[69] The *Trentonian* referred to "The Night 'It' Struck Trenton."[70] "It" was an amalgam of pent-up fury, despair, neighborhood tensions, and utter chaos that consumed everything and everyone in its path.

Dozens of other cities also experienced riots, with nearby Baltimore and Washington among the most heavily damaged. College students responded by staging protests of their own to demand further steps toward racial equality. At Duke University in North Carolina, for instance, fifteen hundred people occupied much of the campus, including the president's house, in a silent vigil. They demanded that the leader of the university resign from a segregated country club, order a day of mourning for King, and agree to a minimum wage for the campus's largely Black maintenance workers.[71] These uprisings seemed to augment the already multiplying numbers of anti–Vietnam War demonstrations on campuses.

"It was a seminal period," concluded Ward. "Those of us coming of age were shaped by that. By the time we got to high school, we were no longer children. We were activists."[72]

. . . .

TWO MONTHS AFTER THE riots and exactly a week after Sam Jr. was presented with his Soroptimist Citizenship Award at a ceremony at Landwehr's restaurant in West Trenton,[73] *The Hy-Liter* published an unsigned editorial of unusual forcefulness. It was for the final issue of the school year, and the last under Sam Jr.'s editorship.

The editorial began with a quote from Judges 21:25: "In those days there was no king in Israel: every man did that which was right in his own eyes." It went on to say, "Those days could well be 1968. Today's laws are broken like New Year's resolutions. Teachers strike, violating the law. Bus drivers, garbage men, doctors, nurses—you name it—strike in knowing and defiant violation of the law. Students over-run their campuses, imprison their professors, rip up their school's property. Everyone demonstrates without permits or in spite of injunctions against their demonstrating. Let alone urban rioting and the violations of law arising out of opposition to the war in Vietnam."

The editorial expressed disgust for the notion that civil disobedience had roots in "our Western heritage." It took umbrage at the idea that some protesters drew inspiration from Thomas More, the Catholic saint who was executed for refusing to follow King Henry VIII's repudiation of the pope. The protesters had no appreciation of how More agonized, how he "twists and turns and talks and delays before breaking one itsy-bitsy law! How old-fashioned! How un-cool! How up-tight!"

A "more fitting explanation for modern practitioners of civil disobedience," the editorial said, came via Simon and Garfunkel, who wrote the lyric "The force can't do a decent job / Cause the kids got no respect / For the law today (and blah, blah, blah)."

The editorial concluded: "'Blah Blah Blah.' It takes only a second or two to say. Just about the time it takes to take out a match, light up a Molotov cocktail, and let fly."[74]

This angry blast—way out of character for *The Hy-Liter*—seemed intended to pierce the serenity of Steinert High. At a fleeting moment before graduation, in the warmth of senior spring, there was a sudden need to warn students of dangers beyond their suburban oasis. Their secure, orderly way of life was under threat, even as their mothers dutifully combed and pressed their graduation gowns.

The solemn biblical verse, stark rejection of any moral rationale for protest, fierce defense of the law, abject dismissal of discrimination as a justification for trammeling other people's rights, and open ridicule of elites who embrace such actions ("how un-cool")—it all seemed a cry from a battle yet to come.

The editorial was entitled "BLAH, BLAH, BLAH."

CHAPTER **3**

The Princeton Mystique

efore the start of the fall term of 1968, Princeton University administrators hosted a reception for certain incoming freshmen. Andy Napolitano, then an outgoing eighteen-year-old from Newark, remembers
it distinctly as a gathering of scholarship students, a group that Princeton
was struggling to integrate. There, Napolitano met a shy valedictorian from
Steinert High School named Sam Alito.[1]

The two had a lot in common, from a curiosity about politics to a sense
that they were carrying the hopes of their Italian American ancestors on
their backs. Admission to Princeton was the surest sign that the Napolitanos and the Alitos had really arrived in the United States. The two
young men were also nervous. To go from a New Jersey public high school
to Princeton, the Ivy League university that was in their state but not necessarily of it, was to make a leap into the unknown, to jump the fence of
the richest, plushest, most beautiful house in town.

That Princeton administrators felt the need to host a special welcome
for these kids was a bit curious. Did they assume that poorer students
would band together, marshaling their defenses against the school's rigid
social hierarchy? Did they expect them to express gratitude for the financial assistance? Or perhaps the reception was merely meant to acknowledge
their achievements, and the students themselves felt singled out because
they didn't fit the Princeton mold.

Throughout much of its then-222-year history, as it ascended the ranks of
the world's finest universities, Princeton wrestled with its own elitism. Even
by the standards of Ivy League universities, all of which were seen as snobbish

in some quarters, Princeton stood out for its emphasis on social cachet and conformity. "For the coming football games, we are ready with charlie caps, white bucks, gray flannels, Princeton ties—naturally all on the rebate system," assured a 1949 advertisement for the Princeton University Store.[2]

Much of the university's mystique stemmed from its so-called eating clubs. In 1855, Princeton banned fraternities, but in doing so, it opened itself to a new form of exclusivity. Unlike many other universities that shunned the Greek system, Princeton wasn't in a city big enough to feed and entertain its students. They soon organized themselves into clubs of like-minded individuals.[3]

At first, the purpose was nothing other than to have a place for meals, but over the decades, the eating clubs evolved into societies as insular and personality driven as any fraternities; the richest among them ruled the campus from Gilded Age mansions lining Prospect Avenue. By 1907, Princeton's president, Woodrow Wilson, was bemoaning the clubs' dominance over university life. They selected members through a process known as "bickering"; the one-third of students who were deemed unworthy of the clubs—the poor kids, the nerds, those of disfavored religions or social backgrounds—lived a life that was, in Wilson's words, "a little less than deplorable." While the clubs provided lifelong bonds for privileged students, they conferred shame and worthlessness on others.[4]

Despite Wilson's admonitions, however, the clubs thrived—and in just thirteen years, they became subjects of swooning envy among admirers of Princeton grad F. Scott Fitzgerald's romantic bestseller *This Side of Paradise*. Initially a far bigger hit than *The Great Gatsby*, *This Side of Paradise* provided a primer on the manly attributes of the various Princeton clubs: "Ivy, detached and breathlessly aristocratic; Cottage, an impressive mélange of brilliant adventurers and well-dressed philanderers; Tiger Inn, broad-shouldered and athletic . . ."[5]

By the late 1950s—just a decade before Alito and Napolitano were to arrive on campus—the university had given up its attempts to quell the clubs' influence and aspired to what it hoped would be a happy equilibrium: with more than a dozen clubs of varying interests, every student could find a place of welcome. That optimism quickly dissolved with the "Dirty Bicker" of 1958, in which twenty-three students were turned away from every club. Most of those given the universal thumbs-down were Jewish, adding a patina of antisemitism to Princeton's reputation.[6]

The university hastened to establish a non-competitive dining hall, shrewdly named for Princeton grad Adlai Stevenson II.[7] He was a scholarly governor of Illinois whom the Democratic Party had nominated for president twice in the previous six years. The name sent multiple messages: not all Princeton men were card-carrying Republicans, but then again, Stevenson's liberalism had twice been rejected at the polls. This would be the home for the other half—a group that inevitably came to include outcasts, principled objectors, and some nice, modest kids who simply had no patience for the bickering and pomposity of the eating clubs.[8]

The arrival of a non-competitive dining option accompanied a shift in Princeton's demographics. Its all-male student body had long been drawn mostly from northeastern preparatory schools, many of which were associated with Protestant denominations. But the university's youthful new president, Bob Goheen—nicknamed BoGo by students[9]—pushed for steadily increasing admissions from public high schools.[10]

This wasn't merely a progressive reform; it was a realization that some of the best minds were coming out of the postwar middle class. The meritocracy that had elevated the likes of Sam Alito was starting to make inroads at Princeton. By Alito's class of 1972, public school boys—some, admittedly, from very wealthy communities—outnumbered prep school graduates 481 to 344.[11]

Students' political preferences began to change as well. In 1960, Princeton men favored Republican Richard Nixon over Democrat John F. Kennedy by a robust 70–30 margin. Just four years later, in the last election before Alito's arrival, Democrat Lyndon Johnson outpaced Barry Goldwater 66–27. For the first time since campus polling began in 1916, a Democrat had come out ahead.[12]

The clash of old traditions and new viewpoints was starting to be felt, like the advance tremors of an earthquake. Princeton's tectonic plates were shifting in ways that would scramble the experiences of just about everybody on campus. For some, the turbulence would be energizing. "It was a great era to be in college in the United States, especially at Princeton," enthused Richard Balfour, who was an editorial writer for *The Daily Princetonian* in the class of 1971. "You cannot imagine more going on in a four-year period."[13]

Those same upheavals would leave deep and lasting bruises on the shy boy from Mercerville. The collision of wealth, class, and politics on the bucolic campus shaped his worldview. As Princeton became more agitated, older alumni began to blame the democratization of the admissions process—all those public school kids came to Nassau Hall with liberal politics in their steamer trunks. Alito saw essentially the opposite: his discomfort with his wealthier classmates was conflated with his distress over the campus's leftward shift. In his assessment, the rich kids felt free to challenge authority because they had nothing to lose. Their position in the global hierarchy was secure. They didn't need good grades, so they skipped exams to rail against injustices toward others. He, the superior student, relied on good grades to prove his mettle. But those same privileged kids went on to question the value of the entire grading system. It was just the start of feelings of unfairness and distrust that he would carry forward from his Princeton years.

"I saw some very smart people and very privileged people behaving irresponsibly, and I couldn't help making a contrast between some of the worst of what I saw on the campus and the good sense and decency of the people back in my own community," he would say at his confirmation hearing, casting his Princeton years as a period of disruption after his frictionless upbringing in Mercerville.[14]

Later, he would elaborate: "One thing I saw was at the time, there was a feeling among a lot of college students, including my fellow students at Princeton, who came from much more privileged backgrounds than I did, that there was something wrong with their parents' values and the kinds of lives that their parents lived—that they had sold out, that they had taken advantage of other people, that they had bad values, that they were very materialistic, that they were very status conscious. I didn't feel that way at all about my parents or about my family. They weren't privileged. By that point they were solidly middle class, but everything they had achieved, they had achieved on their own through hard work and sacrifice. So I thought that entire view of the generation to which my parents belonged was false."[15]

A different perspective isn't a falsehood, however. Alito's later ruminations were an illustration of what many classmates saw in him at a very young age: the tendency to reduce complicated issues to a choice of right or wrong, a simple equation with a clear answer.[16] Other students, for their part, would dispute the idea that their activism was a manifestation of privilege. Yes, they were asserting different values from their parents, but their parents weren't the main issue. The issues were poverty, discrimination, and a bloody war in Vietnam that made them ashamed to be Americans. Maybe everyone on campus needed to pause and take a breath a little more often, but meaningful lines were being drawn. And while they were drawing lines, so too was Sam Alito.

. . . .

WITH HIS SLIGHT BUILD, tortoiseshell glasses, and inscrutable gaze, the Sam who arrived at Princeton in 1968 was a quiet presence.[17] He didn't seek to make a splash like Napolitano, who turned himself into the face of campus conservatism, defending both the Vietnam War and the newly elected Nixon administration in the pages of *The Daily Princetonian*.[18] At the same time, if Sam had thought he could lead by example the way he did at Steinert, most of Princeton wasn't paying attention. He studied hard and was viewed by those who knew him as intelligent, even compared to his classmates.[19] But he didn't try to dominate the campus. Unlike the extracurricular dynamo of his high school years, he cut his activities to one: debating.

He opted out of eating clubs. Stevenson Hall was a better fit.[20] Large numbers of Catholics, Jews, and public school kids ate there, and when in his sophomore year Princeton consented to allow women on campus as full-fledged students, a fair number of them landed at Stevenson as well.[21] Housed in a defunct eating club replete with Gothic dormers, Stevenson Hall was a short walk from Sam's real comfort zone: the Woodrow Wilson School of Public and International Affairs.[22]

He was, by varying descriptions, "a nice guy, bordering on humble,"[23] and "a real dweeb, a person you should steer clear of."[24] He was doubly shunned, by eating club aristocrats and the free spirits at his own dining establishment. But he made friends with a group of guys of similar backgrounds who studied at the Wilson School and aimed for careers in the law. "Five of us . . . were good old-fashioned Catholics, and two of us were Protestants," said Mark Dwyer, who would become Alito's roommate. "We Catholic guys were different—we were cultural Catholics, repressed, a bit shy, aware of being in a non-Catholic universe. . . . At Princeton, it was never that we had intellectual limitations. But it was obvious that the preppies from Andover and Exeter had been invited there and fit in with the traditional culture of the Ivies."[25]

The gap between Alito and the dominant culture was visible. On some Sunday mornings, while hungover classmates staggered out of their eating clubs after a night of partying, Alito would be on his way to Mercerville to attend services at Our Lady of Sorrows.[26] He may have felt out of step, but he wasn't contentious about it. It was as if he didn't see the point of expending energy on dorm-room bull sessions when he could be studying or practicing for his formal debates.

Princeton, as it happened, had a storied debate club under the umbrella of the Whig-Cliosophic Society. It traced its origins back through multiple iterations to the days when James Madison was a member, and it operated out of the handsomest clubhouse on campus, Whig Hall.[27] The building's pillared facade resembled that of the Supreme Court Building. The society's purpose was "to train students in the techniques of argument, persuasion, and public speaking."[28] But in a tacit acknowledgment that such an apolitical approach to debating was out of tune with the passionate 1960s, the club also published journals and staged events to allow students to air their own views. Liberal Whigs would push one side of an issue; conservative Clios would act as counterpoints.[29]

Two of Sam's friends quickly emerged as outspoken leaders—Mark Dwyer of the Whigs and Andy Napolitano of the Clios.[30] But Sam himself was more drawn to formal debating, traveling the Northeast to take on other colleges. On one occasion, the *Princetonian* reported that he went all the way to Smith, the all-women's college in Northampton, Massachusetts, to take on a "pipe-smoking team" of female students on the freighted issue of women's lib.[31] Alito and two other Princeton men were assigned to defend the movement; Smith debaters—including Alito's sister, Rosemary—were stuck arguing the other side. The men prevailed. The debate-panel journal *Princeton Style* reported, tongue in cheek, that they "managed with amazing ease to convince their audience that women's lib was good."[32]

In the society's marquee event, the annual Class of 1876 Prize Debate, Alito won second prize and a hundred dollars for defending Vice President Spiro Agnew, who had stirred up a ruckus with his attacks on the media ("an effete corps of impudent snobs"[33]) and other allegedly liberal-infected institutions.[34] At the time, many people found his salty language and bitter partisanship to be undignified for a vice president.[35] Hence the debate question: "Should Vice President Agnew be censured for his speeches in the 1970 election campaign?"[36]

Later, after Alito's ascendency to the Supreme Court, his exploits would be recounted in a glass display case in the society's museum in Whig Hall, alongside those of other Princeton worthies such as Adlai Stevenson, John and Allen Dulles, and John Rawls.[37] It's where Alito's personal stamp remains visible at the university he attended for four years. But in his own recounting, his Princeton tenure was notable less for what he did than for what others did and the impressions they left on him.

....

THE FIRST GASH IN Princeton's culture was over sex, not war. Princeton's peer institutions were moving rapidly to admit women, and Princeton didn't want to be left behind. It wasn't, for the most part, a matter of fairness and equality, but rather a desire to create a campus atmosphere that better resembled the world outside. While many alumni cherished their all-male traditions, the president and trustees felt that some of them were holding the university back.[38] Playful practices that helped to create bonds among classmates up through the 1950s seemed juvenile and embarrassing in the more sophisticated 1960s. It was time to build a more mature culture.

Unlike some of its Ivy cousins, Princeton did not have a women's college abutting its campus. There was no sister school for dating on weekends or cross-registration to allow for gentle, incremental steps toward coeducation. For much of its history, it was as much of a male enclave as a navy ship at sea, albeit with weekend shore leave in New York. Women who visited for social events were dubbed "imports," and found themselves in uncomfortable settings.[39] They weren't allowed in bedroom suites.[40] Eating clubs permitted them to dine as guests, in an outwardly chivalrous, polite setting. But after dessert, when their escorts guided them to the door, club members responded by banging spoons on the table. The visitor might feel flattered, but the inside joke was that the louder the noise, the prettier the date: pity the man whose girlfriend generated only a few faint vibrations.[41]

By the late 1960s, many chaperones had lost their will to separate the sexes; thus, dormmates felt free to sneak in overnight guests and hide their presence, often leading to a boudoir farce of mixed-up toothbrushes and locked doors.

All this history combined to frame the debate over whether to admit women around questions of dating, sex, and—for socially conservative doomsayers—pregnancy and abortion. Bob Goheen, the president who pushed hard to admit women, issued a commonsense appeal to normalize campus life: no more running to Manhattan on Saturdays in search of companionship. "The need is for the presence of both sexes in the day-to-day life of the university as something natural and accepted, as against the forced and frenetic weekends that have become too much a part of the Princeton experience in recent years," Goheen explained to skeptical alumni.[42]

Tiny numbers of women had attended classes at Princeton as early as 1963. They were part of a Critical Languages Program that allowed students from other colleges to study Russian, Arabic, Japanese, Chinese, and other languages, thereby boosting attendance in lightly enrolled courses; women were included at the insistence of the coed liberal arts colleges that partnered with Princeton. The Critical Languages women quickly received the nickname "Critters."[43]

But Critters were never fully credentialed Princeton women. To test the concept of coeducation, the university invited eight hundred women college students to visit the campus for a week in February 1969—the middle of Sam Alito's freshman year.[44] To make the women feel welcome, administrators ousted male students from their dorms and put potted plants in bathroom urinals.[45]

Even *The Daily Princetonian*—ostensibly a force for coeducation—framed the visit in terms of dating and socializing. "To our fellow Princetonians, we can only say: beware. Older and wiser heads than ours have been turned from scholarly pursuits by the sight of nubile femininity," the newspaper opined. "Perhaps the reactionary alumni are right. Perhaps the presence of women is merely disruptive. We don't think so, but it's up to us to prove to the skeptics that business and pleasure can indeed be mixed together."[46]

A columnist followed up: "How refreshing a pause it will be in the middle of a boring art lecture to stare casually at the curvature of real feminine knees and compare their aesthetic value. A 'Princeton gentleman' is appreciative of natural beauty. And our old gigantic elms are nice, but . . ."[47]

Sophomoric humor aside, coed week was successful enough that Goheen and the trustees authorized the admissions office to accept women for the class of 1973, and for women to transfer into the earlier classes.[48] That gave Alito's class of 1972 a special distinction: it was the last all-male class to enter Princeton.

The women who arrived the following fall encountered a distinctly second-class experience, piled into makeshift dorms like Pyne Hall, excluded from clubs, whistled at by classmates.[49] Susan Squier, who transferred into Alito's class of 1972 en route to becoming a gender studies professor, described brutally sexist scenes in which women were "made fun of" in classes and steered clear of eating club events for fear of being molested.[50] By contrast, Stevenson Hall was a haven. Most of the men there had attended public high schools with girls, and some were even able to see women as peers. Alito's precise views on coeducation would become a point of contention in later years, but he claimed to have been unfazed by female classmates because of his experiences at Steinert.[51] In contrast to the randy club members, the bookish Alito was seen as "safe" by women.[52] But even he was prone to red-faced, innuendo-filled jokes to cover up the awkward feelings that were pervading the campus.

During his debate club trip to Smith College, he unleashed a series of double entendres using the language of economics to describe Princeton's thinking in admitting women: "With the price of imports rising and the quality of goods declining, university officials thought it time for Princeton to foster its own infant industry."[53]

....

THE JOKESTERS WEREN'T ENTIRELY off base. Princeton's social life began a painful period of adjustment, especially around the area of sex. Male-female interactions changed substantially. When couples saw each other only on weekends and at heavily chaperoned events, sex was something to be approached furtively or avoided entirely. Having men and women share a campus and see each other every day introduced the prospect of stable, longer-term relationships between partners with no plans for marriage. Dorm-room conversations began to revolve around how to handle this new mode of dating, including which forms of contraception to use and, in a worst-case scenario, what to do in the event of pregnancy.

For teenaged boys from devout Catholic families, these conversations were discomfiting. It wasn't simply the prospect of premarital sex, with all its wonders and taboos; it was the need to defend chaste beliefs that were once the default position on campus but now seemed outmoded or prudish.

For people in immigrant families of Sam Sr. and Rose's generation, sex outside of marriage led to disastrous outcomes. An unplanned pregnancy obliged a man to propose marriage instantly; failure to do so rendered him a fugitive from the community and damaged his girlfriend's chances of marrying another man. Equally important, it violated the unspoken rules of a happy family life—the magical progression from boyhood and girlhood to husband and wife to parents and grandparents, as sanctified by a host of rituals and social norms. The Catholic Church deemed premarital sex a mortal sin. There was no ambiguity in the lessons handed down to boys and girls at Our Lady of Sorrows. However sympathetically it was presented, the answer was an absolute, door-slamming no.

And yet here were students at Princeton openly challenging these notions—in some cases fecklessly, in others boldly—with many using the language of liberation. In some conversations, even more challenging acts, like sex among men or women, crept under the umbrella of sexual privacy.

The whole idea of the bedroom as a private sanctuary had been given voice by the Supreme Court just a few years earlier. In the 1965 case of *Griswold v. Connecticut*, a Planned Parenthood board member named Estelle Griswold was arrested for distributing birth-control information and devices to married women; the state of Connecticut had outlawed contraceptives since 1879. But many married couples chafed at the restriction, arguing that the state had no legitimate reason to oblige them to give up sex if they couldn't afford more children.

Seven of the nine justices agreed that the state was unjustified in telling couples how to handle their marital relations. The majority opinion created a newly named right to privacy based on personal liberty as expressed in multiple places in the Constitution's Bill of Rights; Justice William O. Douglas, who wrote the majority opinion, used the term "penumbra" to describe the shadow of privacy emanating from the First, Third, Fourth, and Fifth Amendments.[54] Though the new right didn't yet apply to unmarried couples, the court was strongly signaling that lawmakers should tread carefully when approaching people's bedrooms.

Like most states, New Jersey heavily restricted abortions, but its political temperature was changing fast. Next-door New York was already in the process of legalizing the termination of pregnancy. Like clockwork, the combination of legalization and women arriving at Princeton led to a spate of abortion ads in *The Daily Princetonian*. One ad, entitled "Your Questions on Abortion," included a series of queries such as

"How promptly can surgery be scheduled?" with the answer "Within 24 hours." A procedure that had long been spoken about in whispers was suddenly blaring in newspaper type.[55]

At nineteen, Sam Alito found himself talking about not only subjects his church considered sinful but also his own achingly personal responses to them. In dorm-room conversations, he defended his belief in refraining from sex before marriage, according to three classmates.[56] At least one of his roommates shared his views.[57] It was a mature decision, but not the one that many others were making on the cutting edge of morality. Once again, he was out of step with the dominant culture at Princeton.

CHAPTER 4

War Within and Without

The grainy TV show appearing on the night of December 1, 1969, wasn't a typical holiday-season special: it was almost a matter of life and death for families with sons born between 1944 and 1950. Live from Washington, DC, the Nixon administration was staging a lottery to determine the order in which young men would be drafted to serve in the Vietnam War.[1]

The war had shown its brutal face in 1968, the year Sam Alito graduated from high school: almost seventeen thousand Americans had been killed. Now, in 1969, deaths were declining—they would end up just short of twelve thousand—but few people expected the fighting to end quickly.[2]

Beyond the casualty list was the destructive toll on families. Like Sam, many of the young men who were exposed to the draft had fathers who'd served in the Second World War. While some of those dads were profoundly affected by combat disorders, the stakes of that global conflagration, and way the country had rallied to victory and emerged with new power on the world stage, made it a unifying event. Mobilizing against a common enemy had broken the barriers separating white men of all classes, religions, and nationalities; only the race barrier was enforced by the military. For many immigrants, the Second World War was a chance to indelibly bond with their adopted nation—to stand on equal footing with those who traced their ancestry through the *Mayflower*.

The messages those proud veterans handed down to their sons varied, of course. Many were deeply reluctant to send another generation off to war. But most couldn't help seeing parallels between their own patriotic duty and that of their offspring. Fighting for your country was part of becoming a man.

But the Vietnam War wasn't the Second World War; it was a proxy fight against communism, though the seriousness of the threat posed by North Vietnam was a matter of intense dispute. Many Americans rejected the notion that allowing communism to take root in Vietnam would lead to its spread throughout Southeast Asia—the so-called domino theory that underpinned the American intervention. Appalled by photographs of US soldiers gunning down Viet Cong villagers, some wondered what was so wrong about communism in a country that had long been a colonial pawn. In their eyes, Americans were the outsiders, the aggressors, the killers.

Young men with reservations about the war had no good options. Would they dare to defy their family and country and bolt for Canada? On the other hand, what if they submitted to the draft to satisfy their parents' idea of honor and ended up under a tombstone in the family plot?

The contours of the Vietnam debate were elusive, with each decision point seemingly leading to a fresh moral conundrum. The only refuge was in absolutes: End the war now, for some, or stand by America without reservation, "Love it or leave it."

Princeton men were in a precarious position. By dint of a policy that insulated the privileged classes from the horrors of jungle warfare, the military had granted deferments to men enrolled in higher education. Now the inequities of this policy were starting to be noticed. The government removed most deferments for graduate schools, meaning that most of those whose birthdates were pulled out of a glass bowl would be eligible for a ticket to Vietnam immediately after college.[3] News stories laid out the implications of this system: those whose birthdays emerged relatively early in the lottery—"the first 140–150," according to *The Daily Princetonian*—might well prepare themselves to be measured for khakis upon graduation.[4]

This arbitrary, casino-like spectacle seemed destined to breed discord. Its very strictures cast military service as a grim obligation—fateful, and possibly fatal—that fell to the unlucky. The mood at Princeton was anxious as everyone turned on their radios. "We were all listening intently," recalled Richard Clifton, a friend and classmate of Alito's who went on to become a federal judge.[5] *The Daily Princetonian* cast the proceedings in solemn terms: "Never before has a 'fish bowl' meant so much to so many. . . . Depression and relief were the order of the day."[6]

Alito himself wasn't conflicted about the war. He resolved any doubts in favor of pure loyalty to country.[7] Whatever his thoughts about the conduct of the war, they paled compared to his sense of alarm at the defiance and lawlessness of the anti-war protestors: this was not the way to change policies in the United States. Like his father, he was prepared to do his duty.

The broadcast began with Alexander Pirnie, a sixty-five-year-old Republican congressman from New York, pulling the first capsule with an unlucky birthday: September 14.[8] Thus began a grim roll call as capsules were fished out of the bowl one by one, while families at home clutched their hands and exhaled after every selection. On the thirty-second pick, the capsule read April 1—Alito's birthday.[9] This was a strikingly high number. While some questioned *The Daily Princetonian*'s alarming assertion that draft numbers up to 150 could face service, no one doubted that those at number 32 were likely to be called.

So Alito made a practical decision: he would join campus ROTC—the Reserve Officers' Training Corps—and prepare to be an officer. This would give him more control over his ultimate assignment. He could also gain Princeton course credits in the process. "Sam figured quite rationally that he was going into the army, and he figured he'd rather be an officer than an enlisted man," explained Dwyer, his future roommate.[10]

There were complications, however. For decades, Princeton students and faculty had frowned on giving credit for ROTC classes. A 1931 *Daily Princetonian* editorial compared the practice to giving academic points for "carpentry or industrial glass-blowing."[11] Those objections reached a crescendo as students and faculty groped for ways to express their opposition to the Vietnam War.

This put the tiny sliver of ROTC students—only twenty-seven would graduate in Alito's class—under a spotlight.[12] It made them as much of a symbol of militarism as the ROTC itself.

It wasn't just that those students' opinions were different from many of their classmates'. It was the perception that they stemmed from precisely the kind of blind loyalty that so many young people were rejecting. The protesters might have had more respect for such choices if they seemed to be freely made. But no: the war supporters were just applying the dogma handed down by older generations. That made the views of Alito and other ROTC members not only less legitimate but also more dangerous, in the sense that if everybody followed the old precepts as obediently as they did, the whole country would be on a runaway train to hell. To the growing numbers of protesters, that made Alito and his ilk a big part of the problem, beyond even the merits of the war he was in training to enter.

Alito was outnumbered. But among his own cohort, there was a righteousness of their own. It was not, precisely, the Nixon administration that they were defending—Andy Napolitano's broadsides in *The Daily Princetonian* aside.[13] It was the American system of governance, the rules that everyone must play by. In this reading, the protesters themselves were more dangerous than what they were advocating for. Yes, there were points to be made against the administration's war policy. The danger to America wasn't necessarily that the war would be stopped. The danger was in the fury in the streets, in the whole evil anarchical idea that you could impose your will on others simply by being loud and angry and—deliberately or not—conveying a threat of violence.

Alito and the protesters were on that rarest of trajectories: a collision course without an end. Each would carry their convictions against the other for far longer than the Vietnam War would last. And the fierce passions of 1969 would linger, submerged, simply because the stakes were so high and the choices so personal.

....

PRINCETON WAS IN TURMOIL. The threat of disorder proved all too real. It was as if the old, carefree, drunkenly aristocratic campus of Fitzgerald's day had been swallowed up and spit out in a mad purging of all that was smug and self-satisfied.

The Daily Princetonian's headlines reflected the extent of the upheaval. Titles like "Activists Challenge Princeton to Modernize with the Times"[14] and "Students Arrested in Armory Arson"[15] replaced social write-ups and profiles of faculty leaders. In the four years before Alito's arrival, the word "protest" had appeared in 360 articles in the campus paper; similarly, the word popped up in 366 articles in the four years following his graduation. But during his time at Princeton, from the fall of 1968 to the spring of 1972, there were a whopping 643 such articles—the greatest display of militancy in campus history.[16]

Political activist groups had started to pop up as early as the second semester of Alito's freshman year. They were hardly overrunning the campus, but it was difficult to ignore the harshness of their messages. About 350 East Coast members of Students for a Democratic Society (SDS), a national group that drew a line between civil rights, the anti-war movement, and socialism, converged on Princeton in February. They drew up a manifesto demanding an end to the ROTC, war-related research, and military recruiting on campus, while pushing progressive reforms like open university admissions.[17]

That same month, the Association of Black Collegians led a one-day strike to commemorate the anniversary of Malcolm X's assassination while pushing to end the war and divest university assets from racist South Africa. "This Friday boycott is for black students," one strike leader declared in an edgy aside. "We do not especially urge whites to cut classes unless they feel a genuine spiritual unity with us."[18]

When administrators tried to impose a new speech code to rein in demonstrations, SDS and the Association of Black Collegians joined the mainstream student government in condemning it in sweeping revolutionary terms: "This policy is designed to stop those of us who believe that the University cannot be allowed to act as the apologist, researcher, and personnel producer for the rulers of this country . . . We are to be destroyed because we represent a growing threat to a system that defines its 'rationality' in the charred limbs of Vietnamese freedom fighters and the racist and class oppression of most Americans—on the one hand—and the profits and power of the country's ruling class on the other."[19]

The following winter, Nixon's secretary of the interior, Walter Hickel, showed up on campus to deliver a speech and was greeted by seventy-five

SDS members dressed in Native American costumes. It was an apparent reference to Hickel's oversight of reservations at a time when tribes were trying to assert more independence. The "Hickel heckle" drowned out Hickel. (He would later be fired by Nixon for saying the administration's war policy had alienated young people.)[20] A furious President Goheen threatened disciplinary action while protesters shouted the slogan "Today's pigs, tomorrow's bacon! Nixon and Hickel better start shakin'!"[21]

There wasn't much of a counterbalance. A close friend of Andy Napolitano's named T. Harding Jones established an activist group called Undergraduates for a Stable America.[22] It backed Nixon and opposed the protests. The group's support came from far less privileged students—a harbinger of conservatism to come—but no one seemed to pay it much attention; conservatives of any stripe were largely invisible in the ruckus. Alito wasn't active in the group—studying and debating were his twin obsessions—but Napolitano and other friends felt he shared its goals.[23]

The salient emotion wasn't love of Nixon but hatred of the protesters. George Carpinello, an Italian American friend and classmate of Alito's who identified as politically liberal, said that even he was bothered by the snide tone of the protesters. The ease with which they presumed to speak for the university reeked of class bias and insensitivity to those simply trying to get a Princeton education.

"For someone like me, and for someone like him, I think there was a feeling of people really abusing a privilege they had been given, denigrating and disrupting such an august institution," Carpinello said. "Coming from the same kind of ethnic background—Catholic, Italian—you have a tendency to be on the more conservative side."[24]

....

ON APRIL 30, 1970, President Nixon shocked the country by revealing that the United States was sending troops into Cambodia, a next-door staging ground for communist fighters in Vietnam.[25] The goal was to roust the Viet Cong, the president assured in a televised speech, not to make war against neutral Cambodia. But this expansion of fighting ran counter to the administration's assurances that it was training South Vietnamese fighters to take the place of Americans, and thus making progress toward an "honorable peace."[26]

Soon, the full dimensions of Nixon's strategy would become known, including the fact that the US had been secretly bombing Cambodia for more than a month. This threw toxic new questions into the Vietnam mix: Did Nixon have the power to invade a non-combatant country without congressional approval? What was the endgame here?

In an explosion of visceral anger, Princeton students poured out of their dorms within an hour of the president's announcement to join a pre-planned anti-war rally. More than twenty-five hundred people piled into the Princeton University Chapel, a massive cathedral built in the fourteenth-century style, with many students jammed cross-legged in the aisle.[27]

With its towering arches, enormous stained-glass windows, and memorial plaques, the chapel resembled an Americanized version of London's Westminster Abbey; some of the pews were carved out of wood from Sherwood Forest. In this Gothic fortress, under windows depicting Jesus Christ and various signers of the Declaration of Independence, rage over war, injustice, government secrecy, and the looming threat of death in combat brought the pulsating spirit of protest into the beating heart of the university.[28]

The dean of the chapel, a Scottish Presbyterian minister named Ernest Gordon, presided from a sixteenth-century pulpit imported from France.[29] Gordon was a muscular liberal, a survivor of three years in a Japanese prison camp who once hosted Martin Luther King Jr. in his campus home. After being driven to campus from the Trenton train station in Gordon's battered Peugeot, the civil rights leader quizzed his host's young children on their favorite books and sports while Gordon assured the kids that they were talking to a giant, "one of the rare prophetic voices in the land."[30]

Now Gordon was bringing his ministerial gravitas to another cause, at another moment of crisis. It was unclear to what extent he led the crowd or the crowd led him, but a turning point had been reached. After fiery speeches, the giant congregation voted to stage an immediate strike against all academic and social functions of the university.[31] But then a strange thing happened, redolent of all the pent-up aggression: University police alerted Gordon that they had received a bomb threat against the chapel.[32] Immediately, he urged that the meeting be moved to the fountain plaza outside the Woodrow Wilson School.[33] As the crowd pressed outward, one frenzied student rushed to the altar and handed his draft card to Gordon, yelling to the departing students, "You're all hypocrites if you don't do the same."[34]

At the massive rally at the fountain plaza, which began at 11:50 p.m. and bled into the wee hours of May 1, protest leaders announced plans to picket classes and ticked off their demands: end ROTC, cease all connections with the Defense Department, terminate contracts for the Institute of Defense Analyses (a federally funded research center), and ban military recruiting.[35]

"Nixon pushed everybody over the brink," recalled Richard Balfour, who was *The Daily Princetonian*'s editorial page editor at the time.[36] His paper endorsed the strike and gently goaded students into backing it to refute the university's reputation for complacency: "It would be selfish and cruel for Princeton students to spend the weekend drinking beer and frolicking in the Wilson School pool while their brothers are dying in Vietnam and Cambodia, or demonstrating for the Black Panthers in New Haven."[37]

....

JUST TWENTY-FIVE HOURS AFTER the fountain rally broke up, at 3 a.m. on Saturday morning, two Princeton students, aided by two comrades from nearby colleges, tossed half-gallon Molotov cocktails through the windows of Army and Navy ROTC offices at the campus armory.[38] The small bombs set off fires and caused smoke damage that the university estimated would cost $15,000 to repair—or $120,000 in 2025 dollars.[39]

Strike leaders condemned the firebombing but proceeded with a "multi-media" program at the chapel that afternoon.[40] Drama heaped upon drama: the schedule included anti-war films, a student-penned play entitled *Antithesis*, and a passion play produced by a popular English professor.[41] But that was just a warm-up for the real theatrics—the climactic moment that

Princeton students still carry in their hearts with warmth or anger. In his "roaring baritone"[42] with its Scottish intonations, Dean Gordon stood at the pulpit and called upon students "to place your draft cards on the altar as a gift to God."[43] One by one, 175 young men stepped up to deposit their documents in a silver collection plate.[44] There the papers sat, like offerings for a future service. Later, more students returned to the chapel with their own cards, adding to the pile. Gordon, back in his office, explained that he would convene a meeting on Tuesday, May 5, to decide what to do with them.[45]

"Of course I could do nothing else," Gordon told *The Daily Princetonian*, as if moved by an overpowering sense of religiosity and submission to a higher power.[46] The following day, at a music concert, another sixty-nine students surrendered their draft documents.[47] The idea of placing draft materials in the protective hands of a man of God, as if it were within his mystical power to stop the violence, spread across the country. Soon, Gordon was receiving mailed-in draft cards from the University of Texas, Union College, Kenyon College, and many more.[48]

The following day—Sunday—more than a thousand students joined an emergency meeting of the University Council that lasted for seven hours, only breaking up at midnight.[49] The product of one of President Goheen's reforms, the University Council was meant to democratize governance of Princeton by bringing together administrators, students, faculty members, and even a small cadre of graduate students.[50] At the end of the marathon session of nearly nonstop speeches, council members unexpectedly voted to expel ROTC from campus: no training, no course credit, no use of university facilities.[51] This wasn't a shocking act—not after years of stirring around the topic—but it sent a powerful signal: military service wasn't a suitable match for higher education, and student soldiers should look elsewhere for any succor. A month later, the Princeton trustees would ratify the council's decision.[52]

On Monday, more than 80 percent of students refused to show up for classes.[53] Most gathered with the rest of the Princeton community for a special planning meeting instead. As they crowded into Jadwin Gym, the beloved home of the Princeton Tigers basketball team, to vote on whether to continue the strike, word began to spread that National Guardsmen had shot and killed four unarmed students at Kent State University in Ohio.[54] The specter of blood darkening a campus lawn, of screaming and crying protesters, and of a phalanx of rifle-carrying guardsmen in riot gear didn't deter anyone at Princeton.[55]

Shell-shocked professors in bow ties joined militant students in condemning the government in harsh terms. When the crowd voted on the merits of the strike, only a paltry 181 out of 3,769 voters favored a return to classes, the proposal put forward by the Anti-Strike Committee.[56] The majority opted to continue the strike as a redirection of energy outward from the university, a way to grapple with the dire events in Washington and Southeast Asia. The university itself wasn't the target; it was the war makers. The purpose was to marshal Princeton's institutional energy "to work against the expansion of the war."[57]

"It was a godsend for me," conceded one strike organizer, Grif Johnson, who acknowledged that he was so wrapped up in the protests that he hadn't studied for exams.[58]

Most students continued to boycott classes and activities. Every new day brought more protests. On May 6, nine hundred people marched on the campus headquarters of the Institute for Defense Analyses.[59] Seizing on rumors that the institute had recommended the use of the defoliant Agent Orange—blamed for torching villages and injuring innocent children in Vietnam—student leaders set up pickets at its headquarters; it was a symbol of all that was immoral in the war.[60]

The following day, students succeeded in shutting down the institute's supercomputer, defaced windows and walls with slogans and caricatures of Nixon, and dropped stink bombs into the ventilation system.[61] But then President Goheen, who had previously expressed cautious support for the students' views, decided to get tough. On May 11, protesters were met with police in riot gear.[62] The clash of cultures that exploded at Kent State had reached Princeton as well.

The crackdown didn't stop the violence, however; it may even have triggered it. One day after the riot police arrived on campus, amid a growing sense of crisis, a student arsonist set fires at both the Institute for

Defense Analyses and Nassau Hall.[63] Built in 1756 as the largest stone building in the American colonies, "Old Nassau" was steeped in history and beloved by generations of students. Freed from British control by George Washington in the Battle of Princeton, Nassau Hall went on to become the de facto Capitol building of the United States, hosting the Continental Congress in 1783. This magnificent structure wasn't just an emblem of Princeton; to many people, it *was* Princeton.[64]

Now it was a target.

. . . .

ALITO DID NOT PARTICIPATE in the protests, and his silence conveyed a deep disapproval. That much was clear to his friends.[65] But what came next offended him even more. Princeton's faculty, in a mixture of sympathy for the protesters and resignation over their failure to attend class, agreed to postpone exams until the fall.[66] In addition, the university created a two-week break from classes in the fall term to let students campaign for candidates in the 1970 midterm elections. This transparent effort to help anti-war candidates was credited to a group of students at Alito's own dining hall, Stevenson.[67]

Unlike most of his classmates, Sam had attended every class and spent his evenings buried in his schoolwork. He was ready for exams, and if the pattern of a lifetime held, he'd probably ace them.[68] While liberal faculty members believed that delaying exams signified that there were more important things in the world—and more to education than testing, for that matter—Alito focused on how they had allowed irresponsible students to get off scot-free for skipping class.

"Sam was prepared [for exams] and he knew the proposals being discussed, which ultimately permitted lots of things to be kicked off until next October," said his friend Clifton. "Well, if you want to take an exam in the class, and the professor elects to do that, you're kind of screwed, because you spent all this time studying for an exam that's going to be taken two weeks from now, and now you're expected to take it five months from now. What's right about that? And so I remember his frustration at not being able to proceed."[69]

Well before the strike, grading was already a subject of complaints from liberals; they felt that judging student performance with a letter grade was subjective and created a false hierarchy. The previous year, a sociology lecturer got attention for revamping his class to "eliminate the artificial distinction between student and teacher."[70] *The Daily Princetonian* featured a picture of the casually dressed instructor, replete with mustache and a pipe in his mouth, leaning back in his chair with his legs atop his desk.

In Alito's mind, the strike essentially obliterated a semester of education. And it had taken direct aim at his own ROTC chapter. This meant he would have to travel to Trenton State College—his parents' alma mater— to take military courses, a serious logistical hurdle.[71] When students scattered for the summer, many to continue strategizing to end the war, Alito had his own rigorous activity in store: six weeks of officer training at Fort Knox, Kentucky. An army press release from the time proclaimed that he would "train as a small unit leader and instructor in realistic exercises, and [would] receive command experience and the opportunity to apply classroom knowledge in the field."[72]

At Fort Knox, he would meet a very different kind of student. Many came from large public universities and families who supported the military like his own. These ROTC members often needed their stipends to cover the cost of their education, unlike most of his Princeton classmates. They were humble. They were loyal. And they, too, believed they were doing what was best for their country.

....

FOR MOST PEOPLE AT Princeton, the story ended, along with the strike, in the summer of 1970. The campus dispersed, and it returned more or less as usual in the fall.

Though no one seemed to shift allegiances, and sentiments remained overwhelmingly liberal, there was a change that became more noticeable only in retrospect. Undergraduates for a Stable America, the tiny conservative group co-chaired by T. Harding Jones and Andy Napolitano, began to get noticed.[73] This was partly through a strange union with much older conservative alumni.[74] In some ways, these wealthy, steadfast Republicans bore little resemblance to the strivers that Jones and Napolitano purported to represent: they were men of a different era, cosseted by their memories, frank in their prejudices in a way that could never survive the generational changes to come.

But the older alums and the younger conservatives shared a disdain for liberalism, and in their yearning to provide balance on campus, they found some intriguing common ground. In the fall of 1970, Jones and Napolitano received some encouragement from a nascent group of conservative alumni that eventually named themselves Concerned Alumni of Princeton (CAP).[75] The first co-chairs were both scions of old-monied Princeton families: Asa S. Bushnell III '21 and Shelby Cullom Davis '30.[76] Davis was also the university's largest donor, and he expressed deep pain over the arrival of women and people of color. "May I recall, and with some nostalgia, my father's 50th reunion, a body of men, relatively homogenous in interests and backgrounds, who had known and liked each other over the years during which they had contributed much in spirit and substance to the greatness of Princeton," Davis wrote in CAP's magazine. "I cannot envisage a similar happening in the future with an undergraduate student population of approximately 40% women and minorities, as the Administration has proposed."[77]

Also part of the CAP inner circle was William Rusher '44, the publisher of the conservative journal *National Review* and a close associate of that magazine's editor, William F. Buckley.[78]

With alumni encouragement, Jones and Napolitano scored a coup in getting Buckley himself to visit Princeton that fall.[79] He had shot to fame with *God and Man at Yale*, his 1951 book denouncing his own alma mater as a cradle of liberalism, and he knew how to energize Ivy Leaguers who felt out of step with the left. His patrician manner and pedantic speaking style mimicked those of the older Princeton alums, but he was far nimbler and more willing to engage with liberals. When he wrote, cheekily, of guilty-liberal student protesters—"Could it be that there is in the picture a strong streak of psychological masochism?"[80]—people felt entertained by his elaborate syntax, which also took the edge off ideas that many found offensive. In his own inimitable way, he was freshening the old anachronistic views and giving them new zest.

At Princeton, he offered a veritable greatest-hits speech. He tweaked the Black Panthers—whose murder trial in New Haven attracted national attention—as existing "primarily for the satisfaction of white people rather than blacks"; white liberals who "like to strut their toleration"; and "absolutizers," who "in their struggle against what they call repression" make the Constitution "incoherent."[81] With high-toned references to Thomas Jefferson and counterrevolutionary theory, Buckley was lampooning liberals in what seemed like a parody of their own language. Later, Alito would cite him as a formative figure.[82]

The following spring brought tangible evidence that student views were turning rightward. Just a year after ROTC was booted from campus, students voted 1,239 to 945 to allow it back as an extracurricular activity. Cadets wouldn't get course credit for their military classes, but they could use university facilities for their training.[83] A year later, the army and air force would agree to return on those terms, though other branches refused.[84]

. . . .

THE SEEMING TURNAROUND IN feelings about ROTC emboldened conservative alumni. CAP was now officially a thorn in the side of the Princeton administration, to the point that an exhausted President Goheen would resign in 1972 and be replaced by William Bowen.[85] Goheen insisted that alumni pressure played no role in his decision, but he expressed bitterness toward CAP for years after.

Though predominantly an alumni group, CAP helped boost its small cadre of like-minded students. It hired T. Harding Jones to edit its magazine, *The Prospect*, through which it routinely hammered the university on coeducation, inclusion of minorities, and student-health policies that seemed to encourage abortion.[86]

In a 1974 manifesto, Jones wrote: "Alumni are concerned, upset, enraged, sickened, or doubtful about some or all of the following: admissions policy, coeducation, athletics, radicals on campus, the Gay Alliance of Princeton, the refusal to allow alumni trustee candidates to speak out on the issues, the abolishment of almost all rules, the oneness of mind of the Board of Trustees and their apparent failure to act independently of President Bowen, the Alumni Council's ties with the administration rather than its existence as an independent entity, and the failure of the administration to take the leadership in the moral and spiritual development of undergraduates."[87]

In interviews, Jones said coeducation had destroyed Princeton's sense of camaraderie and called it "the fad of the moment."[88] CAP accused the administration of reneging on a commitment to maintain eight hundred men in each incoming class, suggesting that men's slots were being taken by women.[89] *The Prospect* featured numerous columns by Buckley and more incendiary fare. It reprinted a *Daily Princetonian* column by a student who claimed that "many people have homosexual tendencies," but "normal people learn to outgrow this stage and eventually reach sexual maturity." Continuing along the gay path, the writer wrote, was "a crime against God and society."[90] Another piece, entitled "In Defense of Elitism," opined, "People nowadays just don't seem to know their place. Everywhere one turns, blacks and Hispanics are demanding jobs simply because they're black and Hispanic. The physically handicapped are trying to gain equal representation in professional sports. And homosexuals are demanding the government vouchsafe them the right to bear children."[91]

New York Knicks basketball star Bill Bradley, a Princeton legend from the class of 1965 and future US senator, initially expressed support for CAP but repudiated it in 1972 after three issues of *The Prospect*, saying it was "filled with innuendo and unsupported allegations."[92]

Alito identified as a CAP member as late as the mid-1980s, but when confronted on it years later, at his Senate confirmation hearings, he claimed to have "racked my memory" to figure out why.[93] People who knew him at Princeton doubt that he was so conflicted. They remembered feeling that he supported CAP in his own quiet way.[94] In any case, CAP was such a flashpoint that few could be unsure where they stood on it as late as the 1980s.

Alito concluded that he must have joined CAP because of his anger over the university's treatment of ROTC, not coeducation.[95] That rang true enough for those who knew him, but it didn't capture the full extent of how Princeton shaped his later philosophy.

College years are always formative; they're when episodes of conflict or emotion, of secret hurts or private triumphs, combine to form an adult character. Shy, bookish, devoted to his studies, Alito seemed to wear the same nonpartisan mask as his father; it was okay to have strong values and clear political preferences, but advertising them diminished your credibility as a scholar, an independent assessor of facts. And Alito clearly wanted to be remembered for his scholarship, not his politics. The mask slipped only once: when the strike prompted the cancellation of exams. Then, his friends say, he was truly perturbed.[96]

Alito would speak often of a sense of class anxiety, or at least class awareness, at Princeton, a university where "a generation earlier, I think, someone from my background probably would not have felt fully comfortable."[97] Class was everywhere at Princeton; it infused the air above the eating clubs on Prospect Avenue and fertilized the ivy growing on Nassau Hall.

Liberals, too, expressed discomfort with Princeton's class biases. Both they and the nascent conservatives contrasted their alertness and attentiveness to the changing world of the 1960s with the lack thereof among upper-class club members. Though Princeton's archives suggest that most eating clubs supported the strike by postponing social events until after graduation in that fateful spring of 1970,[98] George Carpinello, who agreed with Alito about the delayed exams, insisted, "There were a lot of parties at a lot of eating clubs after that suspension."[99]

The point seemed to be that the Princeton elite, their positions secure, scored the postponement of exams as a victory: exams were what gave up-and-comers like Carpinello and Alito the credentials to storm their citadel. Alito, who carried with him all the hopes of Rose and Sam Sr., and the whole scrapbook of accomplishments that suggested a great future to come, certainly lived up to the meritocratic ideal of earning his place through hard work.

However, he seemed more bothered by liberals than elitists. Perhaps he perceived, as others did, that the old Princeton aristocrats were already a bit enervated—that the heyday of the Asa Bushnells and Shelby Cullom Davises and their progeny had passed, and that of the Sam Alitos and Andy Napolitanos lay ahead.

The only obstacles were the people who sought to alter the path to success, challenge his heartfelt beliefs, and discredit vehicles like grades that helped to establish his standing in the world.

CHAPTER 5

"The Wages of Crying Wolf"

I f Princeton marked Sam Alito with a lifelong sense of bitterness from watching his classmates "behaving irresponsibly," so too did it steer him toward his lifelong vocation.[1] Out of chaos there was order. He spent much of his collegiate days and evenings squeezed into a study carrel at the Wilson School.[2] With its focus on theory—mapping political geography from thirty thousand feet—the Wilson School was an effective antidote to the frothing, roiling ocean of anger on the campus below. And he soon gained a loyal and encouraging mentor, Professor Walter F. Murphy, who infused legal study with a political scientist's sense of detached analysis.

Murphy was the McCormick Professor of Jurisprudence, a chair that traced its lineage back to the man for whom the school was named, President Woodrow Wilson. Princeton didn't have a law school, but the university prided itself on its ability to assess the legal system in the larger context of American governance. Murphy himself wasn't a typical law professor. For one thing, he had a PhD, not a law degree, and his eclectic interests ranged so widely that he wrote a bestselling potboiler about a young man from an Irish family who became a hero in the Korean War and chief justice of the United States before being elected pope.[3]

Murphy may have been telling an idealized version of his own story. He was a Korean War hero, as well as an unexpectedly influential constitutional scholar. "He pioneered the study of judicial politics within the Supreme Court—the politics of putting together a coalition on the court to reach a decision," said Sotirios Barber, a political science professor at the University of Notre Dame.[4] This was a fresh look at a cloistered institution. Lawyers, with their focus on reaching the "right" outcome, would not accept the notion of a Supreme Court justice as a savvy political operator; it was anathema to them.

Alito seemed every inch the devoted pupil. As always, he typed up his homework and kept harsh judgments to himself. And Murphy sensed the potential in him as few people at Princeton did. Where others saw a hard worker, a grinder who pushed his way onto the honor roll, Murphy saw an expansive intellect. As a law professor, Murphy seemed to sense that Alito's studiousness wasn't a sign of submission or passivity or grade-grubbing—it was a sign of his determination to master the material before sounding off. He wasn't looking to be part of the conversation at Princeton; Princeton would give him the credibility to assert himself at a time of his choosing. Decades later, when Alito was named to the Supreme Court, Murphy was perhaps the only Princetonian who wasn't surprised to see him make such a big leap. In touting his enthusiasm for Alito, Murphy disparaged others whom he considered far less able—including the man who appointed him, President George W. Bush, and Alito's future colleague Clarence Thomas.

"I confess surprise that a man so dreadfully intellectually and morally challenged as George W. Bush would want a person as intellectually gifted, independent, and morally principled as Sam Alito on the bench," he opined.[5] After commentators suggested that Alito's approach to the law was similar to Justice Thomas's—a compliment in conservative circles—Murphy was having none of it. "It's a gross insult to say [he's] in the mold of Clarence Thomas," he countered. "Their IQs are so radically different . . . We're not talking about someone in Sam's intellectual league."[6]

Murphy's appreciation of Alito was even more noteworthy because he was not himself a conservative. He noted that he had a "fundamental difference" with his protégé on "what is euphemistically (and foolishly) called 'original understanding.' We don't know and, more crucially, can't know how white American males 'understood' the Constitution in 1787–1788 beyond what the text itself says in the Preamble."[7]

In retrospect, Alito's work with Murphy at the Wilson School offered glimmers of his future interests and convictions about the law, but with a more youthful, open-minded, and even searching approach. He chaired a Wilson School conference on privacy,[8] in which students produced more than a dozen essays on various threats to personal privacy and proposed practical responses. This forward-looking task force covered topics like government surveillance, data gathering, and data protection. In his "Report of the Chairman," Alito mentioned the threat of the nascent "cybernetic" revolution and the risk of the government's breaching the walls of the bedroom. This latter concern followed the Supreme Court's assertion of the right to privacy in the contraception case of *Griswold v. Connecticut*. "The Conference believes that no private sexual act between consenting adults should be forbidden," Alito wrote in his report, and that "discrimination against homosexuals in hiring should be forbidden."[9] He did not, however, acknowledge whether he personally endorsed those conclusions.

When pre-law students went to Washington in the spring of 1971 to meet an illustrious Princeton graduate on the Supreme Court, Justice John Marshall Harlan II, Alito engaged him in a conversation about "the law of the case"—a doctrine Harlan invoked that calls on judges to tailor their rulings narrowly to the facts of the case.[10] In the 1960s and early 1970s, this was a conservative position: Harlan meant to suggest that the Warren Court was going beyond the confines of the cases at hand to assert its own power. But in later years, the same charge of going further than what was strictly necessary to resolve cases would be leveled at Alito, most notably in his *Dobbs* decision.

Alito's senior thesis was a labor of love, the product of a summer spent in the country his father and grandparents had left behind nearly sixty years earlier. It was a chance to bond with his ancestral homeland and test his ability to capture the intricacies of Italian law. His 134-page assessment of the Italian Constitutional Court—as much a work of journalism as legal scholarship—was crisply written and delved into areas of later interest. In one pointed passage, he noted that "the myth of the judge as automaton, as disinterested finder of the law, is probably stronger today in Italy than in America. To study the court as a political body still seems to many Italians almost profane."[11]

This observation lent itself to many interpretations. Was he saying he believes courts are indeed political bodies? Was he chiding the Warren Court for making Americans lose faith in judges as disinterested finders of facts? Or was he merely referencing Professor Murphy's approach of viewing judicial decisions as exercises of political skill?

Elsewhere in the thesis, Alito foreshadowed his interest in the law surrounding religion, reviewing dozens of Italian cases touching on the freedom to worship. With a barely discernible sense of approval, he took note of cases granting the Catholic Church extra protections from government interference because it reflects the "ancient uninterrupted tradition of the Italian people."[12]

How to give force to long-standing traditions and practices would be a later obsession of Alito's. Maybe he was schooling himself for it by studying Italian precedents, hoping to glean insights from a country that more explicitly acknowledged the intertwining of its religious and national roots. But only one thing was clear: at the dawn of his interest in the law, in the safe confines of the Wilson School, he exhibited an open-mindedness that would be less evident later in his life.

. . . .

FEARS OF AN AUTOMATIC induction into the military for the class of 1972 proved blissfully unfounded. In the months following graduation, the Vietnam War was winding down. Nixon, facing reelection, was determined to show that peace was just around the corner. He accelerated negotiations with the North Vietnamese, leading to a drawdown of forces.[13] This not only spared most of Alito's classmates from the draft but also enabled him to delay his ROTC commitment until after he finished his schooling.

Princeton's yearbook, the *Nassau Herald*, carried a striking prophecy under the name of Samuel Anthony Alito Jr.: "Sam intends to go to law school and eventually to warm a seat on the Supreme Court."[14] In later years, he acknowledged writing it but claimed it was a joke.[15] Friends attest that his humor was indeed bone dry, but the expression of confidence caught even them off guard.[16]

In fact, he was one of six students from his class at Princeton—the "Princeton Six," all Wilson School denizens—who would enroll at Yale Law School.[17] The move from leafy Princeton to gritty New Haven may have been a shock to the senses, but the arrival at an institution grappling with internal dissension was eerily familiar.

Even more than Princeton, Yale Law School had been a hotbed of strife for five years and was only then, in the early 1970s, moving aggressively to quell its fires. Yale's place in the constellation of law schools was secure enough: compared to the much larger Harvard Law School, which served as a portal to corporate firms, Yale prided itself on having an academic rather than pre-professional approach to the law.[18] This made it a good fit for a student hoping to "warm a seat on the Supreme Court," except that the line between academic and pre-professional tended to break along liberal and conservative lines. Liberals wanted to infuse legal education with larger themes of fairness and justice and challenge students to critique the system based on those ideals; conservatives preferred the rigor of learning how legal precedents emerged, case by case. Alito was in the conservative camp. He may not have been dreaming of a partnership in a corporate firm, but he wanted to learn the law straight—to get a grip on important precedents and understand precisely how they developed.[19]

At Yale, the residue of half a decade of chaos was all around him and his fellow Princeton grads, including Richard Clifton, Mark Dwyer, and George Carpinello. Yale's constellation of legal thinkers had been caught off guard by the student revolt of the 1960s. Faculty members, most of them schooled in the New Deal era, considered themselves liberals and were unprepared for an assault from the left.[20] These teachers viewed the progress of the Warren Court approvingly. In their minds, the Supreme Court was demonstrating that the Constitution was strong enough to accommodate dramatic changes in social views. Like Justice Brennan in *Abington School District v. Schempp*, the case prohibiting Bible readings in public schools, they felt that the Constitution was elastic, not static. It was a living document. It should be read in terms of its "broad purposes, not specific practices,"[21] and thus readily adapted to changing times. With stepped up legal advocacy for those disadvantaged by the law—such as the poor, racial minorities, and women—the Supreme Court could stay ahead of the political branches in advancing social change.

But starting in the mid-1960s, greater and greater numbers of students weren't buying it. Whatever Brennan and the other justices believed, the Supreme Court was not a force for social change: it was, at best, a lagging indicator. Many students rejected the notion that the Supreme Court could simply shake off decades of decisions that were infected with the biases and exclusions of earlier eras. Such a situation called for a more radical stance than that of the tired New Dealers, who'd become, in their older years, as inured to their privileges as any corporate malefactor.

The law school community lived and learned on top of itself in Sterling Hall, yet another Gothic campus building designed like a miniature medieval palace, a doll-house version of Hampton Court. Law students walked into the building under a stone arch inscribed with the words "Law is a living growth, not a changeless code." There was a courtyard in the middle, perfect for spending an idyllic afternoon on a blanket reading a casebook.[22] But nothing was idyllic or even normal anymore.

Starting in 1967 and reaching a peak in 1969, students routinely and ostentatiously snubbed the faculty. In 1968, they stalked out of an Alumni Weekend panel entitled "Law and the Urban Crisis" in opposition to the idea that white professors could fairly analyze the plight of inner-city ghettos. (They offered their own discussion panel with the cheeky title "Law Is the Urban Crisis.")[23] Emboldened, they were soon rejecting the whole idea of faculty rule, demanding instead that a council with equal faculty and student representation take control over everything from the curriculum to tenure decisions. Liberal faculty members were appalled. "The Student Negotiating Committee Friday received what many of its members considered a rude slap in the face from the faculty, in the form of a faculty resolution effectively rejecting regular student participation in faculty meetings," reported a short-lived law school newspaper, the *Yale Law Advocate*.[24]

Later that month, to avoid a repeat of the previous year's walkout, faculty agreed to hold a special panel on Alumni Weekend to air student grievances. Students didn't hold back. They accused the faculty of "inertia and self-satisfaction" and said Yale was no longer the "very progressive institution at the very frontier of legal education" that it once was. A female student decried the "serious underrepresentation of women." A speaker from the Black Law Students Union declared the minority presence at the school to be no more than a "token" and warned ominously of violence. "You can go on for only so long and there's going to be a fire," another Black student told alumni.[25]

It was a dangerous time. There were indeed fires when classes resumed in the fall—cooking fires. Several dozen peace-loving students set up a commune in the law school courtyard, saying they wanted to demonstrate what real, open, non-hierarchical living looked like. About twenty tents furnished with sleeping bags lined the courtyard. While most of the faculty looked on with distaste, one funky professor, Charles Reich, who had spent the Summer of Love in the hippie haven of San Francisco, sometimes joined the campout.[26] Students later speculated that his presence helped forestall a police raid, since administrators didn't want the bad press of rounding up a tenured faculty member alongside a bunch of student protesters.[27]

WHILE THE LAW SCHOOL communed within itself, a rude shock came from the outside. In May, a trout fisherman found the body of a nineteen-year-old Black man, Alex Rackley, floating in a marsh in Middletown, Connecticut. Gauze strictures bound his wrists. Wire from a hanger circled his neck. Burns singed much of his body, and gunshot wounds penetrated his head and chest.[28]

Rackley was a member of the Black Panthers, the extremist group that was expanding in urban areas around the country. While the group's calls for violent uprisings against racist institutions frightened most people, Black and white, its Marxist–Leninist asceticism appealed to some student radicals. Even students who didn't support violence felt compelled to reckon with the group's message.

It didn't help that the FBI director, J. Edgar Hoover, had dubbed the Panthers the biggest threat to America and let it be known that his office was aggressively moving to infiltrate the group. Rackley, it emerged, was suspected of having informed on the Panthers' New Haven chapter, which was based in a dilapidated housing complex a short distance from the Yale campus. After a months-long investigation, which involved testimony from Black Panther members gleaned in exchange for lenient sentences, prosecutors issued a shocking indictment: Panther members had tortured Rackley with boiling water inside the headquarters, leading him to confess; the order to kill him had come from none other than Bobby Seale, the national chairman of the Panthers, who had been in New Haven to deliver a speech at Yale. Ericka Huggins, the founder of the New Haven chapter, was a part of the conspiracy. In an expression of outrage, the state vowed to seek the death penalty against both Seale and Huggins.[29]

The fact that the attack on Rackley had happened so close to Yale, and that its primary defendant, Seale, had been the university's guest speaker, drew students closer to the proceedings.[30] For many people throughout the university, the case was hopelessly compromised by the larger clash between law enforcement—embodied by Hoover—and the Panthers, with their communist beliefs. The evidence obtained from cooperating witnesses seemed tainted by bias—even though this was a common prosecutorial tactic—and the charge against Seale reeked of political retribution.[31]

Yale students threatened to go on strike to concentrate their energies on the trial. The university's president, Kingman Brewster, negotiated a compromise. The faculty and administration, while remaining "neutral" on the merits of the case, would nonetheless agree to incorporate the wide-ranging issues raised by the trial into classroom discussions. This seemed like a magical solution, a way to preserve the educational mission of the university at an extraordinary moment. But to some faculty members, Brewster went too far—and violated the university's neutrality—

when he announced, "I am skeptical of the ability of black revolutionaries to achieve a fair trial anywhere in the United States."[32]

On April 27, 1970, a fire started in the cluttered basement of the international law library in the law school building, destroying five hundred books. No one claimed credit for it, and it was ultimately determined to be accidental, but many initially believed it was an act of protest.[33] Four days later, while Princeton students were crowding into the chapel to protest the US incursion into Cambodia, more than fifteen thousand people rallied outside the gates of Yale to support Seale and his co-defendants.[34] They included thousands of Yale students led by the university's chaplain, Rev. William Sloane Coffin.

For conservative students in the quiet of their dorms, the events surrounding Brewster's concessions to student protesters marked an indelible turning point. "Kingman Brewster and Yale University capitulated to the radicals and abandoned the whole notion of academic freedom," recalled John Bolton, the future White House national security advisor, who was then a Yale undergraduate before matriculating at the law school and overlapping with Alito. "To me, it was the collapse of intellectual integrity in higher education."[35]

Law students made it their business to police the fairness of the trial; some showed up at the courthouse every day. Others, including a second-year student named Hillary Rodham, joined committees to protect demonstrators from harassment.[36] In the end, while three people were convicted, Seale and Huggins's jury was deadlocked, with the majority favoring acquittal. The charges were dismissed, and they were not retried.[37]

While the brutal facts of Rackley's murder turned some Panther sympathizers into critics, the larger issues surrounding the trial—Hoover, racism, and whether Seale and Huggins were targeted for political purposes—made it an enduring flashpoint. The Panther leaders were unrepentant; Huggins published a book of jailhouse poetry, while Seale ran for mayor of Oakland, California.[38]

For some of the liberal students, the spectacle of the trial represented an escape from convention and a journey into forbidden places; many would remember it as a time of bracing energy and vitality. They tended to gloss over the details of the murder the way some veterans block out the horror of war and recall only the sense of adventure. But for a different kind of student, the anarchy was frightening—a threat to their well-being and the secure future they envisioned as lawyers.

Faculty members toggled between their own urges to break free of the classroom and their fears of losing their platforms. At this rattled moment, Yale Law School needed to choose a new dean for a five-year term starting in 1971. Students wanted a conciliator with whom they could share power; faculty opted for a hard-liner. He was Abraham Goldstein, the forty-five-year-old son of a pushcart peddler and expert in criminal law. Goldstein wasn't a fan of Brewster's concessions to the protesters; he summoned all his expertise to refute the university president's famous quote about fair trials. He said he could "see no evidence yet that the New Haven Panthers cannot get a fair trial here."[39]

He also set about purging the junior faculty of leftists. In law schools, unlike the humanities, assistant professors usually received tenure; with even one law review article under their belt, they could gain permanent membership in the academy. But at Yale, senior faculty believed their junior colleagues had played a role in emboldening the students to take on the institution. Thus began a chain of six rejections of junior faculty—all of whom believed they were being purged for their liberal views.[40]

Goldstein was suspected of weeding out radicals among incoming students as well. At the start of his tenure, in 1971, he allegedly told an alumni group that he wanted a different type of student than the group just graduating.[41] Charles Reich, the faculty member who had sometimes hung out with students in the commune, complained that the school was adjusting admissions standards to increase "the numbers of straight law students"[42]—meaning those committed to a pre-professional path.

At least one of the six Princeton graduates admitted to the first class accepted under Goldstein's regime—Alito's class of 1975—wondered whether they were chosen for their conventional interests.[43] The six were from strictly middle-class backgrounds. Only one had been a major participant in student protests.[44]

. . . .

THE YALE LAW SCHOOL that greeted Sam Alito was benumbed, weary of the feuding that had marked the late 1960s and the Black Panther trial. Yet it was still in the thrall of campus liberalism. Bill Clinton and Hillary Rodham, deeply involved in social issues, were in the third-year class (Rodham had stayed an extra year to be with her boyfriend).[45] Clarence Thomas—still sporting moderate to liberal politics—was in the second-year class, along with the self-described reclusive conservative John Bolton.[46] But Alito didn't interact much with any of them.

The first year of law school can be notorious for its rigidity, but Yale—to soften the blow—assigned each student to a small class where they could interact closely with a senior professor. Alito's assignment would lead to a life-long resentment. His small section was in constitutional law, and his teacher was Charles Reich, the backer of student radicals.[47]

At forty-four, Reich had a tangle of graying curly hair above soft eyes and a boyish smile that could convey kindness and smugness at the same time—a little like author Norman Mailer.[48] Within the legal community, Reich was known for his highly influential 1964 article "The New Property," which began, "The institution called property guards the troubled boundary between individual man and the state."[49] The notion of what constitutes personal property was shaped by the government to safeguard certain forms of ownership, Reich noted. Therefore, he argued, the government could enforce a right to other forms of property, such as social-welfare payments for food and rental assistance.

"The New Property" and others of Reich's writings pointed toward a holy grail of liberalism: a constitutionally protected right to a subsistence level of income and services. It was a foursquare example of how the law could adapt to new visions of rights and responsibilities, a creed that appealed to New Dealers and radicals alike.

For many liberals, this seemed like a logical extension of the Supreme Court's recent jurisprudence—especially after the court, in 1970, mandated that welfare benefits were an entitlement and could not be revoked without a hearing.[50] For conservatives, though, it marked a slippery slope down which a rogue court could govern the country like a super-legislature.

By Alito's arrival at Yale in the fall of 1972, Reich had extended his fame beyond the legal world. Two years earlier, he had published an enormous bestseller called *The Greening of America* that predicted a revolution was coming. "It will not be like revolutions of the past," he wrote. "It will originate with the individual and with culture, and it will change the political structure only as its final act."[51] The book became a cultural touchstone, an attempt to translate to all Americans just what was happening on the nation's campuses. Reich's newfound celebrity put a spotlight on his offbeat teaching methods. A 1971 *Doonesbury* cartoon by Garry Trudeau introduced a character based on Reich whose lecture class consisted of "Be free and freaky, and don't get into an anxiety bag. Stay or leave—do what comes the most naturally for you. Class dismissed."[52]

In Alito's later telling, Trudeau wasn't far off the mark. Alito portrayed Reich as ludicrously, clownishly irresponsible. "He began by saying that his thesis was there were no livable lives to be lived in the law," Alito said in an interview with conservative journalist William Kristol. "That was his phrase. So he went around the room and he'd say, 'Why did you come to law school?' And in those days nobody would say, 'I came to law school because I want to become a partner at a Wall Street firm and make a million dollars,' so everyone would say, 'I came to law school because I think it's a way of achieving social reform or helping society' or something like that. And then he would engage in a long debate with each student to try to prove that this was not a good reason for going to law school . . . And this went on for weeks. And then he went on to other subjects. That was my Con Law course."[53]

But by his own account, Alito's disdain preceded Reich's classroom antics. He told Kristol that he tried to get out of the class as soon as he realized he'd been assigned to Reich: "I had read *The Greening of America*, and I really was not interested in being in his class."[54]

Alito wanted instead to be in the constitutional law class taught by Robert Bork, the bearded conservative iconoclast who loved to mix it up with students, but in a more conventional way. Bork, a specialist in antitrust law, had seen his star rise amid the turmoil of the late 1960s; he co-taught con-stitutional law with his friend Alexander Bickel, a sharp critic of the Warren Court.[55] The two provided a robust counterpoint to all that was going on around them. Alito was especially eager to learn from Bickel, whose career he had followed, but Bickel underwent cancer treatment during Alito's first year and died before his graduation.[56] In Bickel's absence, Alito yearned for Bork. But Yale administrators were affronted by his request. "Never in the history of Yale Law School has anyone ever switched a class," he claimed he was told, as administrators forced him to endure Reich's escapades.[57]

In 2012, Alito told a Federalist Society 30th Anniversary Gala that someone once brought wine to class. "He [Reich] began to chant, 'Who put the acid in the wine, who put the acid in the wine,' and that was the end of the class for the day."[58]

The fact that Alito would choose, many decades later, to unload on Reich in so many conservative settings—the Federalist Society, the Kristol interview, the Heritage Foundation—suggested that Reich's class was more than just a bad memory. It was a defining moment. Reich was the deranged hippie of conservative nightmares, the freaky flower child of a future that conservatives were hell-bent on avoiding. His casual manner suggested a lack of seriousness, an absence of standards, and the feckless-ness with which liberals impugned other people's values and treasures, such as their property rights.

Alito's antipathy toward Reich reflected his own much more conventional expectations. The punch line of some of his Reich stories is that the professor mentioned only one Supreme Court decision all semester—*only one decision in the entire history of constitutional law.* It was *Hammer v. Dagenhart,* which struck down laws to protect child laborers.[59] "I don't know why it came up but that was it," Alito concluded in a 2022 Heritage Society interview.[60]

"So I'm self-taught," he told Kristol. "A lot of people say, 'This ex-plains a lot.'"[61]

Not everybody at Yale disdained Reich. One student who attended the law school in the same period as Alito portrayed him as a bracing antidote to the rote learning demanded by other professors: Reich respected the fact that intelligent students could read and analyze the important constitutional cases on their own; he wanted to break the shackles of legal precedent and force these future leaders to look at the law through a moral lens.[62]

And so the battle lines were drawn. Liberals wanted to refresh the system with new values and updated thinking. Conservatives like Alito wanted to understand the black-letter law down to the precise nuances on which a decision might turn. Using theory to gloss over the nuts and bolts of constitutional law was specious. Theory was a tool for radicals. A healthy respect for Supreme Court precedents wasn't just a boring concession to the past; it was a way to rein in the runaway ponies of American liberalism.

. . . .

LIKE THE FACULTY OF Yale Law School, the Supreme Court of 1972 was engaged in retrenchment. Earl Warren had been retired for three years. His replacement as chief justice was the Nixon appointee Warren Burger. With his mane of gray hair and chiseled features, he personified judicial normalcy. A judge who approached his job with the pragmatic eye of a practicing lawyer, Burger wanted to restore a sense of reasoned centrism.[63]

And yet the court was confronting one of the thorniest social issues of all time: abortion. This, too, was the product of changing values of the 1960s. Spurred by demands from many quarters—including the women's movement—a few states such as New York moved quickly to remove or reduce criminal penalties for abortion.[64] But most states weren't budging, and women seeking to terminate unwanted pregnancies saw a right to abortion as a logical extension of their recently granted right to contraception.

Despite fierce passions on both sides, abortion was not a partisan issue; Democrats and Republicans each had a mixture of constituencies who favored and opposed abortion rights.[65] Public opposition, however, often centered on Catholicism. For some Catholics, rejecting abortion wasn't just a matter of adhering to church teachings—it was a visceral reaction to the old saw that large families were the result of failures in planning or, worse, attempts by the lower orders to dominate white Protestants.[66] To certain eyes, this made the abortion rights movement the first cousin of the detested eugenics movement of the early twentieth century. Alarms about ever-larger immigrant and African American families had been sounded in varied ways over the decades, sometimes by white Protestants who opposed abortion on the grounds that family planning would lead to the dwindling of their own numbers. Catholics and African Americans, presumably, would continue reproducing, tipping the population scales in their favor.

"The greatest of all curses is in the curse of sterility, and the severest of all condemnations should be that visited upon willful sterility," declared former President Theodore Roosevelt, a father of six, in 1910. "The first essential in any civilization is that the man and the woman shall be father and mother of healthy children, so that the race shall increase and not decrease."[67]

After some wrangling, the justices determined that *Roe v. Wade* would be the main case testing their views on abortion; it was brought by two women attorneys representing an unmarried pregnant mother of two who did not want another child but was unable to obtain a legal abortion in Texas. A companion case, *Doe v. Bolton*, featured a married husband and wife from Georgia who wanted to have "normal sexual relations" but were warned that carrying a pregnancy to term could endanger the wife's life.[68]

The all-male justices of the Supreme Court were thus called upon to consider the proper nature of marital relationships, the physical burdens of pregnancy, the psychological weight of unwanted motherhood, and all the medical complications of aborting a fetus. Traditional Dick-and-Jane conceptions of family life collided with women's liberation and the stark reality that many pregnant women lacked family support or financial security. The justices were plainly uncomfortable, exchanging numerous memos and private messages before ordering a second set of arguments so that two new justices could have their own grab at the hot potato.[69]

In later years, entire Supreme Court nominations would turn on how candidates felt about abortion rights, and whether their judicial philosophies would support the holding of *Roe v. Wade*. But this court, significantly, was not geared to take a stance on the issue. The justices, for the most part, were not party to any movements within the law. Only two of them—William

O. Douglas, the last surviving pick of Franklin D. Roosevelt, and Thurgood Marshall, a Lyndon Johnson appointee—were regarded as progressives at the time of their appointments. And while Douglas was indeed a creature of the left, FDR's other eight appointees, including the centrist academic Felix Frankfurter and the segregationist politician James F. Byrnes, had been all over the political map. Political considerations had played a role in the appointments, but judicial philosophy wasn't usually the decisive factor.

Six of the justices were appointed by Republican presidents, including four by Richard Nixon, but only one—William Rehnquist—identified as a doctrinaire conservative. Most of the justices had switched places on the ideological spectrum during their years on the court—the Kennedy appointee Byron White moved to the right and the Eisenhower appointee William Brennan moved to the left, for example, among many other shifts and epiphanies. Brennan's nomination, in fact, had been considered a concession to Catholic voters. While he insisted he was influenced by a Catholic sense of human dignity, it apparently steered him away from his church's position on *Roe*.

Many feminists, including the pioneering women's-rights attorney Ruth Bader Ginsburg, hoped that the justices would base their decision on the Constitution's equal protection clause.[70] Women's ability to function on an equal footing to men in the family and in the workplace depended on controlling their pregnancies. There was constitutional weight behind such an approach. Equality was a fundamental underpinning of the law; no one could claim the court was making up rights out of whole cloth. The justices would be applying the same clause that had been so powerfully vindicated in the segregation case of *Brown v. Board of Education*.[71]

But society wasn't comfortable equating women with men, and vice versa. The two sexes were different; God made them so. If feminists were to seize on the equal protection clause to secure the right to abortion, what was next? Shared restrooms? Mothers of newborns being drafted into jungle warfare? If it tried to draw equivalences between women and men, the Supreme Court would be offending biology and nature while poking its nose into the barracks and locker rooms of America.

The court seemed eager to remove abortion from a strict gender analy-sis, and the obvious vehicle for that was the right to privacy asserted in the *Griswold* contraception case. The various justices still saw different constitu-tional roots for the right to privacy—the Ninth Amendment, the liberty and due process clauses of the Fourteenth Amendment, the "penumbra" of other rights—but to some, this only reinforced the existence of a zone of personal freedom. And pregnant women weren't the direct targets of abortion laws. Those facing prosecution were often medical professionals, most of them men.

Justices searched their own experiences for sources of wisdom. Harry Blackmun, the Nixon appointee from Minnesota in his third year on the court, was assigned by Burger to write the opinion. He understood the stakes of an unplanned pregnancy from his own family life: one of his three daughters had dropped out of college and entered an unhappy marriage to her twenty-year-old boyfriend because she got pregnant.[72] She subsequently suffered a miscarriage and got a quick divorce. In addition, the highlight of Blackmun's professional life had been his nine years as counsel to the famed Mayo Clinic, working with some of the finest doctors in the land. Many physicians and medical organizations felt strict abortion laws disrupted the doctor–patient relationship.[73]

Deferring to the judgment of medical professionals sat well with the court, especially Chief Justice Burger,[74] and at least partly sidestepped the issue of women's rights. Of course states would retain some interest in regu-lating abortion, just like other medical practices. The question became when that interest would kick in. Blackmun, in consultation with Lewis Powell and other justices, developed a timetable based on the progress of a wom-an's pregnancy.[75] For the first three months, women would be free, with a doctor's approval, to terminate a pregnancy; in the last trimester, with the fetus at or near the point of viability, the state could act to protect "potential life."[76] In the middle trimester, women would retain the right to an abortion, but the state would also have a greater rationale for imposing regulations.

This formula satisfied seven of the nine justices, including five of the six Republican appointees. Only White, who privately avowed his own liberal views on abortion but felt the opinion treaded too heavily on state legislative territory,[77] and the conservative newcomer Rehnquist dissented. White, who carried the distinction of being both a Rhodes scholar and a member of the Pro Football Hall of Fame, made clear that he believed the court had badly overstepped its bounds. "I find nothing in the language or history of the Constitution to support the Court's judgment," he declared. "The Court simply fashions and announces a new constitutional right for pregnant mothers and, with scarcely any reason or authority for its action, invests that right with sufficient substance to override most existing state abortion statutes."[78]

....

THE SUPREME COURT ANNOUNCED its *Roe v. Wade* decision on January 22, 1973. In newspapers, it took second place to the sudden death of former President Lyndon Johnson at his Texas ranch. Linda Coffee, one of the two lawyers who brought the case, remembers being inundated with messages from celebrants.[79] But the reaction from abortion opponents was more dramatic, opening a wound that would never heal. Terence Cooke, the archbishop of New York, called the decision "tragic," while the head of a Connecticut pro-life group said it facilitated "the wholesale slaughter of unborn children." A Catholic lay group in Virginia called for the excommunication of William Brennan, the only Catholic on the court.[80] Two days later, when Harry Blackmun flew to the small Iowa city of Cedar Rapids for a long-planned mid-winter speech to the local chamber of commerce, he was greeted by a swarm of picketers.

"The rest of Harry Blackmun's life had begun," wrote his biographer.[81]

At Yale Law School, reaction to *Roe v. Wade* was skeptical, and among some professors, sharply negative. Bork was a strong dissenter. So, too, was the highly respected John Hart Ely. Unlike Bork, Ely did not identify as a conservative; he purported to share the New Deal politics of most of the faculty. But like the ailing Alexander Bickel, he was distressed by the state of the Supreme Court. He quickly penned a scathing critique of the abortion decision with the grandly mysterious title "The Wages of Crying Wolf."

"The opinion strikes the reader initially as a sort of guidebook, addressing questions not before the Court and drawing lines with an apparent precision one generally associates with a commissioner's regulations," Ely wrote, declaring that *Roe* is "not constitutional law and gives almost no sense of an obligation to try to be."[82]

At least one student of that era, John Bolton, remembered that criticisms like Ely's were rampant at Yale Law School. Academics found Blackmun's majority opinion unpersuasive as a work of legal craftsmanship. It "read like a sociological essay" rather than a robust statement of constitutional law, Bolton said, summarizing the Yale reaction.[83]

For supporters of abortion rights, this esoteric criticism was beside the point. Certainly, feminists like Ginsburg would have preferred for the court to view abortion as a matter of women's equal protection, tying it to a constitutional pillar that no one could dismiss as the sociological fancy of a group of justices. But the plain fact was the court *had* recognized the rights of women to control their bodies, and that was a breakthrough no matter how circuitous the route chosen by the justices.

For those who did not support abortion rights, however, the offense against the unborn and the purported injury to the Constitution became one and the same.

Sam Alito, entering the second semester of his first year of law school, heard all the chatter about *Roe v. Wade*. He carried a deep and steadfast opposition to abortion from his family and religious background—as his mother, Rose, would later attest.[84] He was also, by his own account, an opponent of the Supreme Court's activist stance on social issues.[85]

A flame of interest had been ignited. A half-century later, when he picked up his pen to write the majority opinion in *Dobbs v. Jackson Women's Health Organization*, the first citation after *Roe v. Wade* itself would be to John Hart Ely and "The Wages of Crying Wolf."[86]

THE MOVEMENT

CHAPTER **6**

A Society of Their Own

Despite coming three and a half years after Earl Warren's retirement, *Roe v. Wade* would be remembered as the last gasp of the Warren Court's judicial activism. The next time the justices confronted a divisive social issue, in 1978's affirmative action ruling in *Regents of the University of California v. Bakke*, their tentativeness was evident. One could only barely discern a ruling by digging through the six different opinions. The decision was muddled. The justices had lost their appetite for dramatic pronouncements.[1]

The court's pullback had the immediate effect of emboldening the academic left. Out was the argument that the law could refresh itself. In was the radical view of the system as hopelessly, fatally embodying the injustices of the past. And now that view had a name: critical legal studies. Its philosophy was simple: "At the root of it is the question of, 'Who does the law serve, and who isn't served?'" said Clare Dalton, a Northeastern University law professor and early adherent.[2]

Its target was mainstream liberalism. Leaders of critical legal studies (CLS) were only too aware of the fate of previous left-wing critiques of the law. Legal realism, built around the idea that judges weren't applying neutral principles but rather their own preferences, had morphed into a toothless analysis deployed by much of the academic left; Yale Law School embraced legal realism even as it drove out radicals.[3] There was also the Law and Society Association of the early 1960s, which charted social influences on the law. It was devoted to objective analysis and lacked any political agenda.[4]

The Crits, as adherents of CLS were known, vowed to keep their edge, even if it meant casting aside potential allies. True Crits should be devoted to toppling the system, not merely studying it. That meant even such radicals as Alito's old antagonist Charles Reich weren't entirely welcome;[5] Reich's seminal tract "The New Property" was progressive enough to terrify the right but still advocated working within the system.[6] The Crits were adamant: the system was the problem.

Youthful energy was their calling card. Two of CLS's leading apostles, Duncan Kennedy and Peter Gabel, wore jeans in the classroom when other law professors donned suits and bow ties. Kennedy and Gabel luxuriated in the flowing, neck-length hair of 1970s teen idols.[7]

"The meetings that occurred had a lot of energy," observed Mark Tushnet, a legal scholar and early Crit. "Two of the figures, Duncan [Kennedy] and Peter Gabel, you could feel a certain kind of, I would say, erotic energy directed to them when they were speaking."[8]

Sex appeal and exclusivity gave CLS a cultish allure. It was where the beautiful kids hung out. Kennedy and Gabel came from vastly different places than Alito and his friends. Gabel hailed from the world of showbiz. He was the only son of a ubiquitous celebrity mother, Arlene Francis, who appeared regularly on the prime-time game show *What's My Line?*, and an award-winning actor father, Martin Gabel. An avowed creature of the counterculture who nonetheless attended old-line Deerfield Academy and Harvard, Gabel described his beginnings in the movement this way: "We came together out of solidarity in a sense that we were going to rebel against the received wisdom of the way we were educated."[9]

Kennedy grew up in the academic enclave of Cambridge, Massachusetts, attended a progressive elementary school, and considered himself a part of the "impoverished gentry"; his father was an architect and his mother a reader at a publishing house.[10] His feelings about the law were shaped by his disillusion with Yale Law School, which he attended from 1967 to 1970, shortly before Alito's arrival. He was one of the radicals who rejected the school's New Deal liberalism and decided that the rigid, hierarchical structures of law schools, combined with their uncritical reverence for legal precedents, turned lawyers into tools of the capitalist system.[11]

As early as 1968, Kennedy put these feelings into writing in a work with the blunt title "How the Law School Fails: A Polemic," in which he attacked law professors as "smug" and "narcissistic."[12] More than a decade later, he would expand his critique into a small book, self-published as a leftist pamphlet, that called for radical reforms such as replacing admissions committees and picking students through a lottery system with quotas for "women, minorities, and working class students," as long as they had "minimal skills."[13] Kennedy was inspired to write the text in part after reading revolutionary pamphlets, and he described the cover as a bit like Mao's *Little Red Book* and a bit like French socialist poster art.[14]

Kennedy accused law schools of blinding students to larger considerations of justice and injustice through "endless attention to trees at the expense of forests."[15] He added that the law school format "encodes a message of the legitimacy of the whole system into the smallest details of personal style, daily routine, gesture, tone of voice, facial expression, a plethora of little p's and q's for everyone to mind."[16] His prescriptions included equalizing salaries for everyone employed by law schools and having secretaries and janitors spend a month teaching classes while professors performed their jobs.[17]

These ideas were all gestating when he, Gabel, Tushnet, and others gathered at the University of Wisconsin Law School in Madison for a summit of left-wing legal activists in 1977. It brought together CLS forces with members of the Law and Society Association and radicals with their own distinctive theories.[18] The mood was more tense than collegial. By the account of one participant, David Trubek, "Law and Society people were very much turned off by the then-emerging CLS crowd . . . Let's call it the yippie-acting-out mode versus the serious-academic-in-conservative-suits mode."[19]

But Gabel, for one, remembered it as a time of "common dawning awareness."[20] The group would go on to meet eight more times, including in Boston, San Francisco, Buffalo, and Camden, New Jersey.[21] The young people who tried to close down universities in the 1960s were making their professional marks in those very institutions in the 1970s. It was easy for them to imagine the world bending to their vision as they gained further leverage in the 1980s and 1990s, after those who came of age under FDR died off. New age radicalism was percolating through the legal world. People were taking notice.

················

THE RISE OF THE Crits coincided with Alito's final years at Yale. Kennedy's dismissal of law schools as failing institutions was felt in the conversational breezes surrounding the New Haven campus. But while the Crits were building on the recent radical past, Alito was proceeding as if the radical past never existed.

His good grades qualified him to be an editor on the *Yale Law Journal*, and his "note" (the term for an academic paper published by a student) adhered tightly to law review norms: the "p's and q's" that Kennedy disdained. About half the words were footnotes, and the piece was rigorously, painstakingly neutral in its methodology.[22]

Alito's political passions were visible only in retrospect, in the subject he took on: the Supreme Court's behind-the-scenes handling of cases limiting religious activity in and around public schools. Once again, as in his Princeton thesis, he was delving into the clash between law and religion. He seemed to view Italy's special relationship with the Catholic Church as an intriguing contrast to the separation of church and state in America, and his note in the *Yale Law Journal* explored the roots of that separation. His starting point was a 1948 case called *McCollum v. Board of Education*, which, Alito informed his readers, "four cardinals and ten bishops of the Roman Catholic church" had decried as a "victory for 'doctrinaire secularism.'"[23]

Following his mentor Walter Murphy's approach of exploring how the justices negotiated among themselves to cobble together a majority, he used the letters and papers of deceased justices to re-create their private deliberations.[24] He bored in on their conflicting views on a once-common practice of public schools allowing voluntary "released time" for students to gain religious education. The justices, Alito made clear, got seriously bogged down in trying to decide how far public officials could go in facilitating religious teaching. The focus of their debate was the Constitution's establishment clause, which bars the government from establishing a state religion.[25]

McCollum put the country on a path toward banning Bible readings in public schools—the decision that stung Alito's own mother in her teaching career. It was a big change in American life, but it grew out of a series of almost trivial disagreements about issues such as whether taxpayer money could be used to pay the bus fare for kids traveling to Bible classes.[26]

Mindful of legal norms, Alito betrayed little evidence of his personal opinions, even though the net effect of his labors was to raise questions about the court's rigid interpretation of the establishment clause. But he also showed his faith in the Supreme Court as an institution. He listed numerous legal scholars who had accused the justices of imposing pre-existing "value judgments" on the religious cases, but then, surprisingly, concluded that the record did not support those accusations.[27] His assessment would have pleased Murphy: the cases were not clashes of deeply personal values but turned on the tangled mechanics of judicial decision-making. Or so he believed.

....

ALITO'S FIRST STEPS ON the career ladder were straight out of the professional playbook criticized by the Crits: summer internship at the New Jersey public defender's office in Trenton; summer associate's position at a corporate partnership; six-month clerkship at a politically connected New Jersey firm. This was followed by the big step up, the chance to clerk for a federal judge on the Court of Appeals for the Third Circuit.[28]

His post–law school career also featured time in the military to fulfill his delayed commitment to ROTC. He was on active duty in the US Army Signal Corps from September to December of 1975. Service in the reserves followed, culminating in an honorable discharge.[29]

The judicial clerkship in Newark was a plum. His boss was Judge Leonard I. Garth, a shopkeeper's son whose life was textured by

Depression-era hardships and combat in the Second World War. A Nixon appointee, Garth was not an ideological judge. He was known to scrutinize the factual record and closely follow precedent.[30]

"My own personal predilections have no place in the decisions that I make, and they should not have a place," Garth once declared. "If there is one thing I feel strongly about, that is the major, major thing."[31]

Garth saw Alito as a kindred spirit. The two would take afternoon walks from the Newark courthouse to a nearby coffee joint to discuss cases. Garth was impressed by Alito's seriousness and took it as a sign that he, too, believed cases turned strictly on precedent and the text of statutes, not a judge's view of an appropriate outcome.[32]

Three decades later, when Alito was nominated for the Supreme Court, Garth considered himself a crucial character witness, telling the Senate Judiciary Committee that Alito was a legal purist who would never prejudge a case: "I can tell you with confidence that at no time . . . has he ever expressed anything that could be described as an agenda, nor has he ever expressed any personal predilections about a case or an issue or a principle that would affect his decision. Make no mistake: he is no revolutionary."[33]

After impressing Garth with his legal acumen, Alito aimed for the ultimate reward: a clerkship on the US Supreme Court. He scored an interview with Justice Byron White, one of the two dissenters in *Roe v. Wade*, but didn't get the job.[34] Instead, he settled for another mark of mainstream success—a post as a federal prosecutor working under the US Attorney for the District of New Jersey.

His mentor was Maryanne Trump, the eldest child of New York real estate magnate Fred Trump and his wife, Mary Anne. A pioneering woman attorney, she graduated from Mount Holyoke College in 1958 before earning a master's degree in government from Columbia and a law degree from Hofstra.[35] By 1977, she was chief of the appellate division of the US attorney's office in Newark. For four years, she and Alito were two of the three assistant US attorneys who handled criminal appeals.[36]

It was a tough job, as Trump acknowledged. Almost all defendants in high-profile cases appealed their convictions, and any letup by Trump, Alito, or their team could put a criminal back on the streets.[37] Often, they had to defend the government's position under tough questioning.

Alito's ability to rebut the defense lawyers in a dispassionate way was noticed by Trump and others in the office.[38] He outfoxed those who wielded claims of bias or errors by police or trial courts. And he spent almost every day working alongside Maryanne, bringing him closer to the Trump family.

She was between marriages and cast a very different image than her flamboyant brother Donald. While he was cutting a swath through New York's social scene, she was earning a reputation for discipline and probity in the legal world. Her calm competence contrasted with his mercurial style. But the siblings remained on decent, if not close, terms, with Maryanne officiating at weddings of Donald's children. He would sometimes express pride in his sister, but he also claimed credit for her later judicial appointment—which deeply wounded Maryanne. Only much later, when their niece Mary Trump surreptitiously recorded conversations with her aunt, did it come out that Donald's older sister considered him reckless and unreliable.[39]

For Alito, who would spend four years with Maryanne in the US attorney's office and six more serving alongside her on the Third Circuit bench, she put a friendly face on the Trump name. Their relationship provided a warm, personal link between the young man from Mercerville and the famous family from Queens.

. . . .

By 1980, as he entered his fourth year working under Maryanne Trump in Newark, Sam Alito could take pride in his accomplishments but also assess their limits. He had been enough of a star at Steinert High to make it onto the success track at Princeton and Yale, though he often felt hemmed in on two sides: not part of the traditional Ivy League aristocracy, and not part of the liberal intelligentsia being forged by his fellow meritocrats.

While two mentors, Walter Murphy and Leonard Garth, regarded him as brilliant, they were self-made men from similar backgrounds to his, and they projected their own profiles onto his still-malleable frame.[40] Among his peers—the people he would work alongside for five decades— there was less effusiveness; in their view, he was smart, that much was clear, but trapped in a shy, recessive personality.[41] At key moments, the colorless Alito failed to show himself in the best light.

But then came an event that would provide an impetus, a jolt, that would propel the rest of his career. In 1980, Ronald Reagan became the first true conservative to win the presidency since the 1920s. Reagan's con- servatism had a dynamism—a charismatic quality—that no previous Re- publican had projected. Black hair slicked back, head cocked at a jaunty angle, he was America's storyteller-in-chief. At the height of the Cold War, he conveyed a reverence for the United States as a beacon of freedom. In his telling, America was a story not of struggle but of endless victories, and the Declaration of Independence and US Constitution were sacred docu- ments, models of free and fair governance for the entire world.

While the early days of the Cold War motivated Americans to em- brace social change and fully live up to the country's self-image of equal opportunity, the later Cold War triggered the opposite impulse: a push toward triumphalism. Probing the distance between America's ideals and its reality smacked of weakness, of self-flagellation. And some efforts to close that gap, such as affirmative action and Supreme Court rulings to prevent any one religion from dominating the public square, were simply wrongheaded; they violated American traditions.

Reagan's hearty and emotionally moving message resonated with many children and grandchildren of European immigrants. His truth was their truth; it dovetailed with everything they had heard from their older rela- tives. This was Alito's truth as well, and he was eager to find his place in the new administration. He quickly gained a choice position in Reagan's Jus- tice Department, in the office of the solicitor general, putting him in line to argue on behalf of the administration before the Supreme Court.[42]

Meanwhile, some like-minded individuals emerged to carry Reagan's message into barren corners of academia where just a few years earlier, few conservatives had dared to venture. Many of them had backgrounds and perspectives similar to Alito's. One was a Yale law student named Steven Calabresi. Eight years younger than Alito, he also carried a sense of family destiny. His father and uncle fled the fascist grip of Italian dictator Benito Mussolini in the late 1930s to become giants in the fields of medicine and the law. Steven remembered spending the better part of a Boston Red Sox game at Fenway Park in 1970 with his uncle Guido, a Yale law professor, debating the merits of the Vietnam War. Twelve-year-old Steven concluded that the war was worth fighting; Uncle Guido didn't agree.[43]

As an undergraduate, Steven befriended two classmates whom he met at the Yale Political Union.[44] One was Lee Liberman, the conservative granddaughter of Jewish immigrants from Russia,[45] and the other was David McIntosh, a liberal who was raised in Indiana along with three siblings by a plucky widowed mother on her nurse's salary.[46] Calabresi considered himself a centrist at the time. Despite their political differences, the three students hit it off. Each felt that hard work and sacrifice were part of their family's story, and that vindicating those values would be their mission in life.

After graduation, all three went to Washington. Calabresi and Liberman got jobs with Republican senators and lived in a group house with two other foot soldiers of the Reagan Revolution.[47] It was a heady time. Calabresi compared Reagan's impact on young people to that of the civil rights movement a decade or two earlier.[48] But unlike civil rights protesters, who operated at arm's length from lawmakers, Reagan's supporters were engaged at all levels of politics. The Reagan Revolution combined grassroots organizing with ideological clarity and an electoral gameplan. It wasn't out simply to change minds—it meant to put ideas into action.

There were three strands to Reaganism: a hard-line anti-communist stance growing out of an unflinching belief in the American system, a commitment to cutting the federal budget to unleash the virtues of capitalism, and a social agenda based on a conservative view of Christian faith. It was a potent cocktail, each ingredient flavored by the America of an earlier age—the place of deeply rooted values depicted in the Golden Age of Hollywood, when Reagan was a star.

Evangelical Christians, in particular, shifted strongly into the Republican camp. They and their parents had been Democrats for most of the twentieth century, but a series of Supreme Court rulings supported by Democratic administrations turned the tide. Decisions banning racial segregation, outlawing Bible readings in public schools, and granting rights to contraception and abortion struck them as assaults on their values.

By some accounts, the founders of the largest religious group backing Reagan, the Moral Majority, were most offended by President Jimmy Carter's threats to revoke the non-profit tax status of religious schools that refused to enroll Black students. Many such schools had been established after the Supreme Court banned segregation in public schools; white parents who opposed integration moved their kids into all-white religious schools. Now Carter was threatening to force those private schools to accept Black kids as well. Rev. Jerry Falwell, co-founder of the Moral Majority, was among those who created a so-called segregation academy.[49]

In polls, most Americans did not support the Moral Majority's positions on many, if not all, of their issues. But when Reagan lumped their issues together as examples of government interference—condemning the Internal Revenue Service for monkeying around with "independent" schools, for example—he struck a different note. Rather than opposing policies that most people supported, he was standing up for the rights of individuals to make their own choices.[50]

This made the courts an inevitable foil for the Reagan administration. After a year in Washington, a city frothing with conservative energy, Calabresi, Liberman, and McIntosh—by now a convert to Reagan's movement—went on to law school: Calabresi to Yale and Liberman and McIntosh to the University of Chicago.[51] Each was dismayed to discover that while conservative ideas about the law were percolating, they were still the province of a tiny minority. More needed to be done to give Reaganism its place in the legal academy. They intended to do it.

....

EARLY SUPPORTERS OF THE Federalist Society take pride in how outnumbered they were in the legal world; the very thinness of their ranks casts their later success in a glowing, almost miraculous light.

"There were probably ten constitutional law professors in the country who were suspected of voting for Reagan, even in the primary," observed former Ambassador Grover Joseph Rees III, who attended the first Federalist Society meeting while a law professor at the University of Texas.[52] Former National Security Advisor John Bolton recalled that when Robert Bork left Yale Law School to join the Nixon administration, faculty quipped that the headline should have read that Nixon had taken "20 percent of all conservatives at Yale Law School."[53]

This was true enough. But unlike some other minorities, conservative legal activists didn't lack resources or support. In 1971, while working as a corporate attorney, Lewis F. Powell Jr. authored a memo to the US Chamber of Commerce entitled "Attack on the Free Enterprise System." It accused business leaders of "appeasement, ineptitude, and ignoring the problem" of liberal dominance in American institutions.[54] Declaring that nothing less than capitalism itself was at stake, Powell trained his fury not on the far left but on the professional people in politics, academics, and law who were systematically chipping away at the liberties of business owners. His prescription was for corporations to fight back by funding networks of conservative scholars and regulators to attack the problem at its grass roots. In his opinion, he wrote, "the judiciary may be the most important instrument for social, economic, and political change."[55]

Within months, Powell himself was appointed to the Supreme Court, where he quickly showed his libertarian streak by pushing the court further in favor of abortion rights in Roe v. Wade.[56] Even if his own tenure didn't satisfy later conservatives, Powell's memo inspired deep-pocketed donors to invest in grassroots organizing. John M. Olin, who expanded his father's chemical fortune through innovations in the manufacture of arms and ammunition, said Powell's memo "gives reason for a well-organized effort to reestablish the vitality and importance of the American free enterprise system." Beer maker Joseph Coors Jr. was also inspired by Powell's memo.[57]

In 1980, a foundation started by banking heir Richard Mellon Scaife commissioned a report by Michael J. Horowitz that zeroed in on the need to refresh the legal brainpower on the right. He, too, suggested investing in a pipeline that would carry potential conservative judicial nominees from law school to the high court.[58]

Thus, in early 1982, when Calabresi, McIntosh, Liberman, and their friends started planning the first conference of a new organization of conservative law students, the Federalist Society, the grant-makers didn't take much persuading: Olin's foundation and another controlled by conservative intellectual Irving Kristol ponied up enough money to fly in and put up sixty students and twenty professors.[59]

. . . .

THE "SYMPOSIUM ON FEDERALISM: Legal and Political Ramifications" was a mythical moment, a time when the past, present, and future seemed to converge, and a tunnel of light—or darkness, depending on one's perspective—emerged between the stuffy portraits adorning the walls of Yale Law School's largest classroom, room 127.[60]

"I went to the Woodstock Rock Festival, but when I went, I didn't know it was going to be Woodstock with a capital W and an exclamation point," recounted Rees. "I just thought it was going to be a really interesting rock festival with a lot of interesting musicians. And that's exactly how the first Federalist Society conference was. You didn't go there with a sense of making history. You went there with the sense that you were going to hear Nino Scalia and Lino Graglia on a panel together arguing about originalism."[61]

Scalia, the University of Chicago professor who was in line for a circuit court appointment, played a key role in bringing people together. "He'd done things," Liberman said. "He'd been in government."[62] Calabresi gave the same credit to Bork, who had just joined the US Court of Appeals for the DC Circuit. "It was Bork who had the star power," Calabresi insisted.[63] Graglia, a professor alongside Rees at the University of Texas, was also a powerful presence.[64] But then there were Harvard's Charles Fried and the newly minted Seventh Circuit Appeals Court Judge Richard Posner, along with Reagan administration luminaries such as Ted Olson and Michael McConnell.[65]

These figures all leaned to the right, but in different ways. Some, like Posner, were focused on economics. As a professor, he had advocated for a cost–benefit analysis of protections against personal injuries.[66] Others, like John Noonan of the University of California, Berkeley, were focused on social issues. He had been a consultant to the Vatican and urged Federalist Society members to back a constitutional amendment banning abortion.[67]

Organizers knew that they would have to knit together social conservatives like Noonan with libertarians, who abhorred most forms of government regulation, and federalists, who believed that the national government should surrender power to the states. What they shared was a fear of the left—not only of the perceived excesses of the Warren Court but also the current musings of Kennedy, Gabel, and the critical legal studies movement. It wasn't that the Crits were so persuasive, but they represented a new frontier for legal activism—a sense of what could happen without any checks on law professors' liberalism.[68]

One powerful voice for unity belonged to the most unusual participant in the conference. He wasn't a student or a professor or a lawyer. Rather, he was there because he specialized in building organizations and had hosted Liberman and McIntosh at his training programs.[69] He was Reagan's special assistant, Morton Blackwell, who had turned the College Republicans into a powerful national organization.[70]

An unassuming forty-two-year-old man in a business suit, Blackwell looked like a traveling salesman who'd stumbled into the Gothic corridors of Sterling Hall by accident. But he offered the attendees some wisdom that set them apart—and not just from their left-wing counterparts, who were busy attacking each other in the name of ideological purity. "Study how to win," he told the gathering. "At least 25 percent of the Federalist

Society training efforts should be discussing practical action, not the fine points of doctrine and legal philosophy." Blackwell presented the group with a list of eight priorities, from "How to get the right people into the study of law" to "How to make sure the right people get to be judges." This was politics, not academia; a battle of results, not ideas.[71]

"Back in the Goldwater days, when I first became politically active, conservatives had the belief that being right, in the sense of being correct, was sufficient to prevail," he told the crowd. "We believed in the Sir Galahad theory: 'I shall win because my heart is pure.' But that is not the way the real world works."[72]

Looking back more than four decades on his bracing warning, Blackwell said, "The truth is, I believe it is possible to organize almost anything on a college campus . . . I suggested what they needed to do was set up a program to go to every campus and recruit members."[73]

....

IF BLACKWELL'S ADVICE RANG the loudest in retrospect, the main attraction for many in the room was the contrasting presentations by the two lions of conservatism, Scalia and Bork. Each man was known as an engaging professor, willing to bat around ideas, but also trenchant in what he believed. Scalia, however, had a politician's sense of the moment and a deeper desire to be liked. As such, he played a role akin to genial toastmaster.

His prepared remarks floated above any contentiousness in the room. He locked in on the term "federalism," saying that as a governing principle, it was "midway between two extremes," the disunity of independent states and the heavy hand of the federal government. "As such it can be used to beat either dog," he offered.[74] It was an unfortunate metaphor, but his point seemed to be that he was skeptical that returning power to the states was a magical cure to the problems worrying conservatives. "I urge you then—as Hamilton would have urged you—to keep in mind that the federal government is not bad but good," he concluded. "The trick is to use it wisely."[75]

When Noonan made his push for a constitutional amendment banning abortion, Scalia sagely pointed out that such an amendment could itself be viewed as a violation of federalist principles: it would tie the hands of the states.[76] Plainly, he wanted to encourage wide-ranging debate. Most of the audience—schooled by Buckley's *National Review* in how simply expanding the national discussion could benefit the right—was happy to play along. A belief in debate as a means of acknowledging conflicts and showing respect for multiple opinions would become a Federalist Society trademark. It refuted critics who claimed the conservative legal movement was monolithic or prone to top-down thinking. It also served to keep people of varying opinions in the conservative camp.

Bork was less magnanimous. At fifty-five, he was nine years older than Scalia and had been a professor for the better part of two decades. Despite having been confirmed to the bench two months previously, he was accustomed to speaking freely and challenging orthodoxies. His critique was sweeping and aimed squarely at the Supreme Court: "We now have a Court—and I think it is not improper to say it—we have Court which is creating individual rights which are not to be found in the Constitution by any standard method of interpretation." This, he said, amounts to "nothing more than the imposition of upper middle class values on the society."[77]

Bork's class-based analysis—claiming the court was mimicking the values of the reporters and professors to whom its opinions were directed—might have been applauded at the critical legal studies confab in Madison. But in Bork's telling, these were affectations not of bourgeois capitalism but of "left liberal" thinking: "They want sexual freedoms; they want freedom for abortion; they want the death penalty outlawed and so forth and so on," Bork insisted. "They want every kind of expressive behavior, or any kind of behavior that can remotely be called expressive, protected by the First Amendment."[78]

In later years, participants in the conference would claim not to recall any mention of abortion.[79] But there was Noonan's plea for a constitutional amendment, and there was also Bork, who cited *Roe v. Wade* as the epitome of all that was wrong: "We are seeing not merely a shift from democratic to judicial rule, but a shift from local, diverse moral choices to a nationalization of morality through the creation of new constitutional rights . . . *Roe v. Wade* is the classic instance."[80]

In his prepared remarks, Bork didn't address the court's stated ratio-nale for abortion rights—the right to privacy as expressed in multiple amendments, as applied to a woman's desire to control her reproduction.[81] In discussions, he dismissed the court's reasoning as "made up."[82] This fol-lowed a pattern of conservative critics rejecting *Roe* as unconstitutional without grappling with the points raised by Blackmun, Powell, or other justices, let alone by women's rights attorneys. It was as if giving voice to them would indulge a dangerous habit.

Bork's edgy speech left the students in the room with a sense of direc-tion—legally and politically—and a feeling for what might be at stake in future debates. But it would soon boomerang on the man who delivered it.

. . . .

As HE MOUNTED THE lectern in Sterling Hall, Ralph Winter, the con-servative Yale Law School professor and later judge, quipped that "in al-most 20 continuous years of association with Yale, this has to be the most extraordinary gathering that I have seen, and that includes some Black Panther rallies in the 1970s."[83]

By coincidence, the Black Alumni of Yale Law School were having a conference at the same time, with Judge A. Leon Higginbotham Jr. of the Third Circuit Court of Appeals as the keynote speaker. Higginbotham had been a civil rights aide to Lyndon Johnson, who appointed him a judge on the federal district court. Jimmy Carter elevated him to the circuit court.[84] *The New York Times* covered both conferences as bookends of legal thinking.

Organizers of the Black alumni event noted that having to cover their own expenses, only 40 of 220 members were able to attend. Meanwhile,

Federalist Society members had their flights and hotel rooms comped by right-wing foundations. "This is the poor people's conference," said one organizer.[85]

While conservatives were stressing how outnumbered they were, Higginbotham sensed the beginning of a tide that could wash away many of the gains achieved by Black people. "Anything that talks about a dilution of federal involvement," he told the *Times*, "can be translated as a reduction in resources particularly for the weak, the poor, and Blacks as a class."[86]

CHAPTER 7

Robert Bork's America

There was something intoxicating about Reagan's Washington. Liberals didn't feel it, but young conservatives swooned over what speechwriter Peggy Noonan, who was born the same year as Alito, called "the authentic sound of the Reagan Revolution, buzzing around me."[1]

The implicit promise of Reaganism was to turn back the clock to the days before John F. Kennedy's assassination—before the messes of Vietnam and Watergate, but also before campus protests and Lyndon Johnson's Great Society programs. In Noonan's telling, Reagan's nostalgic vision made Baby Boomers think of their childhoods and grandparents who "taught us to go to church and pray to God and if you work hard you can be somebody. Show respect, love your country, stop complaining."[2]

Noonan also mused that "like most Baby-boomers, I live this paradox: Nothing really memorable happened in my childhood, yet I think about it all the time." That was because life seemed simpler, more elemental; Noonan, the Irish Catholic daughter of an appliance salesman, romanticized her hard-working forebears as much as Alito did.[3]

While many on the outside regarded the administration's agenda as simply cutting programs and letting the chips fall where they may, those on the inside felt differently. They were changing policy for the better, improving people's lives. Young Reaganites had the zestful confidence that liberals felt in their own moments of creation, during the New Deal and the New Frontier.

For Alito, the Washington of the early 1980s was a perfect antidote to years spent in the wilderness as a conservative on campus. For once, he could function as a member of the majority. He could put forward frankly conservative positions and have them validated by colleagues.

The Justice Department, where he worked, was more than simply a network of federal prosecutors. Its backroom offices played crucial roles in setting the national agenda by choosing which battles to fight and whose side to be on. Alito's first posting was in one of the most visible and prestigious of those offices: that of the US solicitor general. He was charged with defending the administration before the Supreme Court.[4]

Alito worked mainly under Reagan's first solicitor general, Rex Lee, whom he would later honor by choosing his son Mike as a clerk, helping him on the path to becoming a US senator from Utah. Later still, he would pick Mike's son, James Rex Lee, for a Supreme Court clerkship.[5]

Solicitor General Lee was not the doctrinaire conservative that his son would become. He was true to his Mormon faith but also known for taking a balanced approach to the law; he was more in sync with the career staff of the Justice Department than the White House aides who pushed a conservative agenda.[6]

Arguing cases before the Supreme Court was the public face of the office's work. When Alito, at age thirty-two, made his first appearance in a low-stakes case regarding military contracts, he acquitted himself well.[7] He later expressed thanks that his opening question from the bench was a softball from Reagan's first appointee, Justice Sandra Day O'Connor.[8]

Less visible was his advice to the administration on how to achieve its own priorities. In this behind-the-scenes work, he showed the extent of his nascent conservatism. He was unabashed in his desire to restrain First Amendment protections for the media, preserve latitude for police to use deadly force, and limit abortion rights.

In a memo to Lee marked "Important and Urgent," he "strongly recommended" that the Reagan administration not file a brief in support of a man who wrote to Reagan raising concerns about a job candidate. When the candidate failed to get the job, he sued the letter writer for libel; the letter writer claimed he deserved absolute immunity under his constitutional right to petition the government. The Justice Department's Civil Division sided with him, reasoning that people would be reluctant to give the president honest advice if they were under threat of libel. But Alito felt that restricting libel suits might have the unintended consequence of helping the media.

"I strongly recommend against amicus participation," he wrote, using the legal term for a friend-of-the-court brief. He added, "I think adoption of the petitioner's argument would go far toward abolishing libel and slander for political speech. That is not a development that I think we should support."[9]

Alito's opinion sparked a forceful blowback from the Civil Division, where the deputy assistant attorney general penned her own memo sharply rebutting Alito's.[10] In the end, Alito's position won out. The Reagan administration stood down, and the Supreme Court rejected the letter writer's claim.[11]

Alito's view did not prevail, however, in a high-profile case involving a police officer who shot and killed an unarmed fifteen-year-old boy as he fled a burglary scene in Memphis, Tennessee. Both the officer and the suspect were Black.[12] The officer had responded to a burglary call; when he saw young Edward Garner sprinting from the scene, he called, "Police, halt!" but the boy attempted to climb a chain-link fence. His arms and hands were visible and free of any weapons. Nonetheless, the officer shot the boy in the back of the head to prevent him from fleeing.[13]

Garner's grieving family sued the police on the grounds that they had violated his Fourth Amendment rights against unwarranted search and seizure. The Garners claimed officers shouldn't be allowed to shoot suspects simply to prevent them from running away. It had all the earmarks of a landmark case, fraught with racial tension, and would become one of the most high-profile Supreme Court decisions of the era.

Alito backed the police. In his memo, he wrote, "Any rule permitting the use of deadly force to stop a fleeing suspect must rest on the general principle that the state is justified in using whatever force is necessary to enforce its laws."[14]

Alito's advocacy for "whatever force is necessary" proved controversial even within Reagan administration; another Justice Department lawyer wrote a memo reaching the opposite conclusion.[15] Once again, the administration did not intervene in the case. But the Supreme Court went against Alito's position: by a vote of 6–3, the justices ruled that officers must have a legitimate fear for their lives or the lives of others before using deadly force.[16]

Later that same year, 1984, the court prepared to reopen, if only slightly, the closed door known as *Roe v. Wade*. The court planned to review the constitutionality of laws in Pennsylvania and Illinois that required doctors to give women seeking abortions detailed information about the procedure and the gestational progress of the fetus. Ostensibly, this was to help them make an informed choice, but abortion providers thought the requirements were framed to discourage women from exercising their rights.[17]

People in the White House saw this as a showcase moment for their full-frontal assault on the right to privacy—the "made-up" right that Bork and others so forcefully disdained. Alito, however, viewed it as an opportunity to defend the laws as consistent with a narrower reading of *Roe* itself; if the court were to agree that women's rights weren't violated by having to receive information about the fetus before undergoing their procedure, it would open the door to other laws aimed at discouraging abortions.

"No one seriously believes the Court is about to overrule *Roe v. Wade*," Alito wrote. "There may [instead] be an opportunity to nudge the Court toward the principles in Justice O'Connor's *Akron* dissent, to provide greater recognition of the states' interest in protecting the unborn throughout pregnancy."[18]

Rex Lee had just been replaced as solicitor general by Charles Fried, a Harvard professor who was a frontline soldier in the growing conservative legal movement. He had spoken at the first Federalist Society conference and was more eager than Lee to promote a conservative reading of the Constitution.[19] He showed Alito's memo to other Reagan officials with a cover sheet reading, "I need hardly say how sensitive this material is, and ask that it have no wider circulation."[20] In the end, Fried didn't take Alito's advice. He attacked *Roe v. Wade* head-on, and the court headbutted back. It declared that statutes that discouraged abortions under the guise of providing neutral information were unconstitutional.[21] *Roe* carried the day, but only by a 5–4 vote. As Alito predicted, O'Connor was among the dissenters.

Two decades later, when Alito was nominated to the Supreme Court, his once-secret memo surfaced again. While some observers suggested it reflected his desire to overturn abortion rights, others noted that he was writing for a client, the Reagan administration, which was committed to overturning *Roe v. Wade*.[22] One defender, Charles Fried himself, pointed out that Alito was urging a position more supportive of *Roe* than the full-frontal assault that he, Fried, eventually mounted.[23]

But Alito's memo didn't support *Roe*. Rather, it recommended what he considered a smarter and more fruitful approach to undermining a case that he felt was wrongly decided.

....

In 1985, Sam Alito took a bride. She was Martha-Ann Bomgardner, whom he had met six years earlier while working in the Newark US attorney's office before moving to Washington. She was the courthouse law librarian but defied stereotypes about her profession. Lively and vivacious, Martha-Ann overflowed with all the emotions that her husband-to-be kept bottled up. They met in the late 1970s, when she was charged with cataloguing volumes of legal cases. On many afternoons, only she and Alito, the extra-diligent assistant US attorney working under Maryanne Trump, were in the small space.[24]

Intrigued, she hoped he would say hello. But true to his taciturn nature, he stayed buried in his texts. "I thought, 'What have I done?'" she would later recall. "I could usually engage anyone in conversation. This went on for a good year."[25]

Finally, he noticed her and found much to appreciate. She was a homebody who also liked to have a good time. She had the loquaciousness of the daughter of an air force controller who moved around frequently, meaning she always had to make new friends. She had spent her early years in Kentucky and her high school years in Mount Holly, New Jersey, before heading back to the Bluegrass State for college and a master's degree in library science at the University of Kentucky.[26]

She was neither a feminist nor a war protester; as a high school senior at the height of Vietnam War protests in 1971, she was one of nineteen New Jersey winners of the Betty Crocker Search for the All-American

Homemaker of Tomorrow. The award was based on "written knowledge and attitude examination," according to the *Times of Trenton*.[27]

For her part, Martha-Ann appreciated Alito's intelligence. One day, she overhead someone in the office tell him, "I hear you learned Russian this weekend," and "my eyes and my whole being went [*gasp*] 'a really smart one,'" she later quipped while introducing her husband at an award banquet.

"I met him in March 1979, and I told my friends in April 1979 that I would be getting married in April 1980," she added. "And because Sam is a deliberate man, we married in February 1985."[28]

Martha-Ann had been raised Presbyterian but converted to Catholicism. The wedding took place at Our Lady of Sorrows in Mercerville. Alito's father, Sam Sr., was listed as best man.[29]

In the years to come, Martha-Ann Alito would become the other half that complemented and, in some ways, completed her husband's personality. She eagerly embraced the role of his helpmate, maintaining friendships with former clerks and colleagues, sometimes via warm handwritten notes on pink paper with her hyphenated first name stenciled on top.[30]

One person who interacted with the Alitos described their union as "one of those marriages where one party does 90 percent of the talking"—in this case, Martha-Ann.[31] But if her conversations sometimes veered in directions he wouldn't go, she always viewed herself as speaking for the Alito team. Soon enough, that team would expand to include a son, Philip, and a daughter, Laura.

. . . .

THE EASY CONFIDENCE OF the first Reagan term, and the considerable star power of its leader, quickly cemented the Reagan coalition as a dominant force in American politics. But not every part of the team felt it was being equally served. The religious right wasn't entirely pleased with what it saw, especially on the legal front.[32] Its galvanizing issue—keeping the IRS from meddling in admissions for its largely white Christian academies—continued to be a source of irritation. In January 1982, the administration announced it was dropping the antidiscrimination requirements for tax-exempt institutions, only to backtrack under fire a few weeks later.[33]

Meanwhile, with Alito's help, Rex Lee was amassing an impressive record of winning cases at the Supreme Court,[34] but that was because he often seemed reluctant to push the court too strongly in a conservative direction. His boss, Attorney General William French Smith, was part of a recent trend of presidents picking their personal lawyers to run the Justice Department; Smith had represented Reagan in California. He was a trusted conservative but operated with some of the cautiousness of a practicing attorney. Sound, reliable advice was his calling card, not upending the system to advocate for churches.

Then there was the Supreme Court. In his eagerness to appoint the first woman justice, Reagan had been charmed by Sandra Day O'Connor. She told a feisty personal tale of being raised on a cattle ranch and going on to become a state judge and Republican political leader in libertarian Arizona. She learned how to fire a rifle and brand a cow before she was ten years old.[35] But she was almost completely unknown among East Coast conservatives. The exception was William Rehnquist, the most conservative member of the Supreme Court. They had been classmates at Stanford Law School, where they went on a few dates.[36] Much later it would emerge that Rehnquist had been so infatuated with this brainy Westerner that he had proposed marriage.[37] Having the stalwart Rehnquist vouch for O'Connor helped assuage the concerns of many conservatives that she would be a moderate justice at best.

Rev. Jerry Falwell, however, wasn't assuaged. He voiced his displeasure to members of the administration.[38] His main contact was Reagan's longtime aide, Edwin Meese. Meese had grown up in the Missouri Synod Lutheran Church, which believes the Bible represents truth in history and science, before becoming a professor at a small Catholic law school. Meese had worked hard to get the IRS to change its policy of revoking tax exemptions for racially segregated schools, only to watch helplessly as moderates persuaded Reagan to back off.[39]

It was a rare defeat for Meese, whose closeness to Reagan dated to when he served as executive assistant to the then-governor of California.

To career Washington insiders trying to understand the president, Meese was almost Reagan's alter ego. But because of his long service behind the scenes, unprepossessing appearance, and lack of East Coast credentials, he was viewed more as a political fixer than a principal—let alone a person capable of great national influence.

That changed when Reagan won reelection in 1984 and rewarded Meese with the nomination to succeed Smith as attorney general.[40] Suddenly, the Justice Department became ground zero for the administration's social agenda. As a former campaign aide, Meese understood the political importance of keeping religious conservatives happy. He knew that the abortion issue, long considered a Catholic obsession, was starting to gain traction with evangelical Christians, especially when used as an example of elitist contempt for religious values. Thanks to *Roe v. Wade*, there was starting to be a lot of connective tissue between the elite Ivy League conservatives of the Federalist Society and working-class Catholics and evangelicals. All disdained the holding of *Roe*, whether opposing abortion or the idea of an activist Supreme Court.

. . . .

MEESE'S RISE CAME JUST three years after the first conference of the Federalist Society, and after Sam Alito himself had joined as an early member of its inaugural DC chapter of practicing lawyers. This made him part of a network of movement-driven conservatives who could be counted on to fill administration jobs or challenge liberal norms in court.[41] To emphasize the informality of the group—and its sense of itself as composed of youthful outsiders—the DC chapter hosted events in Chinese restaurants. The atmosphere of gold lacquer and painted dragons created a noticeable contrast with the blandly institutional banquet rooms in which more established legal groups convened.

Alito became a regular participant and bonded with fellow members over fortune cookie jokes. At one event, he ran into his new boss, Charles Fried, who quipped, "Oh, what a surprise to see you here. This is like meeting a friend at a bordello."[42]

The rampant expansion of the Federalist Society caught even its co-founders off guard. Back in 1982, Calabresi, Liberman, and McIntosh had announced their conference in an ad in *National Review*. They were shocked when mail started pouring in from like-minded students across the country. "The point of announcing the thing in the *National Review* was to let people know about the conference, people in the area who might want to come," recalled Liberman. "In fact, what happened was that we started getting letters from all around the country saying, 'How do I start a chapter of the Federalist Society?'"[43]

By 1984, the year of Reagan's reelection, there were chapters at thirty-two law schools.[44] The previous year, Liberman had recruited a fellow Yale graduate named Eugene Meyer to serve as national director. Meyer had a unique pedigree. His father, Frank Meyer, had been a communist in the 1930s who became a pivotal figure in the development of conservatism in the 1960s and 1970s. His theory, fusionism, envisioned an alliance of small-government libertarians and traditionalists. Frank Meyer died of cancer while Gene was in college, but Gene quickly incorporated his father's ideas into the development of the Federalist Society.[45]

Students who started chapters got a how-to manual penned by McIntosh and Liberman and access to national speakers through Meyer. Attorney General Meese was especially eager to bolster the Federalist Society. He not only hired Calabresi, Liberman, and McIntosh to positions in his Justice Department, but he also spoke at events, lending gravitas to the ragtag student chapters.[46]

Meese's speeches served another purpose: they tied the frayed strands of conservative legal thinking into an actionable agenda. The Federalist Society may have been a big tent—an analogy Reagan himself used to describe the uniting of disparate Republicans[47]—but Meese sought to concentrate all of the factions on targets like the Supreme Court, judicial activism, and godless social liberalism.

Up until then, the Federalist Society had toggled between calls for restraint by judges and officials—a "dispersal of political power," as one speaker at the first conference put it[48]—and robust action to roll back liberal gains.

Meese pushed the envelope in the activist direction but used the language of historical restoration: this was a revolutionary program that supporters could nonetheless claim was merely correcting the mistakes of the past.

On July 9, 1985, four months after taking office, Meese used the occasion of an American Bar Association meeting in Washington to train his sights on the Supreme Court, which he called "a political body." He sought to prove his case with a lacerating critique of the "utterly unpredictable" Burger Court's failure to "yield a coherent set of decisions."[49]

He stated that his team would be pushing for consistency in the court's rulings. "It has been and will be the policy of this administration to press for a Jurisprudence of Original Intention," he announced. "In the cases we file and those we join as amicus, we will endeavor to resurrect the original meaning of constitutional provisions and statutes as the only reliable guide for judgment."[50]

For some conservative lawyers, this was almost like a founding moment: Calabresi and another former Meese lieutenant called his comments on originalism "two of the most important sentences ever spoken by an attorney general."[51]

Meese kept pounding the cudgel, deepening his critique of the Supreme Court and adding items to his agenda. Before the Christian Legal Society in San Diego on September 29, he blamed the court's decisions on separation of church and state—such as those limiting religious expression in public school classrooms—for creating "an attitude of hostility towards religion in our country."[52]

On November 15, the attorney general visited Alito's DC chapter of the Federalist Society, taking the podium at the Golden Palace Chinese restaurant. Seizing on a chance to preach to the converted, Meese offered a detailed analysis of what a jurisprudence of original intent would entail: "The approach of this administration is rooted in the text of the Constitution as illuminated by those who drafted, proposed, and ratified it." Like all of Meese's speeches, it had a high tone, with references to Founding Fathers and quotations from the Federalist Papers. He cast his ambitions as a matter of historical fidelity, or even inevitability.[53]

The following fall, Meese journeyed to Tulane University to speak before its Federalist Society chapter. It was a great honor for students to be able to attract such an important figure, as one future federal judge, Bill Pryor, remembered.[54]

Meese devoted his talk to "the necessary distinction between the Constitution and constitutional law." The Constitution was the supreme law of the land; constitutional law, as laid down by the Supreme Court, was far more fallible. It was always subject to change and, in Meese's view, must therefore be challenged.

"The Supreme Court would face quite a dilemma," Meese declared, "if its own constitutional decisions really were 'the supreme law of the land,' binding on all persons and government entities, including the court itself, for then the court would not be able to change its mind."[55]

The message to Pryor and other students couldn't have been clearer: it's time to remake constitutional law, and that means changing the court.

. . . .

ALITO GOT HIS OWN wake-up call to Meese's new direction for the Justice Department. Under Rex Lee, the solicitor general's office was perceived as being "not with the program," as Chuck Cooper, a key Meese lieutenant, put it. Cooper had been in the DOJ's Civil Rights Division in Reagan's first term and recalled numerous quarrels with Lee's staff over how aggressively to challenge affirmative action quotas. There was one crack in the wall of resistance: Sam Alito. He was "very friendly and simpatico with the direction we were trying to move the department and the law," Cooper recalled.[56]

Cooper, a former law clerk to William Rehnquist, and Alito were close in age and soon became friends. So when Meese elevated Cooper to head the Office of Legal Counsel (OLC)—the inner sanctum where decisions were made about the extent of the president's power—Cooper decided he wanted Alito as his principal deputy. There was only one problem: no one in Meese's inner circle knew or trusted Alito, given his close ties to Lee.[57] And Meese made it clear that merely being a good lawyer wasn't enough to make it into an important policy position. Only proven conservatives need apply.[58]

Cooper asked Alito to write a memo explaining his own evolution as a conservative and even helped him to craft it.[59] It would be a fateful document. The assignment from Cooper pushed Alito out of his self-protective crouch—his reluctance to assert his own political voice, modeled on his father's strict nonpartisanship—and put on paper the kinds of doctrinaire beliefs that could easily trip up a judicial candidate facing tough scrutiny.

"I am and always have been a conservative and an adherent to the same philosophical views that I believe are central to this administration," Alito began, sounding a bit like a witness before a committee dedicated to rooting out communists.

He further attested: "I believe very strongly in limited government, federalism, free enterprise, the supremacy of the elected branches of government, the need for a strong defense and effective law enforcement, and the legitimacy of a government role in protecting traditional values." He described William F. Buckley as an early influence on his political thinking. He cited his membership in the Federalist Society and his steadfast participation in the Washington chapter's lunch meetings at Chinese restaurants. But then he went a step too far, declaring himself to be a member of Concerned Alumni of Princeton, the group founded by older men who couldn't get their minds around the idea of women students at their alma mater.[60]

While his last comment would put him in hot water in later years, the pleading tone of the memo seemed to satisfy the attorney general and his aides. Alito soon found himself at the beating heart of Meese's revolution. He was among fifteen members of Meese's Legislative Strategy Working Group, alongside the attorney general's closest aides. The group was charged with finding ways to advance Reagan's agenda through the law. This included enhanced use of presidential signing statements to assert Reagan's interpretation of statutes—the subject of an Alito memo—along with efforts to limit affirmative action rules, thwart "Judicial Usurpation of Power," and toughen criminal sentencing, among other priorities.[61]

Eventually, Alito landed in the middle of one of the most contentious issues of the decade: whether employers could fire people who were suspected of having AIDS. This was a source of widespread pain and rejection. Doctors insisted the disease could not be transmitted by casual contact, but some bosses chose to root out those suspected of being infected, including large numbers of gay men.

Their lifeline was a 1973 law that prevented handicapped people from being unjustly fired from federally funded programs. When asked to consider whether Congress intended to protect people with infectious diseases, Alito determined that it did not. With his laser-like focus on original intent, he discerned that members of Congress were concerned only about physical handicaps, not diseases. The Supreme Court disagreed. In a 7–2 decision involving a Florida teacher who was fired because of her history of tuberculosis, the court declared that Congress had crafted the law broadly, to cover people suspected of having impairments of any cause.[62]

While advocates for people with AIDS cheered and expressed hope that private employers would also get the message about nondiscrimination, Alito was unpersuaded. "The Supreme Court disagreed with us," he acknowledged to a New Jersey newspaper. "But there was nothing in the legislative history to suggest that Congress was thinking about contagious diseases when they passed the law."[63]

The AIDS question was an exception to the rule that Alito's work was largely invisible to the public. The most far-reaching product of his and Cooper's tenure at OLC was developed behind the scenes: the so-called unitary executive theory. It was designed to fight back against Congress's efforts to create offices such as the Environmental Protection Agency and the Federal Communications Commission to make independent policy determinations. The idea behind such agencies was to bring scientific or economic thinking to bear on matters requiring special expertise; by putting the agencies under the control of commissioners appointed to set terms by both the president and Congress, lawmakers hoped to insulate them from political pressure.

But Cooper and his team felt that these structures contravened the Constitution, which vested executive power in the president. In their view, that meant the president had personal control over all executive functions of the government; the only limitation on his power was in defining what was and wasn't an executive function. In creating independent agencies, Congress had treaded too heavily on the president's turf. Richard Nixon's imperial presidency had given way to a reign of outside experts.

The unitary executive theory would outlive the Reagan administration. It would become a major talking point in two of the Republican administrations that followed, those of George W. Bush and Donald Trump, where it was used to defend those presidents' unilateral authority. Of the seemingly endless paper trail of memoranda that bore Alito's stamp or crossed his desk during his years in the Justice Department, the unitary executive theory would be the issue with the most relevance to his later work on the Supreme Court.

"We were strong proponents of the unitary executive, that all federal executive power is vested by the Constitution in the president," Alito said at a 2000 Federalist Society panel discussion. "And I thought then, and I still think, that this theory best captures the meaning of the Constitution's text and structure."[64]

Cooper attested that Alito was fully supportive of the unitary executive theory, calling it "a fundamental tenet, if you will, of the values of that administration, and the values of that Justice Department and, rest assured, the Office of Legal Counsel."[65]

Another such tenet was the pressing need for members of the conservative legal movement in federal judgeships. And the task of determining which potential nominees were best aligned with Meese's priorities fell largely to Cooper, Alito, and their team at OLC.

They were determined not to miss the opportunity to remake the judiciary.

．．．．．．．．．．．．．．．

GROVER JOSEPH REES, THE young University of Texas professor who attended the first Federalist Society conference and sometimes sacked out on Calabresi's couch in New Haven, said he "knew the Federalist Society had really arrived" when he saw lawyers whom he considered "non-ideological opportunists" who were "suddenly touting their membership."[66]

There was an understandable reason for this: Reagan was seeking proven conservatives for federal judgeships, and those appointees, in turn, wanted conservative students for clerkships. Like Alito, they all used the Federalist Society as a stamp of authenticity. Membership had its privileges. That included a leg up for desirable jobs.

This marked a big shift from the practices of earlier administrations. For over a century, presidents had used the choice of federal judges as a way of rewarding senators for supporting policies entirely unrelated to the justice system. As with most mossy Washington political traditions, there was a practical rationale for this process. Senators sometimes did know who the best judges for their states would be. But there was a smell of political grease as well.[67]

To be sure, both the White House and senators understood that federal judges had to be competent. When a politician tried to use a judgeship to reward an unqualified crony, the American Bar Association stood guard. It maintained a system of rating judicial candidates based solely on their legal qualifications. This became a useful tool for rooting out incompetent nominees before they could be confirmed by the whole Senate.[68]

Some presidents regarded judgeships as a patronage tool and had little interest in who was appointed on their watch. Others would aim for judges who shared a few key precepts. Franklin Roosevelt wanted a Supreme Court that would approve his New Deal programs, but beyond that, he chose a mix of moderates, liberals, and conservatives who adhered to no common blueprint. Likewise, Richard Nixon wanted judges who were tough on crime, but his appointees ended up diverging widely on social issues, with three of them in the majority on *Roe*.[69]

The difference in the Reagan administration's approach was that Meese wanted nominees who shared his originalist ideology and considered themselves part of his movement. His aim was to change the way the judiciary understood its mission, and how it determined the state of the law.

To discourage senators from thinking they could control the process, Meese's staff solicited three recommendations for each district court opening, hoping that one might turn out to be an acceptable conservative. If none fit the bill, the staff could find a suitable candidate on their own.[70] "Unless there was something very unusual," Cooper said, senators "couldn't just call up and say, 'My college roommate wants his judgeship. How long will it take you to get the nomination?' Those days were over in the Reagan administration."[71]

Meanwhile, Cooper said, he, Alito, and the rest of the staff at OLC conducted "a very rigorous process" to find like-minded conservatives for the most important positions: the Supreme Court and the federal appeals court.[72] But in ridding the proceedings of politics as usual, they were imposing their own ideological test—another form of politics. It was perhaps the strictest test in history. Only true believers got a passing score.

Meese's aides didn't shy away from touting the revolutionary nature of this change. Calabresi and Gary Lawson, in their memoir of their time in Meese's Justice Department, said they were "looking for [appeals court] candidates who were not only opposed to *Roe v. Wade*—and opposed to it for constitutionally correct reasons—but who were also willing to challenge the New Deal revolution of 1937, and its abandonment of basic constitutional principles of limited federal power and of the separation of powers." In this, Calabresi and Lawson believed, the Reagan administration was "uniquely successful."[73]

Many of the appeals court nominees from the early Reagan years were academic progenitors of the movement who spoke at the first Federalist Society conference, including Bork, Scalia, Winter, Posner, and John Noonan.[74] Once those worthies were securely on the bench, the Meese team began cultivating its next generation of originalists, who would be all the more reliable simply because they emerged as part of a movement. There was an obvious difference between those who came to conservatism through the lonely path of Bork or Scalia and those who were funneled through the pipeline laid down by Meese. The younger conservatives were part of a community of like-minded thinkers; they lacked the hard-won independence of those whose views were tested before a phalanx of liberal colleagues in the heat of the 1960s. Younger nominees were more like executives hired to implement a strategy. If they deviated from the plan, their fellow Federalist

Society members stood ready to nudge them back into line. There were also costs to violating originalist principles. It would deprive them of support for the ultimate prize: a seat on the Supreme Court.

. . . .

DEMOCRATIC INSIDERS WERE ONLY too aware of the changes in the judicial process, but they were uncertain how to respond. Their initial test came with the first Supreme Court opening of the Meese era. In the summer of 1986, Chief Justice Burger announced his intention to resign, and Reagan decided to promote William Rehnquist to his position. At sixty-one, Rehnquist had already served fourteen years on the court, holding down its right flank. His elevation opened another slot, and Reagan and Meese chose to nominate Antonin Scalia.[75]

Ralph Neas, a former Senate aide to moderate Republicans Edward Brooke of Massachusetts and David Durenberger of Minnesota, was then the director of the Leadership Conference on Civil Rights, a group dedicated to building upon the Warren Court's legacy of expansive civil rights protections. He saw both appointments as looming threats.[76]

In meetings with key Democratic senators and liberal activists, Neas suggested they concentrate their energies on Rehnquist, not Scalia. Though he was considered by other justices to be a fair and generous colleague, the rather charmless Rehnquist carried a long record of seeking to narrow civil rights and voting rights protections. There was also his dissenting opinion in *Roe v. Wade*. Scalia, meanwhile, was a smiling new face on the national scene. The proud father of nine children, he was as ebullient as the colorful dad on a TV sitcom. If opponents wanted to strike a blow against Reagan's attempts to remake the law, Rehnquist was the fatter target; as a Supreme Court clerk in 1952, he had gone so far as to author a memo supporting *Plessy v. Ferguson*, the notorious segregation case.[77]

"We made an institutional decision," Neas said, noting that the Republican chairman of the Senate Judiciary Committee, Strom Thurmond of South Carolina, was pressing ahead with early hearings. "We couldn't do two Supreme Court justices at once, and we had a much better chance with Rehnquist, who had been filibustered by Senator Brooke and others in 1972," when he was first nominated.[78]

Neas worked with Democratic senators to press the case that Rehnquist's record was unsupportive of women and minorities, and out of step with the preferences of most Americans. In the end, though, they could muster only thirty-one of the forty-one Senate votes needed to block the nomination through a filibuster.[79]

Much of America, including some Democratic senators, clung to the idea that judicial nominees should be judged on their legal acumen, not the substance of their record. It was hard to persuade these people that Rehnquist, having ably handled his Supreme Court work for more than a decade, was unqualified to be chief justice. And if his record was conservative, well, he would be replacing a man, Burger, who was at least somewhat to the right of center; the court's fragile equilibrium wouldn't be tilting that much further to the right with Rehnquist as chief.

Scalia, meanwhile, sailed to confirmation by a vote of 98–0.[80]

. . . .

EMBOLDENED BY THEIR SUCCESS, Reagan and Meese soon had a chance to shift the court further in their direction. In the following summer of 1987, Lewis Powell announced his retirement. Powell, whose Chamber of Commerce memo called on business leaders to fight judicial activism, had proven to be a surprisingly centrist jurist. His laissez-faire attitudes about business extended into the personal realm with his support for civil liberties, including abortion rights. Some went so far as to call him the court's swing vote.[81] Now Meese could move the pendulum rightward by replacing Powell with a social conservative.

Robert Bork, whose spirited class at Yale Law School Alito had begged to get into, loomed over the conservative movement like a demigod. Back in the days when many conservatives dared not speak their name, he had blasted away at every perceived liberal excess, including popular cases such as *Griswold v. Connecticut*, which established the right to contraceptives.

Burly, blunt, and often dismissive in his language, the bearded, chain-smoking Bork was a born debater. He had a gentleness behind a gruff exterior, but he never expressed any self-doubt. Over his more than three-decade career in academia and government, he had trashed hundreds of Supreme Court decisions. They included most of the Warren Court canon dating back to *Brown v. Board of Education*. He was every bit as skeptical of affirmative action and civil rights laws as Rehnquist, and even more emphatic about it.[82] But having seen Rehnquist receive the Senate's endorsement with relatively little fuss, Reagan and Meese couldn't help but press their luck with Bork. The Senate had shifted to Democratic control, but the White House believed that many Democrats, particularly in the South, would acknowledge that Bork's legal credentials were impeccable, much as they had with Rehnquist.

In his diary, Reagan expressed confidence: "We'll get Bork confirmed to Supreme Ct. But it will be a battle with left-wing ideologues."[83]

The left was prepared for the fight. Their leader was Sen. Edward Kennedy, the brother of the late president and longtime liberal troubadour. He took to the Senate floor within hours of the appointment and delivered a denunciation so sweeping that it shook the turf under Bork's feet.[84]

"Robert Bork's America is a land in which women would be forced into back-alley abortions, blacks would sit at segregated lunch counters, rogue police could break down citizens' doors in midnight raids, schoolchildren could not be taught about evolution, writers and artists could be censored at the whim of the government, and the doors of federal courts would be shut on the fingers of millions of citizens for whom the judiciary is the only protector of the individual rights that are at the heart of our democracy," Kennedy thundered.[85]

It was a surprise attack. Most people in the White House had assumed that Kennedy would express grave concerns about Bork but reserve his judgment for the hearings. That was the usual pattern for a senator of the opposing party. But here he was, putting his clout on the line to oppose this nomination at all costs. The NAACP leader, Benjamin Hooks, quickly threw his lot in with Kennedy, saying at the group's convention the following week that he would fight Bork "'til hell freezes over."[86]

Republicans complained that Kennedy had mischaracterized Bork's record. He did indeed believe, as did many legal conservatives, that constitutional rights should cover only what they were understood to cover in the time of the framers. He objected to court-ordered rights to abortion and contraception, but that didn't mean he opposed abortion and contraception. It meant only that he believed elected officials should make the determination, not judges. It was a crucial distinction. Everyone at the meetings of the Federalist Society understood it. But would it come through to average voters?

Two and a half months later, when Bork finally took the witness chair before the Senate Judiciary Committee, he struggled to convince people that his passion was for restraining the judiciary, not removing legal protections that most people took for granted. Within minutes of taking the stand, he found himself in a defensive crouch, trying to justify a lifetime's worth of academic observations, up to and including his fiery speech before the inaugural Federalist Society conference.[87]

Back in the 1950s, when the Supreme Court outlawed segregation, it confronted an odd problem: the basis for the court's ruling was the equal protection clause of the Fourteenth Amendment, which applied to states. But the District of Columbia wasn't a state. So could segregation continue in the nation's capital? The Supreme Court ruled it could not, because the Fourth Amendment's due process clause incorporated equal protection.[88] Bork, like many conservatives, rejected the notion that "due process" conferred substantive rights, rather than merely fair procedures. This was precisely the kind of open window through which liberal judges could shove all kinds of unwarranted orders. So, asked Pennsylvania's Republican senator, Arlen Specter, did that mean that Bork, as a Supreme Court justice, would not vote to prevent segregation in Washington?

"I have not thought of a rationale for it because I think you are quite right, Senator," Bork replied, referring to Specter's suggestion that he opposed substantive due process.

Bork's answer stunned his White House handlers, who seized on a break to urge him to recant. Though often stubborn—"I'm a lawyer, not a politician,"[89] he told Republicans who suggested he show more emotion—Bork quickly agreed to back down on segregation. "My doubts about the substantive due process approach . . . [do] not mean that I would ever dream of overruling" the ban on segregation, he said. But the question remained: How could he make that claim if due process rights were, as he insisted, a completely illegitimate means of interpreting the Constitution? That question, and others like it, cast a pall over the entire conservative legal agenda.[90]

Conservatives were getting manhandled, and there was a lot of blame to go around. Some latched on to the surprising ruthlessness of Democrats, for one. "A perversion of the process," complained John Bolton, then one of Meese's assistants.[91] There was also the somewhat dubious attempt to present Bork, who was nothing if not an iconoclast, as an open-minded moderate; Republicans' efforts to soften his image were contradicted by his ornery demeanor and finger-wagging lectures. If they had presented him in a different light—as a fiery advocate for forgotten Americans, perhaps—they might at least have presented a truthful image.[92]

Bork went down to a crushing defeat, 58–42, with an angry Reagan accusing Democrats of "a spectacle of misrepresentation."[93]

Bork's humiliation—being forced to endure five days of questioning on national television as senators tore into his record—would haunt judicial nominees for the next four decades. Forever after, Republicans would claim that Ted Kennedy had turned judicial confirmations into a gladiator sport; Democrats would counter that Meese and Reagan had tried to game the system by packing the court with ideological allies.

Many people in both parties would mourn the day that nominees stopped being judged by their credentials and became targets for political attacks. Ralph Neas, who helped bring about the defeat of Bork, later admitted that liberals took the fight to a new level.[94] But in their view, the notion that qualifications alone were enough to merit confirmation assumed that presidents would choose nominees on the same criteria.

Reagan had not. He and Meese wanted a conservative in the originalist mold, not the best-qualified candidate of any stripe.

Bolton blamed the White House staff, who had been distracted by that summer's Iran-Contra scandal, for a flawed strategy. "They thought his intellect alone would dazzle the Democrats," Bolton said of Bork. "They were going to score political points, and we were conducting a seminar and that just didn't cut it."[95]

The Bork fiasco left an indelible mark on the conservative legal movement. It would never again attempt to defend itself solely on the merits of overturning flawed legal precedents; rather, its leaders embraced the idea that removing those precedents would clear the way for conservative social priorities. Their critique of the activist Supreme Court was subsumed into the anti-abortion movement, the anti–affirmative action movement, and other political drives propelled by right-wing constituencies. The purely intellectual concept of judicial restraint became conflated with social conservatism. This meant that future nominees would be carried on the shoulders of the religious right, the gun lobby, and fellow activist groups that appealed to blue-collar conservatives.

Once the model of academic rectitude, Bork himself adapted to the new reality. He accepted the need for allies wherever he could find them. He quit his seat on the DC Circuit Court of Appeals and embraced his admirers on the religious right. Unaffiliated with any church at the time of his Supreme Court battle and reported to be agnostic, he was baptized a Catholic at the age of seventy-six.[96] He became a caustic presence on conservative talk shows and authored books with doomsday titles, including *Slouching Towards Gomorrah: Modern Liberalism and American Decline*.[97]

CHAPTER 8

Alito Rising

After Bork's defeat, Sam Alito called him "one of the most outstanding nominees of this century."[1] Alito was speaking in his new role as US attorney for New Jersey, back in the Newark courthouse where he'd begun his government career and met his wife.

The role of prosecutor suited Alito's personality. His native reserve dovetailed perfectly with a prosecutor's need for discretion, and his tendency to find simple truths in complicated issues made him an effective communicator.

Despite his decade in the Justice Department, Alito was not a surefire pick to run its operations in the Garden State. Rep. Jim Courter, the leading New Jersey Republican, had pushed hard for his own candidate for the job, going so far as to lobby the White House to intervene with the Justice Department. But Alito had won Meese's confidence, and both of the state's Democratic senators, Bill Bradley and Frank Lautenberg, spoke well of him as a professional prosecutor, not a political guy.[2]

Sam Sr.'s bipartisan reputation may also have given his namesake a boost, as the now-retired father popped up in the *Trenton Times* to declare that he and Rose were "proud as peacocks" of their son.[3] Just a little more than two months later, on May 20, 1987, Sam Sr. would pass away at seventy-three, plunging his family into grief. The *Trenton Times* cited his nonpartisanship in the very first paragraph of his obituary, touting the hard work that propelled this immigrant boy's journey from Calabria to Trenton and his lasting contribution to New Jersey's structure of government. His successor as head of the Office of Legislative Services said, "He brought the whole concept of nonpartisan professional staff services a long way."[4]

....

ALITO TOOK THE HELM of the New Jersey US attorney's office at a propitious time. The office had long been focused on political corruption and organized crime, the state's twin plagues, which sometimes intersected. But the 1980s had brought the most serious crackdown against the Italian Mafia in a generation. The campaign was fueled by Reagan's decision to partner with Benito Craxi, Italy's socialist prime minister, to break the international supply lines that connected the Sicilian mob to the families controlling drug dealing in New York and New Jersey; all together, the Sicilian Mafia exported about half the heroin entering the East Coast of the United States.[5]

This was treacherous work, given the Mafia's use of violence to intimidate prosecutors and witnesses alike. In Italy, the leader of the crackdown was an ambitious magistrate named Giovanni Falcone. Smiling and confident, Falcone accepted the risks in the name of patriotism. He believed he was ridding his native Sicily of a centuries-old curse. "I grew up in the same neighborhoods as many of them," he said of the mobsters. "I understand how a Sicilian mind works."[6]

He knew his life was in danger. From the moment he agreed to the assignment, Falcone surrounded himself with armed guards, bulletproof vehicles, and sandbags in front of glass windows. In 1986, Falcone took on his greatest challenge, putting 452 defendants on trial for a multitude of crimes, ranging from heroin trafficking to murder. The trial played out under intense security: the alleged Mafia chieftains were held in thirty barred cells—described as "grilled cages" in *The New York Times*—in the back of a specially constructed courtroom. From behind the bars, they cursed at prosecutors and witnesses alike, while supporters in the audience echoed their catcalls. About 3,500 police officers stood guard on the streets of Palermo. In the end, 338 of the 452 defendants were convicted, with 19 getting life terms.[7]

Falcone's team was part of the Italian-American Working Group, through which Sicilian prosecutors shared information with the US attorneys in New

York and New Jersey.[8] In the Southern District of Manhattan, the US attorney was a self-described crimefighter named Rudolph Giuliani, who courted the city's tabloids with stunts like donning sunglasses and a leather vest to go undercover and show how easily someone could buy crack cocaine.[9]

Giuliani became a household name across the Hudson River for convicting seventeen mobsters for importing heroin and cocaine from Sicily via Brazil in the so-called Pizza Connection trial. The conspirators allegedly laundered tens of millions of dollars in profits through a network of Italian restaurants.[10] Giuliani's big win came just as Alito was taking office. He gamely called Giuliani "one of the great prosecutors of our time," and suggested he'd be satisfied being a lesser light in the tri-state constellation.[11]

In fact, Alito's low-key diligence won him admirers among those who disdained Giuliani's showboating. When an FBI special agent was shot and seriously injured while interrogating a suspect in a Plainfield, New Jersey, motel room, Alito decided to handle the case himself. It wasn't an easy win: the shooter claimed his automatic weapon had fired on its own. But Alito brought in a ballistics expert to rule out any possibility of an accidental discharge.[12] He gained a conviction and the gratitude of his office. Here was a man who put his own reputation on the line to stand up for his team.[13]

New Jersey's big mob case was already well underway when Alito took office. On August 22, 1985, federal prosecutors had indicted twenty-six members of the Lucchese crime family for drugs, gambling, and credit card fraud. This case had its own colorful details stemming from four years of wiretapping of mob hangouts, including the Hole-in-the-Wall luncheonette in Newark.[14] But the trial was proving to be problematic. Health problems kept popping up among the defendants, jurors, and their family members, extending the proceedings for a whopping twenty-one months.[15]

In the end, all twenty of the remaining defendants were acquitted in just fourteen hours. It was a stunning defeat, but Alito was stoical. "It's not going to change our plans to fight as hard against the Mafia as we can," he said. "We have other cases. We will have other cases in the future."[16]

While Alito and his team pointed to a flawed jury instruction from the judge,[17] a likelier explanation for the big loss emerged five years later. Michael "The Fat Kid" Taccetta, the lead defendant in the case and acting head of the Lucchese family, and Michael Perna, a co-defendant and lieutenant, admitted to bribing a member of the jury. Alito's successor as US attorney, Michael Chertoff, called the news "a sucker punch."[18]

But the Lucchese trial wasn't Alito's last chance against the Mafia. In 1989, he launched the prosecution of a powerful underboss named John Riggi, who allegedly controlled labor unions and large segments of the state's construction industry.[19] Riggi would have a later claim to fame as the reputed inspiration for the TV character Tony Soprano.[20]

After a highly publicized trial, Riggi was convicted of extortion, although the jury declined to find him guilty of the broader charge of racketeering.[21]

Decades later, Alito would seize on an event celebrating the Rutgers University Italian Studies program to lace into *The Sopranos* for creating a negative image of Italian Americans. "You have a trifecta—gangsters, Italian-Americans, New Jersey—wedded in the popular imagination," he said.[22] Instead, he urged students to think of the Italian immigrant experience in terms of people like his father and grandparents, who retained their ethnic pride while embracing America in all its virtues. "They grew up in homes that were distinctly Southern Italian," he said, "and I grew up in a home that was distinctly American."[23]

Alito would return to the same theme the following year, when the Supreme Court honored the courage of Giovanni Falcone, the Italian magistrate who oversaw the mob crackdown in Sicily. In 1992, Falcone was killed, along with his wife and four other people, when the Mafia blew up his bulletproof car with two thousand pounds of explosives planted along a highway near Palermo.[24]

"The international community lost a very great man," Alito said, before going on to accuse the media of using mobsters to "slander Italian Americans." Hollywood, he charged, created a "perversely romantic" image of the Mafia and "shamefully promulgated" it at the expense of recognizing the real achievements of the Italian people.[25]

. . . .

Bork's martyrdom was a setback that put the conservative legal movement on a path to dominance. The impressive show of resistance by liberals had the perverse effect of reminding conservative political donors and activists of the importance of judicial nominations, and the fusion of law and politics moved closer to completion.

Reagan, however, struggled to fill the seat left open by Bork's rejection. Douglas Ginsburg, a forty-one-year-old Meese lieutenant who had spent less than a year on the DC Circuit Court of Appeals, was the president's next pick. For a moment, it looked like the whole contretemps might end with a justice who was as conservative as Bork but twenty years younger. But Ginsburg's youth quickly began to haunt him. First, it came out that he had acknowledged smoking marijuana, which older Americans associated with the hippie culture. Then it emerged that as a Harvard student, he had co-founded Operation Match, the nation's first computer dating service. While in a later era, that would have made him a tech pioneer, many social conservatives regarded computer dating as a form of promiscuity. ("Nominee Left College to Be Matchmaker," headlined *The New York Times*.)[26] Ginsburg withdrew his nomination.[27]

Reagan eventually sought refuge in a more experienced and broadly acceptable nominee, Anthony Kennedy. Notably, the fifty-one-year-old Kennedy had spent nearly thirteen years as a federal appeals court judge. A Gerald Ford appointee, he was not associated with the conservative legal movement and carried a reputation as a thoughtful moderate.[28] He was confirmed 97–0.

While Justice Kennedy was the immediate fruit of the Bork fight, the greater harvest would come later, from the seeds planted by the Federalist Society. "It was tremendously energizing for conservatives, having a martyr, basically," said Calabresi.[29]

This served two functions. It attracted new people to the movement, including wealthy donors who were not previously focused on the law but wanted to avenge Bork's defeat; within four years, the Federalist Society's budget had doubled. And it created a stronger bond among Federalist Society members who felt a personal connection to Bork.[30]

For young conservative lawyers, Bork's brainy mixture of certitude about the Constitution and confidence in tearing down liberal precedents was galvanizing. If he went further than his contemporaries, plunging into academic critiques with the kind of reckless abandon that had tripped him up in the hearings, it was because of his unusual commitment to the conservative cause. Plus, Ted Kennedy's success in simplifying Bork's constitutional theories to "back-alley abortions" and "segregated lunch counters" hit right-wing intellectuals where they lived. It cast their studied faith in a limited Constitution as a form of prejudice toward women and minorities. It made Bork's martyrdom, in some sense, their own.

"People felt a tremendous loyalty to him," Calabresi said of Bork. "In fact, I named my oldest son Robert, I'm sure because of my admiration for him . . . There were a lot of people who felt this way and nursed their sense of grievance, and it became a martyrdom situation."[31]

In the ten years after Bork's defeat, the number of Federalist Society chapters would roughly triple, as would its budget.[32] Its annual National Lawyers Convention, inaugurated the year of the Bork fight, became a must-attend networking event for anyone seeking a legal post in a Republican administration. Federalist Society members who were already on the bench would attend as well, with Supreme Court justices delivering keynote speeches in packed hotel ballrooms.

Meanwhile, the DC chapter continued its regular lunches, holding forth from Tony Cheng's, the glitziest parlor in Chinatown, with its gold walls and gaudy mirrors.[33]

....

LIFE WASN'T SO PUNGENT on the other side of the ideological spectrum. Critical legal studies received a burst of attention in the first years of the Reagan era, as a sharp swing in one direction motivates some people to pull harder in the other. But it struggled to grow. Its center of gravity remained firmly, almost stubbornly, in Cambridge, Massachusetts. By 1984, a story in *The New Yorker* suggested that the Crits had amassed enough clout on the Harvard Law School faculty to influence tenure decisions.[34]

That proved to be mistaken, since opposition to CLS began to mobilize in earnest around that time. In fact, that very *New Yorker* story prompted two board members of the conservative Olin Foundation to sound the alarm. At a series of meetings culminating on May 31—just two months after the *New Yorker* piece was published—the foundation's trustees voted "to support scholars at leading universities who are able to advance the intellectual case against the CLS movement through public lectures and debates, publication and research."[35] The following spring, the Olin board approved a grant of $917,000 over three years to fund a law and economics program at Harvard itself.[36]

Harvard accepted the money to rebut all the Moscow-on-the-Charles talk that was preoccupying the media. President Derek Bok, a former law dean, was antsy about his school being so identified with a radical movement; Harvard's hegemony would be weakened if it tilted too far in any direction.[37]

It didn't help that the Crits were fighting battles on so many fronts: against the New Deal liberals who were their main target, against conservative plotters like the Olin Foundation members, and against some of their would-be allies within the feminist and African American communities.

Duncan Kennedy and another important CLS leader, Roberto Unger, were unapologetic about the movement's Marxist roots, which prioritized class-based analysis over race or gender. This was a point of contention between the 1960s radicals who founded the movement and slightly younger Crits like Clare Dalton, a British-born scholar who joined Harvard's faculty in 1981.[38] By the late 1980s, however, the movement began to broaden its base. Derrick Bell, a pioneering Black professor, used the tenets of CLS to help develop critical race theory, which is based around the idea that civil rights victories weren't sufficient to erase the built-in racial biases in the law.[39] Feminist scholar Mary Joe Frug, the wife of Harvard law professor and CLS pioneer Gerald Frug, dedicated herself to showing how the law served to sexualize and marginalize women in the ways it addressed prostitution, among other gender-infused topics.[40]

A CLS power couple, the Frugs often hosted spontaneous get-togethers in their big old house in Cambridge, at which Dalton, Bell, Kennedy, Martha Minow, and other intellectuals would eat, drink, and discuss legal theories late into the night.[41] A feeling of social and sometimes romantic camaraderie had always coursed through the movement, and Minow, a young liberal on the fringes of CLS, compared those evenings to "expatriates Ernest Hemingway and Ezra Pound living in Paris in the 1920s," according to *The Boston Globe*.[42]

The rest of Harvard Law School was less bedazzled. Starting in the mid-1980s, liberal junior faculty members started to be denied tenure, culminating in the faculty's rejection of Dalton in 1987.[43] She fell three votes short of the required two-thirds majority. After an outcry—in which she, her fellow Crits, and some students insisted that she was being pilloried for her left-wing views as well as her gender—Bok initiated an investigation but ultimately did not overturn the faculty's verdict.[44] Dalton sued for gender discrimination, collected a $260,000 settlement, and moved across the river to join the faculty of Northeastern University Law School.[45]

In 1988, President Reagan spoke before the Federalist Society in Washington and credited it with slaying the dragon of critical legal studies. His apocalyptic language suggested the extent to which fear of the Crits had propelled the growth of the conservative legal movement.

"Just a few years ago, the Critical Legal Studies movement stood virtually unchallenged like some misplaced monster of prehistoric radicalism," Reagan said. "Today, you are vexing the dog masters to the left. The Federalist Society is changing the culture of our nation's law schools. You're returning the values and concepts of law as our Founders understood them to scholarly dialogue, and through that dialogue to our legal institutions."[46]

Conservatives believed they were the only ones willing to take on the Crits, but that wasn't so. The following year, Derek Bok, the ultimate establishment figure, cemented Harvard's crackdown on the group by appointing a corporate law specialist named Robert C. Clark as dean; though not a member of the conservative legal movement, Clark was a traditionalist with an interest in law and economics.[47]

Then came a shocking crime: the murder of Mary Joe Frug on a cold April night in 1991. The forty-nine-year-old Frug, a professor at New England Law School, was walking to a convenience market in one of the wealthiest neighborhoods in Cambridge. An assailant leapt from the bushes and viciously stabbed her to death, plunging a seven-inch knife deep into her chest and thighs. Choir members practicing at the Holy Trinity Armenian Church heard her screams and rushed outside to find her collapsed in a pool of blood. Other witnesses reported having seen a white man in his early twenties hovering in the shrubbery shortly before the attack.[48]

Based on the severity of Frug's wounds and the fact that nothing was stolen, Cambridge police decided it was premeditated murder. Two possibilities loomed large: Could this feminist scholar, who often depicted men as oppressors, have antagonized someone enough to kill her? Or was the killer someone who knew her socially, perhaps even among her circle of family and friends?

"We interviewed people who disagreed with her politics," said one Massachusetts State Police investigator. "But people say, 'Look, when I disagree with someone, I write an article saying how stupid they are and what I believe is right. I don't go out and kill them.'"[49]

Police then turned their attention to members of the Crit community and their associates, including a third-year law student who had been a friend and confidant to Frug's husband, Gerry. There was also the thought that a student may have had an unrequited crush on the victim. Christopher Edley, a professor at Harvard Law, suggested that "students get crushes on people all the time, but Mary Joe got that more than the average professor."[50]

Harvard Law School was unsettled. The police activity, on top of the existing tensions around critical legal studies, made the movement seem radioactive. At this fraught moment, Gerry Frug asked the student-led *Harvard Law Review* to publish an early version of his late wife's opus, "A Postmodern Feminist Legal Manifesto (An Unfinished Draft)." Its claims were sexually charged and focused on how the "terrorization" of the female body featured in the law.[51] Conservative students objected, claiming the highly unconventional piece was only finding the light of day because of people's collective grief over its author's murder.[52]

Skeptics used the law review's April Fool's humor issue to make fun of Frug's ideas, dubbing her the "Rigor-Mortis Professor of Law." The cruelty of the parody ("Then we go out at night to hunt down some hunky men and rip their clothes off"),[53] combined with the inflammatory subject matter, set the Boston legal community at war with itself.

"They engaged in a necrophiliac gangbang upon the living body of her work," charged Elizabeth Spahn, one of Frug's friends from New England School of Law.[54] Alan Dershowitz, Harvard Law School's reigning civil libertarian, shot back that the puffed-up furor over the parody was "a reflection of the power of women and blacks to define the content of what is politically correct and incorrect on college and law school campuses."[55]

At Frug's memorial service, her grieving twenty-year-old son, Stephen, an undergraduate student at Harvard, delivered a moving eulogy: "And she would take walks. Long walks, short walks, bicycle rides, walks during the day, walks at night. And that is how she died."[56]

Later, he would muse about how his mother helped keep CLS together, and how it came unstuck after her death. When the movement was accused of neglecting women, she organized the "Fem-Crits" and held women-only meetings at her house (she banished her son to his room while urging her daughter to join). These confabs were an extension of her regular rotation of intellectually charged dinner parties.[57] Cook, hostess, den mother—she played many roles. Her death, and its brutal circumstances, seemed to destroy the sense of unity among her friends.

As years went by, Stephen Frug could only wonder whether his mother's murder might have been the random act of a deranged person. Duncan Kennedy, for his part, would say he had no ideas, no theories on how his close friend met her sad end.[58]

He did, however, know who killed the critical legal studies movement: Derek Bok and the center-left. Conservatives, he acknowledged, used CLS as a red cape to attract right-wing bulls to their own movement, but it was the ostensibly liberal Harvard Law School, fearful of its declining rankings, that stomped out the Crits for good.

"By the mid-1990s, the radicals had disappeared, and the liberals had just been pummeled: they were scared, they were intimidated, they had lost their self-confidence," Kennedy concluded.[59]

. . . .

IN THE SUMMER OF 1988, Meese's reign in the Justice Department ended prematurely after a fourteen-month independent counsel investigation into conflicts of interest in his business dealings. The report did not recommend criminal prosecution, allowing him to claim vindication. But he had already been weakened by his role in the administration's Iran-Contra scandal, which only gave fodder to those who felt he was too enmeshed in politics to be effective as the nation's chief law enforcement officer.[60]

The following year, Reagan was succeeded by his own vice president, George H. W. Bush, who was not close to Meese and was eager to turn down the thermostat on judicial nominations. So when Justice Brennan retired in 1990, Bush opted for a little-known New Hampshire judge named David Souter. So modest that he lived alone in a rustic farmhouse in the small town he grew up in, Souter was an emblem of judicial rectitude carried to recessive extremes. But he seemed an antidote to both the judicial activism of the 1960s and Meese's counterrevolution of the 1980s. After a quiet Senate hearing, he was confirmed 90–9, with only a small cadre of liberals in opposition.[61]

When a seat opened on the New Jersey–based Third Circuit Court of Appeals, with the retirement of a Brennan-like liberal named John Gibbons, Bush nominated Alito in a similar spirit, as a model of low-key competence.[62] Alito had been laying the groundwork for the appointment for at least four months, sending his résumé to the White House through Federalist Society co-founder Lee Liberman with a note saying, "Many thanks for your help."[63]

Alito played the part of the nonpartisan professional. He told the Senate Judiciary Committee that he would not allow his years as a prosecutor to influence his judicial decisions. "After a career as a government lawyer, I am not under the illusion that the government's litigation position is always correct," he said. He further vowed to be "open-minded," and never to allow his personal opinions to influence his decision-making.[64]

He was greatly assisted, once again, by the support of New Jersey's Democratic senators, Bradley and Lautenberg. Lautenberg hailed him as "impartial, thoughtful, and fair," while Bradley went even further. The former Princeton basketball star said he backed Alito "100 percent" and predicted that he would "make a contribution that will stand the test of time." None other than Ted Kennedy assured Alito, "You have a distinguished record."[65]

The Senate confirmed him by voice vote. In an instant, the forty-year-old Alito was serving alongside his mentor Leonard Garth on a court ranking just below the US Supreme Court.

Still, he projected modesty. Like many people who tense up around those who have power over them, Alito relaxed noticeably with his own clerks. He seemed to enjoy playing the role of big brother: he was one part mentor, taking an interest in their lives and careers, and another part pal. The clerks remember him as calm, studious, and easy-going. When cases called for him to sit in Philadelphia, the biggest city in the Third Circuit, he would pile into one clerk's ramshackle car.[66] There was no sign of ego—nor of an abiding political passion. "During the entire time I clerked for him, we never talked about politics," said one. "There were no red-button issues." Rather, his favorite subjects were Newark history and baseball.[67]

The office was hardly a sweatshop. Usually, it would wrap up business early so everyone could leave the dangerous Newark neighborhood before sunset. As the father of two young children, Alito liked to be home for dinner. Martha-Ann would sometimes visit the office, brightening the mood with her boisterous spirits.[68]

Alito's humor was drier. When another judge put statues of lions outside the door to her office, prompting some raised eyebrows around the courthouse, Alito's clerks gave him a pair of pink flamingos to adorn his own chambers. They became among his most prized possessions, along with a baseball card from a Philadelphia Phillies fantasy camp he attended as a gift from Martha-Ann.[69]

"He handled his cases with human decency and common sense," said one former clerk, who remembered him showing concern for a person who was denied Social Security benefits on a technicality and for a defendant who faced a long mandatory-minimum prison sentence based on faulty math about the amount of money he had skimmed from his employer.[70]

The sense of ease and good feeling extended to his fellow judges as well. Garth and the circuit's chief judge, Ed Becker, were especially fond of the polite and unprepossessing Alito; they cast him as a diligent judicial fact finder, not an ideologue.[71]

But while colleagues marveled at his lack of pretentiousness, Alito was amassing a very conservative voting record—one that fully foreshadowed his record on the Supreme Court. His restrained personality among the big egos in the courtroom distorted people's perceptions of him; it led colleagues to mistake his modesty for moderation.

The role of a federal circuit court judge is to apply precedents handed down by the Supreme Court. But at many junctures, Alito sought to stretch those precedents to cover conservative priorities, from abortion restrictions to gun rights to public displays of religious symbols to fewer constraints on police tactics.

When, a year after taking the oath of office, he was part of a three-judge panel reviewing a Pennsylvania law requiring women seeking abortions to notify their husbands, he alone thought the law did not impose an "undue burden" on the right to abortion.[72]

The spousal notification law was highly controversial. Critics maintained that women in troubled marriages would be so reluctant to consult their husbands that they would be deterred from pursuing abortions altogether. Alito, however, suggested that very few women would be in that situation and questioned whether a provision affecting such a small number of people could be considered an undue burden. He noted that the law contained exceptions for women who faced spousal abuse, and that others who might initially have been reluctant to tell their husbands about their pregnancies might do so and never regret it.[73]

He based his legal analysis of what constituted an undue burden largely on Justice O'Connor's rulings in previous abortion cases. But when the case went to the Supreme Court, the court—in an opinion co-authored by O'Connor—ruled the spousal notification provision unconstitutional.[74]

Then came a case in which a machine-gun owner challenged a federal law banning average citizens from owning such weapons. Alito took the opportunity to question the constitutional basis for most federal gun control laws. The gun laws were a product of Congress's power to regulate interstate commerce. A conservative reading of the Constitution would suggest that any commerce occurring exclusively within a state would be outside federal regulatory control. But in a string of cases going back many years, the Supreme Court had ruled that because economic activity within a state had a natural impact on other states, Congress could regulate anything within the larger stream of commerce. The court's majority upheld the machine-gun ban, but Alito disagreed.

"In sum," he wrote, "we are left with no congressional findings and no appreciable empirical support for the proposition that the purely intrastate possession of machine guns, by facilitating the commission of certain crimes, has a substantive effect on interstate commerce, and without such support I do not see how the statutory provision at issue here can be sustained."[75]

In 2000, the guardian of a public school student in New Jersey filed suit against officials who moved a poster the boy had painted expressing thankfulness for Jesus to a less conspicuous spot in the classroom and, in a separate incident, declined to let him read a Bible story in class. The entire Third Circuit heard the case and split 6–6 on the merits. Alito sided with the child and his guardian.

"I would hold that discriminatory treatment of the poster because of its 'religious theme' would violate the First Amendment," he wrote. "I would hold that public school students have the right to express religious views in class discussion or in assigned work, provided that their expression falls within the scope of the discussion or assignment."[76]

Four years later, a mother and her ten-year-old daughter sued Pennsylvania police officers who strip-searched them without a warrant; the police had obtained a warrant to search the premises for methamphetamines, but only the woman's husband was listed as a suspect.

The court's majority ruled that the police had overstepped their bounds in submitting the mother and daughter to a humiliating ordeal. Alito, however, suggested that a broader reading of the warrant would have included all occupants of the residence, and even if it did not, a police officer "certainly could have thought that the warrant conferred such authority."[77]

These cases weren't outliers; Alito's positions on religious expression and police conduct, in particular, placed him well to the right of his colleagues. His fellow members of the Federalist Society started to take notice. Here was a respected veteran of Meese's Justice Department and a steadfast conservative whose low-key demeanor gave him some middle-of-the-road credibility. It wasn't long before Sam Alito's name started to rise on their lists of possible Supreme Court nominees.[78]

CHAPTER 9

A Conservative Revolt

After Alito had spent about a decade on the Third Circuit, a talented young law school graduate approached his mentor, a professor who had served in Meese's Justice Department, to ask for advice. The newly minted lawyer had received two offers of clerkships, one with Alito and one with another circuit court judge. He wasn't sure which to take. The professor told him it was an easy call: Go with Alito. He'll be on the Supreme Court someday.

The would-be clerk was baffled; there wasn't even a Republican in the White House at the time. "I saw that there was this conservative network out there, making a list," the clerk later recalled.[1]

In the intervening years, judicial nominations had only gotten more political and more combative. While Souter cruised to confirmation, George H. W. Bush's next pick, Clarence Thomas, saw his Senate Judiciary Committee hearing turn into one of the most dramatic clashes in congressional history, an opera waiting to be written.

Thomas, who had overlapped with Alito at Yale Law School, served during the Reagan administration as chairman of the Equal Employment Opportunity Commission (EEOC), the agency established in the Civil Rights Act of 1964 to monitor workplace discrimination. Thomas's assistant for his first year on the job was a young lawyer named Anita Hill. After Thomas left the EEOC, Bush nominated him for the DC Circuit Court of Appeals.[2] He was confirmed just two months before Alito.[3]

When Thurgood Marshall, the only Black justice on the Supreme Court, retired in 1991, Bush chose Thomas as his replacement. Both men were Black, but their experiences and judicial views couldn't have been more different. Marshall was a legendary liberal who, as head of the NAACP Legal Defense Fund, won the case overturning legal segregation, *Brown v. Board of Education*. On the Supreme Court, Marshall was a reliable supporter of affirmative action programs and abortion rights. Thomas was a noted skeptic of the Warren Court and felt race-based laws placed a stigma on Black people. That made him something of a hero to the overwhelmingly white conservative legal movement: a living refutation of the assumption that Black people either needed or wanted robust government protections.

Politicians on both sides expected Thomas's confirmation to turn into a Bork-like game of cat and mouse. But the hearings took an unexpected turn when Hill, who had become a law professor at the University of Oklahoma, accused Thomas of repeatedly sexually harassing her while they worked together at the EEOC.[4] Hill's riveting testimony and Thomas's explosive reaction—he called the hearing "a high-tech lynching for uppity Blacks who in any way deign to think for themselves, to do for themselves, to have different ideas"[5]—left much of the country in shock. In sheer drama, the Thomas hearings outstripped even Bork's, and generated even more corrosive feelings.

Thomas eked his way to confirmation, 52–48, but was deeply marked by the struggle. While he was considered an affable, talkative judge during his year and a half on the DC Circuit bench, he barely spoke for his first quarter-century on the Supreme Court, at one point going ten years without asking a single question.[6] And while most advocates for women in the workplace regarded his confirmation hearings as a travesty[7]—with Anita Hill as the true victim—the majority of conservatives agreed that he was unfairly targeted for violating liberal dogma.[8] It was an early example of how people could view the same events differently based on their personal assumptions.

After President Bill Clinton succeeded Bush in 1993 and secured a healthy Democratic margin in the Senate, the judicial wars receded a bit. Clinton's two Supreme Court appointees, Ruth Bader Ginsburg and Stephen Breyer, sprinted to confirmation by margins of 96–3 and 87–9, respectively.[9]

But the drama shifted to the lower courts. After Republicans took control of the Senate in 1995, they either delayed or denied hearings to many of Clinton's choices, forcing twenty to withdraw. These included a disproportionate number of women and minority candidates, ratcheting up frustration on the left.[10] In all, an unusually high 105 Clinton nominees failed to make it to Senate hearings, while 378 were confirmed.[11]

Conservative media, then in its infancy, used anecdotes to sound alarms about liberal nominees: Judith McConnell, a California state judge from San Diego, granted custody of a sixteen-year-old boy to his late father's same-sex partner. Sam Paz, a noted California civil rights attorney, represented teenagers in a police brutality case. Peter Edelman, a Clinton friend and former aide to Robert F. Kennedy, wrote an article suggesting that people had a right to a minimum income. All were denied appointments.[12]

By the 2000 presidential election, judgeships were a salient campaign issue. Republican nominee George W. Bush, son of the former president, vowed to appoint only those who agreed "to interpret the law, not to legislate from the bench."[13] It was a politically useful phrase—one Bush continued to invoke throughout his eight-year presidency—because it could be read in different ways. To some, it was a call for judicial restraint, a lowering of the temperature while judges receded into a more limited role of resolving conflicts and tying up loose ends. But to conservatives in tune with the originalist ideology, it meant only that courts would not create new rights or issue complicated orders. When it came to rolling back rights that were already granted, judges would be entirely free to shake things up.

....

ALITO'S TERM ON THE Third Circuit coincided with the longest stretch without a Supreme Court vacancy in history. For eleven years after Breyer's confirmation, the same nine justices settled into a comfortable routine.[14] Rehnquist, Scalia, and Thomas anchored the right; Ginsburg, Breyer, and John Paul Stevens anchored the left. The others—Kennedy, Souter, and O'Connor—were swing votes. O'Connor seemed to find herself in the middle the most often—a role that suited the well-liked former majority leader of the Arizona Senate.

O'Connor was the antithesis of a justice who felt pressure to conform to ideological expectations. She viewed her work on the court as a quest for fairness and justice and, above all, a reasonable outcome. If a rule made sense, she stuck with it. Practicality was a consideration.[15] She didn't reject originalism as much as acknowledge its limitations; parsing the Federalist Papers for clues to the thinking of the Founding Fathers didn't solve every case.

"Those who would renegotiate the boundaries between church and state must therefore answer a difficult question: Why would we trade a system that has served us so well for one that has served others so poorly?" she wrote in one of her last cases, in which she cast the deciding vote against allowing framed copies of the Ten Commandments to be displayed in Kentucky courthouses.[16] Her point was that separation of church and state in the United States allowed religion to flourish, while countries with state-sponsored religions often had far less spiritual activity. Needless to say, an originalist wouldn't consider whether a rule was working—only whether it was supported by the original understanding of the First Amendment.

So when O'Connor announced her retirement on July 1, 2005, more than the usual attention focused on the court. She was the swing vote, which led many to call for Bush to appoint a widely acceptable centrist, another O'Connor. She was also one of only two women on the court, and she herself expressed hope for a female successor.

The opening on the court—the first in fourteen years to be filled by a Republican president—provoked intense interest within the Federalist Society and the tight network of Meese DOJ veterans who considered themselves custodians of the originalist movement. They saw a meaningful chance to move the court to the right. O'Connor had been no one's idea of a true conservative, and neither had Souter. In fact, "No more Souters" was something of a rallying cry within the movement, a psychological prod to Bush to avoid the weaknesses of his father.[17] "For him it was important that he not make the same mistake as his father did with Souter," said Alberto Gonzales, Bush's Texas confidant who was also his first White House counsel and second attorney general.[18]

In fact, Gonzales envisioned himself as the nation's first Hispanic justice. He had served on the Texas Supreme Court before coming to Washington, but he wasn't part of the conservative movement. Bush had some interest in

Gonzales, too, but members of the conservative legal movement sussed it out and initiated what Gonzales depicted as a "whisper campaign" against him.[19] He wasn't imagining things. Behind the scenes, Meese and Leonard Leo, the Federalist Society vice president and power broker, privately advised Bush that conservatives would not support Gonzales. They offered up four other names, including Alito's, as acceptable alternatives.[20]

When Gonzales tried to mend fences by speaking at a conservative event, members of the audience booed when he talked about the role of the Supreme Court as arbiter of the nation's laws. The boos may have been aimed at the court, but Gonzales felt the sting as well.[21]

So when Bush's team—Attorney General Gonzales, White House counsel Harriet Miers, Vice President Dick Cheney, and Chief of Staff Andy Card—gathered to discuss how to fill the O'Connor opening, Bush quickly pulled Gonzales aside.

"I'm not going to put you on the court," Bush told him.[22]

Gonzales said he understood. Tensions over the White House's handling of the war on terror, including allegations of torture, had made Gonzales's confirmation as attorney general harder than expected, and he knew he would face more of the same if he were tapped for the court.

"I said, 'That's fine. I'm happy where I am.'"[23]

. . . .

For Alito, the opening was both a window of opportunity and a last chance. He had spent fifteen years on the Third Circuit, making himself as much a fixture in the Newark courthouse as the pink flamingos outside his office. By now, the job felt less like a stepping stone and more like a destination. At fifty-five, he was already on the far end of the age spectrum for Supreme Court nominees. Conservatives wanted someone who could carry their flags for decades—the younger the better.

What's more, the unusually long delay between Supreme Court openings had created a crowded field of conservative jurists who aspired to the court, a generation that had aged in place for about a decade. There were a handful of men and women with solidly conservative lower-court records who would be acceptable to movement leaders and important constituencies such as the religious right.

During his four years as White House counsel, Gonzales had been intermittently building a list of potential nominees, including Alito, and meeting with them privately. Gonzales's first question for Bush when the opening finally came was whether he wanted to go to war for a nominee who was beloved on the right but would stir up anger among Democrats, particularly over opposition to *Roe v. Wade.* "In the end," Gonzales said, "the president did not want to have that war."[24]

That cut down the field considerably. Fifth Circuit Judge Edith Jones was an obvious contender for a seat vacated by a woman. But she was fervently pro-life and had seized on a suit brought by Norma McCorvey, the woman at the center of *Roe v. Wade,* to inveigh against the Supreme Court's abortion rights decision in forceful language. Tenth Circuit Judge Michael McConnell was popular on the right but had once signed a petition calling for a constitutional amendment that would overturn *Roe.*[25]

There was also Fourth Circuit Judge Michael Luttig, considered by many to be the front-runner, but he was outspoken in a way that conjured memories of Robert Bork. Karl Rove, the president's close adviser, thought he had a sense of entitlement.[26] And Gonzales called him "a conservative's conservative" but advised Bush he could provoke a serious confirmation battle.[27]

Alito's studious manner, along with his unpretentiousness, distinguished him from some of the more showboating figures on the right. At the same time, his unwavering conservative record separated him from some candidates who were suspected of being susceptible to liberal influences, such as Fourth Circuit Judge J. Harvie Wilkinson III. ("The more we looked into him, the more he might be another [Anthony] Kennedy," Rove said of Wilkinson.)[28]

But when Alito made a secret trek to Washington to meet with Bush's inner circle—Cheney, Gonzales, Rove, and Miers—his old bugaboo, his nerves, betrayed him. Gonzales would later recall that he had such short, crisp answers to every question that the interview wrapped up well before its allotted time.[29] Rove had even more dramatic memories: "He is quaking. I mean literally, the table is like [*shakes table*]—I felt for the guy . . . You could tell he was enormously nervous."

He added: "It was comical."[30]

Later, Rove would say that he found Alito's discomfort endearing. "It humanized him," he said. "It was tough for him. It emphasized that this guy is really a judge's judge. He's used to studying these issues seriously."[31]

In the end, Alito made the cut. He was among the five candidates granted a chance to make their case to Bush. While the president relied heavily on advisers, he also trusted his gut, particularly if he felt a spark that created a sense of connection. That's what he hoped for when he sat down with the five finalists: "I went into the interviews hoping that one person would stand apart."[32]

One did.

It was John G. Roberts Jr.

Roberts was five years younger than Alito and a fellow Federalist Society favorite who had spent six years in the Reagan administration. He had followed a similar path in life to Alito's: He came of age in a devout Catholic household in Indiana, where his father managed a steel mill. His upbringing was largely devoid of politics, but he recognized his political inclinations when he went to Harvard and felt himself to be out of sync with his liberal classmates.[33] His conservative baptism was less dramatic than Alito's, however, because campus furors had cooled considerably in the five years between Alito's time at Princeton and Roberts's at Harvard. Rarely had five years make such a difference in the American mindset. But Roberts had been a circuit court judge for only two years, compared to Alito's fifteen. His greatest asset was his lighthearted personality: Roberts conveyed an aura of warmth and ease that Alito did not.

Pretty soon, the youthful, attractive Judge Roberts would start to win over others the way he had charmed Bush.

. . . .

THERE WAS ANOTHER POLITICAL factor at work in the confirmation process: angst over a filibuster. Under Senate rules, a bloc of forty-one senators could impose a filibuster to prevent a vote from happening. In practice, that meant a nominee might need sixty votes to win confirmation. Filibusters were originally a rare occurrence but had become more commonplace through the embittered judicial fights of the Clinton and Bush years. During Bush's presidency, the Senate was closely divided, giving Democrats the power to quash overly conservative nominees if they could keep enough of their own members in line. But the tactic provoked extreme anger in the chamber; many in the GOP began hyping what they called the "nuclear option" of eliminating the filibuster for judicial nominations.[34]

Senate moderates, along with some old-time institutionalists, worried that such a move would change the world's greatest deliberative body for the worse; it threatened to turn confirmations into partisan rubber stamps. So they formed their own caucus—seven Democrats and seven Republicans—and dubbed it the Gang of 14, and then came together to forge a compromise. Under the terms of their deal, the seven Democrats agreed to vote against a filibuster except in "extraordinary" circumstances, while the seven Republicans agreed to keep the filibuster rules in place.[35]

The Gang of 14 presented an obstacle for liberal Democrats and their activist allies as they strategized against John Roberts. They wanted to portray Roberts as dangerously conservative, despite his affability. But even if they succeeded, the filibuster tool was probably out of reach. And the Gang of 14, by its mere existence, put a thumb on the scale in favor of confirmation. It seemed to frown on the role of politics in judicial nominations. It communicated the idea that the system worked best when nominees were confirmed, not rejected.

Ralph Neas, who had played a major role in derailing the Bork nomination, was ready to fight. He saw Roberts as a stalking horse for the right wing and tried to sound the alarm for how he would tip the court away from the moderation that most Americans appreciated in O'Connor. Roberts had clerked for Rehnquist, then the court's most conservative member, and helped author many of the Reagan administration's conservative legal doctrines.[36]

But no one saw that side of Roberts as he prepared for his confirmation hearing. Even *The New York Times* dubbed him "pragmatic" and "always conservative, but never doctrinaire."[37] Bush was so pleased with Roberts's reception—a rare win in a season that included Hurricane Katrina and escalating war in Iraq—that when Rehnquist died of cancer three days before Roberts's confirmation hearing, Bush renominated him to chief justice.[38]

The hearing went ahead as scheduled.

Led by the Senate Judiciary Committee chairman, Arlen Specter of Pennsylvania, a relatively rare pro-choice Republican, the questioning quickly zeroed in on abortion. In recent years, such hearings had devolved into nominees solemnly refusing to discuss matters before the court but offering euphemisms—the right to privacy, the importance of precedent— to reassure supporters of Roe v. Wade.

But Roberts went further than most Republican nominees in providing such assurances. He attested to his support for a right to privacy, called Roe v. Wade "settled" law, and expressed deep reservations about overruling such a precedent. "I do think that it is a jolt to the legal system when you overrule a precedent. Precedent plays an important role in promoting stability and evenhandedness," he said. "It is not enough that you may think the prior decision was wrongly decided."[39]

And when a senator alluded to Roberts's Catholic faith, he offered that there is "nothing in my personal views based on faith or other sources that would prevent me from applying the precedents of the court faithfully."[40]

Roberts was so persuasive that even the ranking Democrat on the Judiciary Committee, liberal stalwart Patrick Leahy of Vermont, announced his support. "I actually ended up writing two speeches over the weekend: one for him and one against him," Leahy told a reporter. "And I felt far more comfortable for him. In this case, I was genuinely having questions in my mind. I mean, John Roberts is undeniably brilliant. He is a very likable person. But is he going to be an ideologue? I'm convinced in my own mind he will not be."[41]

To Neas's fury, fully half of the Democratic caucus joined Leahy in clambering aboard the Roberts train.[42]

He was confirmed 78–22.[43]

....

THERE WAS STILL, OF course, the matter of O'Connor's replacement. For Alito, back in New Jersey, this was a possible source of reclamation. But the confirmation of another white male to the court upped the pressure on Bush to choose a woman. Even the president's wife, Laura Bush, let it be known publicly that she, too, wanted another woman on the court.

The Bushes had already established that they were on different sides of abortion rights.[44] In many ways, their diverging opinions were politically useful as a means of reassuring moderates that they could respect each other's views on such a contentious matter. Now Laura seemed to be campaigning for a more moderate justice—one who would at least pause to consider a woman's options before overturning *Roe v. Wade*. And the president himself, while stopping short of saying he'd encouraged her to speak out, expressed profound respect for his wife's opinion. "This was a rare occasion when Laura's advice spilled out into the public, but far from the only time I relied on her thoughtful counsel," Bush said. "Laura had an instinctive feel for the pulse of the country."[45]

Bush asked his White House counsel, Harriet Miers, to add more women to the list of potential nominees: he was eager to find a suitable female candidate. But the perfect person didn't emerge.[46] Finally, Bush started thinking outside the box. What about Miers herself? She had been his longtime lawyer and loyal aide, rising to head the White House Counsel's Office. But she was also a pioneer: the first woman lawyer in her large Dallas firm, the first woman managing partner, the first woman president of the Dallas Bar Association, and the first woman president of the Texas Bar Association.[47] Along the way, she had been elected to the Dallas City Council, giving her a little O'Connor-like exposure to the give-and-take of electoral politics.

By historical standards, this was more than enough to qualify her for the Supreme Court. In the late nineteenth century, it was common for a president to choose a nominee whose primary experience was as a corporate attorney. Presidents also were apt to choose Supreme Court nominees from among their top deputies: William McKinley, Theodore

Roosevelt, Woodrow Wilson, Calvin Coolidge, Franklin D. Roosevelt, and Harry Truman all elevated their attorneys general to the high court.[48] And the notion that every nominee had to be a distinguished scholar and judge didn't bear scrutiny: among the nation's seventeen chief justices, for instance, were a former president, a former Republican nominee for president, a former governor of California, a former Ohio senator, and a former US representative from Kentucky.[49] Especially if one gave credit for the unusual obstacles in her path, coming of age in the suburban-style neighborhood of North Dallas in the years before the women's movement, the sixty-year-old Miers was a plausible choice.

The Senate Democratic leader, Harry Reid of Nevada, claimed to have first mentioned Miers as a potential candidate to Bush.[50] Rove, however, maintained that the president was already thinking of Miers.[51] In any case, Reid's surprising endorsement indicated she might have an easy path to confirmation. Rove suspected members of the conservative legal movement would be a harder sell. They had their hearts set on what Notre Dame law professor Richard Garnett, writing in *National Review*, called "the farm team"—judges such as Alito, Luttig, Jones, and McConnell, who had been planted and nurtured like hothouse flowers by fellow members of the Federalist Society.[52]

Rove placed an early phone call, one day before Bush planned to announce Miers's nomination, to James Dobson, founder of Focus on the Family and, after the ailing Jerry Falwell, the nation's preeminent leader of the religious right. Rove emphasized to Dobson that Miers had attended an evangelical Christian church in Texas and urged him to talk to Miers's close friend Justice Nathan Hecht of the Texas Supreme Court, who had introduced her to that church. The call served its purpose. Flattered by being taken into the White House's confidence, Dobson dutifully endorsed Miers. But he would also attract unwanted attention by bragging on his radio show, "When you know some of the things that I know—that I probably shouldn't know—you will understand why I have said, with fear and trepidation, that I believe Harriet Miers will be a good justice."[53]

Dobson could have been referring to secret information leaked in his call with Rove, or to a larger briefing for religious right leaders with Hecht and another Miers friend who allegedly included assurances that Miers was "pro-life."[54]

Had Rove intimated that Miers would overturn *Roe v. Wade?* Dobson seemed to think so.

....

HARRIET ELLAN MIERS STEPPED before the public with the beaming endorsement of George and Laura Bush, who together had delivered her the news about her nomination at a private White House dinner on Sunday, October 2.[55] Eager, as always, to be of help to her friends the Bushes, she took the greatest leap of what had been a career marked by caution. She was careening into the unknown.

But while White House aides warned her of the usual sources of hostility—ruthless Democrats, unappeasable liberal activists, a media that would scrutinize every detail of her life going back to her grade school report cards—they failed to gird her for her ultimate enemy: the conservative legal movement. This was the grizzly bear that had grown up during the years she was representing private clients, and in taking a Republican-nominated seat on the Supreme Court, she was stealing one of the berries its life depended upon.

The day after her nomination, Randy Barnett, a Boston University law professor and respected Federalist Society leader, took to the pages of *The Wall Street Journal* to fire the first shot. Ever the originalist, he cited none other than Alexander Hamilton in the Federalist Papers in warning against a president's "spirit of favoritism" and casting Miers as a cipher elevated by Bush for cronyism alone.[56]

That same day, another erudite conservative, George F. Will, laced into Miers for the same reason, but with a more withering tone. If one hundred constitutional experts had been asked "to list 100 individuals who have given evidence of the reflectiveness and excellence requisite in a justice," Will wrote from his perch at *The Washington Post*, "Miers's name probably would not have appeared in any of the 10,000 places on those lists."[57]

That morning, Bush made his first attempt at damage control. Calling her "a woman of principle and deep convictions," he said, "She shares my philosophy that judges should strictly interpret the law and not legislate from the bench." But he stepped on his message by saying he could not recall ever discussing abortion rights with her and declaring, "I have no litmus test."[58]

That sounded like a signal that Miers—hailed by the White House as a pioneering woman, chosen to offer the perspective afforded by her gender, never married while ruggedly pursuing a high-powered career—was likely, after all the constitutional arguments played out, to find a path to supporting *Roe v. Wade.*

....

For Ralph Neas, news of Bush's nomination of Miers was greeted with excitement: Bush had capitulated. Liberals had done their job. They had raised enough of a ruckus about O'Connor's being the swing vote that even a conservative president could see the country was hungry for a moderate justice, not a Federalist Society fellow traveler. News footage from that morning showed a beaming Neas in the office of People for the American Way, the liberal activist group he headed, accepting congratulatory calls from supporters.[59]

The New York Times's liberal editorial page shared Neas's reaction. On the same day that Barnett and Will were laying into Miers from the right, *The Times* claimed that the nomination was provoking "sighs of relief." The newspaper strongly implied that Miers, whom it called a "stealth nominee," was the best that liberals could hope for; yes, she was largely unknown, but that at least suggested her mind would be open. "Many of the best justices have taken odd routes to the court," *The Times* concluded. "Ms. Miers could prove to be a pragmatic, common-sense justice who ends up making this court the Miers Court, the way Justice O'Connor made the last one the O'Connor Court."[60]

Democratic senators, having to answer to their liberal constituents, took a different tack. They weren't ready to support a woman that Bush, after all, claimed would share his views to a Texas T. Ted Kennedy was cautious, saying "the record we have so far is simply insufficient to assess the qualifications of this nominee."[61] To close observers, this gentle scolding was far more of an endorsement than the thunderhead of criticism he'd poured over other conservative nominees, but it gave little succor to Miers's defenders: Kennedy might go easy on her, but he wouldn't actually vote for her.

Harry Reid was curiouser still. He believed himself to have been the originator of the Miers nomination, and he seemed, at first, to be trying to clear a path for her confirmation. He sought to mitigate her greatest weakness by casting her extensive experience as a private lawyer as an important credential, one that kept her closer to the real life of the nation, and her lack of judicial experience as "a plus, not a minus."

But reporters noted something dodgy about Reid from the start, pointing out that he had also praised Roberts before voting against him. Reid's spokesman, Jim Manley, furthered this line of thinking by saying that Reid's personal good feelings toward Miers didn't preclude his opposition or even a filibuster.[62]

Many players would come forward to say Reid was simply messing with the Republicans. Specter, who had a similar tendency to stir the pot, said he discerned Reid's intentions from the start: "Reid did not comment on her qualifications, noting only that she was a nice person and returned telephone calls promptly—hardly the strongest substantive recommendation."[63]

Rove, who never trusted Reid—a handwritten note in his files at the Bush presidential library in Dallas includes a scribbled "I hate Harry Reid"—said of him, "I think he knew he was poison."[64] In other words, Reid would praise Miers just enough to raise the hackles of the right—*See? The Democrats are thrilled with her!*—but then pull back at key moments to leave her hanging by herself.

Reid was also influenced by animus toward Rove, who was already under siege for allegedly having revealed the CIA background of the wife of one of Bush's principal Iraq War critics.[65] When Dobson intimated that he knew things he "probably shouldn't know," Reid joined with his deputy, Chuck Schumer, and key liberals like Dick Durbin to demand an investigation. "This is not a game of wink and whisper," said Schumer. "This is serious business."[66]

For his part, even Manley, Reid's spokesman, found it difficult to figure out his boss's intentions: "I remember at one point, I had to pull him aside and say, 'What the hell is going on here?'" But it was characteristic of Reid to set things in motion and then wait for more data points to recalibrate the political equation. "He had a theory of politics to throw some things up in the air and see how they land," said Manley. "Reid threw it out there and then he took a step back and watched the Republicans publicly and privately attack the woman."[67]

For a tough combatant like Reid, who built a robust Democratic machine through labor unions in politically divided Nevada, watching the GOP descend into disarray brought satisfaction. But it did nothing to help Miers, let alone to advance the cause of a balanced and moderate Supreme Court.

....

THE YEAR 2005 WAS buffeted by a new form of political communication—blogging. From their think tanks and academic enclaves, conservative intellectuals exchanged posts, offered comments, and helped to develop a real-time narrative of their feelings about the Harriet Miers nomination. In quick order, the case against her took form.

First, there was the implication made by Barnett and Will that she was a crony pick. This carried some weight across the political spectrum because Bush had indeed been known to boost his inner circle; just a few months earlier, he had elevated two other Texas intimates, Gonzales and Margaret Spellings, to his cabinet.

Then, equally quickly, came the notion that Miers was another squish in the line of Souter, O'Connor, Kennedy, Burger, Blackmun, and Powell—in short, a Republican who would support abortion rights and gradually shift to the left as she acclimated to Washington culture. "I can't stomach another 'trust me' from a Republican," groused conservative organizer Paul Weyrich.[68]

The whole point of amassing a farm team of proven conservative judges like Alito, Luttig, and Jones was to avoid the risk inherent in a person like Harriet Miers. The movement existed to provide benchmarks and guardrails, to separate the true believers from the pretenders. And then, of course, to decorate those chosen few with the finest credentials and support them as they climbed the ladder.

The next step in the throttling of Miers was to challenge her own qualifications. John Podhoretz posted in *National Review* that Miers's writings as president of the Texas Bar Association were so "utterly inane" as to call into question her fitness for the Supreme Court. "Let me offer you an analogy. I was a talented high-school and college actor . . . But if you took me today and gave me a leading role in the Royal Shakespeare Company where I would have to stand toe to toe with, say, Kenneth Branagh, Kevin Spacey, Meryl Streep, Kevin Kline and others, I would be hopelessly out of my depth."[69]

In an opinion piece in *The Washington Post*, conservative columnist Charles Krauthammer wrote, "The issue is not the venue of Miers's constitutional scholarship, experience and engagement. The issue is their nonexistence."[70]

Robert Bork chimed in that the choice of Miers was "a disaster."[71]

. . . .

MIERS'S NOMINATION WAS ALREADY faltering when some old testimony from a voting-rights lawsuit during her days on the Dallas City Council surfaced. In it, she appeared to disrespect the Federalist Society.

At the time, she testified that she "tried to avoid memberships in organizations that were politically charged," and she listed the Federalist Society as among those that she shunned. "It's better to not be involved in organizations that seem to color your view one way or the other for people who are examining you," she said of the society, in particular.[72]

That was sixteen years before her nomination, and the group had since grown into a dominant force. Bush's spokesman, Scott McClellan, rushed to atone for the insult: Miers, he said, regarded the Federalist Society as "a great ally on many important issues, particularly when it comes to the federal judiciary."[73]

The bleeding didn't stop. Specter and Leahy, the chairman and ranking member of the Senate Judiciary Committee, rejected Miers's initial answers to their fifty-seven-page pre-hearing questionnaire, making a public show of giving her extra time to amend her responses.[74] The implication was clear: she was in over her head.

David Frum, a former Federalist Society chapter head and Bush speechwriter, said a group he had formed would run ads on Fox News and Rush Limbaugh's radio program opposing Miers. "Even the best leaders make mistakes," the ad began. "Conservatives support President Bush, but not Supreme Court nominee Harriet Miers."[75]

The following day, Miers told Bush she planned to withdraw her nomination.[76]

. . . .

THE FAILURE OF THE Miers nomination was a forgotten turning point in legal history. It sketched the limits of consensus and moderation in a polarized atmosphere: one side, Bush's own, wouldn't stomach her because she wasn't a product of their carefully orchestrated movement; the other side, the Democrats, was hesitant to extend a lifeline for fear of alienating its supporters. How would it look if a liberal senator voted to confirm a woman who abetted a conservative takeover of the court?

The defeat of Miers established the conservative legal movement as a boldly independent, almost upstart force in right-wing politics. It wasn't lost on many Republicans that Rove was able to count on Dobson and the religious right but not the intellectuals in the Federalist Society. Texans like Bush and Rove and Gonzales saw the attacks on Miers in class terms: Ivy League conservatives could be just as contemptuous of their perceived lessers as the liberal elites that Republicans loved to rail against.

Bush felt the chafe of a "largely unspoken" allegation: "How could I name someone who did not run in elite legal circles?"[77]

Declared Rove, "I think how unfair is this, that because she didn't go to Harvard or Yale or Princeton or Columbia that she is somehow unworthy of the high court. She was a major partner of a major Texas law firm, first bar president, brilliant lawyer."[78]

Gonzales was more blunt: "The Washington legal establishment is a little snobbish if you're not from here, working on K Street from an Ivy League school."[79]

The Federalist Society would come out of the battle stronger. By completely dismissing Miers's credentials, its members narrowed the field of prospective jurists to those who fit their own pipeline: people groomed for judgeships at an early age and then monitored to fulfill certain ideological requisites. Gone was the notion that a politician or practicing attorney might provide needed ballast; Gonzales claimed to have begun his search with over one hundred names, but it essentially ended with the four put forward by Meese and the Federalist Society's Leonard Leo.[80]

The missed opportunity was by Democrats. Reid spoke for many in his party by complaining, after Miers had withdrawn, that the "radical right wing of the Republican Party drove this woman's nomination right out of town."[81] But Democrats of all stripes, from liberals like Leahy to centrists like Dianne Feinstein, poured gasoline on the flames lit by conservatives. Bush himself would say, "When the left started criticizing Harriet, too, I knew the nomination was doomed."[82]

Nathan Hecht, the respected Texas jurist who had taken heat for vouching for his friend Miers, would think of her seventeen years later, when abortion rights were overturned by one vote, with Chief Justice Roberts agreeing to sustain Mississippi's ban on abortion after fifteen weeks of pregnancy but stopping short of what he called "the dramatic step of altogether eliminating the abortion right first recognized in *Roe*." Would Miers have shifted the ruling in the other direction? Hecht couldn't know for sure, but he thought the moderate path sketched out by Roberts was something Miers might have found appealing, and she would have given serious consideration to the weight of settled precedent.

"Even today, people will argue, oh, well, I thought *Roe* was wrongly decided at the time, just thought Justice Blackmun got it wrong," said Hecht. "But would I upset the country by changing it today? I don't know."[83]

America will never know.

CHAPTER 10

"The Solemn Responsibility"

eorge W. Bush wasn't drawn to Sam Alito. They'd had a face-to-face interview in July, in the White House family quarters. It hadn't gone especially well.

An aide told Alito to go to a DC street corner early on a Saturday morning and wait for a Chrysler 300 to pull up and flash its headlights. Alito got in and was whisked away to the White House. "I felt like a spy," he later said.[1] At that meeting, their oil-and-water personalities were on full display. The straitlaced Alito, in a business suit and tie, was ushered into the president's living room, only to find a young man sitting across from him, lacing up his sneakers. This was, Alito figured, a friend of one of Bush's daughters. Then Bush's terrier, Barney, came bounding in, sniffing Alito's shoes. He was followed by the casually dressed president. Bush hoped they would mesh, even going so far as to show the baseball-loving Alito the White House TV where he watched Texas Rangers games.[2] But the bonding didn't take.

After the Miers blowup, Alito's appeal stood out in sharper relief. Federalist Society members demanded a highly credentialed jurist with a long record. And they wanted a proven conservative, someone who wouldn't go soft in Washington. No one doubted Alito's conservative bona fides. Bush, for his part, needed someone who could withstand the confirmation gauntlet. Alito was that.

The White House had monitored Alito closely, starting with his first interview with Alberto Gonzales five years earlier. A classified dossier prepared at that time reported, "There are no apparent problems with Alito's character, ethics, or temperament."[3] It confirmed that Alito's judicial record was conservative and had been covered that way by the media. It did, however, predict that "a few of Alito's opinions are almost certain to be the focus of controversy if he is nominated to the court."

The dossier pointed specifically to his dissent in *Planned Parenthood of Southeastern Pennsylvania v. Casey*, which maintained that the requirement that women notify their husbands before having an abortion was not an "undue burden." There was also a case in which Alito "argued that an Iranian feminist's asylum petition should not be granted because she did not have a well-founded fear of persecution upon deportation to Iran." That, the report said, "might draw the ire of women's organizations." The dossier also predicted flatly that "the criminal defense bar likely will oppose Alito's nomination," citing multiple cases in which he had voted to uphold heavy-handed police tactics.[4]

An addendum to the report zeroed in on *Roe v. Wade*: "Based on a review of his judicial opinions, news articles, and his legislative testimony as United States Attorney for the District of New Jersey, Judge Alito has not commented directly on the decision in *Roe v. Wade*. However, his judicial opinions in this area would be the subject of intense scrutiny in any confirmation hearing and would be portrayed as very conservative." The report added that Alito had not taken a position on the right to privacy or abortion as a matter of social policy.[5]

To Bush's team, this was all good news. Alito's record fit the complicated political dynamics of the moment: he was someone conservatives could trust to oppose *Roe v. Wade*, but he had left no obvious footprints, nothing definitive that liberals could point to. Conservatives would recognize the strength of his convictions, just as they had seen the lack of conviction in Miers; but for others, his zeal would be hidden behind his prim judicial temperament. The same couldn't be said of the other judges deemed appropriate by Federalist Society, so Alito stood out as more confirmable.

Under the rules established by the Gang of 14, a filibuster could be invoked only under "extraordinary" circumstances. Mere suspicion of a judge's intentions on abortion rights wouldn't be enough.

....

ALITO WAS IN THE kitchen of his midsize suburban house in West Caldwell, New Jersey, thinking that his big chance had passed him by.[6] He had reached his destination. It was, on the whole, a good place to be. On this tree-lined street, Sam and Martha-Ann had raised their kids, Philip and Laura, and Martha-Ann, whose conversion to Catholicism was fervent and heart-felt, taught religious classes at the family church of Our Lady of Blessed Sacrament in nearby Roseland.[7] West Caldwell and Our Lady of Blessed Sacrament strongly resembled Mercerville and Our Lady of Sorrows, down to the color of brick on the facades of the two churches. Alito had replicated his happy childhood, an hour from where he grew up.

But then the phone rang. It was Bill Kelley, deputy White House counsel to Harriet Miers. He had a surprising message: Miers would be dropping out, which was not yet public, and President Bush was thinking seriously of nominating Alito. Kelley's call was followed by one from White House Chief of Staff Andy Card and finally Bush himself. Even on the telephone, the two men seemed to misunderstand each other. After Bush extended the offer and Alito expressed gratitude, Bush asked, "Well, do you accept?" and Alito replied, "Yes, of course I accept."[8]

In that very instant, Sam Alito's life changed. For years afterward, he and Martha-Ann would bemoan the disruption of their simple, happy routine. The Washington political and social pressures were daunting, even overwhelming at times. The emotionally driven Martha-Ann came to see herself as the unwitting target of vicious, unprincipled enemies. But at his moment of truth, Sam would draw on all his studied instincts to shrewdly navigate one of the toughest confirmation battles of his era. And convincing the public that he was a nose-to-the-grindstone legal nerd—a professional so dedicated to the details of cases that he couldn't possibly carry an agenda—would be his first order of business.

At a press conference on Halloween afternoon in the Cross Hall of the White House, Bush praised Alito's skills and joked about them both having married librarians. Alito was on message in accepting the president's nomination. "Every time that I have entered the courtroom during the past 15 years, I have been mindful of the solemn responsibility that goes with service as a federal judge," he said. "Federal judges have a duty to interpret the Constitution and the laws faithfully and fairly, to protect the constitutional rights of Americans, and to do these things with care and restraint, always keeping in mind the limited role that the courts play in our constitutional system."[9]

....

IN HOPES OF PERSUADING the Senate to hold confirmation hearings before the holidays, Alito rushed to visit individual senators on Capitol Hill. Harriet Miers, always the team player, offered him tips.[10] Meanwhile, conservative operatives fanned out across New Jersey to recruit his friends for what would amount to a truncated national political campaign. Bill Agress, Alito's old Steinert High debating partner, told the operatives that he hadn't stayed in touch over the years. No matter, they said; people who knew Alito were being sent to states with undecided senators to do radio and TV and meet with local influencers. Their authenticity mattered more than the currency of their ties to Alito. Thus, Agress, who took part in Revolutionary War reenactments of New Jersey battles, found himself being grilled on subjects like gun control and abortion rights in places like Fargo, North Dakota, and Helena, Montana.

"One guy said, 'You know, we're very concerned about the Second Amendment, because here in Montana, we take our gun rights very seriously,'" Agress, the reenactor, recalled. "And I just couldn't resist what I said next. I said, 'Well, I'm from New Jersey, and most of my friends have rifles and a couple of cannons.'"[11]

In a noteworthy gesture, all fifty-four of Alito's former clerks signed a joint letter endorsing his fitness for the Supreme Court. They were mostly white male and conservative, but they also included self-described liberals such as Katherine K. Huang, an Asian woman, and David J. Stoll, a gay man who advised Lambda, the legal services organization dedicated to gay rights. "We collectively were involved in thousands of cases," the letter said, "and it never once appeared to us that Judge Alito pre-judged a case or ruled based on political ideology."[12]

The White House press office drafted internal briefing documents addressing what the administration feared would be the biggest "allegations" against Alito. The aim was to rebut the argument that he was too conservative. "Allegation: As a former prosecutor, Judge Alito has been insufficiently protective of constitutional safeguards against unreasonable searches and seizures. Facts: Judge Alito has never shrunk from invalidating convictions based on unlawfully obtained evidence," said one such document, which cited two cases in which Alito ruled against police, one of which was an unjustified stop and search of two Black men driving in a sports car. Other briefing documents covered employment discrimination, free speech rights, and abortion.

Another one, entitled "Religious Liberties," stated, "Allegation: Judge Alito is an extreme religious conservative who supports governmental endorsement of religion. Facts: Judge Alito's judicial opinions demonstrate his steadfast commitment to the free exercise of all religions without governmental burdens or discrimination."[13]

But while the White House was delivering its spin, so too were liberal activist groups. They had been tracking Alito for almost as long as the administration had, and they thought they had him pegged. They were ready to attack him not only on abortion and police searches, but also on his support for the Reagan administration's allowing employers to fire people suspected of having AIDS and his narrow view of employment discrimination generally.[14]

Liberal Democratic senators, including some who had backed John Roberts, showed no hesitation in voicing their concerns about Alito. Leahy, for one, accused Bush of caving in to the very people who'd torpedoed his friend Miers. "Instead of uniting the country through his choice, the president has chosen to reward one faction of his party, at the risk of dividing the country," Leahy said.

Ted Kennedy struck a similar note, saying that all Democrats had to do was look at the way conservative activists were celebrating the Alito nomination to know there was something wrong. "They are shouting from the mountaintops for Alito," he said.

And Chuck Schumer said it was all in the record for people to see: "Many of the opinions that he has written over the past 15 years cast real doubt on whether he can be a fair, mainstream, albeit conservative, judge."[15]

. . . .

ALITO WASN'T THE ONLY one being judged, however.

While most of the senators seemed to agree that a nominee must be open-minded and offer no foregone conclusions about the big issues of the day, they also weren't girding for a fight. The whole hullabaloo about the "nuclear option" of removing the filibuster had made most senators—including some liberals—deeply conscious of the need for decorum, deference, and respect. It was as though the Senate itself was being scrutinized for fairness and objectivity.

This precarious balance was deeply troubling to the activists who saw only danger in Alito. Ralph Neas, for one, felt that Alito's intentions were plain to see. "I thought the best case was being made by Alito himself as to why he should be opposed," Neas said. "It wasn't because he was undecided on *Roe v. Wade*, like John Roberts, [but because] he was extraordinarily committed to overturning *Roe v. Wade* and a lot of other things."[16]

Earlier in the year, seizing on Bush's promise in the 2004 campaign to appoint judges in the mold of Scalia and Thomas, Neas's People for the American Way had produced a report called "Courting Disaster" that looked at all the legal precedents that could be overturned if Bush fulfilled his promise. But when Neas was invited to join some fellow activists at dinner with Barack Obama, the newly elected Democratic senator from Illinois, he was stunned when Obama singled him out for a scolding. "I think you've been performing a disservice to the United States Senate and to the people of the United States, because you've been engaging in hyperbole," Obama told Neas, as the rest of group looked on in silence.[17]

This shouldn't have been too much of a surprise, since Obama's campaign had focused heavily on the need to break down political barriers and restore civility; much of what passed for debate in Washington struck Obama as hyperbole, and he often seemed eager for opportunities to call out his own side. But the encounter illustrated the difficulty faced by those opposing Alito: they needed to raise serious doubts about his record without appearing to have prejudged him.

Two unrelated episodes early in the nomination process also set the opposition back on their heels.

At ninety, Rose Alito was still a redoubtable figure, hale and hearty and bursting with maternal pride. So when reporters from news outlets around the country knocked on her door at 137 Fenwood Ave.—the same house where she'd raised her two children—she politely invited them in. She happily took out her bursting scrapbook. This was the ledger where, for the better part of six decades, she had recorded the many triumphs of Sam Jr. And she regaled the reporters with expressions of excitement over his Supreme Court nomination.

"I cannot be prouder of him," she exulted. "I am happy I am healthy enough to see this." She spoke of his resemblance to his father, and of how she and Sam Sr. instilled in him and his sister a sense of pride and achievement from the earliest ages.

When the reporters asked about his views on national issues, Rose demurred—except once. "He is against abortion," she said. "We both are."

In short order, the phone rang and Rose picked it up. Sam was on the line.

"Oh, Sam, there are people over the house and in front of the house," she said. Then she looked sad and worried.

"I hope I did not do anything wrong," she said into the phone. "Now I'm upset. Call me back later, Sam."

She quickly shooed the reporters out of her house.[18]

The encounter yielded some news—Alito's mother's testimony of his abortion views—but it also showcased a competitive press corps at its least appealing: taking advantage of an elderly woman's hospitality. The image of reporters cramming into Rose Alito's modest living room to try to extract information about her son didn't further the cause of civility.

Meanwhile, the well-known TV pundit Chris Matthews was raising hackles in Washington. The former Capitol Hill staffer was known for his emotive style. On his NBC show *Hardball*, he inveighed against petty injustices like an angry bartender fused with an Old Testament prophet. And on the day of the Alito nomination, he thought he smelled a rat.

"I'm sitting here holding in my hands a pretty disgusting document," he said. It was a briefing paper that "comes from the Democrats." While it included a long rundown on past Alito opinions, it also derisively called him "Judge Scalito"—suggesting he would be an echo of his fellow Italian American jurist—and featured the talking point that "Alito Embarrassed Government by Failing to Obtain Crucial Mafia Conviction."

Matthews was indignant: "Why would they bring up this ethnically charged issue as the first item they raise against Judge Alito?" He cited Alito's "incredible record" as a "prosecutor, as a judge, as a Yale law grad," and offered, "I'm telling you, this is going to hurt the Democrats for putting this out."[19]

It was never clear where in the Democratic universe this memo came from. Howard Dean, the Democratic National Committee chairman, disclaimed it on Matthews's show.[20] But it once again shifted the focus from Alito to the ruthlessness of his critics.

....

FOR ANYONE CAUGHT IN a maelstrom, the picture looks worse from the inside. People in Washington might not bat an eye at the mocking tone of "Scalito" or the rank unfairness of blaming him for the failed Lucchese family prosecution or even the flimsiness of highlighting his neglect to recuse himself in cases involving Smith Barney and Vanguard, two giant brokerages that happened to hold his stock accounts.[21] But judges aren't politicians, no matter how much political fire is in their furnace. Many come from the same pool of poli-sci majors who went into politics, but they were drawn to the law for its distance from the slings and arrows of the public square. Insults don't wash off their backs. And in the terror of the confirmation process—when their every action going back to high school is scrutinized—nominees are intensely aware that one side will use any means to defeat them and the other will deploy any argument to save them. Rarely are friends and enemies so clearly delineated. And so it was with Alito.

Despite all this—and the disturbances felt by Rose and Martha-Ann and the rest of his family—Alito was no naif. He plowed ahead like a man who had thought through this process for years and was determined to prevail, no matter which obstacles were placed in his path. Unlike Bork, who had assumed his brilliance would carry the day, Alito would prove his brilliance by effectively parrying the claims against him.

Alito's private meetings with Democrats and other undecided senators—one of the few opportunities to turn down the temperature—tended to focus squarely on abortion rights, with senators probing for signals of a sort that might not emerge in a public hearing. In the closed meetings, Alito sought to explain his *Casey* dissent, perhaps because it appeared to establish his opposition to abortion rights. In fact, he insisted to Illinois Democrat Dick Durbin, he had agonized over the proper interpretation of Justice O'Connor's "undue burden" standard, striving to get the law right regardless of its implications for abortion rights.

"He said he had spent more time worrying and working over that decision than over any other decision he made when he was a judge," Durbin said.[22]

To Ted Kennedy, Alito said, "I am a believer in precedents," a fairly standard line for any judge. But he then appeared to make his first-ever proclamation on the right to privacy: "I recognize there is a right to privacy," Alito said, according to Kennedy's diary. "I think it's settled."[23]

If Alito offered this assurance privately, with the understanding that Kennedy would not make it public, it might have been a meaningful revelation. But simply believing in a right to privacy doesn't imply that it covers abortion rights; in fact, Alito would acknowledge a right to privacy in his *Dobbs* opinion but reject its application to abortion. Kennedy, in any case, wasn't gulled—he continued to oppose Alito's confirmation.

Lincoln Chafee, the patrician Republican from Rhode Island, was a different species of senator. He supported abortion rights but believed in common sense and moderation above all else. Chafee was born just three years after Alito, and when Alito showed up for a private chat, Chafee strove to remind him of the pain of growing up during the Vietnam War. No one could want to replicate those types of divisions. He asked Alito to take a walk outside the Capitol, where the Supreme Court's mighty facade loomed across the street, and tried to talk man to man, on a human level.

"We went through Vietnam together," Chafee said he told Alito. "We're about the same age. This country doesn't need another rendering of all of our compassions, and that's going to happen over *Roe v. Wade*, if you go there . . . And he kind of looked at me. I remember exactly how he drew himself up and raised his head and looked at me, and it was, you know, 'Thank you very much for your thoughts. But let's get this meeting over with.'"

Chafee realized he had made no impression on Alito. It was not entirely surprising. Alito's judicial philosophy took little account of the kinds of political considerations Chafee raised. But at that moment, Chafee thought: *This is a cold person.*[24]

. . . .

CHAFEE'S VIEWS ASIDE, ALITO could count heavily on the regard of those who knew his workplace manner the best: his fellow judges. And they tended to find him anything but cold. Alito had cultivated a close friendship with Edward Becker, a Reagan appointee and longtime chief judge of the Third Circuit. From the start of Alito's tenure, the two exchanged handwritten notes full of dry humor.

"I am afraid that, while you have been a chief judge par excellence, you have presided over a fattening of the court," Alito joked in one note, referring to the candy Becker provided at judicial conferences.[25]

Becker was seventeen years Alito's senior and seemed to channel some of his own hopes into Alito's career; Becker was battling prostate cancer when Bush nominated Alito to the Supreme Court, but he sprang into action to help his younger friend.[26] He vouched for Alito to a parade of influential officials, including Ruth Bader Ginsburg, prompting Ginsburg to send Alito her best wishes on the confirmation process. "A colleague of excellent judgment, Ed Becker, tells me you are the very best," she wrote to the embattled nominee. "I wish you well in the trying days ahead."[27]

Mostly, Becker pressed Alito's cause to Arlen Specter, the chairman of the Senate Judiciary Committee and the man who most closely controlled Alito's fate. Becker and Specter had been close friends since they rode the elevated train from Northeast Philadelphia to the University of Pennsylvania together in 1950.[28] Like Lincoln Chafee, Specter was a moderate Republican who supported abortion rights, but the resemblance ended there. Specter was no idealist: a former prosecutor, he specialized in sharp cross-examinations of judicial nominees. He also took mercurial stances. He skewered Bork, tore into Anita Hill in defense of Clarence Thomas, and broke with his party to back Bill Clinton in his impeachment trial. The common thread in those matters was that they drew a lot of attention to Specter, and he ended up on the winning side. Everyone agreed: he was a terrible person to have as an enemy.[29]

Most recently, Specter's public comments had raised questions about Harriet Miers's fitness for the court, but he expressed no such doubts about Alito. In fact, at several key junctures, he would leap to Alito's defense.

Becker had hosted Specter and Alito at a dinner party at his home long before the nomination.[30] After the nomination, he worked back channels with Specter on Alito's behalf; Specter apparently shared with Becker a copy of a letter he'd sent to Alito outlining the topics on which he would be interrogating the nominee.[31] The senator also helped facilitate Becker's testimony and that of other Third Circuit judges. "The Sam Alito I have sat with for 15 years is not an ideologue," Becker testified. "He is not a movement person. He is a real judge deciding each case on the facts and the law, not on his personal views, whatever they may be."[32]

....

ONE FAVOR SPECTER DID not grant was an early hearing; after consulting with Leahy, he scheduled the start of the Judiciary Committee's consideration of the Alito nomination for January 9, 2006, giving all sides more time to hone their arguments.

Alito used the time to craft an eloquent opening statement that established a high-minded tone. He paid tribute to his parents and grandparents, and expressed, with sagacious warmth, his reverence for the legal system. At nearly every juncture, he emphasized the importance of keeping an open mind: "Good judges are always open to the possibility of changing their minds based on the next brief that they read or the next argument that is made by an attorney who is appearing before them or a comment that is made by a colleague."[33]

In politics, people use these moments of theater to address criticisms and firm up weaknesses; in dwelling so heavily on open-mindedness, Alito as much as acknowledged that some people felt his mind was closed. But his personal rectitude fortified his stance. He came off as serious, soft-spoken, gentle, and even conciliatory in manner. Americans watching on TV could easily see him as a model of civic virtue.

Early questioning, as expected, focused on *Roe v. Wade*. Contrary to his reputation as a tough cross-examiner, Specter started things off with a series of softballs, almost as if he were eager to get the abortion issue off the table. "The history of the court is full of surprises on this issue," he interjected before asking a question, as if to remind colleagues that Alito could defy expectations and turn out to be a strong proponent of *Roe*.[34] A few months earlier, John Roberts had won broad support by calling *Roe v. Wade* "settled" and attesting to his own willingness to apply its precedent.[35] Alito did not go nearly that far. When Specter fed him lines from the *Casey* opinion about women's reliance on abortion rights and the importance of *stare decisis*—the respect for precedent—Alito said merely that "the doctrine of *stare decisis* is a very important doctrine."[36]

Specter didn't press him further.

Later, under tougher questioning from Durbin, Alito said only that past judicial decisions deserve "considerable respect," and that such respect increases after decisions are reaffirmed in subsequent rulings, as had happened with *Roe*. But he refused to say they couldn't be reconsidered. "If settled means it can't be re-examined, then that's one thing," Alito said, making it clear that he felt the court should be free to revisit the issue. "If settled means that it's a precedent that is entitled to respect as *stare decisis*, and all of the factors that I've mentioned come into play, including the reaffirmation and all of that, then it is a precedent that is protected, entitled to respect under the doctrine of *stare decisis* in that way."[37]

Many viewers at home were probably scratching their heads and reaching for their clickers, but liberal senators took note of Alito's evasive language and kept hammering on the issue; conservative senators then used their questioning time to praise Alito's good sense in refusing to comment further on an issue he would have to confront from the bench.

A couple of weeks before the hearing, the Reagan Presidential Library had released the 1985 memo Alito wrote with the help of Chuck Cooper when he was applying to the Office of Legal Counsel[38]—a document that appeared to have eluded the Bush administration vetters who asserted that Alito had never commented on *Roe*.[39] It was the closest thing to a smoking gun to have emerged since the nomination, and Democrats seized on both Alito's attack on *Roe* and his membership in Concerned Alumni of Princeton, with its record of opposing women and minorities.

When Leahy asked him directly about his CAP membership, Alito humbly disavowed any association. "Well, Senator, I have racked my memory about this issue, and I really have no specific recollection of that organization," he said. "But since I put it down on that statement, then I certainly must have been a member at that time. But if I had been actively involved in the organization in any way, if I had attended meetings or been actively involved in any way, I would certainly remember that, and I don't."[40] Alito went on to speculate that he might have joined CAP because of his anger over the university's treatment of ROTC and its disrespect for the military.[41]

Alito's candor seemed to disarm the questioners; he had almost put the issue to rest when Kennedy, assuming the role of Grand Inquisitor, brought it back.

Judicial nominations were Kennedy's forte; he, as much as anyone, had taken down Bork. And he was loaded for bear. His large staff had spent weeks poring over Alito's record and were convinced that he presented a Bork-like threat to the liberal order.[42]

Kennedy's first questions were scattershot but shrewd: he covered many of the substantive issues that would, indeed, mark Alito's tenure on the court. The senator zeroed in on the unitary executive theory, and what it would mean for a president's ability to imprison US citizens, disrupt the work of independent agencies, or assert through presidential "signing statements" the right to violate laws of Congress.[43]

Alito responded that the president should have full latitude in exercising executive power, but that didn't mean the "scope of executive power" was unlimited; in other words, the debate shouldn't be over whether the president has unitary executive powers, but how far those powers extend. He did not offer any parameters for presidential authority. He did, however, say that the Supreme Court's decision authorizing independent agencies was "settled law"—a position he would later question on the Supreme Court.[44]

Those answers, like many of Kennedy's initial questions, seemed to fly over the heads of most of the audience. But then came the third day of testimony, when Kennedy again commanded the microphone. This was the moment many Alito critics had been waiting for, when Kennedy, the great liberal stalwart, would raise high dudgeon against Alito in a mini version of his famous "Robert Bork's America" oration.

Kennedy didn't disappoint. Brandishing copies of CAP's magazine, *Prospect*, he quoted aloud from the article declaring, "Everywhere you turn, blacks and Hispanics are demanding jobs simply because they're black and Hispanic." He then pulled out another article lampooning the idea of AIDS research: "Now the scientist must find humans—or, rather, homosexuals, to submit themselves to experimental treatment. Perhaps Princeton's Gay Alliance may want to hold an election."[45]

After each quote, Alito responded that he hadn't read the articles and didn't endorse their views.

But Kennedy wasn't done: he noted that a Princeton alumni panel including Bill Frist, the current senate majority leader, had repudiated CAP as far back as 1975. He quoted a 1980 *New York Times* article on CAP's steadfast opposition to women at Princeton.

"In 1980, you were working as an assistant US attorney in Trenton, New Jersey," Kennedy thundered. "Did you read *The New York Times?* Did you see this article?"

Alito, who was actually stationed in Newark at the time, said he hadn't.

"And did you read a letter from CAP mailed in 1984—this is the year before you put CAP on your application . . . which declared Princeton is no longer the university you knew it to be?"[46]

When Alito repeated his claim to have only been drawn to CAP because of its defense of ROTC, Kennedy was ready: the CAP magazine had made only one reference to ROTC, and that was simply to say "ROTC is popular once again."

After a subdued Alito responded that he had addressed all the questions about CAP, Kennedy went in for the kill. "I have to say that Judge Alito, that his explanations about his membership in this sort of radical group and why you listed it on your job application are extremely troubling," he intoned. "In fact, I don't think that they add up."[47]

The ears of the hearing room, and many of the journalists following along, perked up. It was a vintage Kennedy performance, and it fell to Lindsey Graham, the Republican senator from South Carolina, to try to help Alito recover. He walked the judge through several questions distancing him from CAP and its magazine, and then said, "Are you really a closet bigot?"

Alito answered, "I'm not any kind of a bigot."[48]

"No, sir, you are not," said Graham. "And do you know why I believe you when you say you disavow those quotes? Because of the way you have lived your life and the way you and your wife are raising your children. Let me tell you this, guilt by association is going to drive good men and women away from wanting to sit where you are sitting . . . Judge Alito,

I am sorry that you have had to go through this. I am sorry that your family has had to sit here and listen to this."[49]

During Alito's exchange with Graham, an unexpected noise reverberated through the hearing room: the sound of a person crying. Martha-Ann Alito, seated behind her husband and beside his sister, Rosemary, had begun to sob, at first softly and then louder and louder, before fleeing the room in tears.

When NBC's *Today* covered the hearing the next morning, the theme wasn't Kennedy's blistering takedown but a question posed in large letters on the screen: "DEMOCRATS GONE TOO FAR?"[50]

....

MARTHA-ANN'S BREAKDOWN WAS THE fulcrum of the hearing, the moment that sympathy turned in the nominee's favor. In *The Washington Post*, writer Libby Copeland noted that "men tend to get all rubbery" when a woman cries.

"The crying wife is sacrosanct," Copeland wrote, "an argument-ender, and more than a little retrograde, which is why we think of 'I Love Lucy' and Lucy dissolving into tears when Ricky wouldn't let her buy a new coat or some such thing."[51]

Bloggers speculated as to whether Martha-Ann had faked the tears to get her husband off the hook, but that merely attested to the power of the moment. Ed Whelan, president of the conservative Ethics and Public Policy Center, predicted that Americans would always choose a "loving spouse of a smeared nominee" over the "bullying" Kennedy.[52]

Copeland wasn't the only *Post* writer to turn her attention to Martha-Ann Alito that day. Robin Givhan, the paper's fashion writer, had been doing a series of columns on how people in Washington communicate their politics and social attitudes through their wardrobe. And Sam and Martha-Ann Alito were that week's subjects.[53]

Givhan's main point was that the Alitos were presenting themselves as an average, middle-class New Jersey couple, visitors from the real America who weren't kowtowing to the expectations of the capital elite.

That much seemed true enough. But Givhan's pungent lines often bordered on ridicule—and Martha-Ann Alito, in particular, was deeply wounded by the barbs.

"Her clothes were more *Redbook* than *Vogue*," Givhan wrote. "More main floor than designer salon. In her red suit with black trim—so Kasper, so Albert Nipon—she looked average.

"There was something charmingly awkward about her blue cardigan. A cable-knit cardigan! At a Senate hearing! The sweater has all those connotations of Dan Rather informality, ease, and grandmotherly coziness. It is the antithesis of power and strength. The sweater was also baby blue. This isn't clothing as armor, but clothing as security blanket. Remember Linus?"

Givhan compared another of Martha-Ann's outfits to "the upholstery that once covered La-Z-Boys" and said she coordinated colors "with a rigor more commonly found in Garanimals."[54]

The column, like many of Givhan's works, sought to explain how politics pervades all corners of Washington society; later that year, she would be awarded the Pulitzer Prize for Criticism, one of journalism's highest honors (though not for that particular column).

But the Alitos and their allies saw the column differently: it represented everything people hate about Washington—the snobbishness, the elitism, the contempt for average Americans. How could a decent couple feel at home in such a place?

More than eighteen years later, a person would surreptitiously tape the Alitos at a Supreme Court reception, where Martha-Ann sounded off about Robin Givhan and the terrible things she said about her back in 2006.[55]

. . . .

BUT KENNEDY'S ATTACK FIZZLED for reasons other than just Martha-Ann's tears or Givhan's barbed pen. At the end of his propulsive questioning about Alito's association with CAP, Kennedy floridly requested that the committee subpoena records from the Library of Congress that had been donated by William Rusher, the *National Review* publisher who was also a leader of CAP.[56] His iron-fisted demand sent a shiver through the hearing room: Would these documents expose lies about Alito's involvement in CAP?

They did not.

Kennedy, perhaps unwittingly, had violated a key tenet of political advocacy: Don't promise a big revelation without knowing that it exists.

The next day, a clearly irritated Specter made a point of emphasizing Alito's exoneration. "The committee staff, accompanied by representatives of Senator Kennedy, went through the Rusher files yesterday, finishing up their work, I am advised, at about 2 a.m. this morning, and provided me with a memorandum that the committee staff reviewed more than four boxes of documents from the personal files of William Rusher concerning CAP," he said.

"Judge Alito's name never appeared in any document. His name was not mentioned in any of the letters to or from the founder, William Rusher. His name was not mentioned in any of the letters to or from CAP's long-term executive director, T. Harding Jones. His name does not appear anywhere in the dozens of letters to CAP or from CAP. The files contained canceled checks for subscriptions to CAP's magazine, *Prospect*, but none from Judge Alito. The files contained dozens of articles including investigative exposes written at the height of the organization's prominence, but Samuel Alito's name is nowhere to be found in any of them."[57]

. . . .

REPUBLICANS CAME OUT OF the hearings energized. In a speech before the Republican National Committee, Rove sharply condemned the Democrats' "mean-spirited" attacks on Alito.[58] At the annual Right to Life March in Washington, pro-life activists were ebullient. "You can see it everywhere: Every time someone says Judge Alito's name, a roar goes up," said one participant. Another added: "We've made so many strides, waiting to get to the end of *Roe v. Wade*. Now, it's like there's light through the darkness."[59]

After the Judiciary Committee voted along party lines to advance the nomination, there remained the question of a filibuster. In deference to the

Gang of 14, no Democrat seemed willing to call for one—until, from the snowy vistas of Davos, Switzerland, Kennedy's fellow Massachusetts senator, John Kerry, demanded one. It was an odd scene. Kerry, who had been the Democratic presidential nominee in 2004 and lost a close race to Bush, was licking his wounds at the World Economic Forum. His faraway announcement made the filibuster seem like an eccentricity.[60]

The senators quickly voted 72–25 to end the filibuster and then confirmed Alito by a much narrower 58–42 vote.[61] Chafee, in a nod to the odd politics of the moment, voted against the filibuster because Alito's nomination didn't raise any "extraordinary" concerns, the standard imposed by the Gang of 14. But then he turned around and opposed Alito.[62] It was a final irony: if all the senators who opposed Alito had agreed to a filibuster, they could have prevented him from joining the court.

The Alitos were jubilant, none more so than Rose,[63] and immediately began the long process of thanking all who had come to their aid in this moment of extreme vulnerability. Edward Becker was high on the list. Martha-Ann sent him a handwritten note offering "joy, prayers, and love," and thanking him for "your considerable mentoring, shepherding, and joy you've given to us, to Sam, and to the furtherance of his career."[64]

Sam also wrote to those who had helped him and invited old acquaintances like Bill Agress to visit him at his new digs at the Supreme Court.[65]

Meanwhile, the judges of the Third Circuit congratulated themselves. It was they, of course, who had most persuasively attested to Alito's fairness and lack of a political agenda. One of them, D. Michael Fisher, wrote to five of his fellow judges, including Trump, Garth, and Becker, to say, "Your efforts were cited many times in the course of the Senate debate[,] and aside from Martha's tears, it may have been the most important part of the process."[66]

Former US Transportation Secretary William T. Coleman congratulated Becker in particular: "History also some day will record that the association between Becker and Specter and their wives really had a beneficial effect on this great Nation."[67]

Among liberal activists and other Alito opponents, there was only a sense of impending doom. Many of them suggested that if only Kennedy had been able to get his message into the lifeblood of the nation the way he had with Bork, they would have succeeded. Martha-Ann's tears upended their best opportunity.[68]

Chafee, however, believed the result reflected the abject failure of the Democratic Party to mount a serious opposition to Bush, a problem dating back to the 9/11 attacks.[69] This was partly because of Reid's haphazard leadership, he felt, but went beyond that; Democratic senators were almost evenly divided between wanting to build a case against Alito and simply waiting to see how things unfolded.

Like Obama, who ultimately voted against Alito, many Democrats were determined to demonstrate their open-mindedness. But Alito did a better job of showcasing his own. He rose above the proceedings by answering every needling question in a neutral, teacherly manner, as if painstakingly explaining the legal system to uninformed politicians. This posture earned him the benefit of the doubt from some influential legal reporters,[70] and it made real the notion that his devotion was to the Constitution rather than his political predilections.

When, at a key moment in the proceedings, a senator asked the judge about his 1988 comment that Robert Bork was "one of the most outstanding nominees of this century," Alito distanced himself. He replied mildly, "There are issues with respect to which I probably agree with Judge Bork, and there are a number of issues on which I disagree with him."[71]

Bork, of course, had long been a hero of Alito's—the man whose constitutional law class he fought to get into. But at the hearing, Alito did what Bork had refused to do in his own confirmation nightmare: contour his response for the moment at hand.[72]

It was an impressive performance.

BOOK THREE

THE COURT

CHAPTER **11**

Stepping Up, Taking Command

The Supreme Court was halfway through its 2005–6 term when Samuel A. Alito Jr. mounted the majestic steps and navigated his way to the suite vacated by Sandra Day O'Connor, whose files and mementos had been carted upstairs to an empty space used for retired justices.

Alito kept two O'Connor clerks along with his own, to provide continuity in the unusual mid-session transition. The clerks recalled the starkness of sitting at the empty table with the newly minted justice on his first day at the court. There was no orientation session or training in this elite chamber; Alito would have to learn on the job.

"The hierarchy of needs for a Supreme Court justice is first, like, who's even working for me?" recalled one clerk. "Second is where do I go, and am I going to be there at the right time? Third, am I going to have the right papers in front of me? And how do I get them? And how do I even figure that out? This is a long way away from judicial philosophy or approaches to your colleagues, or that sort of thing. You're looking for like food and shelter and water."[1]

There was even a wake-up call of sorts: the court had to vote on an emergency order, and there was irritation throughout the building that Justice Scalia's clerks had refused to wake him overnight while he was traveling in a different time zone. So Sasha Volokh, one of the O'Connor clerks who stayed on, said to Alito, "My first question is, Do we have your standing permission to call you and wake you up when necessary in the middle of the night when you need to do something?"

"Yes," Alito replied.[2]

And the work began.

....

THE MUNDANITY OF THE early days of Alito's tenure masked its status as a turning point in court history. Alito would be the model for the Republican-appointed justices who came after him, and in some sense for the career paths of Democratic appointees as well. After the bruising rejection of Harriet Miers, no chief executive of either party would consider appointing a person whose main experience was as a politician or practicing attorney, and no Republican would deviate from the Federalist Society line. All future GOP appointments would be "proven" conservatives, nominated in consultation with the same leaders who promoted Alito.

The key consultant would be Leonard Leo, one of the landmark figures in the movement who assiduously shied from the spotlight. Leo founded a chapter of the Federalist Society while at Cornell Law School and joined its full-time staff in 1991.[3] As head of the student chapter, he hosted various conservative legal luminaries at the Cornell campus.

Richard Epstein of the University of Chicago was among those who made the trek to the gorges and waterfalls of Ithaca, New York, and came away viewing Leo as a wunderkind. "I said to myself, 'This man has such a command of how these things are talked about. I expect he will do great things in the world,'" Epstein recalled. "And he has."[4]

But over the next thirty-five years, Leo's distinction wouldn't come from legal practice, judging, or politics; instead, he would carve out a role as a relentless fundraiser and kingmaker. Arriving at the Federalist Society at a time when many members feared that their movement had gone down with Bork, Leo brought the political advocacy and financial savvy needed to expand the blueprint that Steven Calabresi and Gene Meyer and others had laid out.

The society would continue with its big-tent approach of welcoming conservatives of all stripes, but Leo would dedicate himself to the cause of elevating originalist judicial nominees whose records suggested they would not stray from the chosen path. This required a delicate balancing act. Whenever it was time to push for a judicial nomination or fight a confirmation battle, Leo would step out of his staff position at the Federalist Society and pay for his efforts through separate donor-funded groups.[5]

His first big foray into judicial politics involved the nominations of John Roberts and Samuel Alito. He would later claim to have spent $15 million—a huge sum for the time—for ads, organizing, and the kind of grass-roots outreach that sent Bill Agress and various former Alito clerks fanning out across the country.[6]

"As long as courts act as political institutions, confirmations will likely resemble political campaigns," Leo told the University of Virginia Federalist Society chapter in 2006, just months after Alito's confirmation. "The stakes are just too high."[7]

One radio spot funded by Leo's network featured an Arkansas minister who warned about liberals who wanted to prevent Christmas celebrations: "Now these extremist groups want our senators to vote against Judge Alito for the United States Supreme Court."[8]

Leo's path to conservatism was similar to Alito's. He grew up in Monroe Township, New Jersey, just twenty minutes from Mercerville. He was born fifteen years after Alito, but like him, he was part of a multigenerational Italian American family. His grandfather's immigrant story, his Catholicism, and his Cold War childhood dovetailed with those of other figures in the conservative legal movement.[9] But his role was unique. As a highly disciplined fundraiser, he created a network of groups—nonprofit, for-profit, and some purely for grant-making—that widened the scope of the movement.

With his half-in, half-out posture toward the Federalist Society, he could draw from donors who were impressed by the society's activities but wanted to pursue a more partisan agenda. Eventually, he would obtain a massive $1.6 billion gift from Barre Seid, the Chicago manufacturing mogul.[10] Although he'd met Seid through Meyer at the Federalist Society, the money didn't go to the society—it went toward Leo's other activities.[11]

Those activities ranged from supporting lawyers who brought cases challenging liberal precedents, to funding study centers aligned with conservative professors, to running advertisements for Republican judicial nominees.[12]

Epstein, for one, said Leo helps fund his Classical Liberal Institute at NYU School of Law, which describes its mission as being "to examine how systems of property rights and contracts advance human welfare within a framework of limited government."[13] Epstein said the money comes with no strings attached, as Leo forbids his donors from dictating its use.[14]

There is nothing unusual or unprecedented about such funding, but the fact that it all traces back to Leo, with his outsize advocacy role, serves to keep scholars—along with judges and legal activists—in a state of gratitude for his indispensable services.

The money helped to turn a movement driven by ideas and professional ambitions into a well-rounded conservative ecosystem; judges, academics, and politicians were now part of one team. While all of them enjoyed a great deal of latitude—and felt themselves to be independent actors—they were continually aware of who had their backs (Leo) and who did not (the liberals).

Federalist Society leaders sometimes kept an arm's length from Leo's fundraising, knowing that it could create unseemly entanglements.[15] But they, too, were dependent on the money. And no one seemed to see it as inappropriate. They believed Leo was merely giving conservatives what liberals had enjoyed all along: an academic cheering section, access to university jobs and study centers, the backing of activist groups.

And they believed that intense politicization of the confirmation process began with Ted Kennedy, not Leo. Leo was belatedly introducing conservatives to the tactics that Ralph Neas and others had already deployed on behalf of the left. As Leo himself put it during his 2006 UVA appearance: "It is sad to see that a judicial confirmation process needs to resemble a political campaign, but that is where we are. We need to be preemptive, rapidly reactive, and very strategic."[16]

For judges, the existence of an ecosystem of conservative friends, colleagues, and thought partners made evolutions in thinking less likely; there would be no more leftward shifts in ideology as had occurred with the Eisenhower- and Nixon-appointed justices, and even with more recent Republican-nominated justices like Stevens, O'Connor, and Souter.

Leo never openly asked anything of the justices he helped, but he never quite left their sides either. In his office, he reportedly displayed a photograph of himself with Sam and Martha-Ann Alito, standing outside the Palace of Versailles.[17]

THE DIFFERENCE BETWEEN THE liberal institutions that Leo sought to counter and the conservative ones that he built himself was that the liberal ones emerged organically. They weren't created with an outcome in mind. The conservative legal movement, by contrast, was more purposeful. Its study centers and educational groups were constructed with ideological guardrails attached. Scholars, activists, and judges who came up through the ranks embraced a common set of values. As a fusion of law, education, and politics, it was almost unique in American history.[18]

Over time, though, it sparked a liberal response. In 2001, a group of left-leaning activists and funders formed the American Constitution Society (ASC). It was dedicated to promoting "a judiciary that reflects the diversity of the public it serves, vindicates fundamental freedoms, protects democratic guardrails, upholds the rule of law, and interprets the US Constitution through a lens of history and lived experience."[19] All of a sudden liberals had a Federalist Society of their own, and the network of supporters that went along with it.

The American Constitution Society would come to boast of having "40,000 lawyers, students, judges, scholars, elected officials, and advocates" at a time when the Federalist Society claimed roughly 90,000 members.[20] The ASC wasn't as big as its conservative cousin, but it served a similar organizing function.

These seesawing movements were reminiscent of only one other chapter in history—a very early one. In 1801, President John Adams stacked the judiciary with loyalists dedicated to supporting and upholding a strong federal government. Adams's legal movement was matched, over time, by a Jeffersonian counterpart dedicated to showing greater deference to state authorities.

Adams's strategy was audacious. When he lost to Thomas Jefferson in the election of 1800, leading to the first transfer of power from one party to another, Adams seized on the long lame-duck period to dramatically expand the judiciary. He then appointed men of his party to fill the new slots.

Sixteen new circuit judgeships were created through the Judiciary Act of 1801; a separate bill added additional judgeships and forty justices of the peace for Washington, DC.[21] The jurists whose nominations were rubber-stamped by the departing Federalist-led Senate weren't, for the most part, party hacks—Adams had higher aims than patronage.[22] Many were respected legal thinkers whose views on the law were consistent with those of the outgoing president and his former ally, Alexander Hamilton. From their lifetime posts, these "Midnight Judges," as angry Jeffersonians dubbed them, could pursue Adams's and Hamilton's vision of a robust national bank and strong Supreme Court for the rest of their days.[23]

Soon after taking office, a furious President Jefferson enacted a repeal of the Judiciary Act, which was followed by a legal firestorm over which of Adams's lifetime appointees could remain in place.[24] The arcane question of whether Jefferson could withhold the undelivered commission of one Adams-appointed justice of the peace, William Marbury, led to the landmark Supreme Court case *Marbury v. Madison*. In a masterstroke, the Adams-appointed chief justice, John Marshall, ruled that the law granting the court jurisdiction over the case was unconstitutional, handing an apparent victory to Jefferson. But by asserting the power of judicial review—the right of the Supreme Court to declare laws to be unconstitutional—Marshall had, in a stroke of his pen, achieved his own party's goal of strengthening the court.[25]

What followed was a spate of judicial appointments by Jefferson and like-minded successors who adhered to their own well-grooved approach of respecting states' rights; these appointees were largely responsible for the infamous *Dred Scott v. Sandford* decision, which hastened the Civil War.[26]

After the war, the country grew tired of dueling judicial philosophies. Politics was still a part of the appointment process, but judgeships were more often used to reward loyalists or appease certain constituencies than to invoke a well-defined philosophy of constitutional interpretation.[27] Some presidents would impose their own criteria for choosing judges, but their appointees wouldn't be the products of organized movements. This was true until Reagan and Meese changed the script.

Like Adams and Jefferson, Reagan and Meese believed that a political party could engrave a theory of constitutional interpretation in its political platform and appoint judges to rule on cases within its rigid framework. Early appointees like Scalia had already blazed their own paths through the legal landscape. But twenty years later, Roberts and Alito would be chosen precisely because of their loyalty to the movement. And their supporters expected them to stay true to their originalist roots.

ANOTHER WAY THAT THE Federalist Society changed the unwritten rules of the justice system was in the choosing of clerks. Before the society emerged in 1982, judges hired their clerks from among students with the highest grades at elite law schools. Usually, the top students would apply to a wide swath of judges, regardless of party affiliation, hoping to be selected for their legal acumen alone.[28]

After the advent of the Federalist Society, however, students tended to apply to judges whose philosophies they shared. Membership in the Federalist Society was a marker that helped students match up with like-minded jurists. The change wasn't absolute; some judges would welcome the intellectual ferment of having clerks with different perspectives. But more often, clerks served as the ideological offspring of the judges and justices they worked with, reinforcing their existing views.[29]

In addition to the two clerks held over from O'Connor's tenure, Alito brought back two strongly conservative clerks from his circuit court days. One, Adam Ciongoli, was a thirty-seven-year-old former official in Bush's Justice Department. His selection attracted immediate attention: Ciongoli had helped to craft the administration's expansive view of Bush's wartime powers. It happened that a major test of those powers was to be argued before the Supreme Court in a matter of weeks.[30]

"Justice Samuel A. Alito Jr., who was so bland and self-effacing at his Supreme Court confirmation hearings last month, made a bold decision on arriving at the court," wrote *The New York Times*. It was an early signal that Alito might not be as "self-effacing" on the bench as he had been in the witness chair.[31]

Ciongoli's selection also raised an issue of favoritism: his father, Dr. A. Kenneth Ciongoli, was the head of the National Italian American Foundation. The older Ciongoli had assisted Alito's confirmation by penning an open letter to the *Times* warning Alito's critics against "ethnic stereotyping."[32] Alito's other clerk, Hannah Clayson Smith, had worked with him on the circuit court and had already clerked at the Supreme Court for Clarence Thomas. Her husband, John, was also a former Alito clerk.[33]

Within two months, Alito would hear the landmark case to determine the legality of the military commissions that Bush had established to try enemy combatants in the war on terror. The case was closely watched because of the administration's refusal to consider detainees like the plaintiff, Salim Ahmed Hamdan, as prisoners of war under the Geneva Conventions.

There were two important issues in the case. The first was whether Bush had the authority to set up the tribunals on his own, without congressional approval. The second was whether the commissions provided sufficient procedural safeguards to satisfy the Uniform Code of Military Justice and the Geneva Conventions, whose treaties had been ratified by the United States. The commissions deviated from procedural norms by failing to allow objections to hearsay evidence and by letting the court consider secret evidence withheld from the defense.

The Supreme Court, by a 5–3 vote, with Chief Justice Roberts recusing himself because of his previous involvement in the case as a DC Circuit judge, voted against the Bush administration on both issues. Alito, along with Thomas and Scalia, dissented. He insisted that the commissions were sufficient to satisfy both military law and the Geneva Conventions.[34]

The case, in which Alito read the commission's rules so narrowly as to foreclose the procedural objections of the court's majority, was an early indication of his jurisprudence. On this politically charged case, he was firmly in line with the court's two most conservative members. The case, known as *Hamdan v. Rumsfeld*, also reflected the shifting dynamics of the court itself; Justices Souter, Stevens, Ginsburg, and Breyer were the liberal bloc, countered by Scalia, Thomas, Alito, and Roberts.[35] In the middle, in the swing role that O'Connor had played for twelve years, was Anthony Kennedy.

This was a more conservative version of the Supreme Court, simply because Kennedy usually landed to the right of O'Connor. And the same ideological configuration would be in place for the succeeding decade, as the court continued to move to the right, albeit with one shocking liberal breakthrough.

....

WHILE STILL IN HIS first year, Alito cast the deciding vote in a 5–4 decision that was widely viewed as a turning point in the court's handling of abortion. The court approved a federal ban on a late-term procedure that critics called "partial-birth abortion."[36]

Described by President Bush as "a terrible form of violence inflicted on children just inches from birth,"[37] the procedure involved compression and extraction of a late-term fetus. The procedure was very unpopular with the public,[38] but Planned Parenthood maintained that banning it would place an "undue burden" on women.[39] The bill signed by Bush also lacked an exception for the health of the mother.[40]

Just six years earlier, the court had struck down a similar ban in the state of Nebraska, also by a 5–4 vote, with Justice O'Connor voting in the majority.[41] In replacing O'Connor, Alito seemingly tipped the scales.

In a majority opinion written by Justice Kennedy, the court reasoned that the government had a "legitimate interest . . . in protecting the life of the fetus that may become a child." The law did not violate the "undue burden" test, he asserted, because alternative methods of abortion were available at earlier stages of pregnancy and evidence was inconclusive whether banning this procedure would have health implications for women.[42]

Ruth Bader Ginsburg, in her dissenting opinion, made it clear that the changes in the court's makeup were weakening its support for abortion rights. "Though today's opinion does not go so far as to discard *Roe* or *Casey*," she wrote, "the Court, differently composed than it was when we last considered a restrictive abortion regulation, is hardly faithful to our earlier invocations of 'the rule of law' and the 'principles of *stare decisis*.'"[43]

Her references to "the rule of law" and "principles of *stare decisis*" were almost direct quotes from Roberts's and Alito's confirmation hearings of the previous year. Her implication seemed obvious: the two new justices were talking a different game on the court than they had before the Senate.

. . . .

THE CHANGED COMPOSITION OF the court drew attention again a month later, in the first major case in which Alito wrote the majority opinion. He was once again the deciding vote in a 5–4 decision—this time, to reverse a jury award to a Goodyear Tire employee named Lilly Ledbetter, who claimed she'd received an unfairly low salary because of her gender. A jury agreed that she'd been a victim of discrimination—all fifteen men in her job category earned significantly more than she did. But Alito ruled that Ledbetter hadn't filed her claim quickly enough; even though she was still receiving the low pay at the time she sued Goodyear, her salary had been set earlier, outside the 180-day window for her to file suit.[44]

Once again, Ginsburg fired off a dissent, claiming that Alito's opinion was not "in tune with the realities of the workplace," and that "the actual payment of a discriminatory wage" was an unlawful act.[45]

Ledbetter said she had been unaware that men were earning more than she was and had decided to file suit as soon as she learned of the disparity. But Alito, deploying the principles of textualism, followed the specific wording of the statute: a person must file a claim within 180 days of a discriminatory act, and in his view, the discriminatory act was the setting of the salary, not the arrival of the check. Ledbetter's plight became a rallying cry on the left, and in 2009, President Barack Obama would sign the Lilly Ledbetter Fair Pay Act, effectively nullifying Alito's ruling.[46]

. . . .

WHILE DECISIONS TO NARROW the scope of gender discrimination and abortion rights merely chipped away at liberal gains, the court's new conservative majority would soon move on to a priority of its own: interpreting the Second Amendment in such a way to provide new protections for individual gun owners.

Broadening the scope of the Second Amendment was a long-standing obsession on the right, a way to shield law-abiding Americans from burdensome gun controls. The notion of a populace defended by its own weapons harked back to the frontier days and had an elemental appeal for rural conservatives in particular.

Indeed, the Constitution was written at a time when most Americans were well acquainted with weaponry. The fact that many of the Founding Fathers grew up with muskets hanging from their mantels gave the idea of an individual right to bear arms a strong originalist appeal: it felt like a return to first principles. Even some liberal critics furthered the vision of an original right to bear arms by lampooning the thought of twenty-first-century Americans being tied to the practices of their eighteenth-century forebears.

But the actual originalist argument for such a right was more difficult to make. The plain language of the Second Amendment—the starting point for any originalist inquiry—wasn't entirely helpful. It reads: "A well regulated Militia, being necessary to the security of a free State, the right of the people to keep and bear Arms, shall not be infringed."[47]

The Supreme Court's initial interpretation of this convoluted language was that it protected militias and not individuals, except in the military context. When the federal government passed its first bill regulating guns in 1934, a conservative Supreme Court ruled that "in the absence of any evidence tending to show that possession or use of a 'shotgun having a barrel of less than eighteen inches in length' at this time has some reasonable relationship to the preservation or efficiency of a well regulated militia, we cannot say that the Second Amendment guarantees the right to keep and bear such an instrument."[48]

This view was reaffirmed in future cases involving gun controls,[49] but it never sat well with conservatives. Thus, when Washington, DC, passed an unusually strict gun-control law, banning all handguns unless the owner was given a special permit by the police, an activist at the libertarian Cato Institute brought together a group of citizens who wanted guns for self-defense to sue for the right to get them. The new conservative majority on the Supreme Court agreed to hear the case.

The result, in *District of Columbia v. Heller*, was another 5–4 decision, a landmark in the historic battles over gun control. Writing for himself, Thomas, Roberts, Kennedy, and Alito, Justice Scalia engaged in a long argument that sought to parse the wording of the Second Amendment. The militia language, Scalia asserted, was merely a preamble to the real meaning of the amendment, which he said was understood by people at the time.

"The Second Amendment is naturally divided into two parts: its prefatory clause and its operative clause," Scalia wrote. "The former does not limit the latter grammatically, but rather announces a purpose. The Amendment could be rephrased, 'Because a well regulated Militia is necessary to the security of a free State, the right of the people to keep and bear Arms shall not be infringed.'"[50]

This was a little curious because no other constitutional amendment includes a "prefatory clause"; the framers did not offer anywhere else in the Constitution an explanation for why they were including a provision. Thus, Justice Stevens, writing for the four dissenters, stated flatly that "the Second Amendment was adopted to protect the right of the people of each of the several States to maintain a well-regulated militia."

What followed was an originalist extravaganza, a duel in which Scalia, for the majority, and Stevens and Breyer, for the dissenters, tried to match each other, detail for detail, in outlining the proper reading of the text and the original understanding of the amendment.

The dissenters rejected the idea of "prefatory" and "operative" clauses, insisting the two parts constituted a single meaning: a state's right to maintain a militia. "The term 'bear arms' is a familiar idiom; when used unadorned by any additional words, its meaning is 'to serve as a soldier, do military service, fight,'" Stevens wrote, citing the *Oxford American Dictionary*.[51]

Scalia preferred to focus on the word "keep," noting that "Webster defined it as 'to hold; to retain in one's power or possession.'" He insisted: "The phrase 'keep arms' was not prevalent in the written documents of the founding period that we have found, but there are a few examples, all of which favor viewing the right to 'keep Arms' as an individual right unconnected with militia service."[52]

The jousting among the justices was entertaining, but it didn't alter the outcome: the conservative justices had dramatically reinterpreted the Second Amendment. What remained was the question of whether the ruling applied only to Washington, as a federal protectorate, or also to the states. It fell to Alito to write that opinion.

In *McDonald v. City of Chicago*, Alito wrote for the same 5–4 majority that an individual right to bear arms was "fundamental to the Nation's scheme of ordered liberty," and that "a survey of the contemporaneous history also demonstrates clearly that the Fourteenth Amendment's Framers and ratifiers counted the right to keep and bear arms among those fundamental rights necessary to the Nation's system of ordered liberty."[53]

The Fourteenth Amendment says nothing about bearing arms. But the opinion showcased Alito's own contribution to originalist jurisprudence: his willingness to incorporate unwritten traditions into the law through the Fourteenth Amendment.

....

ALITO'S SURPRISING BELIEF THAT originalism wasn't the answer in every case started popping up more frequently in his fourth year on the Supreme Court.

No longer was he the newest justice. In 2009, President Barack Obama appointed Second Circuit Judge Sonia Sotomayor, who graduated from Princeton four years after Alito, to replace the retiring Souter. A Democratic-led Senate confirmed her nomination, 68–31. Now Sotomayor, as newest justice, would replace Alito as "doorkeeper" at the court's twice-weekly conferences on Wednesdays and Fridays, receiving papers and documents at the door to the meeting room.[54]

Meanwhile, Alito was staking out an independent position on the court, even compared to his fellow conservatives. In April 2010, he was the sole dissenter in a gruesome case involving "crush videos" showing extreme cruelty to animals. While all the other justices felt that the videos were protected under free-speech doctrine, Alito argued that states could ban them under the same theory that applied to child pornography.[55]

Then, at a hearing on November 1, Alito engaged in a memorable bit of byplay with Scalia while the justices heard arguments in a case involving a California law banning violent video games. This was not a particularly partisan matter; both conservatives and liberals expressed concerns about whether California's law violated the First Amendment's free-speech protections.

Scalia, true to his originalist beliefs, suggested that a ban on depictions of violence was "a prohibition which the American people never . . . ratified when they ratified the First Amendment." Scalia noted that the framers of the Constitution understood they were protecting even violent words and images when they crafted the free-speech guarantee.

Then Alito leaned into his microphone. "What Justice Scalia wants to know," he said, "is what James Madison thought of video games" and "if he enjoyed them."[56] It was a prime example of Alito's dry humor, but with a bite: when the decision came out, Alito registered his forceful disagreement with Scalia's majority opinion.[57]

Unlike Scalia, Alito was never a law professor; he didn't gravitate toward elaborate theories. His conservatism was more instinctive, rooted in his early life. Sometimes, he would deviate from an originalist analysis to raise practical concerns. Usually, these observations served to push him in an even more conservative direction. The video game case was an example of this. He concurred with the result in the case on the grounds that the law's definition of a video game was too vague. But he rejected Scalia's idea that the First Amendment protected violent video content.

"In considering the application of unchanging constitutional principles to new and rapidly evolving technology, this Court should proceed with caution," he wrote in his concurrence. "We should make every effort to understand the new technology. We should take into account the possibility that developing technology may have important societal implications that will become apparent only with time. We should not jump to the conclusion that new technology is fundamentally the same as some older thing with which we are familiar. And we should not hastily dismiss the judgment of legislators, who may be in a better position than we are to assess the implications of new technology. The opinion of the Court exhibits none of this caution."[58]

Scalia and the court's majority, Alito said, believed that "spending hour upon hour controlling the actions of a character who guns down scores of innocent victims is not different in 'kind' from reading a description of violence in a work of literature . . . The Court is sure of this; I am not."[59]

The same year, Alito's frustration with what he saw as a mechanical application of free-speech rights flared again in a case involving the Westboro Baptist Church, an extremist religious sect that protested at military funerals ostensibly to register its disapproval of the military's tolerance of homosexuality. The protesters chose their targets from all military funerals that seemed likely to attract publicity, not just those of suspected homosexuals.

When the father of Matthew Snyder, a soldier who was killed in the Iraq War, sued Westboro Baptist Church for emotional distress, a jury granted him millions of dollars in damages. The Fourth Circuit Court of Appeals reversed the award, saying it violated the protesters' free-speech rights. All eight of Alito's Supreme Court colleagues agreed that while the church's actions were deeply offensive, they represented protected speech. Alito wouldn't accept that holding.[60]

"Our profound national commitment to free and open debate is not a license for the vicious verbal assault that occurred in this case," Alito wrote. "The Court now holds that the First Amendment protected respondents' right to brutalize Mr. Snyder. I cannot agree." He added, "In order to have a society in which public issues can be openly and vigorously debated, it is not necessary to allow the brutalization of innocent victims."[61]

Alito was straying far from the text and history of the First Amendment to express his own horror at the church's disruption of a sacred event: the funeral of a young man killed while serving his country. In his demonstration of outraged passion, he was channeling the feelings of much of America. But one couldn't help noting his willingness to stray from modes of analysis that he considered sacrosanct when his personal passions weren't so exercised.

....

THE ISSUE OF GAY MARRIAGE had been gaining currency since the 1990s, with a huge boost coming in 2004 when the Massachusetts Supreme Judicial Court ruled it to be legally mandated in that state. By 2015, thirty-six states plus Washington, DC, and Guam had all legalized same-sex unions; other states had not, however, creating an odd patchwork in which two people could be united in their assets and family lives in one state but without any legal connection in another. By moving from one state to another, parents might lose their rights to their own children.[62]

An amalgam of legal objections to this situation was consolidated into one case for consideration at the US Supreme Court. And when the court announced its decision at the very end of its term in June, the result—a 5–4 vote in favor of a constitutional right to same-sex marriage—defied its rightward turn. This time, Kennedy swung left, joining with Ginsburg, Breyer, Sotomayor, and Elena Kagan, the Obama appointee who had replaced Stevens in 2010.

Kennedy's argument was succinct: marriage was a fundamental right under the "life, liberty or property" guarantee of the Fourteenth Amendment's due process clause—the same source of authority cited in *Griswold v. Connecticut* and *Roe v. Wade*—and the same amendment also promises "equal protection of the laws."[63] By his own account, Kennedy felt it was "necessary to undertake reading, research, and clerk discussions over the whole history of religious, cultural, and social views of marriage." What he discovered was that the definition of marriage in America and elsewhere had shifted considerably over time, from a system in which women were largely subordinate to men to one of more equal status.[64] Though those unions were still between men and women, the actions of a majority of states were proof of a major shift in understanding that the traditional bonds of marriage could be extended to people of the same sex.

In a majority opinion that evoked the major social changes of the Warren and Burger Courts, Kennedy grasped for soaring language to show that the ruling was as much an endorsement of marriage as of gay rights. "No union is more profound than marriage, for it embodies the highest ideals of love, fidelity, devotion, sacrifice, and family," he wrote in a passage that seemed aimed at his conservative colleagues. "In forming a marital union, two people become something greater than they once were. As some of the petitioners in these cases demonstrate, marriage embodies a love that may endure even past death. Their plea is that they do respect it, respect it so deeply that they seek to find its fulfillment in themselves."[65]

While social progressives exulted over the court's decision, the conservative justices seemed enraged. This was precisely the type of ruling that had spawned their movement in the first place. Men who had choked on the rulings in *Griswold* and *Roe*, for both the substance of the rights involved and the sense of judges scribbling their own views onto the constitutional canvas, felt that their lives' work had at least put a stop to these rulings. For most legal conservatives, the goal was to reverse *Roe v. Wade*, not see its constitutional basis extended into a new realm. The court's decision in *Obergefell v. Hodges* would make it that much harder to overturn *Roe* and put the genie back in the bottle.

Each of the conservatives chose to write his own dissent, registering for posterity his specific objections. Some were quite caustic. Scalia opened his dissent by declaring, "I write separately to call attention to this Court's threat to American democracy."[66]

"This is a naked judicial claim to legislative—indeed, *super*-legislative—power; a claim fundamentally at odds with our system of government,"

Scalia wrote. And then, in a highly personal rebuke, he cited the home states and educational backgrounds of his colleagues as evidence of their unfitness to pass judgment on the feelings of the American people. He took a particular swipe at Justice Kennedy, claiming that court did not include "a genuine Westerner (California does not count)."[67]

Kennedy said his children were wounded by Scalia's attack, and afterward, the two men barely spoke. Finally, Kennedy said, Scalia visited his office to apologize just before heading to Texas on a hunting trip from which he would not return. He died a little over seven months after the *Obergefell* decision came down. His widow, Maureen, later told Kennedy that her husband had been very relieved that their good relations were restored.[68]

Alito did not join Scalia's dissent. He chose to stake out his own ground and write one of his most closely considered opinions. Indeed, his dissent in *Obergefell* can be seen as a precursor of his later decision in *Dobbs*: he was laying the groundwork back in 2015.

"To prevent five unelected Justices from imposing their personal vision of liberty upon the American people, the Court has held that 'liberty' under the Due Process Clause should be understood to protect only those rights that are 'deeply rooted in this Nation's history and tradition,'" he wrote, quoting the same line of a 1997 case rejecting a right to physician-assisted suicide that he would cite in *Dobbs*. "And it is beyond dispute that the right to same-sex marriage is not among those rights."[69]

He then offered one of his purest—and most heartfelt—explanations of his feelings about judicial restraint, writing, "Today's decision shows that decades of attempts to restrain this Court's abuse of its authority have failed. A lesson that some will take from today's decision is that preaching about the proper method of interpreting the Constitution or the virtues of judicial self-restraint and humility cannot compete with the temptation to achieve what is viewed as a noble end by any practicable means. I do not doubt that my colleagues in the majority sincerely see in the Constitution a vision of liberty that happens to coincide with their own. But this sincerity is cause for concern, not comfort. What it evidences is the deep and perhaps irremediable corruption of our legal culture's conception of constitutional interpretation."[70]

These and other passages in his opinion were forceful and critical but aspired to a kind of nobility; this was the unshakable core of his legal philosophy as he saw it. But then he offered a seemingly more personal complaint, one that registered on a different level: in approving gay marriage, he asserted, the court was disrespecting the "rights of conscience" of people who oppose gay marriage.

This, too, was a facet of Alito's jurisprudence: a determination to place the beliefs of social conservatives on the same plane—or higher, if their beliefs stemmed from their religion—as the antidiscrimination protections enacted on behalf of racial or sexual minorities.

"I assume that those who cling to old beliefs will be able to whisper their thoughts in the recesses of their homes," Alito wrote ruefully, "but if they repeat those views in public, they will risk being labeled as bigots and treated as such by governments, employers, and schools."[71]

The *Obergefell* decision ended a chapter in Supreme Court history. Scalia's death was just the start of a period of turnover that would yield a very different—and far more conservative—judicial majority, one in which Alito himself would reign supreme.

CHAPTER 12

Free Exercise

n late January 2010, President Barack Obama delivered his State of the Union address, touting the accomplishments of his tumultuous first year in office while urging Congress to act on the health plan that would bear his name. But there was something else bothering him. Just a week earlier, in an unusual January ruling, the Supreme Court had struck down restrictions on corporations' funding of election campaigns.[1] It was a 5–4 decision, with Justice Kennedy casting the deciding vote in a victory for judicial conservatives.

The facts of the case were mundane, but the impact of the ruling seemed vast. Citizens United was a small non-profit company that wanted to air a documentary attacking Democratic presidential candidate Hillary Clinton. But the Federal Election Commission ruled that such an expenditure violated restrictions on corporate or union spending on campaigns. The 2002 McCain–Feingold Act said that corporations and unions could not spend their own money on political activities. They could, however, set up political action committees and fund them with individual donations from their constituents.[2]

Such limits on campaign spending were growing increasingly popular as Americans feared the potential corruption of candidates who would enter public office beholden to large donors. But the donors who were being reined in—wealthy individuals and corporations—felt their free-speech rights were being curtailed. Why shouldn't they be able to put their money where their mouths were?

In a 1990 case challenging a Michigan law that placed restrictions on election spending by corporations, a 6–3 Supreme Court majority led by

Justice Thurgood Marshall concluded that the government had the power to curb a "different type of corruption in the political arena: the corrosive and distorting effects of immense aggregations of wealth that are accumulated with the help of the corporate form and that have little or no correlation to the public's support for the corporation's political ideas."[3]

But Citizens United wasn't some giant special interest—it was a non-profit conservative group dedicated to making movies that attacked liberals. When it challenged the FEC decision, it argued only that the commission had wrongly included Citizens United among the much larger actors that the law had targeted. But the conservative justices didn't think such a narrow ruling was possible, given the free-speech issues at play. They ordered a highly unusual reargument of the case on much broader, more fundamental grounds. Essentially, the justices were telegraphing their interest in striking down the McCain–Feingold Act as a violation of the First Amendment.

When the decision in *Citizens United v. FEC* came down, it pointedly rejected the legal justifications underpinning not only restrictions on corporate spending but also most other campaign-finance laws. One by one, the majority opinion dismissed the need to offset the distorting effect of huge donations, to fight corruption in the form of disproportionate influence by large entities, and to protect the interests of shareholders who might not want corporate funds spent to benefit certain candidates.[4]

Kennedy's opinion conflated a corporation's right to argue for candidates of its choice with the right of news corporations—which were exempted from McCain–Feingold—to produce journalistic broadcasts and newspapers. In later years, both he and Alito would point to the irony of newspapers editorializing against corporate speech when they themselves were engaging in it.[5] But the First Amendment has a separate grant of freedom of the press written into the text, specifically to disentangle it from freedom of speech.

Nonetheless, Justice Kennedy found the McCain–Feingold Act too restrictive. "When Government seeks to use its full power, including the criminal law, to command where a person may get his or her information or what distrusted source he or she may not hear, it uses censorship to control thought," he wrote. "This is unlawful. The First Amendment confirms the freedom to think for ourselves."[6]

The unusually aggressive ruling caught the immediate attention of the political class, including President Obama. And he was determined to use his State of the Union address to make more Americans aware of the sea change in constitutional law.

"With all due deference to separation of powers, last week the Supreme Court reversed a century of law that I believe will open the floodgates for special interests—including foreign corporations—to spend without limit in our elections," Obama said. "I don't think American elections should be bankrolled by America's most powerful interests, or worse, by foreign entities. They should be decided by the American people. And I'd urge Democrats and Republicans to pass a bill that helps to correct some of these problems."[7]

State of the Union addresses are among the most colorful of American political rituals, with some of the flavor of a costume party. In addition to members of Congress, the House chamber hosts Joint Chiefs in their dress uniforms, dripping with medals, and berobed Supreme Court justices lined up like friars at a medieval banquet.

Sam Alito, sitting with his brethren in the front row, seethed at the president's words attacking the court. While other justices clenched their teeth, he opened his mouth. "Not true," he muttered, as the national television audience looked on.[8]

It wasn't clear which of Obama's words he was disputing—he later suggested it was the "century of law"[9]—but the breach of decorum was noticeable. For most Americans, it was their first close look at Justice Alito since his confirmation. And some were put off.

. . . .

IN LATER YEARS, ALITO would suggest the mumbled words just kind of slipped out spontaneously. ("People thought I said something. I assume they're correct. I certainly thought it.")[10] Yet his retort to Obama seemed pugnacious, a quality no one had previously ascribed to him.

Had something happened? Many people who knew him believe that he came out of the confirmation process a changed man. His hearings were tough, but not on the level of Bork or Thomas. He'd succeeded in winning over some skeptical senators, at least to the standards set by the Gang of 14. He came across as sincere. The heartfelt testimonials of clerks and colleagues helped to seal the deal. But that didn't mean the process left no scars: For years afterward, he'd refer to his confirmation as a once-in-a-lifetime ordeal.

"In retrospect, it was an interesting and at times humorous experience," he said in a 2014 interview with a conservative publication. "At the time it was an absolutely miserable experience." He recounted a laundry list of indignities, including having to prove to skeptical reporters that his father had indeed been born in Italy.[11]

Karl Rove, who had helped steer him through the confirmation, pointed to the treatment of Martha-Ann as something that wounded both Alitos. There was her breakdown in the hearing room. There was her anger over the column mocking her clothing.[12] And afterward, there was the family's need to relocate to Washington, a place that the Alitos associated with their degradation.

"I think he responded to the culture of Washington by becoming defensive," said Rove. "It's an ugly thing to confront. It was difficult for him and his wife to deal with."[13]

For the Alitos, life in Washington bore little resemblance to their days in West Caldwell. In the New Jersey suburbs, they enjoyed a sense of community built around high school sports, jogging in the park, and church on Sundays. They liked nothing better than watching their daughter, Laura, compete on the swimming team for James Caldwell High School.[14]

In Washington, there were no more school-age children at home and no community of suburban parents—even after they moved to Fort Hunt, Virginia, which was once thought to be safe ground for conservatives but had become overwhelmingly liberal in the preceding decades. In New Jersey, no one wore their politics on their sleeves, but Washington was politics incarnate. And for every person who expressed admiration for a Supreme Court justice, there were two who disdained the rightward movement of the court. Liberals didn't have to suffer these everyday slights. Washington was their turf, not Alito's.

But there was also good reason for Washington to be surprised by the seeming distance between the Alito of the Judiciary Committee hearings and the one who arrived on the bench. For his part, John Roberts took a lot of conservative stances and moved the court decidedly to the right, but in his public comments, his demeanor, and the tone of his judicial opinions, he still displayed something of the dignified institutionalist that he had presented at his confirmation hearing. Alito, on the other hand, didn't look much like the man he had presented: the one who said he was prepared to change his mind in the face of any fresh argument, scrap of evidence, or insight from a judicial colleague.

One person who was especially chagrined was his predecessor, Sandra Day O'Connor. She had left the court to spend more time with her husband, who was struggling with Alzheimer's disease, but she had little time with him before his mind deteriorated to the point that he entered memory care.[15] Left alone and lacking the stimulation of the court, O'Connor had second thoughts about her resignation. It felt all the worse to realize that Alito was, in her opinion, an inflexible conservative who was unraveling the compromises she had forged. She confided to friends her distrust of her successor.

"She was furious about Alito," said her friend Walter Dellinger, a prominent Duke University law professor. "She viewed him as a betrayal of all her accomplishments. She told me 'The last thing you needed was a fifth Catholic man.'"[16]

When an interviewer asked her how it felt to see her decisions overruled, she responded, "What would you feel?"[17]

. . . .

For liberals and moderates like O'Connor, it would get worse. After Scalia died in February 2016, they saw a chance to replace a conservative with one of their own; Obama chose the moderate DC Circuit Judge Merrick Garland, in hopes of sidestepping opposition. But Mitch McConnell, the Republican Senate Majority Leader, who was intensely involved in judicial appointments, wasn't about to surrender conservative gains. He refused to hold a confirmation hearing on Garland's nomination. "Let's let the American people decide," he said.[18]

McConnell was referring to the presidential election, still eight months away. It was a political gamble that turned into a masterstroke. The surprise Republican nominee was real estate tycoon turned reality TV star Donald Trump. He was propelled by intense support from blue-collar Republicans and talk-radio listeners but was distrusted—and even disdained—by GOP-leaning professionals. Seizing on that vulnerability, Leonard Leo met with Trump in March at a get-together arranged by Federalist Society member Donald McGahn; Leo pushed Trump to commit to naming a Federalist Society judge to replace Scalia.[19] For Republicans alienated by Trump's boorish behavior, the prospect of another true conservative on the Supreme Court was a major reason to put aside their misgivings.

Trump seemed to catch on quickly. "I'm getting names. Federalist people. Some very good people. The Heritage Foundation," he said in April. "I'm going to announce that these are the judges, in no particular order, that I'm going to put up."[20] The following month, he released the first set of names, saying they were selected "first and foremost, based on constitutional principles, with input from highly respected conservatives and Republican Party leadership."[21]

Trump eventually won the election in a shocking rebuke to Hillary Clinton. The new president, again with the aid of Leo, quickly filled Scalia's seat with Tenth Circuit Judge Neil Gorsuch. When Democrats tried to invoke the filibuster, McConnell detonated the nuclear option and changed Senate rules to eliminate filibusters for Supreme Court nominees. Gorsuch was confirmed by a 54–45 vote.[22] A year and a half later, Justice Kennedy retired, giving Trump a second pick. He elevated DC Circuit Judge Brett Kavanaugh.

Both Gorsuch and Kavanaugh had followed nearly the same professional paths as Roberts and Alito: raised in conservative Catholic families, had their unpopular beliefs tested in the Ivy League cauldron, worked in Republican administrations, attained circuit court judgeships at an early age, and relied on the Federalist Society imprimatur to gain appointment to the Supreme Court.

Kavanaugh's confirmation was rockier than Alito's or Gorsuch's. It was dominated by the allegations of a university professor, Christine Blasey Ford, who claimed that a teenage Kavanaugh had groped and sexually assaulted her at a high school party when he was seventeen and she was fifteen; she said she'd feared for her life. Kavanaugh's bristling denial struck some of the same furious, emotional notes as Thomas's from twenty-seven years earlier—and set off the same reactions. While many liberals found Ford's allegations troubling, conservatives saw them as the smearing of a good man for his conservative beliefs. No longer subject to the filibuster, Kavanaugh won confirmation by a wafer-thin 50–48 margin.[23]

Now Republican presidents had succeeded in installing four consecutive men of similar backgrounds and judicial philosophies, all favorites of the Federalist Society. This was made possible by Leo's success in baiting Trump, along with McConnell's machinations in holding open Scalia's seat and eliminating the filibuster. Thanks to the two of them, the court was poised for a conservative takeover.

But fate—and McConnell—had one more card to play. In September 2020, as Trump was sputtering toward a reelection defeat, Justice Ginsburg lost her long battle with cancer. Having rejected calls to retire when Obama would have been the one to name a replacement, the ailing Ginsburg fought to stay alive long enough for a Democratic president to choose her successor. She died within forty-six days of the election.[24]

This time, McConnell vowed to move to confirmation with alacrity. Trump nominated Seventh Circuit Judge Amy Coney Barrett, a longtime favorite of the conservative legal movement. Beyond her status as the first Republican woman nominated to the court, she differed from the recent male GOP nominees in a few noteworthy ways. She had steered clear of the Ivy League, attending tiny Rhodes College and Notre Dame Law School before clerking for Scalia. But she, like the male nominees who preceded her, grew up in a devoutly Catholic family and became a circuit court judge at an early age. She was also a member of the Federalist Society.[25]

Democrats boycotted the Judiciary Committee's vote on her nomination in protest of McConnell's rush to confirm her before the election. They found his actions particularly disingenuous because of his refusal to allow a hearing on Garland's nomination in the eight months before the previous election. But Republicans had the votes—barely. Barrett was confirmed by 52–48, with all Democrats voting no in anger over McConnell.[26]

Eight days later, Trump lost the election and Republicans lost the Senate.

But the Supreme Court was now prepared to shape the law in all the ways that Ed Meese and his minions had only imagined three decades earlier.

....

FOR ALITO, HIS SPECIAL focus—the issue that animated him the most, dominating his speeches while stimulating his legal mind—was the free exercise of religion. It was the cause of a lifetime, one that evoked every stage of his development.

In Chambersburg, the Catholic Church had been an anchor for his parents and grandparents, a place where their Italian heritage could be embraced without the pressures of assimilation. Growing up in Mercerville, he absorbed religious teachings at Our Lady of Sorrows, only to see them challenged and, in his opinion, denigrated by the social changes and political movements of his college years. And when his liberal peers began demanding—and receiving—special legal protections for people by dint of their race and sex, it struck him that there was an imbalance. While religious people were protected against overt discrimination, they were left on their own when it came to expressing religious precepts that might upset non-believers—or even trigger antidiscrimination claims.

There was a long-standing reason for this. In 1878, the Supreme Court took up the case of a Mormon leader who'd challenged a federal bigamy law as a violation of his exercise of religion. A unanimous court seized on a Thomas Jefferson quote that "the legislative powers of the government reach actions only, and not opinions," to rule that all people had a First Amendment right to their views, but not to violate laws that other citizens live by.[27] There was a compelling logic to this rule: if religious practice were an accepted basis for overcoming the law, various entities might easily claim that their rituals required them to use illegal drugs, disobey environmental laws, engage in sexual practices that might constitute assault, or discriminate against disfavored groups.

That rule remained in place for eighty-five years, until the Warren Court held that the state of South Carolina had unfairly denied unemployment benefits to a Seventh-Day Adventist who refused to work on Saturdays; the state's Employment Security Commission decided that her unwillingness to work on Saturdays showed that she had "failed, without good cause . . . to accept available suitable work." Writing for a 7–2 majority, Justice Brennan ruled that "to condition the availability of benefits upon this appellant's willingness to violate a cardinal principle of her religious faith effectively penalizes the free exercise of her constitutional liberties."[28] This meant that people's religious objections were now reasons to exempt them from laws, unless the government had a compelling interest and there was no way to tailor the law more narrowly.

Just twenty-seven years later, the court veered again. In a 6–3 ruling in a 1990 case called *Employment Division v. Smith*, Justice Scalia authored the opinion holding that a Native American church could not use the hallucinogenic drug peyote in its rituals. Quoting the court's 1878 decision in the Mormon case, Scalia wrote that permitting an individual "by virtue of his beliefs 'to become a law unto himself' contradicts both constitutional tradition and common sense."[29] Thus, when Alito joined the court, the range of free exercise of religion was more or less where it was in 1878: religious people could not violate a law as long as it didn't single them out.

Despite religious conservatives' reverence for Scalia and distrust of Brennan, they strongly preferred the Brennan rule. Alito himself, while serving on the Third Circuit, succeeded in stretching the Scalia precedent by ruling that the Newark Police Department's policy prohibiting beards violated the rights of Muslims because it included exemptions for health and undercover work, but not religion. Thus, Alito decided, it was not neutrally applied.[30]

The Muslim case, which drew significant national attention, was brought by the Becket Fund, an organization dedicated to expanding religious liberties. It was founded by Kevin Hasson, who had worked alongside Alito in Meese's Office of Legal Counsel. Becket would generate a stream of cases challenging laws that interfered with religious practices, giving Alito more opportunities to create carve-outs for religious expression.[31]

On the Supreme Court, Alito waited eight years to put his ideas into practice again, but he finally found a high-profile opportunity. The Obama administration's signature Affordable Care Act required all large employers to provide contraception coverage. But the Green family, owners of the $5 billion Hobby Lobby chain of arts-and-crafts megastores, were evangelical Christians who believed that contraception is immoral. They asked the court to find the Obamacare mandate illegal.

It was 2014, and the court did not yet include the three justices who would eventually be appointed by Trump. So Alito had to work hard to cobble together a majority. First, he seized on the 1993 Freedom of Religion Restoration Act, which required laws to be narrowly tailored to avoid interfering with religious practices. He persuaded the five conservative justices to join his opinion ruling that the Green family—as private owners of Hobby Lobby—were entitled to run their business according to their religious precepts. The law requiring them to provide contraception was not narrowly tailored to achieve a government interest, Alito reasoned, because Obama's health department had already exempted religious non-profits and provided separate means for employees to get contraceptives; it could do the same for Hobby Lobby and other for-profit companies owned by religious objectors.

Though *Burwell v. Hobby Lobby* did not change the court's interpretation of the free exercise clause, it was a landmark all the same. Alito had to overcome numerous hurdles, including whether a for-profit corporation could be considered a "person" under the 1993 statute. In other contexts—such as Lilly Ledbetter's workplace discrimination claim—he had been a stickler for the precise wording of a law, but this time he simply asserted that "no conceivable definition of the term includes natural persons and nonprofit corporations, but not for-profit corporations."[32]

Hobby Lobby was the biggest victory for religious expression in a generation, and it signaled to the public that the court's conservative majority would look generously on claims of free exercise of religion.

After the Trump appointees began to join the court, Alito found more support for free exercise claims. In 2020, with Gorsuch and Kavanaugh joining a 7–2 decision, Alito authored an opinion exempting many employees of religious organizations from antidiscrimination protections. The case involved lay teachers at two Catholic schools in California who lost their jobs. One claimed she was let go because she missed time for breast cancer treatment; the other said she was unfairly fired because of her age. Under a 2012 ruling, the court had exempted ministerial positions from non-discrimination laws but left other employees free to sue for wrongful firing.[33] Alito expanded the exemption to cover any employees whose jobs were connected, even loosely, to an organization's religious mission.[34]

"When a school with a religious mission entrusts a teacher with the responsibility of educating and forming students in the faith, judicial intervention into disputes between the school and the teacher threatens the school's independence in a way that the First Amendment does not allow," Alito wrote.[35]

Justice Sotomayor wrote a dissent noting that neither teacher had any religious training and both had taught non-religious subjects. She couldn't resist using Alito's own precepts against him: "Recently, this Court has lamented a perceived 'discrimination against religion.' Yet here it swings the pendulum in the extreme opposite direction, permitting religious entities to discriminate widely and with impunity for reasons wholly divorced from religious beliefs."[36]

. . . .

THE FOLLOWING YEAR, 2021, the court confronted a more dramatic clash between antidiscrimination efforts and the exercise of religion. A gay couple in Philadelphia attended an information session to be foster parents under a city-funded program operated by Bethany Christian Services, only to be told they were wasting their time: Bethany didn't work with gay couples. After the couple related their story in the media, reporters discovered that another large city contractor, Catholic Social Services (CSS), also refused to engage gay foster parents.

Philadelphia officials checked with all the agencies they worked with, but only Bethany and CSS refused to deal with same-sex couples. Bethany ultimately agreed to lift its ban, but CSS did not. Determining that the Catholic agency had violated the antidiscrimination clause in its contract, Philadelphia cut its funding. The agency sued, claiming the city had interfered with its free exercise of religion.

After the Supreme Court heard the case, all nine justices agreed that Philadelphia had erred. With Roberts writing the opinion, the justices found that the city's antidiscrimination rules allowed for individual exceptions. Thus, the rules weren't evenly applied or narrowly tailored to avoid clashing with religion; the city had violated the test Justice Scalia had set down in the *Smith* case back in 1990. That meant Philadelphia would have to renew its contract with CSS, and the state of the law remained the same.[37]

That wasn't enough for Alito. His agitation had shown itself at the hearing when he told the city's attorney, "If we are being honest about what's really going on here, it's not about ensuring that same-sex couples in Philadelphia have the opportunity to be foster parents. It's the fact that the city can't stand the message that Catholic Social Services and the archdiocese are sending by continuing to adhere to the old-fashioned view about marriage. Isn't that the case?"[38]

In a massive, seventy-seven-page concurring opinion joined by Thomas and Gorsuch, Alito demanded that the *Smith* test be overruled. In language similar to that he would use the following year in his *Dobbs* opinion, he wrote that "this Court's governing interpretation of a bedrock constitutional right, the right to the free exercise of religion, is fundamentally wrong and should be corrected."[39]

Justice Scalia's *Smith* opinion, Alito wrote, "paid shockingly little attention to the text of the Free Exercise Clause. Instead of examining what readers would have understood its words to mean when it was adopted, the opinion merely asked whether it was 'permissible' to read the text to have the meaning that the majority favored. This strange treatment of the constitutional text cannot be justified—and is especially surprising since it clashes so sharply with the way in which *Smith's* author, Justice Scalia, generally treated the Constitution (and, indeed, with his entire theory of legal interpretation)."[40]

Alito was challenging the father of originalism on originalist grounds. But his own analysis, which concluded that "if we put these definitions together, the ordinary meaning of 'prohibiting the free exercise of religion' was (and still is) forbidding or hindering unrestrained religious practices or worship," wasn't the last word on the subject.

Alito's fiery opinion generated its own originalist pushback, illustrating the point that while originalism purports to yield unalterable rules, the parsing of ancient dictionaries and texts often breeds confusion and contradiction. Vincent Phillip Muñoz, an expert on religion and the law from Notre Dame University, said the fact that the framers of the Constitution debated whether to include a conscientious objector protection for the military "strongly suggests" that they "did not understand the Free Exercise Clause to grant religious individuals exemptions from generally applicable laws."[41]

Andrew Koppelman, a law professor at Northwestern, put it more bluntly: "When the Free Exercise Clause of the First Amendment was written, not a single person in America had ever claimed that there should be, or that this provision would entail, a judicially enforceable right to exemption from laws that do not aim at interfering with religion. The doctrines and practices of strict scrutiny, narrow tailoring, and compelling interests came into existence in the 1960s. At the time of the framing, they were as unimaginable as TikTok."[42]

In other words, Alito was relying not on original understanding but on the updated rules of the Warren Court, his longtime foil.

. . . .

IN 2025, ALITO TOOK the reins of the court in an even more highly publicized clash between gay rights and religion. In 2022, public schools in Montgomery County, Maryland, had added one LGBTQ+ text into their approved curriculum for each year from pre-kindergarten to fifth grade. Teachers weren't required to use them, but if they did, they were asked to notify parents and allow them to opt out. The following year, the school system decided to end the opt-outs, partly for convenience but also to avoid any stigma to students who felt the storybooks related to their own families. Allowing other students to walk out, administrators believed, left negative impressions on kids with gay parents.

The court's six conservative justices disagreed; it was the religious kids who were being discriminated against. In an opinion by Alito, the court ordered that the opt-outs be restored to protect free exercise of religion. In making his argument, he glided through texts of children's books, including one featuring "apparently a transgender child" standing in a gender-neutral bathroom and another with a prince whose parents wanted him to find "a kind and worthy" bride, but who determines that he is "looking for something different in a partner."[43]

In her dissent, Justice Sotomayor, along with Elena Kagan and Ketanji Brown Jackson—the 2022 Joe Biden appointee who replaced Justice Breyer—argued that Alito was opening the door to limitless challenges to public school systems, which had hitherto been given wide latitude in forming their curriculums. Alito, she contended, was inventing a right out of whole cloth—doing what he had long accused liberals of—while burdening judges with the responsibility of reviewing minute aspects of public school teachings.

"Casting aside longstanding precedent, the Court invents a constitutional right to avoid exposure to 'subtle' themes 'contrary to the religious principles' that parents wish to instill in their children," Sotomayor wrote, putting scare quotes around Alito's words. "Exposing students to the 'message' that LGBTQ people exist, and that their loved ones may celebrate their marriages and life events, the majority says, is enough to trigger the most demanding form of judicial scrutiny. That novel rule is squarely foreclosed by our precedent and offers no limiting principle. Given the great diversity of religious beliefs in this country, countless interactions that occur every day in public schools might expose children to messages that conflict with a parent's religious beliefs. If that is sufficient to trigger strict scrutiny, then little is not."[44]

....

JANUARY 2020 BROUGHT A surprise that rocked the Federalist Society. The Judicial Conference Committee on Codes of Conduct, which is part of the administration arm of the court system, issued a draft opinion advising that "formal affiliation with the ACS [American Constitution Society] or the Federalist Society, whether in a membership or in a leadership role, is inconsistent with the Code of Conduct."[45] The code provided guidance for judges on matters of integrity, including the "avoidance of impropriety or even its appearance."[46]

Even though the policy would equally impact the liberal American Constitution Society and the Federalist Society, conservatives smelled a rat. A group of 210 judges signed a letter to the Committee expressing their disapproval. According to US senators who weighed in on the opposite side, 93 percent of the objecting judges were Republican appointees.[47] The letter leaned heavily on the idea that the Federalist Society was dedicated to public debate and did not have any kind of agenda.

"Take the claim that the Federalist Society advocates particular policies, rather than the general improvement of the law," the letter stated. "The draft fails to identify a single 'policy position' taken by the Federalist Society. That is because—to the best of our collective knowledge—the Federalist Society has never, in its several decades of existence, lobbied a policymaking body, filed an amicus brief, or otherwise advocated any policy change."[48]

Of course, Leonard Leo, while on and off the society's payroll, had helped to facilitate that type of advocacy through his outside activities. But the judges seemed comfortable with the idea that a man who helped to lead the society could play both roles without implicating the society itself.

The Democratic senators who endorsed the draft rule depicted the group quite differently: "The Federalist Society has become the de facto gatekeeper for judicial nominations in the Trump administration. The President and his former White House Counsel, a prominent Federalist Society member, have stated so publicly. To date, over 86 percent of the

President's appellate court nominees, including both his Supreme Court nominees, have been Society members."[49]

The huge partisan divide over the draft rule effectively killed it. Bipartisan approval is crucial to the US courts; risking it, even in the service of an important ethics rule, is tempting fate. In July, the court system's chief administrator announced that the draft would not be published but also warned judges to "take care to make all membership decisions in a way that is consistent with the highest ideals of the profession."[50]

This effort by the US courts to restrict the Federalist Society flew largely under the radar. But its defeat removed one of the few threats to the society's dominant position in American jurisprudence.

....

JUSTICE ALITO, FOR ONE, had no hesitations about embracing the Federalist Society. While on the Supreme Court, he regularly participated in the group's events. Its annual lawyers' conference that fall was no exception. This time, however, his audience wasn't in a banquet hall. The Covid-19 pandemic continued to rage, and the Federalist Society moved its marquee event online.

Standing in front of a harsh blue background, Alito looked perturbed in a dark, almost funereal suit. He alluded to the recent move to deter judges from joining the society. He made no mention of ethics, or the nonpartisan committee that made the recommendation, or the fact that the rule would also apply to the American Constitution Society, but instead portrayed it in starkly partisan terms, as "an attempt to hobble the debate that the Federalist Society fosters." He cited by name the authors of the letter opposing the move and said, "We should all express our thanks to these defenders of free speech."[51]

Then he proceeded, in his choice of words and topics, to put firmly to rest the idea that sitting judges ought not to inject themselves into political disputes.

The pandemic, he said, had exacerbated "disturbing trends that were already present before the virus struck, trends that we must resist and reverse when the crisis is over." One, he said, was the dominance of "law-making by executive fiat rather than legislation."[52] He was referring not to his own unitary executive theory, which gave the president fiat over large swaths of policy, but rather to the health and safety measures that governors had imposed to prevent the spread of the virus.

At the time, this was throwing gasoline on a growing conflagration of complaints, largely from conservatives, who bristled at wearing masks, being required to show proof of vaccination, or maintaining distance from others in stores. These restrictions, Alito noted, had been supported in courts because of a 1905 Supreme Court decision, but then he offered a critique of the case and his own assessment that it "does not mean that whenever there is an emergency, executive officials have unlimited, unreviewable discretion."[53]

Was he offering a roadmap to those who might challenge vaccine mandates and social distancing? He said he hoped his words would not be "twisted or misunderstood," but why, then, offer a sweeping critique of the one case being used to justify a vast number of restrictions?[54]

His worries over Covid restrictions soon landed close to the heart of his jurisprudence: the free exercise of religion. To his chagrin, the Supreme Court had failed to issue an emergency injunction against a Nevada law limiting church services to fifty or fewer worshippers.[55] But that didn't stop him from sounding off. Nevada, he said in his speech, "blatantly discriminated against houses of worship."[56]

He noted that the state, after initially closing its famed casinos, eventually allowed up to 50 percent of normal occupancy. "Not only did the Governor open up the casinos, he made a point of inviting people from all over the country to visit them. So if you go to Nevada, you can gamble, drink, and attend all sorts of shows to your heart's content. But here's what you can't do: If you want to worship at a church, synagogue, or mosque and you are the fifty-first person in line, you are out of luck."[57]

He ran through many other cases outside the realm of Covid restrictions in which he claimed local officials had hampered the free exercise of religion, including the case of the Colorado baker who refused to make a wedding cake for a gay couple.[58]

Then he moved on to free speech, chiding both colleges and "many big corporations" for curbing political dialogue. He referenced comedian George Carlin's monologue "Seven Words You Can Never Say on Television" and claimed that in today's university and corporate settings, "there would not be just seven items on the list. Seventy times seven would be closer to the mark." His prime example, however, was one he'd cited repeatedly: "You cannot say that marriage is between a man and a woman," he said. "Until very recently, that is what the vast majority of Americans thought. Now, it's considered bigotry."[59]

In wrapping up, Alito took aim at proposals by various Democrats to add more Supreme Court justices or otherwise reorganize the court. He referenced a letter from five senators who filed a brief supporting a New York gun control ordinance that was under Supreme Court review. The senators went beyond the facts of the case and, in Alito's telling, "wrote that the Supreme Court is a sick institution and that if the Court did not mend its ways, well, it might have to be 'restructured.'"

"After receiving this warning, the Court did exactly what the City and the Senators wanted," he added. "It held that the case was moot and said nothing about the Second Amendment. Three of us protested—but to no avail."[60]

After saying that the letter "offered a foretaste of what the Supreme Court will face," he declared, "The Supreme Court was created by the Constitution, not by Congress. Under the Constitution, we exercise 'the judicial Power of the United States.' Congress has no right to interfere with that work any more than we have the right to legislate . . . And it is therefore wrong for anybody, including members of Congress, to try to influence our decisions by anything other than legal argumentation."[61]

After nearly fifteen years on the high court, Alito was feeling his oats and having his say. There was little to stop him except his own, oft-referenced, restraint. Had he gone too far? Even some Republican-appointed judges in his Federalist Society audience found themselves wondering.[62]

Alito's parents faced hardships in the Italian American Chambersburg neighborhood of Trenton, New Jersey. Around 1930, Alito's father's family lived in a small apartment at 231 Pearl Street.

Wed At Church

RIGHT: Devout Catholics, Samuel A. Alito Sr. and Rose Fradusco married at Sacred Heart Church in 1948.

BELOW: Rose Alito, a teacher, took her children's education seriously. When her son was nominated to the Supreme Court, she showed reporters his childhood awards.

Jerome Fritz Photo

Mrs. Samuel A. Alito

The former Miss Rose R. Fradusco, daughter of Mrs. Rosina Fradusco of this city, was married recently to the son of Anthony Alito, also of this city. The ceremony took place at the Sacred Heart Church.

College Club Fetes Residents Of Home

The Alitos valued community life. Young Samuel (*far right*) and his sister, Rosemary (*third from right*), distributed gifts at a Trenton nursing home.

At Steinert High School in suburban Hamilton Township, Alito was a star. He served as student council president and editor of the school newspaper and was a champion debater.

At Princeton, Alito found his values under siege. In spring 1970, the campus exploded in protest over President Nixon's incursion into Cambodia, leading to a student strike and a season of protests.

ABOVE LEFT: Alito said he was deeply influenced by writer William F. Buckley, who spoke at Princeton in December 1970.

ABOVE RIGHT: Alito's was the last all-male class to enter Princeton. By 1970, abortion clinics had begun advertising in *The Daily Princetonian*.

Prospect:

Published by Concerned Alumni of Princeton

Volume X No. 3, Summer 1981

Why Can't
A Woman...

Be More Like
A Man?

1980-81 Speakers List   Funding Abortion: Readers Reply   Southern Discomfort

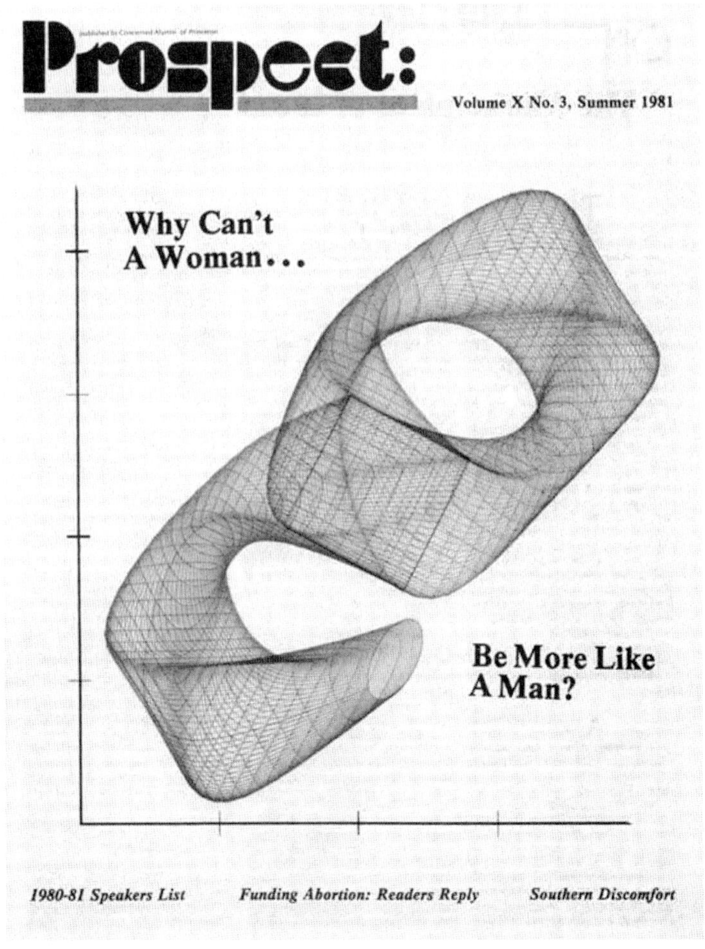

The Concerned Alumni of Princeton group published *Prospect*, a magazine critical of women and minorities on campus. Alito listed himself as a CAP member in a job application.

LEFT: In 1972, Alito's yearbook entry stated that he "intends to go to law school and eventually to warm a seat on the Supreme Court."

BELOW: At Yale Law School, Alito was assigned to a constitutional law class with leftist professor Charles Reich. In 1971, *Doonesbury* lampooned Reich's teaching style.

BOTTOM LEFT: Harvard Law professor Duncan Kennedy was a leader of critical legal studies, a leftist movement that sparked a backlash among conservatives.

BOTTOM RIGHT: Alito had wanted to take a constitutional law class with Robert Bork, whom Ronald Reagan nominated to the Supreme Court in 1987. Bork's failed hearings accelerated the growth of the Federalist Society.

In the 1980s, Alito worked in the Reagan administration, where he met key conservative thinkers at Federalist Society events. Many took place at Chinese restaurants such as Tony Cheng's.

Alito met Martha-Ann Bomgardner while working in Newark as an assistant US attorney. They married in 1985 and have two children.

ABOVE: President George W. Bush nominated his longtime adviser Harriet Miers to the Supreme Court, crushing Alito's hopes. But she soon came under attack from conservatives and withdrew her nomination.

BELOW: On October 31, 2005, President Bush nominated Alito to take the slot vacated by Harriet Miers.

Martha-Ann Alito broke into tears when Democratic senators tried to tie her husband to bigoted statements by Concerned Alumni of Princeton.

18

19

RIGHT: As a Supreme Court justice, Alito has been a regular speaker at Federalist Society events, rejecting efforts to keep judges from appearing at such gatherings.

BELOW: After Alito wrote the decision overturning *Roe v. Wade*, protesters picketed his home in northern Virginia.

20

ABOVE: Alito's support for President Donald Trump's positions on the Supreme Court has led to a backlash, as critics decry growing partisanship in the judiciary.

BELOW: In 2020, Trenton decided to take down a statue of Christopher Columbus in the neighborhood where Alito's parents grew up. He condemned the move, backing Italian American groups fighting against it.

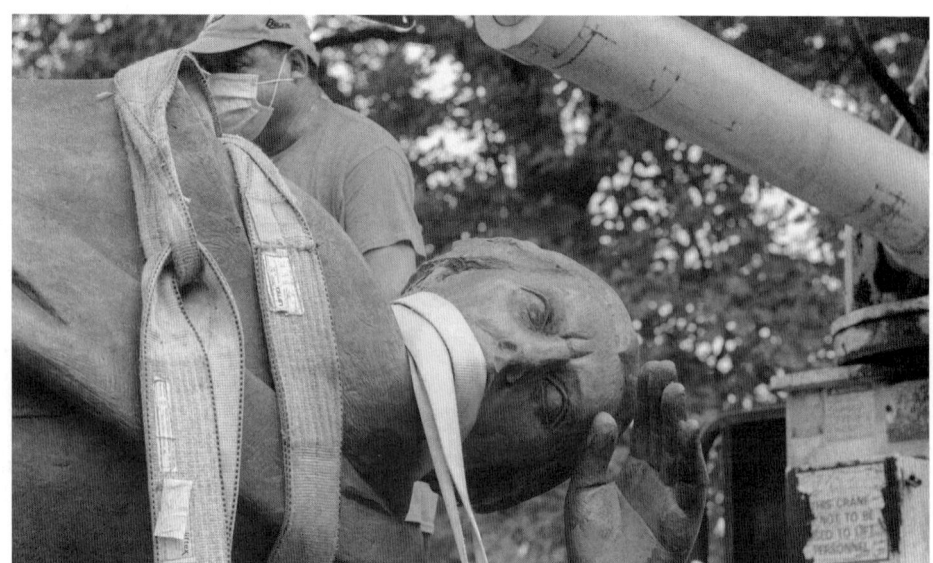

CHAPTER 13

The Backlash

The *Dobbs* decision in 2022 was an epic turning point. It was the moment the conservative legal movement delivered on its promises and paid back its debts. Overturning *Roe v. Wade* had long been the point of connection between the Federalist Society and the religious right, between the intellectual core of the movement and its masses of political supporters. At times, the originalist ideology seemed contoured precisely to overturn *Roe v. Wade*. It would leave no constitutional escape hatch for abortion rights. The movement's political power—the force that drove Bush and Trump to appoint Federalist Society jurists—also sprang from opposition to abortion. Supporters could only wonder whether the fusion of law and politics that allowed the conservative legal movement to flourish could have happened without *Roe*.

Authoring the *Dobbs* decision gave Alito a new status in the legal world. Now his words would be parsed and debated, celebrated and scorned, for as long as students filed into classrooms. But in the immediate aftermath, there were only bursts of emotion from both sides.

While protesters massed outside the Supreme Court building within hours of the leak of the news, Alito quickly canceled an appearance at the Fifth Circuit Judicial Conference planned for three days later;[1] on the Thursday that he would have been at the conference, he awoke instead to discover that supporters had arrived outside his house in Fort Hunt, Virginia, praying and waving signs with messages including "ALITO ROCKS" and "Thank you, Sam."[2]

The following Monday, the other side was heard from. About one hundred pro-choice protesters wearing Covid-19 masks staged a half-mile march to Alito's house, chanting "Alito says post-*Roe*, we say hell no" and carrying a banner saying "Repro-Freedom FOR ALL." Outside the two-story brick house with its white fence and flagpole springing up among a nest of bushes, the protesters handed out candles and delivered speeches through a bullhorn.

"For those people out there that think protesting at politicians' and justices' homes is 'too much,' please keep in mind that these people are actively attempting to take our rights away from us," proclaimed one speaker.[3]

Three police officers stood between the house and the curb of the street, where the protesters gathered. For Alito, the sense of being under siege was shocking, even if the Fox News claims that he had been, in the words of Jesse Watters, moved "to an undisclosed location," were shown to be suspect.[4]

Violent threats against judges had been on the rise even before *Dobbs*; on July 19, 2020, a disgruntled lawyer posing as a delivery man rang the doorbell of US District Court Judge Esther Salas's house in New Brunswick, New Jersey. He shot and killed Judge Salas's twenty-year-old son while critically injuring her husband. Salas and her husband became fierce advocates for judicial safety.[5]

The fact of the *Dobbs* leak further rattled people in and around the Supreme Court. While the leaker's identity and motives were unknown, the breach of ethics and tradition made court officials only too aware of their vulnerability: there were people among them who weren't committed to following the rules.

Alito counted himself as a victim.

"It was a grave betrayal of trust by somebody, and it was a shock because nothing like that had happened in the past," he said in December 2022, referring to the leak. "So it certainly changed the atmosphere at the court for the remainder of last term. The leak also made those of us who were in the majority in support of overruling *Roe* and *Casey* targets for assassination because it gave people a rational reason to think they could prevent that from happening by killing one of us. We know that a man has been charged with attempting to kill Justice Kavanaugh. It's a pending case, so I won't say anything more about that."[6]

Indeed, the person who stalked Kavanaugh before turning themselves in to marshals posted outside the justice's home told police they wanted to kill Kavanaugh because of anger over the leaked *Dobbs* draft. Threats would continue to rise sharply in the years after the decision was announced, with the US Marshals Service logging 562 threats to federal judges between October 1, 2024, and September 30, 2025, up from 509 the previous fiscal year.[7]

The identity of the judges receiving threats remained protected, but Alito, as author of the *Dobbs* decision, would have been a prime target. Beyond the threats, there was online vitriol and condemnations ranging as far as overseas. The Alitos had to learn how to live with constant security.[8]

Fears for their family weighed heavily on Sam and Martha-Ann, who told people that they relied on their religious faith to get them through the period of turmoil.[9]

THE EARTHQUAKE SET OFF by *Dobbs* reverberated through the entire court. It soon exposed one of its long-acknowledged vulnerabilities: its loose ethical requirements. Financial disclosures were designed to reveal potential conflicts of interest, but the justices often seemed more concerned with their own privacy than the public's right to know. For example, they agreed to disclose their spouses' incomes, but not the identity of their spouses' clients; it was the clients who might be seeking to influence the court by hiring a justice's spouse, but they remained invisible.[10] Alito wasn't affected by this because Martha-Ann did not work outside their home.[11] But another loophole helped him avoid revealing a hunting trip he took with backers of Leonard Leo's network.

Justices are required to divulge the sources of expensive gifts and entertainment, but there is an exemption for personal hospitality that they chose to interpret very broadly. The exemption was so broad that Clarence Thomas failed to disclose decades of yacht vacations, private jet trips, and luxury accommodations bankrolled by conservative businessman Harlan Crow, whom he described as a close friend.[12]

Alito chose not to disclose a lavish fishing journey to Alaska arranged by Leonard Leo. It included free air travel on a private plane owned by billionaire hedge-fund operator Paul Singer, who was hoping the Supreme Court would assist his efforts to force the government of Argentina to pay his firm billions of dollars in old debts. The group stayed at a resort owned by Robin Arkley II, a donor to the conservative legal movement. The traveling party also included DC Circuit Judge A. Raymond Randolph, for whom Leo had clerked in the 1990s.[13]

The trip occurred in 2008, early in Alito's tenure, but reporters for the non-profit investigative journalism organization ProPublica contacted him about it in 2023. Rather than respond to them, Alito published an advance op-ed defending his conduct in *The Wall Street Journal*'s opinion pages. It was entitled "Justice Samuel Alito: ProPublica Misleads Its Readers," even though the ProPublica story hadn't yet been published.[14]

Alito said he accepted the flight on Singer's private plane because the seat otherwise would have gone unoccupied. He downplayed the level of luxury at the fishing lodge. He said his decision not to disclose the trip on his ethics filings was consistent with his fellow justices' interpretation of the rules at the time. The *Journal*'s editorial page followed up with an unsigned editorial entitled "ProPublica's Fishing Trip for Justice Alito," which it called "a non-scandal built on partisan spin intended to harm the Justice."[15]

The unorthodox "prebuttal" and the *Journal* editorial page's complicity in it reflected the sense of outrage among conservatives at what they saw as belated attempts to discredit the *Dobbs* decision by highlighting old news as if to expose current-day biases. Alito sought and received refuge on friendly turf—the *Journal*'s opinion pages. This was not unusual for him, since most of his interviews since joining the court had been with conservative think tanks or sympathetic news outlets, and most of his speeches were before conservative or religious audiences. His distrust of mainstream media and academia was palpable.[16]

"I marvel at all the nonsense that has been written about me in the last year," he told the *Journal* a month later. He noted that the traditional expectation of judges has been to "remain mute" and let the legal establishment defend them. "But that's not happening," he said. "And so at a certain point I've said to myself, nobody else is going to do this, so I have to defend myself."[17]

Nonetheless, the ProPublica report was revealing in a way that neither Alito nor the *Journal* acknowledged. The point wasn't strictly that Alito had dodged the disclosure requirements, whether that was because of his own evasiveness (the previous year he had reported "getting $500 of Italian food and wine from a friend," but then neglected to mention the much more valuable fishing trip),[18] or because the court's interpretation of the rules was vague. Rather, he was providing important face time to two supporters of Leo and the conservative legal movement, one of whom had business interests that could easily come before the court. That he presented the trip as entirely personal hospitality—a group of pals heading off for a fun time together—was exactly what his hosts wanted.

In 2014, when Singer's dispute with Argentina went before the Supreme Court, it voted 7–1 in favor of his hedge fund, with Alito in the majority.[19]

. . . .

THE CONCEPT OF CLOSING ranks around the conservative justices, keeping them comfortable in like-minded company, was very much on the minds of religious right leaders. In their view, previous Republican appointees went soft because of the Washington social environment. When erstwhile conservatives started attending big DC social events, hobnobbing with journalists and ambassadors, they began to speak the language of the capital. When their children attended the right private schools and their spouses joined the right charities, they became full-fledged Washingtonians. The culture and values of the liberal elite seeped into their DNA, as if by osmosis.

To counter that, conservative activists sought to create their own cozy social environments, awards dinners, and community of friends who most emphatically did not share the values of the liberal elite. Rev. Rob Schenck, a pro-life leader famed for once handing President Bill Clinton a human fetus in a plastic container, organized events such as the "National Memorial for the Pre-Born and Their Mothers and Fathers," a live Christmas nativity scene at the US Capitol, Bible studies for members of Congress, prayer meetings in front of government buildings, and many others.[20]

But by his account, his prime focus was Operation Higher Court. This was an effort to infiltrate the social lives of the conservative justices. Schenck himself attended Supreme Court hearings, Supreme Court Historical Society events, and social receptions to cultivate relationships with the justices.[21]

His prime initiative was recruiting wealthy couples who shared the social values of the justices and then playing matchmaker.[22] Scalia, Thomas, and Alito were each fat targets in different ways. The first two, Schenck came to realize, enjoyed being wined and dined,[23] living the high life that was a little beyond the means of the justices' generous but not exorbitant salaries ($303,600 in 2025).[24] Sam and Martha-Ann Alito, by contrast, did not have lavish tastes, but they hungered for the companionship of a similarly devout couple. He found one in Don and Gayle Wright of Dayton, Ohio, who were major funders of Schenck's operation. Thus began a series of social encounters in which the Wrights hosted the Alitos, and sometimes vice versa, with the Wrights then secretly reporting back to Schenck.[25]

Don Wright passed away in 2020, but Gayle Wright denied being part of any scheme.[26] Schenck, however, maintained that he coached all the volunteers, including the Wrights, in how to use lines like "the importance of a child having a father and a mother" and "We believe you are here for a time like this."[27] The idea was to reinforce the sense of mission that the religiously inspired justices already felt, but that might be mitigated by exposure to liberal friends and neighbors.[28]

Schenck said he knew from Supreme Court events that Sam Alito was intensely shy—"he would often shrink toward the wall, literally." Martha-Ann, by contrast, was not only the social butterfly in the couple but also the more assertive in her faith. "I always saw her as the religious leader in their relationship, and he followed in her wake," Schenck said. "She was more culturally conscious of what was happening in the conservative stream." He would thus caucus with the Wrights to discuss appropriate gifts for the couple.[29] Schenck called it "our ministry of emboldenment"—spurring the justices to act on their religious beliefs—and Alito was an easy sell.

"Alito, in particular, was quite insular," Schenck said, meaning that he interacted only with people who shared his views. "Oddly, I saw Clarence Thomas as a little more adventuresome in his conversation partners. And then Scalia was more able to entertain how other people saw the core issues and causes, without seeing them as communistic or atheistic . . . Scalia had a degree of humility that the others didn't."[30]

The collapse of Operation Higher Court came not from exposure but from an attack of conscience by Schenck himself. Surprisingly, it wasn't because of the gross betrayal of privacy and friendship inherent in recruiting couples to befriend the justices, but because of something far deeper: he began to question the precepts of the religious right. It started with a nagging sense that his friends weren't on the right side of gun control; some of the same people who grieved for the unborn were unmoved by victims of mass shootings. And pretty soon he was, in his words, "questioning my religious community's positions on guns, abortion, same-sex marriage, and religious liberty . . . I eventually broke with the orthodoxy I had long followed and became a dissenting voice among my culturally and theologically conservative peers."[31]

But he had one more secret to reveal. The Alitos, he claimed, had given the Wrights advance word of the *Hobby Lobby* decision in 2014; Schenck said Gayle Wright called him with the good news weeks before the decision was announced.[32] This was Sam's biggest victory up to that point—successfully persuading his colleagues to stand up for a religious person's right to violate the mandate to provide contraceptives to his workers. But if he or Martha-Ann let the cat out of the bag early, how different was that from the actions of the person who leaked the draft of *Dobbs*?

Alito and Gayle Wright denied it. But Schenck, who testified before Congress and shared details with reporters, insisted that in the privacy of a friendship with fellow religious believers, one or both of the Alitos couldn't resist touting the upcoming *Hobby Lobby* announcement.[33]

Three years after Schenck's testimony, retired Justice Kennedy wrote in his memoir how he never discussed cases with his wife. "Mary, as usual, had no idea the case had been assigned to me and no idea what writing was going on in my home office," Kennedy said of his big opinion in the *Obergefell* case. "We did not discuss pending cases. In my view this could violate my judicial duty and confidentiality."[34]

....

WHILE ALITO'S SHYNESS MADE an impression on Schenck, there was one venue where he felt more comfortable: in the presence of his former clerks. Across the American justice system, there is often a special bond between judges and the young people who assist them. By its nature, the relationship is close and cooperative. The judges and justices then serve as job references for the clerks, and after the justices have left the scene, the clerks can often provide a living record of what transpired in those chambers so many decades earlier.

But while judges and clerks were always connected, recent trends conspired to make Alito's bonds with his former assistants even tighter. Some of these trends played out across the justice system; others were furthered by Alito himself.

Clerks had always been drawn disproportionately from the top law schools. More than half of those who served on the Supreme Court between 1950 and 2024 graduated from either Harvard, Yale, or Stanford.[35] Alito's clerks were no exception: Of his eighty-seven clerks between 2006 and 2025, 51.7 percent went to those three law schools, just a tick below the overall average of 52.6 percent.[36] The numbers were boosted by his own alma mater of Yale Law School, from which he chose a whopping 28.7 percent.[37]

But if the educational backgrounds of Supreme Court clerks were largely the same as ever, their judicial philosophies were not. Adam Feldman, a writer at *SCOTUSblog*, noted that compared to earlier eras, Supreme Court justices were more likely to choose their clerks from circuit court judges who were appointed by the same party as themselves. Only three justices had sizable proportions of clerks who came from judges appointed by the opposite party: Kagan at 26.3 percent, Roberts at 25.0 percent, and Sotomayor at 20.8 percent. By contrast, Alito and Thomas stood out for almost never having chosen a clerk from a judge appointed by the Democratic Party.[38] That meant Alito and Thomas were so committed to their conservative approach to the law that they wouldn't allow a clerk into their chambers who wasn't already exposed to it—or in most cases, committed to it.[39]

This was more likely to be the case because Alito tended to draw older clerks who had more years after law school to establish their conservative bona fides; of the nine justices, Alito's clerks were the third-oldest group after Gorsuch's and Jackson's.[40]

Alito also relied heavily on his former clerks from the Third Circuit. In his first five years on the Supreme Court, he selected eleven former clerks, reflecting his trust in a small inner circle.[41] The other six circuit judges from whom Alito drew the majority of his clerks were all Federalist Society stalwarts, known for their conservatism. They included Judges Thomas B. Griffith, Amul Thapar, William H. Pryor, Thomas Hardiman, Jeffrey Sutton, and—prior to his own elevation to the court—Brett Kavanaugh.[42] This made Alito's chambers a hub of conservative thinking, where different strands of originalism came together.

Not surprisingly, over a dozen of Alito's clerks went on to become officials in Donald Trump's administrations. Others became federal judges, law school professors, and aides to politicians (including Florida Governor Ron DeSantis and Texas Attorney General Ken Paxton). One became a US senator and another joined Elon Musk's DOGE team to cut government spending.[43] Adam Ciongoli, the former Alito circuit court clerk whom he brought to the Supreme Court in 2006, went on to be chief legal and policy officer at Fox Corporation.[44] Hannah Clayson Smith, the other circuit court clerk he brought to the Supreme Court, became a leader of Brigham Young University's International Center for Law and Religious Studies.[45] Two former Alito clerks crossed the aisle to go to work for Biden's administration or campaign.[46] But when it came time for political contributions, all but three former clerks gave only to Republican candidates.[47]

Both Sam and Martha-Ann Alito kept in touch with the former clerks, congratulating them on marriages and the births of their children, while encouraging them to think of themselves as a team. Many remained close friends with Sam, sharing details about their personal lives, careers, and developments in the law. At Supreme Court events, receptions, or formal reunions, the Alitos played host to the entire group, like proud parents welcoming the extended family for a holiday meal.[48]

But for those who didn't entirely share Alito's judicial philosophy, the cocktail-fueled events were a jarring demonstration of groupthink. The most conservative ex-clerks formed a phalanx around the Alitos, cheering on legal and political victories for their side while disdaining the other. These clerks made real what Rev. Robert Schenck had only attempted: they cosseted the justice in a way that left little room for ideological movement without risking the disappointment of those whose validation mattered the most.[49]

....

MARTHA-ANN ALITO WAS ALWAYS the expressive one in her family. Sometimes, it seemed like she would be doing all the talking and feeling and emoting for herself and Sam combined. From old friends to new friends, from court colleagues to clerks, almost everyone got that impression.[50] And one of the ways she registered her feelings defied easy explanation. Like a fairy-tale heroine trapped in a tower, she would send signals in the choice of flag she flew outside her home.

Indeed, the very cul-de-sac on which was the handsome colonial-style home where she and Sam lived often felt like hostile territory, even before her property was rimmed with security. That was because of her mistrust of her liberal neighbors. At the entrance to the cul-de-sac was the most visible house in the neighborhood, and its occupants took full advantage of their corner lot to register their liberal political views through their choice of lawn decorations.

"We always have yard signs during any election, and we would always have bumper stickers on my car—lots of, like, anti-Bush stuff," said Emily Baden, who grew up there.[51] As it happened, Emily and her husband-to-be returned to the neighborhood during the Covid-19 pandemic to shelter with her mother—a time that coincided with the election of 2020. When

Biden was declared the winner, Baden and her family expressed their pleasure by making and displaying a sign that said "Bye, Don" on one side and "Fuck Trump" on the other.

When, some weeks later, the sign blew down in a stiff breeze, a car stopped while Emily was outside. "Thank you for taking the sign down," said an older woman whom she belatedly recognized as Martha-Ann Alito. Emily hadn't realized the sign had fallen, but she had no intention of repressing her feelings about Trump. So, after the woman pulled away, Emily put the sign back up.

On January 6, 2021—Emily remembers it as just hours after the pro-Trump mob overran the Capitol—Emily and her fiancé were in their car when another car pulled up. It was Martha-Ann again, and she just stared angrily at them.[52] Unbeknownst to Emily—because she couldn't see the Alitos' house from her house—Martha-Ann then flew an upside-down American flag, a symbol of the pro-Trump resistance, for several days.[53]

More than three years later, when *The New York Times* reported the story, the feud between the Alitos and the Badens became international news. The notion that a Supreme Court justice would have a pro-Trump flag outside his house during the tense period between January 6 and Biden's inauguration on January 20 was shocking to a great number of people. That was when many Trump supporters with long-shot legal challenges to the election results were desperately trying to get their appeals heard by the Supreme Court. How could a justice who was prepared to review such petitions be displaying the very symbol used by militant Trump supporters?

Alito blamed Martha-Ann and the Badens. "I had no involvement whatsoever in the flying of the flag," he said in an email to *The Times*. "It was briefly placed by Mrs. Alito in response to a neighbor's use of objectionable and personally insulting language on yard signs."[54]

Alito soon elaborated in an interview with Fox News. The neighbor's "vulgar" anti-Trump sign was opposite a school-bus stop, he said, and Martha-Ann had objected for that reason. Then the neighbors turned on her, posting signs blaming her for the January 6 attacks and, in a personal confrontation, using profane language "including the C-word."[55]

Emily Baden, for her part, said there was no sign blaming Martha-Ann for January 6, and that the personal clash was on January 20, the day of the inauguration. That would place it after the upside-down flag flew over the Alito home, not before. She claimed that Martha-Ann had initiated the exchange of bad language. But Emily also acknowledged losing her temper, using the C-word in reference to Mrs. Alito, and then turning on the justice himself: "I was like, 'How dare you? You're a Supreme Court justice . . . and this is how you're behaving and this is how you're treating your neighbors? You should be ashamed.'" Alito, by her account, maintained his dignity. "He kept walking," she said. "He did not respond. And I mean, I understand. I wouldn't if I were him."[56]

The same week as the dust-up over the upside-down flag was unfolding, *The Times* reported that an Appeal to Heaven Flag, a pine-tree symbol often associated with both Trumpian resistance and a desire for a more Christian nation, flew on at least four different dates outside the Alitos' beach retreat at the Jersey Shore.[57] Alito said his wife chose the symbol, which dated from the Revolutionary War, to honor George Washington. He said he was unaware of any pro-Trump connotations.[58]

The flag disputes provoked genuine outrage among liberals, who felt that the justice was hiding his own biases behind Martha-Ann, whom he did not even criticize for her flag choices. But the timing—once again, after the *Dobbs* decision—struck conservatives as an attempt at character assassination. *National Review* ran a piece entitled "The *New York Times*' Specious Crusade Against Justice Alito."[59] Certainly, Sam and Martha-Ann saw the stories as part of the post-*Dobbs* turmoil spilling over into their private lives.

Indeed, after the *Dobbs* decision was leaked, Emily Baden's mother invited her extended family, cousins and all, to come watch the protest march to the Alitos' house. "She put the fire pit in the front yard and she got, you know, chips and dips and stuff like that, and gave it to the protesters," Emily recalled. "Like, to be friendly and like in solidarity."[60]

For the Alitos, there was one more indignity to come. A liberal activist named Lauren Windsor bought tickets to a Supreme Court Historical Society reception and secretly tape-recorded the Alitos. Posing as a Catholic conservative, Windsor goaded Alito into agreeing that there can be no compromise between godly values and secular liberalism. "One side or the other is going to win," he said. "There can be a way of working, a way of living together peacefully, but it's difficult, you know, because there are differences on fundamental things that can't really be compromised."[61]

Martha-Ann was, as usual, far saucier. Having weathered her flag controversy, she told Windsor that "if they come back for me, I'll get them, I'm gonna be liberated." She recounted confronting Robin Givhan about the long-ago column attacking her style of dress. "My heritage is German," she said. "You come after me, I'm going to give it back to you, and there will be a way—it doesn't have to be now—but there will be a way they will know. Don't worry about it. God—you read the Bible—Psalm 27 is my psalm, mine. Psalm 27: 'The Lord is my God and my rock, of whom shall I be afraid?'"

Her husband, she said, doesn't control her. "The feminazis believe he should control me. They can go to hell."

But she acknowledged that Sam begged her not to put up another edgy flag, and she agreed to put it off. She also talked about all the different flags she would like to display.

"I want a Sacred Heart of Jesus flag," she said, "because I have to look across the lagoon at the pride flag for the next month."[62]

. . . .

FOR ALL THE HOSTILE revelations that followed the *Dobbs* decision, the Alitos also enjoyed corresponding outbursts of praise. The overturning of *Roe v. Wade* had deep meaning for those who felt a religious opposition to abortion. They admired Alito's courage. He had achieved what others had only aspired to: he was taking the slings and arrows for them.

Alito's advocacy for the rights of religious people, in the face of fury from feminists and gay-rights supporters, had long given him heightened respect from conservative Catholic organizations. Catholic groups honored him at every stage of his career, from his arrival on the court, after which the Diocese of Trenton gave him its St. Thomas More Society

Award,[63] to his *Hobby Lobby* decision, after which he received the Man for All Seasons Award from the St. Thomas More Society of Maryland,[64] to *Dobbs*, after which he earned an honorary degree from the Franciscan University of Steubenville, Ohio.[65]

There were many similar honors in between, in both the United States and Italy, including a knightship from an ancient Catholic order.[66] This approval from his fellow believers meant a lot to Alito, as he attested in speeches. And it provided yet another social validation for his conservative jurisprudence.

He wasn't the only justice to have taken bows before the faithful, however. In 2004, Justice Ginsburg allowed her name to be used on a lectureship for the NOW Legal Defense and Education Fund, a pro-choice women's group. She accepted awards from Jewish groups, spoke before the American Constitution Society, and appeared in a theatrical movie on her life. By the time of her death, she was an icon of liberal resistance, celebrated in documentaries and in shelves of books with titles such as *I Dissent*.[67]

The loosening of self-restraint across the judicial spectrum—a phenomenon which has paralleled the rise in contentious confirmations and the growth of the Federalist Society and the ACS—has given justices further incentive to stay in their lanes, serve those who appointed them, and emerge with a core of supporters.

As Alito himself alluded to, judges were supposed to keep quiet and let the legal establishment defend them; showing dignity and adhering to ethics were once the path to approval.[68] In later eras, however, approval started to come from larger numbers of agenda-driven supporters.

....

THE SENSE OF A double standard between liberal jurists—who receive approbation from universities and bar associations without any feeling of being compromised—and their conservative counterparts—whose backers are often portrayed as corrupting influences—drives much of the defense of Alito. Even conservatives who shudder at Clarence Thomas's unpaid luxury vacations or the Alitos' flagpole messages feel compelled to defend them; each justice is synonymous with an enterprise larger than himself.

In the years after the *Dobbs* decision, conservative law professors gave respectful attention to Alito's jurisprudence, casting an academic lens on his methods of interpreting the Constitution. They concluded he was not a results-oriented judge, but rather the architect of durable principles that would outlive his time on the bench.

"Samuel A. Alito, Jr. was sworn into office . . . on January 31, 2006," wrote Princeton professor Robert P. George. "As we can say with the benefit of hindsight, that proved to be one of the pivotal moments in the Supreme Court's modern history, with deep and lasting effects on our constitutional law and culture, as well as on the nation as a whole."[69]

In 2023, George, who holds the same position at Princeton that Walter Murphy held in Alito's student days, convened a dream team of conservative academics to write papers analyzing Alito's approach to the law. In his introductory essay, he praised Alito's consistency, modesty—in not seeking attention through "virtue-signaling"—and courage in never "pulling punches to win favor or avoid opprobrium—or even to abate a real and credible risk to his life."[70]

Many sought to distinguish Alito's views from those of other conservative jurists. They concentrated on his belief that the Constitution embodies the history and traditions of the American people up to the time it was written. In *Dobbs* and other cases, he has insisted that the Fourteenth Amendment protects only those rights deeply rooted in the culture at the time of its ratification; he has used a similar rationale to hold that the Fourteenth Amendment confers a right to gun ownership. While other conservatives bored in on the intentions of the framers or the literal meaning of the text, Alito used history and tradition to discern an everyman's understanding of constitutional provisions. This mode of analysis sometimes led him to different conclusions than other conservatives.

Justice Gorsuch, for instance, is an avowed textualist who seized on the word "sex" to hold that an antidiscrimination law covers sexual orientation as well as gender; Alito disagreed.[71] Justice Scalia's intensive focus on the original intentions of the framers led him to side with liberals in free-speech cases and regard police officers who planted a GPS device on a suspect's car as trespassing on private property. Alito, by contrast, favored curbs on deeply offensive speech and felt that police should be free to use tracking devices unless they violated the subject's reasonable expectation of privacy.[72]

In most cases where Alito's analysis differed from that of fellow conservatives, it led him to a more politically conservative outcome.

In a 2019 law review article, Steven Calabresi pointed to how Alito, who had never been a professor, rejected the rote application of theory. Referring to the GPS case, Calabresi and a co-author wrote that unlike Scalia, Alito was more concerned with practical application of the rule than the theory behind it: "To the majority interpretive theory preceded fact. Yet to Justice Alito, fact preceded interpretive theory."[73]

Alito himself expressed admiration for Edmund Burke, the eighteenth-century British political philosopher who defended the American Revolution and backed the Catholic Church against the excesses of the French Revolution.[74] Burke believed that nations were tied together by history and tradition; in his view, radical change was dangerous while well-established practices deserved greater deference.

Thus, Adam White of George Mason University called Alito's conservatism "Burkean and American" and said his sense of tradition was inspired by his immigrant ancestors and skepticism of academia. "He begins with legal principle, and applies legal theories, but he is cognizant of the practical limits of theory, and he understands that practical experience helps to bring the principles themselves into clearer view," wrote White.[75]

White's essay inevitably raises the question of whether Alito's conservatism has any objective standards—or if it is just as open-ended as the theories of liberals who believe in evolving standards of justice. Alito has long accused liberals of interpreting the Constitution in ways that achieve their favored outcomes. Could the same be said of Alito's practical application of history and tradition?

White introduces the idea to dismiss it. As "the new generation of conservative legal scholars and judges moves from a posture of judicial restraint to a posture of judicial creativity," he wrote, the charge of making up rules to suit their own preferences "will apply to them, too."[76]

But Alito, he concluded, is unlikely to go along.

....

DOBBS WAS THE END of the nearly fifty-year fight to overturn *Roe*; it was also the beginning of a string of cases in which the Supreme Court's conservative majority delivered on its long-sought goals.

A year after *Dobbs*, the justices struck down the use of race in college admissions, an issue that was instrumental in the growth of the Federalist Society. Georgetown University law professor Charles F. Abernathy, who was an adviser to his university's first Federalist Society chapter, said it was made up of students whose families were "the minorities of the 1920s," primarily Irish Americans and Italian Americans. They "felt they had overcome discrimination but were now facing discrimination again under affirmative action," he said.[77]

As of 2023, however, affirmative action was over, in a case rejecting the admissions criteria at Harvard University and the University of North Carolina.[78] Alito joined the 6–3 majority, with the three Democratic appointees dissenting.

A year later, the court struck down a forty-year precedent giving deference to independent agencies in interpreting the laws that govern them. In practice, the so-called *Chevron* doctrine enabled the Environmental Protection Agency and its ilk to set rules for industries without the constant threat of litigation (the firms involved wanted a better chance to challenge their fines and regulations in court). For decades, conservative groups had clamored for a change in the law, while the justices delicately skirted around the doctrine.

In 2024, in a case involving fishing companies that were ordered to pay for on-board monitors to enforce their catch limits, the court overruled *Chevron v. National Resources Defense Council*.[79] Quoting the Federalist Papers, Chief Justice Roberts, writing for the six Republican-appointed justices, stressed that the framers of the Constitution entrusted the courts with "the final 'interpretation of the laws,'" and that such a responsibility cannot be delegated to independent agencies.[80]

Justice Kagan, in dissent, argued that the *Chevron* doctrine, which has been applied to thousands of cases, had become part of "the warp and woof of modern government," and that independent agencies have far greater expertise in making intricate policy decisions than courts. By heightening judicial review, she predicted, the Supreme Court would slow down decision-making and hamper the agencies' ability to do their jobs.[81]

Then came the most contentious decision of them all—and yet another instance of the justices splitting exactly along party lines.

Former President Donald Trump, who was campaigning to win back his job, had been charged with crimes by state authorities in New York and Georgia and in two separate federal indictments; in the New York case, he was tried and convicted of falsifying business records to hide payments to an adult film star who threatened to reveal their alleged sexual relationship. But Trump claimed broad immunity from prosecution as a former president. The justices undertook a lengthy review.

When their decision came down, on July 1, 2024, it was seen as a sweeping victory for Trump.[82] Led by Chief Justice Roberts, the six conservative justices granted the former president absolute immunity for his core constitutional functions and a presumption of immunity for official acts beyond his core functions. The court further ruled that official acts could not be used as evidence in cases alleging wrongdoing outside of his official functions.[83] In the federal case involving Trump's actions related to the mob that ransacked the Capitol on January 6, 2021, it could prove difficult to separate official from unofficial acts; so too with the Georgia case involving Trump's alleged attempts to pressure state officials to overturn the election.

The six conservative justices, however, were deeply concerned that a president might be inhibited in performing "the duties of his office fearlessly and fairly" if he had to worry about future prosecutions. Roberts seized on language in a 1982 case granting former President Richard

Nixon immunity from civil lawsuits to justify expanding such immunity to criminal matters.[84] "Potential criminal liability, and the peculiar public opprobrium that attaches to criminal proceedings," Roberts wrote, "are plainly more likely to distort Presidential decisionmaking than the potential payment of civil damages."[85]

Both Jackson and Sotomayor wrote dissents suggesting the court had placed the president above the law. There was no discernible guidance from the framers of the Constitution, no original understanding to draw from: the conservative justices were simply wielding power as they saw fit.

"Argument by argument, the majority invents immunity through brute force," wrote Sotomayor.[86]

But for the foreseeable future, the conservatives had force on their side.

"Things Have Unfortunately Changed a Lot"

On November 5, 2025, exactly one year after Donald Trump's reelection, the Supreme Court convened to hear a challenge to the president's ability to levy tariffs on foreign goods. Imposing large duties on America's trading partners was a centerpiece of Trump's agenda, but it rested on a rickety legal platform: a 1977 law that gave the president the power to regulate imports and exports in the face of "unusual" or "extraordinary" threats.[1] Whether Trump's tariffs were, in fact, a response to unusual threats wasn't the main question before the court. The law itself didn't mention tariffs, and legal experts on the left and the right seemed equally skeptical about whether it would allow a president to impose tariffs in any situation.

The same skepticism was evident on the bench. A federal appeals court had struck down the tariffs, and at the Supreme Court hearing, conservative justices and their liberal colleagues took turns grilling Trump's solicitor general, D. John Sauer. By contrast, Neal Katyal, the attorney representing several educational toy companies that were fighting to avoid the tariffs, was having an easier time. Until Justice Alito peered down from the bench.[2]

He pointed to a 1930 statute that Trump's lawyers hadn't mentioned, but that Alito posited could "provide a basis for all or virtually all of the tariffs that are at issue here."

Katyal seemed taken aback and claimed that the case must be decided on the terms under which Trump issued the tariffs; other arguments shouldn't apply.

"Justice Alito, I think that [argument] is forfeited—forfeited nine ways to Sunday," Katyal said of his claim.[3]

This exchange prompted an unusual editorial from *National Review*, the publication that Alito revered during his formative years. Like some other conservative journals that predated Trump, *National Review* was skeptical of his tariffs and didn't appreciate Alito's jumping in to try to save the day for the president. "Justice Samuel Alito expressed frustration that Trump had not cited other arguable sources of tariff authority, but it is not the Court's job to opine on powers the president has not invoked," the editors wrote.[4] It was a notable swipe at the justice the journal had defended strongly in the wake of the *Dobbs* decision.

It can be foolhardy to read too much into justices' questions from the bench. Often, they raise issues speculatively, only to disregard them when it comes to making a ruling. But the fact that *National Review* would portray Alito as a predictable shill for Trump was noteworthy.

The second Trump administration presented near-constant challenges for the Supreme Court and its conservative majority. During the 2024 campaign, Trump told Fox News host Sean Hannity that he would be a dictator on "day one."[5] Like earlier Trump promises to ban all Muslims or force Mexico to pay for a border wall, the assertion of dictatorial ambitions served Trump's purposes in two ways: voters who wanted a president to rule with a strong hand accepted the comment approvingly, while others waved it off as a show of bombast. Trump didn't talk like a politician, which was good, but it meant you couldn't take everything he said literally.

The dictator comment, however, presaged a spate of unusually aggressive actions that threatened to upend the state of the law. These included the hundreds of billions of dollars in tariffs enacted and retracted at Trump's whims, an attempt to deport Venezuelans without a hearing, an executive order ending birthright citizenship, several commands to overrule state governors in deploying the National Guard in American cities, efforts to unilaterally fire board members of the Federal Reserve and other independent agencies, the dismantling of agencies fully funded by Congress, demands that the Justice Department investigate the president's critics, military attacks on boats suspected of carrying illegal drugs, and many more.[6]

Tasked with determining the legality of these largely unprecedented moves, district court judges issued injunctions at a frenzied pace. Circuit courts rushed to review the district courts. And the Supreme Court often weighed in on an emergency basis.[7] Such a situation presented a challenge to the justices' stamina but also their impartiality. Their decisions would set parameters for presidential power for generations. It would be just as dangerous for them to curtail an important presidential power over Trump's misuse of it as it would be to extend greater presidential discretion in sympathy for Trump's positions.

Throughout the summer and fall, as the court considered emergency injunctions on numerous presidential orders, Alito was a consistent and often vociferous Trump supporter. While Trump's own appointees—Barrett, Gorsuch, and Kavanaugh—appeared willing at times to rein in the president, Alito and Thomas did not. When the court agreed to keep in place a lower-court order blocking Trump from withholding $2 billion in funds owed to USAID contractors whose work was already completed, Alito was outraged.

"Today, the Court makes a most unfortunate misstep that rewards an act of judicial hubris and imposes a $2 billion penalty on American taxpayers," he wrote in dissent.[8]

. . . .

BY THE TIME OF the tariffs case, the conservative legal movement had come into sharper focus: it was not an offshoot of MAGA, no matter how much Trump wanted it to be. It had a power over MAGA that liberalism—their common enemy—did not. It was, in fact, the only force strong enough to restore the legal norms violated by Trump, stopping MAGA in its tracks. But it was not clear if it would do so.[9]

The tension was palpable in November 2025, when the Federalist Society gathered in Washington for its first National Lawyers Convention of the second Trump administration. The awkwardness was felt more in the audience than on stage.[10] In its programming, the society avoided the big points of contention—tariffs, extra-legal killings, birthright citizenship, sharp deviations from Justice Department procedures allowing Trump to assume the role of prosecutor-in-chief. When such issues came up, it was mostly in controlled settings, and the responses were political, not legal.

Deputy Attorney General Todd Blanche agreed to a "fireside chat" with Gene P. Hamilton of the America First Legal Foundation, a group founded by Trump aide Stephen Miller, the architect of the administration's immigration policies.[11] Choosing two unabashed Trump supporters to conduct the conversation was hardly an act of bravery by the convention organizers, and Hamilton obliged by lobbing softball questions about immigration, gun rights, human trafficking, antisemitism, and more.

The two MAGA allies wanted to remind the Federalist Society of all that they, collectively, agreed upon. Nonetheless, Blanche and Hamilton didn't entirely avoid controversy. Hamilton ever so gently alluded to "a lot of criticism of the department today, saying that the department is, in fact, engaged in weaponization of government against its opponents."[12]

The question came about six weeks after Erik Siebert, the interim US attorney for the Eastern District of Virginia, resigned his position. Siebert had resisted pressure from Trump to indict New York Attorney General Letitia James, who had brought civil actions against Trump's businesses,[13] and he had also balked when the department pursued a highly questionable case against another Trump antagonist, former FBI Director James Comey.[14]

Blanche didn't address those matters. Instead, he delivered a full-throated Trumpian attack on Joe Biden's "batshit crazy" Justice Department. He claimed that "nearly every member of President Trump's last administration, some of whom are in this room, had to go in front of a grand jury over one reason or another." So, he added, "when I read now that we're weaponizing, I feel like I'm being gaslit because we're doing exactly the opposite." He later reinforced his point: "This DOJ is not weaponized in any way, shape, or form. It's absolutely not."[15]

Blanche's insistent rhetoric, absent any underlying argument, sounded a warning to Federalist Society members: Trump is their president, and he demands loyalty. Attack Trump and risk a return to Democratic leadership.

For the dozens of federal judges attending the conference—many of them appointed by Trump—the comments likely echoed the president's own oft-stated expectations of their fidelity. When Trump-appointed judges joined their colleagues in blocking some early second-term initiatives, the president erupted in fury against Leonard Leo, who had advised him on his first-term judicial nominations. In an example of his shoot-to-kill rhetoric, Trump mimicked Democratic conspiracy theories about Leo, calling him a "sleazebag" who "openly brags how he controls Judges." Leo's muted response was also telling: he still hoped to exert influence over Trump's second-term judicial choices.[16]

But this uneasy balancing of interests disguised a larger reality: powers granted to Trump would almost certainly be wielded by future Democratic presidents, and conservative judges must therefore be mindful of longer-term considerations. And whatever their common enemies, the Federalist Society and Trump were approaching problems from different angles.

MAGA was heavily blue collar; FedSoc was strictly white collar. MAGA was strongest in the South, Midwest, and mountain states; FedSoc leaders were disproportionately from the Northeast or elite Northeastern institutions. MAGA drew its greatest support from people with the least education; FedSoc members were among the highest-educated Americans.

And now, with the unifying priorities of abortion and affirmative action largely off the table, the Scotch tape that held the two groups together was starting to peel off.

Former Fourth Circuit Judge J. Michael Luttig, once the preferred choice among conservatives for the Supreme Court seat eventually occupied by Alito, was only the most outspoken of right-leaning professors and retired jurists to raise questions about Trump's upending of laws.

"The MAGA movement is a radical movement, and I would not even apply the label of conservative to it," Luttig said. "It is anti-law of the United States and anti-rule of law in the United States."[17]

. . . .

FOR ACTIVE JUDGES AND justices who owed their careers to the conservative legal movement, the question was this: Would they feel free to stand against the person who enabled their success, thus showing that their movement was greater than politics? Or had the intense partisanship of the Trump era so altered their internal feedback loops that they could not see beyond the us-and-them of recent decades?

Like Sam Alito, many of them had grown up with a sense that liberals were upending norms, asserting the supremacy of their values as if by fiat, and twisting American institutions to achieve their aims. While liberals may have viewed themselves as promoting a more inclusive, egalitarian America, conservatives saw the changes through the lens of personal ambition: liberal politicians and jurists were asserting power and lording it over the God-fearing Americans who didn't share their views.

Now those conservatives had the power and could do the same. They could abet Trump's efforts to stretch the law to suit his purposes. Or they could be an originalist bulwark, defenders of the Constitution as written and understood at its framing. But they'd have to decide which came first, conservatism or the Constitution.

Alito was especially vulnerable to a charge of partisanship because of his many strong stances against Biden administration initiatives. In 2023, for example, the states of Texas and Louisiana sued Biden's Homeland Security Department, claiming its policy of prioritizing the arrests of undocumented immigrants who had been convicted of felonies or posed a danger to public safety was too narrow; Congress had anticipated strict enforcement against all undocumented immigrants when it crafted the relevant statutes. Eight justices, led by Kavanaugh, concluded that the states lacked standing to sue over the president's interpretation of the law. Alito, however, stood alone in dissent. He blasted his colleagues for holding "that the only limit on the power of a President to disobey a law like the important provision at issue is Congress's power to employ the weapons of inter-branch warfare—withholding funds, impeachment and removal, etc. I would not blaze this unfortunate trail."[18]

Alito's call for limits on presidential discretion was surprising because he had long been a champion of executive power.[19] His concern over Biden's weakness obviously changed the equation. But would he be similarly moved in a case involving, say, President Trump's decision to dismantle USAID programs approved by Congress?

People who knew Alito before his ascent to power say they assumed he would be a truly equal jurist. The man who stood beside Bush and spoke of the "the solemn responsibility that goes with service as a federal judge" to "interpret the Constitution and the laws faithfully and fairly" rang true, even among those who didn't share his conservative beliefs. They trusted the testimony of his former clerks and Third Circuit colleagues that he wouldn't allow personal views to color the law.[20]

But after twenty years, changes in Alito's public posture and the atmosphere surrounding the court raised significant doubts. Many of his former friends, colleagues, and clerks saw him as a different man than the Sam they once knew.

"When he was on that short list, and a couple of newspaper and TV people came to interview me, and I had remembered saying Sam had a strong moral compass," said Elaine Tarr, the English teacher who came up with the special reading list of great books for her most prized pupil. "That's what I believed at the time—he was straight and narrow. I think he had a sense of right and wrong. Where Sam has picked up all of these ideas now, you've got me . . . How has he become this ultra, ultra conservative? I guess there were always those leanings there, but I had little opportunity to see those."[21]

Tarr has been revisiting her memories of Alito, looking for signs that she may have missed. "He was very responsible, made sure everything was on the dotted line," she recalled. "Even his penmanship was very well formed. There was nothing sloppy about it. He was very methodical, very methodical. Does that equate with rigidity? I'm not going to answer that one. How flexible a thinker was he? I'm not sure about that either."[22]

While most of Alito's Supreme Court clerks, culled from the ranks of the conservative legal movement, remain intensely loyal to him, some of his circuit court clerks have quietly drifted away. They, too, search for clues to how a man they regarded as uniquely committed to the nuts and bolts of the law became something of a revolutionary. "He was so humble," said one. "I'm shocked by who he is today."[23]

What sticks in their minds was their willingness back in 2005 to sign the letter saying it "never once appeared to us that Judge Alito pre-judged a case or ruled based on political ideology."[24] All fifty-four former clerks supported Alito.[25] The unanimity spoke volumes: it was the strongest refutation of the Democrats' claims that Alito had extreme views. If any of the clerks had refused their support, they would have damaged one of the Republicans' best talking points. President Bush even staged a press conference alongside the former Alito clerks to tout the fact that they included among their ranks people with "a wide range of political views. They share two things in common: They all clerked for Judge Sam Alito; and they strongly support his nomination."[26]

No one stuck his neck out further than David J. Stoll, who was active in Lambda Legal, the legal advocacy group for the LGBTQ+ community. Before he died in 2023, Stoll had come to regret his support for Alito.

"David did indeed do a lot of legal and personal work for Lambda and gay rights, and Lambda was very critical, with good reason, of David's support for Alito," recalled his widower, Cornell University professor Ellis Hanson. "I remember David was distressed by this criticism but seemed to find it understandable. Later, it did become clear to him that he had very deep political and legal differences of opinion with Alito, especially on the subjects of abortion, sodomy law, and gay marriage. Alito's opinions about gay marriage were so personally distressing to David that he drafted a letter to him at the time of *Obergefell v. Hodges* to explain his own personal stake in the question . . . I don't know, however, whether the letter was ever sent."

It wasn't just Alito's positions on gay issues that troubled Stoll; the justice's aggressive posture on the bench struck him as a surprise, according to Hanson. "David felt Alito's judgments became more ideologically motivated than he expected they would be."[27]

Andy Napolitano saw things much the same way. Alito's early friend from Princeton has stayed on good terms with the justice, spending time with him and Martha-Ann, even as his own politics evolved in a libertarian direction. Napolitano, who served as a New Jersey Superior Court judge and legal commentator on Fox News, said he too thought Alito became more conservative over time, even compared to when he first joined the Supreme Court.

"Sam is not an originalist," Napolitano said. "Sam is a conservative person who wants a conservative outcome . . . There's nothing wrong with that in the court in which he sits, because it's a court of last resort. If he was on the Third Circuit behaving that way, he'd get reversed a lot. But where he sits, he has the privilege of doing that. So I actually commend his candor, even though I disagree on almost all these issues."[28]

Other Princeton friends who've not kept up with the justice say they're struck by his demeanor most of all. The young man they knew was always polite and quietly witty. They couldn't envision him speaking out with such an edge in his voice.

"He certainly at Princeton, I would say, was just a nice guy, and bordering on humble," said one friend who went on to a legal career. "Nobody would describe him in his written opinions or from the bench as humble or a nice guy anymore . . . I listen to a lot of Supreme Court oral arguments, and sometimes I am shocked at the tone and the nastiness of some of his questions. I just can't believe that's my Sam Alito, but obviously my Sam Alito at the time was holding back, or he's evolved, or some of both."[29]

There are many theories about the sources of that change: bitter feelings engendered by the confirmation process; the cruelty of the Washington social scene; the all-encompassing nature of the conservative ecosystem, with its firm expectations of those it supports and nurtures. But those forces, such as they were, didn't fully explain what some old acquaintances believed was organic to Alito's makeup. And some of the people who grew up alongside him at Princeton and Yale Law School think they know what it is.

"The protests, the disruptions, the overwhelmingly anti-war, liberal atmosphere at Princeton had to have had some influence on him . . . pushing him to an even more conservative viewpoint," said his classmate George Carpinello. "I think he's different in demeanor than the person I knew. Maybe I didn't know him well enough."[30]

Dennis Grzezinski, who, like Carpinello, was at Princeton and Yale with Alito, said, "As I've watched as Sam has proceeded through recent history and become more and more vitriolic and embittered, I think some slice of what is behind Sam being who he is now is a reaction to behaviors and conduct by the probably overwhelmingly privileged rich folks who could do what they wanted without consequences, and doing things that Sam viewed as disrespectful of things that Sam cared about."[31]

....

ON APRIL 11, 2025, Princeton University named a building after and dedicated a portrait to one of its most revered alumni, a distinguished jurist. "With this portrait and naming, your remarkable legacy will be memorialized on campus for generations to come," said President Christopher Eisgruber.

The justice responded, "I am deeply touched to have my name become a permanent part of Princeton. Thank you, Princeton, for all I have become and for all the good your generations of students have brought into this world. My heart is bursting today with joy and gratitude . . . My unexpected life journey started the day I was accepted to attend this university. This is a place that helps make dreams come true, and this is the place from which the improbable happens."[32]

And then the justice, Sonia Sotomayor, stepped back to admire the oil painting and the building, which will house programs to support first-generation, lower-income, transfer, and veteran students.

Sotomayor entered Princeton the fall after Sam Alito graduated, but her class—the class of 1976—had a smoother ride. Women had been at Princeton for three years when she came to campus, and by the time she left, she had been honored with the university's highest undergraduate award, the Moses Taylor Pyne Honor Prize. In her speech accepting the Pyne Prize, the young Sotomayor called for "a new era in which Princeton's traditions can be further enriched by being broadened to accommodate and harmonize with the beat of those of us who march to different drummers."[33]

Sotomayor went on to be a pioneer, the first Hispanic justice on the Supreme Court, and a noted liberal, from her strong support for abortion rights to her forceful dissent in *Trump v. United States*. There was no equivalent honor at Princeton for Samuel Alito, even though he graduated four years earlier and had been on the Supreme Court nearly four years longer. Princeton was Sotomayor's turf, not Alito's.

Visiting the storied campus for the first time, the Bronx-born daughter of parents from Puerto Rico shared many of the same anxieties as the son of an Italian immigrant from the Trenton area. She compared the experience to "a visitor landing in an alien country."[34] But subsequent events, and the different paths of the two students, led the university to embrace one and not the other.

It's part of the paradox of American life since the 1960s. Women, non-white students, and others who "march to different drummers" often felt alienated and out of place jousting with the history and traditions of formerly all-male, all-wealthy institutions. Eventually, moving at varying rates of speed, the institutions evolved in their images. Yet there was another group that felt equally out of place, and the institutions did not move in their direction at all.

The Federalist Society and other conservative institutions that welcomed Alito filled a void that Princeton and its ilk left open. They were the parallel universe in which those who disagreed with a half-century of changes in university life could thrive.

Alito's Supreme Court nomination brought attention to Princeton, but not in a positive way. There was the blow-up over CAP, which reminded the world of the extent to which alumni fought to preserve the old order at the time of coeducation and outreach to minorities. And then there was Alito's unflattering depiction of his own undergraduate years, watching "very privileged people behaving irresponsibly."[35]

"There's an inconsistency," Joanna Friedman, the president of the debate team at the Whig-Clio society, told *The New York Times* in 2006. "We're all very excited for him, but I wonder how Alito feels about us."[36]

For the next twenty years, Alito's friend and admirer Robert P. George taught the fabled undergraduate law course that dated back to Woodrow Wilson's time. A highly respected conservative theorist and beloved teacher, George was proof that the depiction of Princeton as unflinchingly liberal and profoundly unreceptive to conservatives was exaggerated.[37]

While Alito's memories of "very privileged people behaving irresponsibly" were directed at liberals, Princeton liberals used similar terms to critique their own antagonists. When news of Alito's *Dobbs* decision leaked out, many women of the class of 1972 saw it not as a refutation of elitist thinking but as a revival of the old misogyny. The campus they remembered was hardly a progressive paradise. And it galled them that while women later won the Battle of Princeton, they lost the battle for justice.

The fact that their own classmate was the vehicle for this defeat prompted them to spring into action. Thirty-four women from the historic class of 1972—all transfer students—came together to call out Alito. "We, the undersigned women of '72, have been deeply shocked by the leaked Supreme Court draft authored by our classmate Justice Samuel Alito," they wrote in an open letter published in the *Princeton Alumni Weekly*. "As a pioneering class of Princeton women, we find it bitter indeed to see the draft Supreme Court opinion reverse the strides we thought we were making . . . The right to manage one's own health and most intimate personal and family decisions without outside interference is at risk right now and should be preserved to ensure social justice for ourselves, our classmates, and the world Princeton purports to serve."[38]

The letter generated expressions of support from other Princeton alumni, including a group of seventy-nine men from the class of 1972. Their own letter endorsed the views of their "sister classmates" and condemned "the draft *Dobbs* opinion, not Sam personally." But they acknowledged, in a tone dripping with guilt, the struggles that their female classmates had faced back in the day.

"Ours was the last all-male freshman class admitted to Princeton," they wrote. "Our female classmates joined us in the following years, at a time of major transitions and turmoil occurring both on Princeton's campus and in the nation at large. Despite at times enduring heavy headwinds, they have distinguished themselves, our class, and the University during our shared time as students and in all the years since our graduation 50 years ago."[39]

Anger over Alito's *Dobbs* decision further galvanized a group of women from the class of 1972 to begin meeting on Zoom on the third Tuesday of every month, except during the summer, to share experiences from the front lines of social change. They called themselves Friends for Reproductive Justice.[40]

Helena Novakova, who joined Alito's Princeton class after fleeing Czechoslovakia after the Soviet invasion, spent twenty-five years teaching in American schools around the world with her husband, working with young people from Peru to Spain to Kenya to Kuwait to the Philippines and beyond. It was "fascinating to see women's issues in different cultures," said Novakova, who now lives in Miami.

At the monthly virtual get-togethers, she added her perspectives to those of doctors, lawyers, and even a poet. The group discussed Alito at length in the immediate aftermath of the *Dobbs* decision, but then moved into new realms of concern.

"He's very much in our disfavor," she said of Alito, but "the conversations are mainly proactive. What can we do now to help other people understand how the present situation is affecting us? And what can we do to change it in the near future? These women are fabulous, and they are definitely moving ahead and not looking back."[41]

....

WHEN ALITO MOVED AHEAD, he often looked back as well. He spent summers in Italy, practicing the language of his forebears. Even while serving on the Supreme Court, he devoted time to studying Italian.

"It's a beautiful language," he once said, "and I think it's important for Italian Americans to remember their heritage and remember their history—both their history in the United States as immigrants to this country, but also the very rich cultural history that their ancestors experienced."[42]

That sentiment is no doubt the wellspring of his communications with Dr. Gilda Rorro, chairwoman emerita of the New Jersey Italian Heritage

Commission and leader in the effort to restore the Christopher Columbus statue that was removed from Chambersburg in 2020.[43]

Like Alito, Rorro has a strong personal identification with the statue, having seen it for the first time when she met her future in-laws. "I felt that Columbus was looking at me," she said. "I was coming like an immigrant to a new city and a new life. I felt very calm after I saw that statue."[44]

Demographic shifts altered the face of Chambersburg in succeeding decades. Central American immigrants set up shops, churches, and restaurants in spaces vacated by departing Italian Americans. Many of those Latinos objected to Columbus over his alleged misdeeds to their native lands. An African American activist staged a protest, calling the statue "Christopher KKK Columbus"; her proposal was to replace the explorer with a likeness of David Dinkins, the former New York City mayor who was educated in Trenton, in the hopes it would "inspire Black children and bring about positive change in our neighborhood."[45]

When the city hauled away the vandalized remnants of the Columbus statue, Mayor Reed Gusciora tried to appease all parties by giving Columbus Park the new name of Unity Square Park. In so doing, he declared that "our communities rightfully expect that the individuals we celebrate represent the principles of freedom and equality that we all hold dear."[46]

Alito felt it was deeply wrong to remove the Columbus statue on that basis. Gusciora and the critics were misreading the message of the statue; it wasn't to celebrate Columbus the conqueror but to memorialize all the Italians who came in his wake. The statue honored their resilience and the footholds they established in the New World.[47]

Alito strategized with Rorro on how to get Columbus back. She went to the Trenton City Council and read a statement from him calling the removal "an insult to the Italian American community, tantamount to saying that their experience, all that they endured and contributed, accounts for nothing." Rorro said Alito further intervened to ask the city to prove its ownership of the statue.[48]

The fight seemed to trigger his combativeness, his sensitivity to grievance. The wrong to Italian immigrants was personal—a slap in the face of his parents and grandparents. But it also reflected his conviction that diversity was a zero-sum game. One group's claim of discrimination necessitated another's: the aggrieved Central Americans of Chambersburg were trampling on the heritage of Italian Americans the way that gay-rights litigants stifled the free expression of conservative Catholics. There might, of course, be a deeper truth. The experiences of Italian Americans could be a beacon, an inspiration for immigrants who came after them, just like American freedom can allow gay-rights supporters and conservative Christians to live by their own values under the same Constitution. The experiences of Alito's ancestors could be universalized to others who summoned the courage to uproot themselves and make their way to a strange new land, with one group following the footprints and climbing the ladders built by the others. But true to the spirit of the times, no one was making that argument. Not the Columbus critics. Not the Supreme Court justice who joined the battle.

As it happened, the struggle over the statue prompted a reaction from Alito's high school debating rival, Jeffrey Laurenti, the former New Jersey Democratic political operative and congressional candidate. An Italian American and Trentonian himself, Laurenti largely agreed with Alito's sentiments. But he didn't like having Alito involved. Rorro, he said, was making a political mistake in touting the conservative justice's sense of injury.

"He's intervened and sent letters of advice to her, which she has sought to bring to meetings with local officials in Trenton," Laurenti said. "I have tried to squelch it, to make it clear in Trenton that citing Sam Alito is poison if you're trying to deal with Democratic, and particularly Black, politicians."[49]

For her part, as 2025 gave way to 2026, Rorro saw progress in the offing: a chance to buy the statue from the city, restore it, and erect it on another site.[50]

. . . .

As Alito's parents' old neighborhood of Chambersburg evolved through the decades, its changes were more in character and spirit than in physical decline; yes, some of the tenements fell into grave disrepair and others were abandoned, but this was a place that, in its heyday as home to the Roebling plant, was considered noisy and dusty and lacking in upkeep. What changed for Italian Americans was the sense of a common bond among people who lived side by side, without wealth or pretensions, but who left a distinct cultural imprint.

In retrospect, it was easy to give the old Chambersburg a mythic stature, as the neighborhood where no one locked their doors and everyone looked out for each other. But as Alito's own family's history showed, the immigrant experience was never that cozy or secure.

In 2013, a local university professor, Susan Ryan, produced a forty-five-minute documentary on Chambersburg, *From the 'Burg to the Barrio*, and found intriguing connections. "I hope that I have been able to show not only the differences between what much of the Italian community remembers of Chambersburg," said Ryan, "but also a lot of the similarities that they share with the newer residents in terms of their interests in family, food, and work, and religion."[51]

The Spanish and Creole names on the storefronts were jarring to Italian Americans who grew up there, but not in any different way than the Italian names on business signs were shocking to Trenton's Protestant elites in the early twentieth century. One popular mini-market and buffet restaurant, La Sirena on Clinton Avenue, offered a culinary travelogue through the neighborhood's history by serving pizza and meatball parms alongside pupusas, tacos, and mojarra, a fish dish popular in the Caribbean.[52]

Rose Alito, who spent more than three decades in Chambersburg, lived to be ninety-eight. Near the end of her life, her trusted and beloved son, one of the most powerful men in the country, took her on a drive through the old neighborhood. They would have passed by her childhood home at 78 Hudson Street, the remnants of the Roebling plant where her father worked, and the many flats the young Sam Sr. was able to secure for his itinerant family.

There is no record of what Rose thought of all this—what she saw through her wizened eyes. Was it a journey down memory lane or a rude awakening?

Justice Alito, however, shared his reactions. For him, Chambersburg lived mostly in the stories told by Rose and Sam Sr. of their hardships and the faith that overcame them. It also survived in the memory of the nine-year-old boy watching the majestic Columbus statue being raised, with all the music and colors and speeches from priests and Italian diplomats.

While navigating the narrow streets of his mother's youth, Alito was moved but also depressed. He could find no vibrancy, no hope, in the changed tableau before him. The story of Chambersburg was one of loss and decline, a dirge of sadness and regret.

"Things have unfortunately changed a lot," he told *The American Spectator* in one of his many interviews with right-wing publications. "A couple of years ago I drove my mother around the areas of Trenton where she had grown up—"

His interviewer interrupted to recite the famous slogan on the lighted sign on the Lower Trenton Bridge spanning the Delaware River: "Trenton Makes, the World Takes."

The irony was painful as Alito's mind tilted backward. He could find nothing positive to say.

"People joke about it, but it was true," he said. "At one point the city was a model for America. It really has deteriorated."[53]

Acknowledgments

This book would not exist without the work of my two outstanding researchers, Peder Schaefer and Timmy Facciola. Peder is a highly resourceful young journalist who earned a master's degree in intellectual history in Leuven, Belgium, while working on this book. His understanding of law and philosophy is nuanced and deeply impressive, and he quickly became an essential thought partner for me. His dogged reporting and searching through archives from Trenton, Steinert High School, Princeton, and Yale are visible throughout the book. Timmy is an amazing reporter with an innate feel for politics and personal knowledge of Catholic faith and intellectual traditions. He helped to capture the social and political atmosphere surrounding key moments in Justice Alito's career. He also combed the archives of the George W. Bush Presidential Library in Dallas to obtain never-before-published information on the failed Harriet Miers Supreme Court nomination and Bush's choice of Alito to succeed her.

This book also would not exist without the boundless encouragement of Priscilla Painton, legendary editor and jewel of the publishing world. Similarly, I owe enormous gratitude to my dedicated and insightful agents, Wendy Strothman and Lauren Sharp, for their important advice on all aspects of the writing and production of this book. Wendy's record of producing distinguished works of nonfiction is unmatched. Johanna Li of Simon & Schuster helped immeasurably with the editing and production. And Janice Weaver's copyediting along with Michael Trudeau's close oversight made the book better in many ways.

Part of the pleasure in writing this book was to draw on the advice and expertise of close friends of more than thirty years in the legal and journalistic worlds. They include Victor Wolski, Martin Flaherty, Gary Bass, Scott Heller, Mark Caro, Steve Anthony, Bob Manson, Jonathan Nathanson, Gareth Cook, Larry Stratton, James Salzman, David Goldberg, and my brother George Canellos. I also appreciate the long conversations with distinguished thinkers like Liz Magill, John Harrison, Laura Kalman, Richard Epstein, John Bolton, Sasha Volokh, Duncan Kennedy, Grover Joseph Rees, Nathan Hecht, Stephen Frug, Andrew Napolitano, Morton Blackwell, Arthur Aidala, Karl Rove, and Chuck Cooper, along with many other jurists and close associates of Justice Alito who have asked to remain unnamed.

I owe a strong debt of gratitude to the librarians and research directors who helped find important information. They include John Kennedy, Nicole Hawke, and Allen Almodovar at the George W. Bush Presidential Library in Dallas; Robert Schenker, head of the Trenton Public Library's Trentoniana Local History Research Room; Renee Rogers, librarian at Steinert High School; the many special collections librarians at Princeton University and Yale University; and Eleanor Magers Vuono of the Princeton ROTC alumni network.

Friends at *Politico* also offered important input, including Josh Gerstein, James Romoser, Ankush Khardori, Elizabeth Ralph and Alex Keeney, Jonathan Martin, Ben Schreckinger, Stephen Heuser, Mike Zapler, Michael Schaffer, Sasha Issenberg, John F. Harris, and Ian Ward.

Other friends were kind enough to listen to my ideas and share my enthusiasm. A big thanks to Bryan Bender, Aaron Zitner and Ricki Farber, Adam Willis and Lucia Petty, Dan Diamond, Mike Grunwald, Alec Ward, Swanee Hunt, Marty Baron, Aviva Kempner, Mike Rezendes, Katie Kingsbury, Mark Leibovich, Kimber Riddle, Anna Deavere Smith, Farah Stockman, Stefan Fatsis, Judy Abel and Michael Brill, Kate Maguire, Richard Nussbaum, Marietta Robinson, Mark Muro, David Zraket, Phillip Argyris, Indira Lakshmanan, Peter Baker and Susan Glasser, Sean Buffington, Nancy Barnes, Carol Edgar, Nikolas Jaspert and Montse Pascal, David Jaspert, Theo Jaspert, Michael Crowley, Eric Moskowitz, Carlo Rotella, Thomas Medicus and Katharina Uppenbrink, Wendy

Davis, Kevin Baron, Toby Stock and Margy Slattery, Lisa Vollmer, Joanna Weiss, Scott and Roxanne Bok, Maria Rudolph, Charlie Spicer and Jeffrey Steele, Dante Ramos, Dan Gingiss, Chuck Cohen, Amy Davidson Sorkin and David Sorkin, and Matt Kaminski.

My family members—starting with my parents, Jean and George Canellos—offered their endless support and encouragement. They include Diane and Jim Triant, Andrew Canellos and Elizabeth Reluga Canellos, Pamela Brown, Clio Canellos, Evie Canellos, Charlie Canellos, Jeanne Triant, Bill Triant, Craig Estes, Lila Tzitzon, and Elizabeth Herbin.

Finally, this book is dedicated to my second family of more than twenty years, Charlie, Luiza, Will, and Peter Savage, with the greatest of warmth, gratitude, and admiration.

Notes

INTRODUCTION: THE NEW WORLD

1. "Dedication of Columbus Statue Today," *Trenton Evening Times*, October 25, 1959.
2. "Trenton Weather in 1959," Extreme Weather Watch, https://www.extremeweather watch.com/cities/trenton/year-1959.
3. "College Club Fetes Residents of Home," *Trenton Sunday Advertiser*, December 16, 1956.
4. "Story Lady's Sixth Program for Holidays," *Trenton Evening Times*, December 26, 1956.
5. "Columbus Statue Unveiling Sunday," *Trenton Evening Times*, October 22, 1959; "Anthony Alito," *Trenton Evening Times*, December 10, 1963; Erasmo S. Ciccolella, *Vibrant Life, 1886–1942: Trenton's Italian Americans* (Center for Migration Studies, 1986), 79.
6. "100 Units to March in Columbus Parade," *Trenton Evening Times*, October 9, 1959.
7. Dennis J. Starr, *The Italians of New Jersey* (Collections of the New Jersey Historical Society, 1985), 60, 62.
8. "Visit to an Italian Camp," *Daily State Gazette*, July 14, 1903, Trentoniana Room, Trenton Free Public Library.
9. "Little Italy Must Keep Place Clean," *Daily True American*, July 13, 1903, Trentoniana Room, Trenton Free Public Library.
10. "Many Foreign Names on Business Signs," *Trenton Sunday Advertiser*, June 5, 1904, Trentoniana Room, Trenton Free Public Library.
11. "Many Foreign Names on Business Signs," *Trenton Sunday Advertiser*.
12. US Census Bureau, "US Census 1920, Trenton Ward 9, Mercer, New Jersey," National Archives and Records Administration, 1920, Roll: T625_1054; Page: 4B; Enumeration District: 79; US Census Bureau, "US Census 1920, Trenton Ward 10, Mercer, New Jersey," National Archives and Records Administration, 1920, Roll: T625_1054; Page: 1A; Enumeration District: 85.
13. Clifford Zink, "Washington A. Roebling, the Civil War and Building Brooklyn Bridge," *Wire Rope Exchange*, October 2013, 20.

14. *Confirmation Hearing on the Nomination of Samuel A. Alito, Jr. to Be an Associate Justice of the Supreme Court of the United States*, sec. Alito Statement, https://www.congress.gov/109 /chrg/shrg25429/CHRG-109shrg25429.htm.

15. "I-Italy Interviews Justice Samuel A. Alito," *I-Italy*, September 9, 2016, https://www.you tube.com/watch?v=Wwfjh3vxSEU.

16. "Little Italy Must Keep Place Clean," *Daily True American*.

17. George Horne, "Italian Liner Cristoforo Colombo Begins Her Maiden Voyage to U.S.," *New York Times*, July 16, 1954.

18. "Columbus Statue Unveiling Sunday," *Trenton Evening Times*.

19. "100 Units to March in Columbus Parade," *Trenton Evening Times*.

20. "Dedication of Columbus Statue Today," *Trenton Evening Times*.

21. "Dedication of Columbus Statue Today," *Trenton Evening Times*.

22. "Hamilton's Realty Transfers as Filed During Last Week," *Trenton Sunday Advertiser*, November 6, 1949; "Trenton and Mercer County Directory," 1952, Trentoniana Room, Trenton Free Public Library.

23. L. A. Parker, "Columbus Statue Should Leave Trenton and We've Been Saying That for Years," *Trentonian*, June 20, 2020, https://www.trentonian.com/2020/06/20/columbus -statue-should-leave-trenton-and-weve-been-saying-that-for-years-la-parker-column.

24. US Environmental Protection Agency, "Roebling Steel Co. Florence, NJ: Cleanup Activities," Overviews and Factsheets, EPA, accessed July 18, 2025, https://cumulis.epa.gov /supercpad/SiteProfiles/index.cfm?fuseaction=second.cleanup&id=0200439.

25. Lari Robling, "In Chambersburg, Once Trenton's Little Italy, Immigrant History Repeats," *We the Italians/Newsworks*, August 5, 2013, http://wetheitalians.com/single_post /in-chambersburg-once-trenton-s-little-italy-immigrant-history-repeats; David Karas, "Documentary by TCNJ Professor Chronicles Transformation of Trenton's Chambersburg Neighborhood," *Trenton Times*, February 18, 2013, https://www.nj.com/mercer /2013/02/new_documentary_chronicles_a_t.html.; *From the 'Burg to the Barrio* (blog), http://burgtothebarrio.blogspot.com.

26. Peder Schaefer, *Photo of Italian Peoples Bakery and Deli Sign*, January 26, 2025.

27. "Nueva Imagen Barbershop," Google Maps; "Mi Tierra," Google Maps; "El Quetzal Multiservicios," Google Maps.

28. Howard Zinn, *A People's History of the United States* (HarperCollins, 2015).

29. Zinn, *A People's History*, 8–10.

30. The Black Ivy League & Key, "The Renaming Christopher Columbus Park after David Dinkins & Statue Removal," Change.org, June 25, 2020, https://www.change.org/p/statue -removal-and-renaming-park-of-christopher-columbus-the-renaming-christopher-colum bus-park-after-david-dinkins-statue-removal.

31. L. A. Parker, "Vandalism of Trenton's Columbus Statue Upsets Italian Community," *Trentonian*, January 22, 2018, https://www.trentonian.com/2018/01/22/la-parker-vandalism-of-trentons-columbus-statue-upsets-italian-community.

32. Parker, "Columbus Statue Should Leave Trenton."

33. Associated Press, "Christopher Columbus Statue Coming Down in Trenton," WHYY public media, July 8, 2020, https://whyy.org/articles/christopher-columbus-statue-coming-down-in-trenton; Isaac Avilucea, "Trenton Mayor's Mother Was Political Stalwart Who Made Own Historical Culinary Mark," *Trentonian*, January 15, 2021, https://www.trentonian.com/2021/01/15/trenton-mayors-mother-was-political-stalwart-who-made-own-historical-culinary-mark.

34. L. A. Parker, "Goodbye, Columbus: It Was Time for You to Go," *Trentonian*, July 8, 2020, https://www.trentonian.com/2020/07/08/goodbye-columbus-it-was-time-for-you-to-go-la-parker-column.

35. "Samuel Alito (Supreme Court Justice)," *We the Italians*, November 2, 2020, https://www.wetheitalians.com/news/top-american-democracy-american-proud-his-italian-rootswelcome-we-italians-supreme-court-judge-samuel-alito.

36. James E. Goodman and Lee Pasternack, "City Wary After Night of Terror," *Trenton Evening Times*, April 10, 1968; Tony Wilson and Frank Herrick, "Wild Looting, Fires Jar City," *Trentonian*, April 10, 1968.

37. Landon Y. Jones, "Plans for Coeducation: Gift of $4,000,000 Plus Princeton Inn Solves Initial Problems," *Princeton Alumni Weekly*, May 6, 1969, https://paw.princeton.edu/article/day-coeducation-came-princeton.

38. Bill Highberger, "Council Votes End to ROTC, Supports 'Strike,'" *Daily Princetonian*, May 4, 1970.

39. Roe v. Wade, 410 U.S. 113 (1973); John Hart Ely, "The Wages of Crying Wolf: A Comment on Roe v. Wade," *Yale Law Journal* 82 (1973).

40. Interviews with classmates at Steinert High School and Princeton University, January 26, 2024, April 30, 2025, May 8, 2025, May 14, 2025, May 16, 2025, July 9, 2025, July 10, 2025, July 11, 2025.

41. Interviews with classmates at Steinert High School and Princeton University.

42. Adam Liptak, "In Unusually Political Speech, Alito Says Liberals Pose Threat to Liberties," *New York Times*, November 13, 2020, https://www.nytimes.com/2020/11/13/us/samuel-alito-religious-liberty-free-speech.html; Martin Kady II, "Justice Alito Mouths 'Not True,'" *Politico*, January 27, 2010, https://www.politico.com/blogs/politico-now/2010/01/justice-alito-mouths-not-true-024608.

43. "Samuel Alito (Supreme Court Justice)," *We the Italians*.

44. "Samuel Alito (Supreme Court Justice)," *We the Italians*.

45. "Samuel Alito (Supreme Court Justice)," *We the Italians*.

46. "Samuel Alito (Supreme Court Justice)," *We the Italians*.

47. "About Us," Federalist Society, https://fedsoc.org/about-us.

48. Matthew Walther, "Sam Alito: A Civil Man," *American Spectator*, April 21, 2014, https://spectator.org/sam-alito-a-civil-man.

49. *Confirmation Hearing on the Nomination of Samuel A. Alito*, sec. Alito Statement.

PROLOGUE: JUNE 24, 2022

1. "The Scene Outside Supreme Court as Roe Overturned," *Washington Post*, June 24, 2022, https://www.washingtonpost.com/photography/interactive/2022/photos-supreme-court-abortion-ruling.

2. Rebecca Shabad and Fiona Glisson, "'Nonscalable' Fence Erected Outside Supreme Court amid Abortion-Related Protests," NBC News, May 5, 2022, https://www.nbcnews.com/politics/supreme-court/non-scalable-fence-erected-supreme-court-abortion-related-protests-rcna27452.

3. Josh Gerstein and Alexander Ward, "Supreme Court Has Voted to Overturn Abortion Rights, Draft Opinion Shows," *Politico*, May 3, 2022, https://www.politico.com/news/2022/05/02/supreme-court-abortion-draft-opinion-00029473.

4. Linda Greenhouse, *Becoming Justice Blackmun: Harry Blackmun's Supreme Court Journey* (Times Books, 2005).

5. See Griswold v. Connecticut, 381 U.S. 479 (1965), Loving v. Virginia, 388 U.S. 1 (1967), Gideon v. Wainwright, 372 U.S. 335 (1963), and Mapp v. Ohio, 367 U.S. 643 (1961).

6. Michael Kruse, "The Weekend at Yale That Changed American Politics," *Politico Magazine*, September/October 2018, https://www.politico.com/magazine/story/2018/08/27/federalist-society-yale-history-conservative-law-court-219608.

7. Charles A. Reich, "The New Property," *Yale Law Journal* 73, no. 5 (1964): 733–87; Mark Tushnet, "Critical Legal Studies: A Political History," *Yale Law Journal* 100, no. 5 (1991): 1515–44; Duncan Kennedy, *Legal Education and the Reproduction of Hierarchy: A Polemic Against the System* (New York University Press, 2005).

8. Steven Gow Calabresi and Gary Lawson, *The Meese Revolution: The Making of a Constitutional Moment* (Encounter, 2024), 267–89.

9. Chief Justice Roberts concurred in the outcome but made it clear he would not have overturned *Roe* in this case, so by some measures, the vote was 5–4.

10. Walther, "Sam Alito: A Civil Man"; Samuel A. Alito Jr. and John G. Malcolm, "A Conversation with Justice Samuel Alito," Heritage Foundation, December 14, 2022, https://www.heritage.org/sites/default/files/2023-04/HL1332.pdf.

11. Antonin Scalia, *Scalia Speaks: Reflections on Law, Faith, and Life Well Lived* (Crown Forum, 2017), ix–xi.

12. Scalia, *Scalia Speaks*, xi.
13. "Antonin Scalia Delayed the Beginning of His Confirmation Hearing . . ." UPI, August 6, 1986, https://www.upi.com/Archives/1986/08/06/Antonin-Scalia-delayed-the-begin ning-of-his-confirmation-hearing/2962523684800.
14. Vaughn Ververs, "You Say Scalito, I Say Alito," CBS News, November 1, 2005, https:// www.cbsnews.com/news/you-say-scalito-i-say-alito.
15. Samuel A. Alito Jr., "Samuel Alito Job Application 1985," National Archives and Records Administration, November 15, 1985, Records Group 60, Department of Justice, Files of James L. Brynes & Mark Levin, 1983–1988, accession, #060-97-761, box 1, folder Alito, Jr., Samuel A.
16. Samuel A. Alito Jr., "1972 Nassau Herald Yearbook Entry," *Nassau Herald*, Princeton, NJ, 1972, https://pr.princeton.edu/pictures/a-f/alito_samuel_anthony/htm/02nassau _herald_text.htm.
17. George W. Bush, *Decision Points* (Crown, 2010), 98.
18. Bush, *Decision Points*, 98.
19. Randy Barnett, "Cronyism," *Wall Street Journal*, October 4, 2005, https://www.cato.org/ commentary/cronyism.
20. Al Kamen, "Miers's Long-Ago Federalist Slap Still Stings," *Washington Post*, October 20, 2005.
21. Mark Perkiss, "Mom, Neighbors All Love Sam," *Trenton Times*, November 1, 2005.
22. Dobbs v. Jackson Women's Health Organization, 597 U.S. 215 (2022), Thomas, J., Concurring, 1–2.
23. Judi Hasson, "Game of Wits Sparks Debate Tourney," *Trenton Evening Times*, February 9, 1967; Bill Agress, Alito debate partner at Steinert High School, interviewed by Peter Canellos, Timmy Facciola, and Peder Schaefer, January 26, 2025.
24. Alito, "1972 Nassau Herald Yearbook Entry."
25. Dobbs v. Jackson, 1.
26. "90-Year-Old Mother Mum, Except About Topic of Abortion," Newhouse News Service, November 1, 2005, https://www.sunjournal.com/2005/11/01/90-year-old-mother-mum -except-topic-abortion.
27. Dobbs v. Jackson, 1.
28. Dobbs v. Jackson, 5.
29. Washington v. Glucksberg, 521 U.S. 702, 721 (1997).
30. Dobbs v. Jackson, 69.
31. Dobbs v. Jackson, 44.
32. Ely, "The Wages of Crying Wolf."
33. See Alito dissent in Planned Parenthood v. Casey, 947 F.2d 682, US Court of Appeals for the Third Circuit (1991).

34. Dobbs v. Jackson, 56–59.

35. Bill McCarthy, "How a Rumor About Justice Alito in 'Hiding' Jumped to Primetime TV," *PolitiFact*, May 11, 2022, https://www.politifact.com/article/2022/may/11/how-rumor -about-alito-hiding-moved-primetime-tv.

36. Dan Morse, "Details Emerge in Plan to Kill Kavanaugh: 'Break In, Shoot Him, and Then Shoot Myself,'" *Washington Post*, January 3, 2025, https://www.washingtonpost.com /dc-md-va/2025/01/03/nicholas-roske-brett-kavanaugh-assassination.

37. Heidi Przybyla, "Leonard Leo Used Federalist Society Contact to Obtain $1.6B Dona- tion," *Politico*, May 2, 2023, https://www.politico.com/news/2023/05/02/leonard-leo-fed eralist-society-00094761.

CHAPTER ONE: THE LONG JOURNEY

1. RMS (Risk Management Solutions), *The 1908 Messina Earthquake*, RMS Special Report, 2008, 1, https://www.scribd.com/document/123741459/1908-Messina-Earthquake.

2. "150,000 Dead, Cities Gone, More Shocks," *New York Times*, December 31, 1908.

3. RMS, *The 1908 Messina Earthquake*, 6.

4. "150,000 Dead, Cities Gone, More Shocks," *New York Times*.

5. "Churches of the Italian Dioceses, Church of the Santissimo Salvatore," Le Chiese Italiane, https://chieseitaliane.chiesacattolica.it/chieseitaliane/AccessoEsterno.do? mode=guest&code=11324&Chiesa_del_Santissimo_Salvatore__Saline_Joniche, _Montebello_Jonico.

6. "Slow Economic Unification, 1861–1896," in *The Rise and Fall of the Italian Economy*, ed. Carlo Bastasin and Gianni Toniolo (Cambridge University Press, 2023), https://doi.org /10.1017/9781009235303.003.

7. "The Great Arrival, Italian Immigration and Relocation in U.S. History," Library of Con- gress, "Immigration and Relocation in U.S. History," https://www.loc.gov/classroom-ma terials/immigration/italian/the-great-arrival.

8. Yannay Spitzer, Gaspare Tortorici, and Ariell Zimran, "International Migration Re- sponses to Modern Europe's Most Destructive Earthquake: Messina and Reggio Calabria, 1908," Working Paper no. 27506, Working Paper Series (National Bureau of Economic Research, July 2020), https://doi.org/10.3386/w27506.

9. US Census Bureau, "Antonio Alati, US Census 1920, Trenton Ward 9, Mercer, New Jer- sey," National Archives and Records Administration, 1920, Roll: T625_1054; Page: 4B; Enumeration District: 79; "Samuel Alito (Supreme Court Justice)," *We the Italians*.

10. Starr, *The Italians of New Jersey*, 60–62; A. Camera, "A Short Sketch of the Italian Col- ony of Trenton, N.J.," *Columbus Journal*, Trentoniana Room, Trenton Free Public Library; Evelyn Gonzalez, "Trenton, New Jersey," in *Encyclopedia of Greater Philadelphia*, https:// philadelphiaencyclopedia.org/essays/trenton-new-jersey.

11. US Census Bureau, "Antonio Alati, US Census 1920"; "Anthony Alito, US Census 1930, Trenton, Mercer, New Jersey," National Archives and Records Administration, 1930, Page: 27A; Enumeration District: 0041; FHL microfilm: 2341099; "Samuel Alito (Supreme Court Justice)," We the Italians.

12. US Census Bureau, "Anthony Alito, US Census 1930."

13. City of Trenton, "Trenton Tax Assessment, 231 Pearl Street," 1936, Trentoniana Room, Trenton Free Public Library; US Census Bureau, "Anthony Alito, US Census 1930"; US Census Bureau, "Antonio Alati, US Census 1920."

14. "I-Italy Interviews Justice Samuel A. Alito," I-Italy.

15. US Census Bureau, "Rose Fradusco, US Census 1920, Trenton Ward 10, Mercer, New Jersey," National Archives and Records Administration, 1920, Roll: T625_1054; Page: 1A; Enumeration District: 85; "Samuel Alito (Supreme Court Justice)," We the Italians.

16. "Samuel Alito (Supreme Court Justice)," We the Italians.

17. US Census Bureau, "Rose Fradusco, US Census 1920."

18. US Census Bureau, "Rose Fradusco, US Census 1920"; "Rose R. Fradusco Engaged to Wed," Trenton Evening Times, February 17, 1948.

19. US Census Bureau, "Rose Fradusco, US Census 1920."

20. US Census Bureau, "Rose Fradusco, US Census 1920"; Confirmation Hearing on the Nomination of Samuel A. Alito, sec. Alito Statement.

21. Clifford W. Zink and Dorothy White Hartman, Spanning the Industrial Age: The John A. Roebling's Sons Company (Trenton Roebling Community Development Corporation, 1992), 141.

22. Zink and Hartman, Spanning the Industrial Age, 93–99.

23. Now You're Set for Life: Oral Histories of the John A. Roebling's Sons Company (Trenton Roebling Community Development Corporation, 1994), 11.

24. "I-Italy Interviews Justice Samuel A. Alito," I-Italy.

25. Now You're Set for Life, 20.

26. Now You're Set for Life, 3.

27. "I-Italy Interviews Justice Samuel A. Alito," I-Italy; Laurine Purola, New Jersey political consultant who worked with Sam Alito Sr. in the 1970s and 1980s, interviewed by Peder Schaefer, July 9, 2025; David D. Kirkpatrick, "Court Nominee Presents Father as Role Model," New York Times, December 5, 2005, https://www.nytimes.com/2005/12/05/politics/politicsspecial1/court-nominee-presents-father-as-role-model.html.

28. US Census Bureau, "Rose Fradusco, US Census 1920"; US Census Bureau, "Antonio Alati, US Census 1920."

29. Trenton Evening Times, "Rose R. Fradusco Engaged to Wed."

30. "I-Italy Interviews Justice Samuel A. Alito," I-Italy.

31. Trenton Evening Times, "Rose R. Fradusco Engaged to Wed"; "I-Italy Interviews Justice Samuel A. Alito," I-Italy.

32. "I-Italy Interviews Justice Samuel A. Alito," *I-Italy.*

33. "I-Italy Interviews Justice Samuel A. Alito," *I-Italy.*

34. "I-Italy Interviews Justice Samuel A. Alito," *I-Italy; US School Yearbooks,* 1880–2012, Trenton Central High School, 1952.

35. "Samuel A. Alito, Enlistment Records," National Archives, March 11, 1941, https://aad.archives.gov/aad/record-detail.jsp?dt=893&rid=2830769; *Confirmation Hearing on the Nomination of Samuel A. Alito,* sec. Alito Statement.

36. *Trenton Evening Times,* "Rose R. Fradusco Engaged to Wed."

37. "I-Italy Interviews Justice Samuel A. Alito," *I-Italy.*

38. *Trenton Evening Times,* "Rose R. Fradusco Engaged to Wed."

39. "Trenton and Mercer County Directory," 1952, Trentoniana Room, Trenton Free Public Library; "Trenton and Mercer County Directory," 1956, Trentoniana Room, Trenton Free Public Library; *Trenton Evening Times,* "Rose R. Fradusco to Wed."

40. "Wed at Church," *Trenton Evening Times,* May 26, 1948.

41. "Hamilton's Realty Transfers as Filed During Last Week," *Trenton Sunday Advertiser,* November 6, 1949; US Census Bureau, "Sam A. Alito, US Census 1950, Trenton, New Jersey," National Archives and Records Administration, 1950, Roll: 3626; Page: 14; Enumeration District: 33-158.

42. Dale Russakoff and Jo Becker, "A Search for Order, an Answer in the Law," *Washington Post,* January 8, 2006, https://www.washingtonpost.com/archive/politics/2006/01/08/a-search-for-order-an-answer-in-the-law-span-classbankheadsince-his-youth-samuel-alito-jr-has-been-drawn-to-conservative-ideas-on-the-eve-of-confirmation-hearings-the-first-of-two-articles-looks-at-the-forces-that-shaped-the-nominee-span/38efb278-1f81-4b19-80f8-ca9a43e9219d.

43. Workforce New Jersey Public Information Network, "Table 6: New Jersey Resident Population by Municipality: 1940–2000," 2001, 39, https://www.nj.gov/labor/labormarketinformation/assets/PDFs/census/2kpub/njsdcp3.pdf#page=27.

44. Peter Canellos, notes from visit to Mercerville, NJ, January 27, 2025.

45. "Hamilton's Realty Transfers," *Trenton Sunday Advertiser.*

46. Peder Schaefer, *Photo of 137 Fenwood Avenue,* January 26, 2025; Zillow, "137 Fenwood Ave, Hamilton, N.J.," https://www.zillow.com/homedetails/137-Fenwood-Ave-Hamilton-NJ-08619/38972728_zpid.

47. Our Lady of Sorrows, "History of Our Lady of Sorrows Parish," Parish of Our Lady of Sorrows–St. Anthony, https://ols-sa.org/history-of-our-lady-of-sorrows-parish.

48. "Samuel A. Alito and Martha Bomgardner Marriage Record," Our Lady of Sorrows Church, February 9, 1985, Our Lady of Sorrows Church; Peter Canellos, notes from visit to Mercerville.

49. "Memorial of Our Lady of Sorrows," *Roman Catholic Archdiocese of Portland,* https://portlanddiocese.org/memorial-our-lady-sorrows.

50. Russakoff and Becker, "A Search for Order, an Answer in the Law"; "I-Italy Interviews Justice Samuel A. Alito," *I-Italy.*

51. "I-Italy Interviews Justice Samuel A. Alito," *I-Italy.*

52. "I-Italy Interviews Justice Samuel A. Alito," *I-Italy.*

53. Peter Canellos, notes from visit to Mercerville.

54. Bill Agress, interviewed by Peter Canellos, Timmy Facciola, and Peder Schaefer.

55. "Official Family of Trenton Legion Post," *Trenton Evening Times,* January 17, 1947; "Season Opener Tomorrow for Junior Baseball League," *Trenton Sunday Advertiser,* May 13, 1962; "Membership Kick-Off Meeting Is Tuesday," *Trenton Evening Times,* March 8, 1959; "Reverse 1-Way Street Plan, Mercerville Residents Ask," *Trenton Sunday Advertiser,* July 29, 1962; "Traffic Flow Change Likely by Burger Stand," *Trenton Evening Times,* August 8, 1962; "Two Mercer Spelling Bee Contestants," *Trenton Evening Times,* January 3, 1962; "Children's Gift Boosts Camp Fund," *Trenton Evening Times,* September 11, 1961; "Seminar Hopping," *Trenton Evening Times,* November 3, 1966.

56. "Dr. Castells to Address College Club Study Group," *Trenton Sunday Advertiser,* January 14, 1962; "PTA Board Will Meet," *Trenton Evening Times,* November 4, 1957; "More Than 600 Take Part in Hamilton Heart Drive," *Trenton Times,* February 16, 1958.

57. "College Club Fetes Residents of Home," *Trenton Sunday Advertiser,* December 16, 1956; "Story Lady's Sixth Program for Holidays," *Trenton Evening Times,* December 26, 1956.

58. "Children's Gift Boosts Camp Fund," *Trenton Evening Times.*

59. "Didn't Scare Them," *Trenton Sunday Advertiser,* September 15, 1957.

60. "Science Fair Awards Rite Held Tonight," *Trenton Evening Times,* April 3, 1959; "Piano Pupils to Present Recital at YWCA Hall," *Trenton Sunday Advertiser,* May 22, 1960.

61. Paul Hagen, "Q&A with Justice Samuel Alito, a Supreme Phillies Fan," *Philadelphia Inquirer,* April 12, 2010, https://www.inquirer.com/philly/sports/phillies/20100412_Q_A _with_Justice_Samuel_Alito__a_Supreme_Phillies_fan.html.

62. Bill Agress, interviewed by Peter Canellos, Timmy Facciola, and Peder Schaefer.

63. "Hamilton YMCA Midget League Debut Tomorrow," *Trenton Sunday Advertiser,* May 3, 1959; "Al's Cop Sunnybrae Title," *Trentonian,* July 30, 1965.

64. "Al's Cop Sunnybrae Title," *Trentonian.*

CHAPTER TWO: THE GLORIOUS SUBURBS

1. "I-Italy Interviews Justice Samuel A. Alito," *I-Italy.*

2. Dr. James Federici, retired Hamilton Township School District social sciences teacher, interviewed by Peder Schaefer, July 7, 2025.

3. Gideon v. Wainwright, 372 U.S. 335 (1963).

4. Mapp v. Ohio, 367 U.S. 643 (1961).

5. Miranda v. Arizona, 384 U.S. 436 (1966).

6. Dale Russakoff and Jo Becker, "A Search for Order, an Answer in the Law," *Washington Post*, January 8, 2006, https://wapo.st/4fBIbTy.

7. Abington School District v. Schempp, 374 U.S. 203 (1963), 240–41.

8. Abington School District v. Schempp, 241.

9. "Bible Ban Stirs Controversy," *Trenton Evening Times*, September 7, 1963.

10. Russakoff and Becker, "A Search for Order, an Answer in the Law."

11. "Trenton and Mercer County Directory," 1952; "Directory," 1956; "Samuel Alito, 73, Legislative Advisor," *Newark Star-Ledger*, May 21, 1987; "Samuel A. Alito, 73, pioneer in Legislature," *Trenton Times*, May 21, 1987.

12. Alan Steinberg, "I Knew Sam Alito Sr.—A Vivid Contrast to His Son," *Insider NJ*, June 19, 2024, https://www.insidernj.com/i-knew-sam-alito-sr.-a-vivid-contast-to-his-son.

13. "In GOP Challenge Alito Quizzed on Remap," *Trenton Evening Times*, July 24, 1967.

14. Reynolds v. Sims, 377 U.S. 533 (1964); Morris K. Udall, "Reapportionment," Congressman's Report, October 14, 1964, U.S. Congress.

15. Reynolds v. Sims.

16. David D. Kirkpatrick, "Court Nominee Presents Father as Role Model," *New York Times*, December 5, 2005, https://www.nytimes.com/2005/12/05/politics/politicsspecial1/court-nominee-presents-father-as-role-model.html.

17. Alito, "Samuel Alito Job Application 1985."

18. Russakoff and Becker, "A Search for Order, an Answer in the Law."

19. Bill Agress, interviewed by Peter Canellos, Timmy Facciola, and Peder Schaefer.

20. "Rose F. Fradusco Alito," *Trenton Times*, February 12, 2013.

21. Elaine Tarr, former Steinert High School English teacher, interviewed by Peder Schaefer, July 7, 2025.

22. "Samuel A. Alito, U.S. World War II Draft Cards Young Men, 1940–1947," National Archives, St. Louis, Missouri, Record Group: *Records of the Selective Service System*, 147, box 7.

23. Laurine Purola, New Jersey political consultant who worked with Sam Alito Sr. in the 1970s and 1980s, interviewed by Peder Schaefer, July 9, 2025.

24. US Census, "Distribution of Foreign Stock Population," 1970.

25. "Sido L. Ridolfi," *Princeton Alumni Weekly*, December 4, 2013, https://paw.princeton.edu/memorial/sido-l-ridolfi-36; "Ridolfi Chairman For Yule Party," *Trenton Times*, December 4, 1953; John McLaughlin, "Legislature to Get Many New Members," *Trenton Times*, April 30, 1971.

26. Steinberg, "I Knew Sam Alito Sr."

27. Laurine Purola, interviewed by Peder Schaefer; Gayl Mazuco, New Jersey public sector labor relations attorney who worked with Sam Alito Sr., interviewed by Peder Schaefer, July 10, 2025.

28. Laurine Purola, interviewed by Peder Schaefer.

29. *Confirmation Hearing on the Nomination of Samuel A. Alito*, sec. Sen. Durbin Statement.

30. New Jersey former Office of Legislative Services (OLS) staffer, interviewed by Peter Canellos and Peder Schaefer, July 10, 2025.

31. Laurine Purola, interviewed by Peder Schaefer.

32. Laurine Purola, interviewed by Peder Schaefer; Gayl Mazuco, interviewed by Peder Schaefer.

33. New Jersey former OLS staffer, interviewed by Peter Canellos and Peder Schaefer.

34. Russakoff and Becker, "A Search for Order, an Answer in the Law."

35. New Jersey former OLS staffer, interviewed by Peter Canellos and Peder Schaefer.

36. Gayl Mazuco, interviewed by Peder Schaefer.

37. Peter Canellos, notes from visit to Mercerville.

38. *Cresset*, Steinert High School class of 1968; Dr. James Federici, interviewed by Peder Schaefer, July 7, 2025.

39. "474 Get Diplomas from Steinert," *Trenton Evening Times*, June 12, 1968.

40. Dr. James Federici, interviewed by Peder Schaefer.

41. Elaine Tarr, interviewed by Peder Schaefer; *Cresset*, Steinert High School class of 1968, 26.

42. Bill Agress, interviewed by Peter Canellos, Timmy Facciola, and Peder Schaefer; Andrew W. Spisak, "Debaters End Good Season," *Trenton Times*, April 18, 1968.

43. Alito, "Samuel Alito Job Application 1985."

44. *Cresset*, Steinert High School class of 1968, 85.

45. *Cresset*, Steinert High School class of 1968, 34.

46. Jeffrey Laurenti, former Alito debate opponent, interviewed by Peter Canellos and Peder Schaefer, July 31, 2025.

47. Bill Agress, interviewed by Peter Canellos, Timmy Facciola, and Peder Schaefer.

48. *Cresset*, Steinert High School class of 1968, 34.

49. "Dear Slavedriver," *Hy-Liter*, May 14, 1968.

50. "Steinert High Class Night Awards," *Trenton Sunday Advertiser*, June 9, 1968.

51. "Most Popular Seniors Picked," *Hy-Liter*, May 14, 1968.

52. Donna M. Thomas, Steinert High School graduate, interviewed by Peder Schaefer, July 30, 2025.

53. "Poll Appalls Poll-Itians," *Hy-Liter*, April 2, 1968.

54. Samuel A. Alito Jr. "'Gems' Rock 'N' Roll," *Trenton Evening Times*, October 27, 1966.

55. Paul Mickle, "1968: The Trenton Riot," *Trentonian*, 2011, https://www.capitalcentury.com/1968.html.

56. Algernon Ward Jr., Trenton historian and advocate, interviewed by Peder Schaefer, December 18, 2024.

57. Algernon Ward Jr., interviewed by Peder Schaefer.

58. NAACP Legal Defense and Educational Fund, "The Fantastic Case of the Trenton Six," 1951, https://librarycollections.law.umn.edu/racial-justice/trentonsix012.html.

59. Algernon Ward Jr., interviewed by Peder Schaefer.

60. Algernon Ward Jr., interviewed by Peder Schaefer.

61. Algernon Ward Jr., interviewed by Peder Schaefer.

62. Algernon Ward Jr., interviewed by Peder Schaefer.

63. James E. Goodman and Lee Pasternack, "City Wary After Night of Terror," *Trenton Evening Times*, April 10, 1968.

64. L. A. Parker, "Trenton Was Already at the Tipping Point in 1968 before MLK's Death," *Trentonian*, April 7, 2018.

65. Algernon Ward Jr., interviewed by Peder Schaefer.

66. Thomas H. Greer, "Youth, 19, Who Was Killed Active in City Teen Councils," *Trenton Evening Times*, April 10, 1968.

67. Goodman and Pasternack, "City Wary After Night of Terror."

68. Algernon Ward Jr., interviewed by Peder Schaefer.

69. Herb Wolfe, "Flames, Shots, Taunting Laughter," *Trenton Evening Times*, April 10, 1968; Goodman and Pasternack, "City Wary After Night of Terror."

70. Thomas Burnett, "The Night 'It' Struck Trenton," *Trentonian*, April 15, 1968.

71. "Duke University Silent Vigil in Response to King Assassination," Durham County Courthouse Art Wall, http://andjusticeforall.dconc.gov/gallery_images/duke-university -silent-vigil-in-response-to-king-assassination/.

72. Algernon Ward Jr., interviewed by Peder Schaefer.

73. "Samuel Alito Gets Soroptimist Prize," *Trenton Evening Times*, May 31, 1968.

74. "BLAH BLAH BLAH," *Hy-Liter*, June 12, 1968.

CHAPTER THREE: THE PRINCETON MYSTIQUE

1. Andrew Napolitano, former New Jersey state judge and legal commentator, interviewed by Peter Canellos and Peder Schaefer, July 9, 2025.

2. "The U-Store," *Daily Princetonian*, September 28, 1949.

3. Alexander Leitch, "Eating Clubs," in the *Princeton Companion*, Princeton University Press, 1978.

4. Alexander Leitch, "Eating Clubs."

5. F. Scott Fitzgerald, *This Side of Paradise* (Charles Scribner's Sons, 1920), 49.

6. Tablet Studios, "Princeton and the Dirty Bicker of 1958," *Tablet Magazine*, September 13, 2022, https://www.tabletmag.com/sections/community/articles/gatecrashers-podcast -episode-2-princeton-eating-clubs-dirty-bicker; "Princeton Club Body, Target of Attack, Affirms a Moral Duty to Combat Bias," *New York Times*, April 9, 1958.

7. Alexander Leitch, "Stevenson Hall," in the *Princeton Companion*, Princeton University Press, 1978.

8. Luther Munford, class of 1971 at Princeton and Stevenson Hall member, interviewed by Peder Schaefer, December 18, 2024; Greg Conderacci, class of 1971 at Princeton, interviewed by Peder Schaefer, January 23, 2025.

9. Grif Johnson, class of 1972 at Princeton, interviewed by Peder Schaefer, January 23, 2025.

10. Bill Highberger, "Counting Newly Arrived Noses," *Daily Princetonian*, September 8, 1969; "Majority of '59 Attended Public School Systems," *Daily Princetonian*, September 19, 1955.

11. Highberger, "Counting Newly Arrived Noses."

12. David Walter, "Crashing the Conservative Party," *Princeton Alumni Weekly*, January 8, 2023, https://paw.princeton.edu/article/crashing-conservative-party.

13. Richard Balfour, class of 1971 at Princeton, interviewed by Peder Schaefer, May 16, 2025.

14. *Confirmation Hearing on the Nomination of Samuel A. Alito*, sec. Alito Statement.

15. "I-Italy Interviews Justice Samuel A. Alito," *I-Italy*.

16. Alito acquaintance, class of 1972 at Princeton, interviewed by Peder Schaefer, May 14, 2025; Dennis Grzezinski, class of 1972 at Princeton and class of 1975 at Yale Law School, interviewed by Peder Schaefer, July 9, 2025.

17. Samuel A. Alito Jr. "Alito Ad," *Daily Princetonian*, February 5, 1970.

18. Andrew Napolitano, interviewed by Peter Canellos and Peder Schaefer; Bill Highberger, "Poll, Petition Boost Moratorium USA Solicits Aid of Congressmen," *Daily Princetonian*, October 13, 1969.

19. Alito acquaintance at Princeton, interviewed by Peder Schaefer, May 14, 2025; Judge Richard Clifton, class of 1972 at Princeton and judge US Court of Appeals Ninth Circuit, interviewed by Peter Canellos and Peder Schaefer, May 8, 2025.

20. *Confirmation Hearing on the Nomination of Samuel A. Alito, Jr. to Be an Associate Justice of the Supreme Court of the United States*, sec. Sen. Hatch Questioning.

21. Luther Munford, interviewed by Peder Schaefer; Susan Squier, class of 1972 at Princeton and Stevenson Hall member, interviewed by Peter Canellos and Peder Schaefer, April 30, 2025.

22. Judge Richard Clifton, interviewed by Peter Canellos and Peder Schaefer.

23. Alito acquaintance at Princeton, interviewed by Peder Schaefer, May 14, 2025.

24. Susan Squier, interviewed by Peter Canellos and Peder Schaefer.

25. "Alito's Yale Years," *Hartford Courant*, November 20, 2005, https://www.courant.com /2005/11/20/alitos-yale-years-2.

26. Mark Bernstein, "A Tiger on the Court: Sam Alito '72 at Princeton," *Princeton Alumni Weekly*, May 13, 2022, https://paw.princeton.edu/article/tiger-court-sam-alito-72-prince ton; Alito acquaintance at Princeton, interviewed by Peder Schaefer, May 14, 2025; Alito acquaintance, class of 1972 at Princeton, interviewed by Peter Canellos and Peder Schaefer, July 11, 2025.

27. "History," American Whig-Cliosophic Society, January 28, 2016, https://whigclio.prince ton.edu/history.

28. "The Purpose of College Debating," AC023, Whig-Clio Archives, Container 18, Princeton University Archives, Department of Special Collections, Princeton University Library.

29. "The Mods Bite the Dust," *Whig Register*, 1969, AC023 box 15, folder 22, Princeton University Archives, Department of Special Collections, Princeton University Library; "Counter-Protest Letter," *Hallmark*, 1969, AC023 box 15, folder 23, Princeton University Archives, Department of Special Collections, Princeton University Library.

30. "The Mods Bite the Dust," *Whig Register*.

31. "Debaters Triumph," *Daily Princetonian*, March 11, 1971.

32. Bernstein, "A Tiger on the Court."

33. Marjorie Hunter, "Agnew Says 'Effete Snobs' Incited War Moratorium," *New York Times*, October 20, 1969.

34. Princeton University, press release on Alito's debating prize, February 24, 1971, https://pr.princeton.edu/pictures/a-f/alito_samuel_anthony/htm/09release_debating.htm.

35. Charles Holden, "Fifty Years Ago—Spiro Agnew and the 'Des Moines' Speech," *Des Moines Register*, November 10, 2019, https://desmoinesregister.com/story/opinion/columnists/2019/11/10/fifty-years-ago-spiro-agnew-and-des-moines-speech/4166207002.

36. Princeton University, press release on Alito's debating prize.

37. Whig-Cliosophic Society Museum, Oakes Lounge in Whig Hall, Princeton University, accessed January 2025.

38. "Barren Social Life Plagues Students," *Daily Princetonian*, June 15, 1965; Grif Johnson, interviewed by Peder Schaefer, January 23, 2025.

39. Bernstein, "A Tiger on the Court."

40. Judge Richard Clifton, interviewed by Peter Canellos and Peder Schaefer.

41. Greg Conderacci, interviewed by Peder Schaefer; Susan Squier, interviewed by Peter Canellos and Peder Schaefer.

42. Richard Balfour, "Goheen Approves Co-Eds, Hits Student Disruptions," *Daily Princetonian*, February 22, 1969; Stephen Dreyfuss, "Goheen Okays Coed Applications: Admission Remains in Doubt," *Daily Princetonian*, February 12, 1969.

43. Christopher Connell, "Critical Languages, Critical Steps," *Princeton Alumni Weekly*, May 15, 2019, https://paw.princeton.edu/article/critical-languages-critical-steps.

44. "Greetings to the Coeds," *Daily Princetonian*, February 10, 1969.

45. Grif Johnson, interviewed by Peder Schaefer, January 23, 2025.

46. "Greetings to the Coeds," *Daily Princetonian*.

47. Stephen Fuzesi Jr., "The Joys of Feminine Problems," *Daily Princetonian*, February 10, 1969.

48. "The Day Coeducation Came to Princeton," *Princeton Alumni Weekly*, https://paw.princeton.edu/article/day-coeducation-came-princeton; Dreyfuss, "Goheen Okays Coed Applications."

49. Susan Squier, interviewed by Peter Canellos and Peder Schaefer.

50. Susan Squier, interviewed by Peter Canellos and Peder Schaefer.

51. *Confirmation Hearing on the Nomination of Samuel A. Alito, Jr. to Be an Associate Justice of the Supreme Court of the United States*, sec. Sen. Schumer Questioning.

52. Alito acquaintance, interviewed by Peter Canellos and Peder Schaefer, July 11, 2025.

53. Bernstein, "A Tiger on the Court."

54. Griswold v. Connecticut, 381 U.S. 479 (1965).

55. Professional Scheduling Service, "Your Questions on Abortion," *Daily Princetonian*, November 24, 1970; Princeton Council for Abortion Referrals, "Abortion," *Daily Princetonian*, October 4, 1971.

56. Alito acquaintance at Princeton, interviewed by Peter Canellos and Peder Schaefer, July 11, 2025; Alito acquaintance at Princeton, interviewed by Peder Schaefer, May 14, 2025; Susan Squier, interviewed by Peter Canellos and Peder Schaefer.

57. Alito acquaintance at Princeton, interviewed by Peter Canellos and Peder Schaefer, July 11, 2025.

CHAPTER FOUR: WAR WITHIN AND WITHOUT

1. Robert Marston, "Almanac: The 1969 Draft Lottery," CBS News, December 1, 2019, https://www.cbsnews.com/news/almanac-the-1969-draft-lottery-vietnam-war.

2. "Vietnam War US Military Fatal Casualty Statistics," August 15, 2016, National Archives, https://www.archives.gov/research/military/vietnam-war/casualty-statistics.

3. Neil Sheehan, "Most Deferments to End for Graduate Students," *New York Times*, February 17, 1968; Bill Highberger, "How New Call-Up System Will Work," *Daily Princetonian*, December 2, 1969.

4. Highberger, "How New Call-Up System Will Work"; David E. Rosenbaum, "Lottery Is Held to Set the Order of Draft in 1970," *New York Times*, December 2, 1969.

5. Judge Richard Clifton, interviewed by Peter Canellos and Peder Schaefer.

6. Frank LaMay, "Undergrads Draw First, Last Places in Monday Lottery," *Daily Princetonian*, December 3, 1969.

7. *Confirmation Hearing on the Nomination of Samuel A. Alito, Jr. to Be an Associate Justice of the Supreme Court of the United States*, sec. Sen. Leahy Questioning.

8. Marston, "Almanac: The 1969 Draft Lottery."

9. "Vietnam Lotteries," Selective Service System, https://www.sss.gov/history-and-records/vietnam-lotteries; "Justice Samuel Anthony Alito, Jr.," Supreme Court Historical Society, https://supremecourthistory.org/supreme-court-justices/associate-justice-anthony-alito-jr.

10. Mark Dwyer, "Profile of Supreme Court Nominee Samuel Alito," C-SPAN, January 6, 2006, https://www.c-span.org/program/interview/profile-of-supreme-court-nominee-samuel-alito/152553.

11. Ray Ollwerther, "ROTC Past: Change Through Controversy," *Daily Princetonian*, February 13, 1969.

12. "Class of 1972 Commencement Program—ROTC Commissions," Princeton University, https://pr.princeton.edu/pictures/a-f/alito_samuel_anthony/htm/06commencement_rotc.htm.

13. Joe Schubert, "Students Vote to Retain ROTC," *Daily Princetonian*, April 5, 1971.

14. Jay Johns, "Activists Challenge Princeton to Modernize with the Times," *Daily Princetonian*, January 21, 1970.

15. Luther Munford, "Students Arrested in Armory Arson," *Daily Princetonian*, May 2, 1970.

16. Analysis of keyword searches for "protest" between 1963 and 1978 in *Daily Princetonian* archive at the Princeton University Library, https://papersofprinceton.princeton.edu.

17. "'Smash the Military,'" *Daily Princetonian*, February 3, 1969.

18. Tom Crocker, "ABC, SDS to Protest in Separate Boycotts," *Daily Princetonian*, February 19, 1969.

19. Peter Kaminsky and Douglas Seaton, "Attack on Protest Policy," *Daily Princetonian*, February 5, 1969.

20. Dennis Hevesi, "Walter Hickel, Nixon Interior Secretary, Dies at 90," *New York Times*, May 8, 2010, https://www.nytimes.com/2010/05/09/us/09hickel.html.

21. Bill Highberger, "Goheen Promises Discipline," *Daily Princetonian*, March 6, 1970.

22. Tom Crocker, "Moratorium Committee Schedules Decisive Meeting," *Daily Princetonian*, October 7, 1969; Bill Highberger, "Poll, Petition Boost Moratorium USA Solicits Aid of Congressmen," *Daily Princetonian*, October 13, 1969.

23. Andrew Napolitano, interviewed by Peter Canellos and Peder Schaefer.

24. George Carpinello, Princeton class of 1972, Yale Law School class of 1975, and lawyer, interviewed by Peder Schaefer, August 15, 2025.

25. A. J. Langguth, *Our Vietnam* (Simon & Schuster, 2002), 566.

26. Richard Nixon, "Address by President Nixon," Washington, DC, March 29, 1973, https://history.state.gov/historicaldocuments/frus1969-76v38p1/d6.

27. Jeff Collier, "Mass Chapel Meeting Votes University Strike," *Daily Princetonian*, May 1, 1970; Steve Orso, "1969–70: From 'Beat Rutgers!' to 'On Strike!,'" *Daily Princetonian*, June 20, 1970; Editorial Board, "Striking Back," *Daily Princetonian*, May 1, 1970.

28. Peter Canellos and Peder Schaefer, notes from visit to Princeton University, January 2025; Princeton University, "Princeton University Chapel History," https://chapel.princeton.edu/chapel/chapel.

29. "Princeton University Chapel History."

30. Grif Johnson, class of 1972 at Princeton University, interviewed by Peder Schaefer, May 16, 2025; Alastair Gordon, "Prophet in Our Land: A Personal Reminiscence of Martin Luther King," *Medium*, January 17, 2017, https//medium.com/@alastairgordon/prophet-in-our-land-a-persona-reminiscence-of-martin-luther-king-c9d03c56d32f.

31. Collier, "Mass Chapel Meeting Votes University Strike."

32. Collier, "Mass Chapel Meeting Votes University Strike"; Orso, "1969–70: From 'Beat Rutgers!' to 'On Strike!'"; "Bomb Threats Made," *Town Topics*, May 7, 1970.

33. Collier, "Mass Chapel Meeting Votes University Strike"; Orso, "1969–70: From 'Beat Rutgers!' to 'On Strike!'"

34. Collier, "Mass Chapel Meeting Votes University Strike."

35. Collier, "Mass Chapel Meeting Votes University Strike"; Editorial Board, "Striking Back."

36. Richard Balfour, interviewed by Peder Schaefer.

37. Editorial Board, "Striking Back."

38. Munford, "Students Arrested in Armory Arson"; "Strike Roundup: Rally Draws 500, Bombing Decried," *Daily Princetonian*, May 3, 1970.

39. Munford, "Students Arrested in Armory Arson."

40. "190 Draft Cards Surrendered at Chapel Rite," *Daily Princetonian*, May 3, 1970.

41. Steve Orso and Princetonian Staff, "Anti-War Strike Begins," *Daily Princetonian*, May 2, 1970.

42. Grif Johnson, interviewed by Peder Schaefer, January 23, 2025.

43. "190 Draft Cards Surrendered at Chapel Rite."

44. "190 Draft Cards Surrendered at Chapel Rite."

45. "190 Draft Cards Surrendered at Chapel Rite."

46. "190 Draft Cards Surrendered at Chapel Rite."

47. Dave Elkind, "69 Surrender Draft Cards at Festival," *Daily Princetonian*, May 4, 1970.

48. Grif Johnson, interviewed by Peder Schaefer, January 23, 2025.

49. Bill Highberger, "Council Votes End to ROTC, Supports 'Strike,'" *Daily Princetonian*, May 4, 1970.

50. Jim Dorsey, "University Council Acts as Advisory Body to Trustees," *Daily Princetonian*, June 19, 1971.

51. Highberger, "Council Votes to End ROTC"; Grif Johnson, interviewed by Peder Schaefer, May 16, 2025.

52. Alexander Leitch, "R.O.T.C.," in the *Princeton Companion* (Princeton University Press, 1978).

53. Orso and Princetonian Staff, "Anti-War Strike Begins."

54. Bill Highberger, "Back War Opposition 'as Institution,'" *Daily Princetonian*, May 5, 1970.

55. Tim Johnson, "500 Mourn Kent State Deaths at University Chapel Service," *Daily Princetonian*, May 6, 1970.

56. Highberger, "Back War Opposition 'as Institution.'"

57. Kyla Morgan Young, "Even Princeton: Vietnam and a Culture of Student Activism, 1967–1972," Princeton University Archives, https://universityarchives.princeton.edu/2016/02/even-princeton-vietnam-and-a-culture-of-student-activism-1967-1972.

58. Grif Johnson, interviewed by Peder Schaefer, January 23, 2025.

59. Jerry Raymond, "900 Marchers Protest War Research at IDA," *Daily Princetonian*, May 7, 1970.

60. Alvin L. Young, *Agent Orange: A History of Its Use, Disposition, and Environmental Fate*, Final Report nos. AAD19-02-D-0001 (Washington, DC, 2008), 4; Grif Johnson, interviewed by Peder Schaefer, January 23, 2025.

61. Jerry Raymond, "Strikers Besiege IDA: Computer Halted," *Daily Princetonian*, May 8, 1970.

62. Jerry Raymond, "Protestors Yield to Restraining Order," *Daily Princetonian*, May 12, 1970.

63. "Early Morning Fires Strike Nassau Hall, IDA," *Daily Princetonian*, May 13, 1970.

64. Princeton University, "Nassau Hall," Princetoniana, https://princetoniana.princeton.edu /campus/nassau-hall.

65. Andrew Napolitano, interviewed by Peter Canellos and Peder Schaefer; George Carpinello, interviewed by Peder Schaefer; Judge Richard Clifton, interviewed by Peter Canellos and Peder Schaefer; Alito acquaintance at Princeton, interviewed by Peder Schaefer, May 14, 2025.

66. "Departments Implement Strike Decisions," *Daily Princetonian*, May 6, 1970; Richard Balfour, interviewed by Peder Schaefer; Judge Richard Clifton, interviewed by Peter Canellos and Peder Schaefer.

67. "Editorial," *Daily Princetonian*, May 2, 1970; Luther Munford, interviewed by Peder Schaefer.

68. Judge Richard Clifton, interviewed by Peter Canellos and Peder Schaefer.

69. Judge Richard Clifton, interviewed by Peter Canellos and Peder Schaefer.

70. Tom Henderson, "Lecturer Revolts Against Grades," *Daily Princetonian*, February 5, 1969.

71. *Confirmation Hearing on the Nomination of Samuel A. Alito*, sec. Sen. Hatch Questioning; Bernstein, "A Tiger on the Court."

72. Press release on Alito's ROTC training, Princeton University, June 30, 1970, https:// pr.princeton.edu/pictures/a-f/alito_samuel_anthony/htm/10release_cadet.htm.

73. Undergraduates for a Stable America, "Buckley, Banfield, Jones," *Daily Princetonian*, November 5, 1970; Jerry Raymond, "Buckley Impugns 'Revolutionist' Doctrine," *Daily Princetonian*, December 3, 1970; Jerry Raymond, "USA Seeks Calm Expression of Moderate Campus Views," *Daily Princetonian*, June 20, 1970.

74. Andrew Napolitano, interviewed by Peter Canellos and Peder Schaefer.

75. Andrew Napolitano, interviewed by Peter Canellos and Peder Schaefer.

76. David D. Kirkpatrick, "From Alito's Past, a Window on Conservatives at Princeton," *New York Times*, November 27, 2005, https://www.nytimes.com/2005/11/27/politics/politics /special1/from-alitos-past-a-window-on-conservatives-at.html.

77. Chanakya Sethi, "Alito '72 Joined Conservative Alumni Group," *Daily Princetonian*, November 18, 2005.

78. Kirkpatrick, "From Alito's Past, a Window on Conservatives at Princeton."

79. Undergraduates for a Stable America, "Buckley, Banfield, Jones."

80. William F. Buckley, "The New Protestors," *Princeton Business Today* (Winter 1970), AC 364, box 16, Princeton University Publications Collection, Princeton University Archives.

81. Raymond, "Buckley Impugns 'Revolutionist' Doctrine."

82. Alito, "Samuel Alito Job Application 1985."

83. Schubert, "Students Vote to Retain ROTC."

84. Jeff Rosenzweig, "Board Endorses Pacts, 30–4," *Daily Princetonian*, January 17, 1972.

85. Dave Elkind, "Goheen to Step Down, Discloses No Future Personal Plans," *Daily Princetonian*, March 25, 1971.

86. *Prospect Magazine* in ser. 1, Alumni Publications, Princeton University Publications Collection, AC364, Princeton University Archives.

87. T. Harding Jones, "CAP: We Will Continue Toward Our Goals," *Daily Princetonian*, May 20, 1974.

88. Marine Lepeles, "Conservative Alumni Act to Alter Princeton's Image," *New York Times*, March 3, 1974.

89. Lepeles, "Conservative Alumni Act to Alter Princeton's Image."

90. Chris Daniel, "The Case Against Homosexuality," *Daily Princetonian*, reprinted in *Prospect Letter*, April 15, 1979, in Princeton University Publications Collection, AC364, Princeton University Archives.

91. "In Defense of Elitism," *Prospect Magazine* (1983), in Gregg Lange, "Rally 'Round the Cannon: New Lies, Old Lies . . ," *Princeton Alumni Weekly*, April 22, 2018, https://paw.princeton.edu/article/rally-round-the-cannon-new-lies-old-lies.

92. Tom Feyer, "Alumni Magazine 'Prospect' Gets Mixed Reception," *Daily Princetonian*, December 6, 1972.

93. *Confirmation Hearing on the Nomination of Samuel A. Alito*, sec. Sen. Hatch Questioning.

94. Jennifer Epstein and Matt Davis, "CAP's ROTC Advocacy Died Down in 1980s," *Daily Princetonian*, January 13, 2006; Alito acquaintance at Princeton, interviewed by Peter Canellos and Peder Schaefer, May 14, 2025; Dennis Grzezinski, interviewed by Peder Schaefer.

95. *Confirmation Hearing on the Nomination of Samuel A. Alito*, sec. Sen. Leahy Questioning.

96. Judge Richard Clifton, interviewed by Peter Canellos and Peder Schaefer; Andrew Napolitano, interviewed by Peter Canellos and Peder Schaefer; Alito acquaintance at Princeton, interviewed by Peder Schaefer, May 14, 2025.

97. *Confirmation Hearing on the Nomination of Samuel A. Alito*, sec. Alito Statement.

98. Morgan Young, "Even Princeton: Vietnam and a Culture of Student Activism, 1967–1972."

99. George Carpinello, interviewed by Peder Schaefer.

CHAPTER FIVE: "THE WAGES OF CRYING WOLF"

1. *Confirmation Hearing on the Nomination of Samuel A. Alito*, sec. Sen. Leahy Questioning.

2. Bernstein, "A Tiger on the Court."

3. Bruce Weber, "Walter Murphy, Author and Princeton Political Scientist, Dies at 80," *New York Times*, May 1, 2010.

4. Ruth Stevens, "Leading Constitutional Scholar Walter Murphy Dies at Age 80," press release, Princeton University, April 22, 2010, https//www.princeton.edu/news/2010/04/22/leading-constitutional-scholar-walter-murphy-dies-age-80.

5. Stuart Taylor Jr., "Alito: A Sampling of Misleading Media Coverage," *Atlantic*, December 2005, https://www.theatlantic.com/magazine/archive/2005/12/alito-a-sampling-of-misleading-media-coverage/304478.

6. Chanakya Sethi, "Nominee's Missing Thesis Recovered," *Daily Princetonian*, November 9, 2005.

7. Christian Burset, "Alito '72 Tapped for High Court," *Daily Princetonian*, November 7, 2005.

8. Bernstein, "A Tiger on the Court."

9. Samuel A. Alito Jr., *Final Report*, Conference on the Boundaries of Privacy in American Society, Princeton University, 1971–72, 2, 6, https://archive.epic.org/privacy/justices/alito/princeton.

10. Bernstein, "A Tiger on the Court."

11. Samuel A. Alito Jr., "An Introduction to the Italian Constitutional Court," senior thesis, Princeton University, 1972, 2, https://dataspace.princeton.edu/handle/88435/dsp01cz30pt46d.

12. Alito, "An Introduction to the Italian Constitutional Court," 90.

13. Office of the Historian, US State Department, "Ending the Vietnam War, 1969–1973," https://history.state.gov/milestones/1969-1976/ending-vietnam.

14. Samuel A. Alito Jr., "1972 Nassau Herald Yearbook Entry."

15. "I-Italy Interviews Justice Samuel A. Alito," *I-Italy*.

16. Alito acquaintance at Princeton, interviewed by Peter Canellos and Peder Schaefer, July 11, 2025.

17. "Class of 1972," *Princeton Alumni Weekly*, October 24, 1972, 8, https://www.google.com/books/edition/_/kRlbAAAAYAAJ?gbpv=1.

18. Laura Kalman, professor of history at UC Santa Barbara and author of *Yale Law School and the Sixties*, interviewed by Peter Canellos and Peder Schaefer, June 20, 2025.

19. Samuel A. Alito Jr., "Samuel Alito on the Supreme Court, Recent Court Decisions, and His Education." *Conversations with Bill Kristol*, July 10, 2015, https://conversationswithbillkristol.org/transcript/samuel-alito-transcript.

20. Laura Kalman, interviewed by Peter Canellos and Peder Schaefer.

21. Abington School District v. Schempp, 374 U.S. 203 (1963).

22. Peter Canellos and Peder Schaefer, notes from visit to Yale Law School, July 2025.

23. Laura Kalman, *Yale Law School and the Sixties: Revolt and Reverberations* (University of North Carolina Press, 2010), 1.

24. "Faculty Rejects Proposal," *Yale Law Advocate*, April 3, 1969.

25. Kalman, *Yale Law School and the Sixties*, 1–2.

26. Kalman, *Yale Law School and the Sixties*, 163.

27. Kalman, *Yale Law School and the Sixties*.

28. John Darnton, "8 Black Panthers Seized in Torture-Murder Case," *New York Times*, May 23, 1969; Paul Bass, "50 Years Later, Panther Murder Echoes," *New Haven Independent*, May 20, 2019, https://www.newhavenindependent.org/2019/05/20/50_years_after_murder_panther_.

29. Bass, "50 Years Later, Panther Murder Echoes."

30. Kalman, *Yale Law School and the Sixties*, 209–10.

31. Bass, "50 Years Later, Panther Murder Echoes."

32. Kalman, *Yale Law School and the Sixties*, 204–10.

33. Kalman, *Yale Law School and the Sixties*, 210–12.

34. Megan Vaz, "Memories of May Day: A Look Back at Black Panther Protests at Yale," *Yale Daily News*, February 18, 2022, https://yaledailynews.com/blog/2022/02/18/memories-of-may-day-a-look-back-at-black-panther-protests-at-yale.

35. John Bolton, Yale Law School graduate and former White House national security advisor, interviewed by Peter Canellos and Peder Schaefer, July 25, 2025.

36. Robert Farley, "She Did Not 'Help' the Black Panthers," *PolitiFact*, February 15, 2008, https://www.politifact.com/factchecks/2008/feb/15/chain-email/she-did-not-help-the-black-panthers.

37. Bass, "50 Years Later, Panther Murder Echoes."

38. "Not Asking for Freedom—but Free: Ericka Huggins' Poems from Prison," Verso, https://www.versobooks.com/blogs/news/2883-not-asking-for-freedom-but-free-ericka-huggins-poems-from-prison; "Reading Defeats Seale Easily for Oakland Mayor," *New York Times*, May 17, 1973, https://www.nytimes.com/1973/05/17/archives/reading-defeats-seale-easily-for-oakland-mayor.html.

39. Kalman, *Yale Law School and the Sixties*, 209, 229–30.

40. Kalman, *Yale Law School and the Sixties*, 228, 239; David Trubek, email communication on Yale Law School purge with Peder Schaefer, August 21, 2025.

41. Kalman, *Yale Law School and the Sixties*, 231.

42. Kalman, *Yale Law School and the Sixties*, 231.

43. Judge Richard Clifton, interviewed by Peter Canellos and Peder Schaefer.

44. Dennis Grzezinski, interviewed by Peder Schaefer.

45. John Heilemann, "The Making of Hillary Clinton and Barack Obama," *New York Magazine*, October 12, 2007, https://nymag.com/news/features/39321.

46. John Bolton, interviewed by Peter Canellos and Peder Schaefer.

47. Alito, "Samuel Alito on the Supreme Court, Recent Court Decisions, and His Education"; Alito and Malcolm, "A Conversation with Justice Samuel Alito"; Josh Blackman, "Recap of Federalist Society 30th Anniversary Gala Dinner with Remarks by Justice Alito," November 16, 2012, https://joshblackman.com/blog/2012/11/16/recap-of-federalist-society-30th-anniversary-gala-dinner-with-remarks-by-justice-alito-fedsoc2012.

48. Sam Roberts, "Charles Reich, Who Saw 'The Greening of America,' Dies at 91," *New York Times*, June 17, 2019, https://www.nytimes.com/2019/06/17/books/charles-reich-dead.html.

49. Charles A. Reich, "The New Property," *Yale Law Journal* 73, no. 5 (1964): 733–87.

50. Goldberg v. Kelly, 397 U.S. 254 (1970).

51. Charles Reich, *The Greening of America* (Random House, 1970), 2.

52. Garry Trudeau, "Doonesbury for November 3, 1971," *Doonesbury*, November 3, 1971, https://www.gocomics.com/doonesbury/1971/11/03.

53. Alito, "Samuel Alito on the Supreme Court, Recent Court Decisions, and His Education."

54. Alito, "Samuel Alito on the Supreme Court, Recent Court Decisions, and His Education."

55. John Bolton, interviewed by Peter Canellos and Peder Schaefer.

56. Lawrence Van Gelder, "Alexander M. Bickel Dies; Constitutional Law Expert," *New York Times*, November 8, 1974.

57. Alito, "Samuel Alito on the Supreme Court, Recent Court Decisions, and His Education."

58. Blackman, "Recap of Federalist Society 30th Anniversary Gala Dinner."

59. Hammer v. Dagenhart, 247 U.S. 251 (1918).

60. Alito and Malcolm, "A Conversation with Justice Samuel Alito."

61. Alito, "Samuel Alito on the Supreme Court, Recent Court Decisions, and His Education."

62. Yale Law School graduate, interviewed by Peter Canellos, July 14, 2025.

63. Linda Greenhouse, "Warren E. Burger Is Dead at 87; Was Chief Justice for 17 Years," *New York Times*, June 26, 1995, https://www.nytimes.com/1995/06/26/obituaries/warren-e-burger-is-dead-at-87-was-chief-justice-for-17-years.html.

64. "Historical Abortion Law Timeline: 1850 to Today," Planned Parenthood, https://www.plannedparenthoodaction.org/issues/abortion/abortion-central-history-reproductive-health-care-america/historical-abortion-law-timeline-1850-today.

65. Andy Sullivan, "Explainer: How Abortion Became a Divisive Issue in US Politics," Reuters, June 25, 2022, https://www.reuters.com/world/us/how-abortion-became-divisive-issue-us-politics-2022-06-24.

66. Sarah Churchwell, "Body Politics: The Secret History of the US Anti-Abortion Movement," *Guardian*, July 23, 2022, https://www.theguardian.com/books/2022/jul/23/body-politics.

67. Teddy Roosevelt, "The Man in the Arena," April 23, 1910, Theodore Roosevelt Center, https://www.theodorerooseveltcenter.org/Learn-About-TR/TR-Encyclopedia/Culture-and-Society/Man-in-the-Arena.aspx.

68. Roe v. Wade, 128.

69. Greenhouse, *Becoming Justice Blackmun*, 75–101.

70. Meredith Heagney, "Justice Ruth Bader Ginsburg Offers Critique of Roe v. Wade," University of Chicago Law School, May 15, 2013, https://www.law.uchicago.edu/news/justice-ruth-bader-ginsburg-offers-critique-roe-v-wade-during-law-school-visit.

71. Brown v. Board of Education, 347 U.S. 483 (1954).

72. Greenhouse, *Becoming Justice Blackmun*, 74–75.

73. Greenhouse, *Becoming Justice Blackmun*, 74, 90–91.

74. Roe v. Wade, 207.

75. Greenhouse, *Becoming Justice Blackmun*, 96–97.

76. Roe v. Wade, 150.

77. Greenhouse, *Becoming Justice Blackmun*, 94.

78. Roe v. Wade, 221.

79. Eleanor Klibanoff, "Linda Coffee Argued Roe v. Wade. Now, She's Watching Its Demise," *Texas Tribune*, July 12, 2022, https://www.texastribune.org/2022/07/12/linda-coffee-abortion-texas-roe.

80. Lily Rothman "'A Stunning Approval for Abortion': Roe v. Wade Reactions," *Time Magazine*, January 22, 2015, https://time.com/3669867/roe-v-wade-history.

81. Greenhouse, *Becoming Justice Blackmun*, 101.

82. Ely, "The Wages of Crying Wolf."

83. John Bolton, interviewed by Peter Canellos and Peder Schaefer.

84. "90-Year-Old Mother Mum, Except about Topic of Abortion," *Newhouse News Service*, November 1, 2005, https://www.sunjournal.com/2005/11/01/90-year-old-mother-mum-except-topic-abortion.

85. *Confirmation Hearing on the Nomination of Samuel A. Alito, Jr. to Be an Associate Justice of the Supreme Court of the United States*, sec. Sen. Kohl and Sen. Grassley Questioning.

86. Dobbs v. Jackson, 2.

CHAPTER SIX: A SOCIETY OF THEIR OWN

1. Regents of the University of California v. Bakke, 438 U.S. 265 (1978).

2. *The Crits*, directed by Jeannie Suk Gersen and Jackie Mow, 2021, https://vimeo.com/241232271, 00:47.

3. Laura Kalman, professor of history at UC Santa Barbara and author of *Yale Law School and the Sixties*, interviewed by Peter Canellos and Peder Schaefer, June 20, 2025.

4. G. Edward White, "From Realism to Critical Legal Studies: A Truncated Intellectual History," *SMU Law Review* 40, no. 2 (1986): 819–43; Lawrence M. Friedman, "The Law and Society Movement," *Stanford Law Review* 38, no. 3 (1986): 763–80.

5. Duncan Kennedy, professor emeritus at Harvard Law School, interviewed by Peter Canellos, March 7, 2025.

6. Charles A. Reich, "The New Property," *Yale Law Journal* 73, no. 5 (April 1964): 733–87.

7. *The Crits*, 5:33.

8. *The Crits*, 5:33.

9. *The Crits*, 5:33; *What's My Line? Peter Gabel as Mystery Guest*, https://www.youtube .com/watch?v=RZW8BDgOzNk; Peter Gabel, "Curriculuum Vitae," https://static1 .squarespace.com/static/5a6f69d67131a5a670d8d03d/t/5a838c2c08522971783bf127 /1518570540623/Peter+Gabel+CV.pdf.

10. Tol Krever, Carl Lisberger, and Max Utzschneider, "Law on the Left: A Conversation with Duncan Kennedy," *Unbound* 10 (2015): 1–35, 1.

11. Duncan Kennedy, interviewed by Peter Canellos; Krever, Lisberger, and Utzschneider, "Law on the Left."

12. Duncan Kennedy, "How the Law School Fails: A Polemic," *Yale Review of Law and Social Action* 1 (1970): 71–90.

13. Duncan Kennedy, "Legal Education and the Reproduction of Hierarchy," *Journal of Legal Education* 32, no. 4 (1982): 591–615, 615.

14. Kennedy, *Legal Education and the Reproduction of Hierarchy*, 209–10.

15. Kennedy, *Legal Education and the Reproduction of Hierarchy*, 591.

16. Kennedy, *Legal Education and the Reproduction of Hierarchy*, 602.

17. Kennedy, *Legal Education and the Reproduction of Hierarchy*, 615.

18. Mark Tushnet, "Critical Legal Studies: A Political History," *Yale Law Journal* 100, no. 5 (1991): 1515–44, 1523; John Henry Schlegel, "Notes Toward an Intimate, Opinionated, and Affectionate History of the Conference on Critical Legal Studies," *Stanford Law Review* 36, no. 1/2 (1984): 391–411.

19. *The Crits*, 4:15.

20. *The Crits*, 3:15.

21. Schlegel, "Intimate, Opinionated, and Affectionate History of the Conference on Critical Legal Studies."

22. Samuel A. Alito Jr., "The 'Released Time' Cases Revisited: A Study of Group Decision-making by the Supreme Court," *Yale Law Journal* 83, no. 6 (1974): 1202–36.

23. Alito, "The 'Released Time' Cases Revisited," 1202.

24. Alito, "The 'Released Time' Cases Revisited," 1204.

25. Alito, "The 'Released Time' Cases Revisited," 1203.

26. Alito, "The 'Released Time' Cases Revisited," 1207.

27. Alito, "The 'Released Time' Cases Revisited," 1204, 1236.

28. Samuel A. Alito Jr. "Questionnaire for US Senate Committee on the Judiciary," US Senate Committee on the Judiciary, November 30, 2005, https://cdn.factcheck.org/Uploaded-Files/Alito-2005-Questionnaire1.pdf.

29. Alito, "Questionnaire for US Senate Committee on the Judiciary."

30. Stephen P. Warren, "In Remembrance: Hon. Leonard I. Garth," *Federal Lawyer*, March 2017, 20-23, https://www.fedbar.org/wp-content/uploads/2019/10/Garth-Hon-Leonard-I-aspx-1.pdf.

31. Warren, "In Remembrance: Hon. Leonard I. Garth."

32. *Confirmation Hearing on the Nomination of Samuel A. Alito, Jr. to Be an Associate Justice of the Supreme Court of the United States*, sec. Judge Garth Statement.

33. *Confirmation Hearing on the Nomination of Samuel A. Alito*, sec. Judge Garth Statement.

34. Samuel A. Alito Jr., "Interview with Supreme Court Justice Alito," C-SPAN, September 2, 2009, https://www.c-span.org/program/c-span-specials/supreme-court-justice-alito/205566.

35. Sam Roberts and Maggie Haberman, "Maryanne Trump Barry, Retired Judge and Donald Trump Sister, Dies at 86," *New York Times*, November 13, 2023, https://www.nytimes.com/2023/11/13/us/politics/maryanne-trump-barry-dead.html.

36. *Confirmation Hearing on the Nomination of Samuel A. Alito, Jr. to Be an Associate Justice of the Supreme Court of the United States*, sec. Judge Maryanne Trump Barry Statement.

37. *Confirmation Hearing on the Nomination of Samuel A. Alito*, sec. Judge Maryanne Trump Barry Statement.

38. *Confirmation Hearing on the Nomination of Samuel A. Alito*, sec. Judge Maryanne Trump Barry Statement.

39. Mary L. Trump, *Too Much and Never Enough: How My Family Created the World's Most Dangerous Man* (Simon & Schuster, 2020); Roberts and Haberman, "Maryanne Trump Barry, Retired Judge and Donald Trump Sister."

40. Sethi, "Nominee's Missing Thesis Recovered"; *Confirmation Hearing on the Nomination of Samuel A. Alito*, sec. Judge Leonard I. Garth Statement.

41. Alito acquaintance at Princeton, interviewed by Peter Canellos and Peder Schaefer, July 11, 2025; Alito acquaintance at Princeton, interviewed by Peter Canellos and Peder Schaefer, May 14, 2025.

42. Alito, "Questionnaire for US Senate Committee on the Judiciary."

43. Jonathan Riehl, "The Federalist Society and Movement Conservatism: How a Fractious Coalition on the Right Is Changing Constitutional Law and the Way We Talk and Think about It," PhD thesis, University of North Carolina at Chapel Hill, August 2007, 60, 63.

44. Riehl, "The Federalist Society and Movement Conservatism," 60.

45. "Paid Notice: Deaths James B. Liberman," *New York Times*, June 24, 2000, https://www .nytimes.com/2000/06/24/classified/paid-notice-deaths-liberman-james-b.html; US Census Bureau, "Deen Freed, US Census 1930, Greenwood Lake, Orange, New York," National Archives and Records Administration.

46. Riehl, "The Federalist Society and Movement Conservatism," 60; Mike Pence, "Tribute to Mrs. Jean Marie Slough McIntosh, Mother of Former U.S. House Representative David M. McIntosh," Congressional Record, Volume 153, Part 7, 2007, https://www.gov info.gov/content/pkg/CRECB-2007-pt7/html/CRECB-2007-pt7-Pg9518-4.htm.

47. Riehl, "The Federalist Society and Movement Conservatism," 61–62.

48. Riehl, "The Federalist Society and Movement Conservatism," 64.

49. Randall Balmer, "The Real Origins of the Religious Right," *Politico Magazine*, May 27, 2014, https://www.politico.com/magazine/story/2014/05/religious-right-real-origins -107133.

50. Balmer, "The Real Origins of the Religious Right."

51. Riehl, "The Federalist Society and Movement Conservatism," 59–62.

52. Grover J. Rees III, former chief justice of High Court of American Samoa and former ambassador to East Timor, interviewed by Peter Canellos and Peder Schaefer, August 8, 2025.

53. John Bolton, interviewed by Peter Canellos and Peder Schaefer.

54. Lewis F. Powell Jr., "Attack on the Free Enterprise System," memo to US Chamber of Commerce, 1971, https://scholarlycommons.law.wlu.edu/cgi/viewcontent.cgi?article=1000& context=powellmemo.

55. Powell, "Attack on the Free Enterprise System."

56. Greenhouse, *Becoming Justice Blackmun*, 96–97.

57. Gary Gerstle, *The Rise and Fall of the Neoliberal Order: America and the World in the Free Market Era* (Oxford University Press, 2022), 109.

58. David Daley, "The Other Memo That Started the Conservative Legal Movement," *Atlantic*, July 30, 2024, https://www.theatlantic.com/ideas/archive/2024/07/michael-j-horo witz-report-1980/679236.

59. Zoya Haq, "How the Federalist Society Shaped America's Judiciary," *Yale Daily News*, November 4, 2024, https://yaledailynews.com/blog/2024/11/04/how-the-federalist -society-shaped-americas-judiciary; Marcia Chambers, "Yale Is a Host to 2 Meetings About Politics," *New York Times*, May 2, 1982, https://www.nytimes.com/1982/05/02 /nyregion/yale-is-a-host-to-2-meetings-about-politics.html.

60. Michael Kruse, "The Weekend at Yale That Changed American Politics," *Politico Magazine*, September/October 2018, https://politi.co/2wsW1TL.

61. Grover J. Rees III, interviewed by Peter Canellos and Peder Schaefer.

62. Riehl, "The Federalist Society and Movement Conservatism," 71.

63. Riehl, "The Federalist Society and Movement Conservatism," 72.

64. Grover J. Rees III, interviewed by Peter Canellos and Peder Schaefer.

65. "Special Issue: A Symposium on Federalism," *Harvard Journal of Law and Public Policy* 6 (1982).

66. Richard Posner, *Economic Analysis of Law* (Little, Brown, 1986).

67. Nicholas D. Sawicki, "John T. Noonan: Catholic Author, Teacher and Judge Who Embraced the Paradoxes of Faith," *America Magazine*, November 23, 2022, https://www.americamagazine.org/faith/2022/11/23/john-noonan-legal-scholar-244086; John T. Noonan, Jr., "The Hatch Amendment and the New Federalism," *Harvard Journal of Law and Public Policy* 6 (1982): 93–102.

68. Richard Epstein, professor of law at New York University, interviewed by Peter Canellos and Peder Schaefer, September 5, 2025.

69. Morton Blackwell, conservative organizer and trainer and special assistant to Ronald Reagan, interviewed by Peter Canellos and Peder Schaefer, August 7, 2025.

70. Morton Blackwell, "Student Organizations and Activism," *Harvard Journal of Law and Public Policy* 6 (1982): 135–47.

71. Blackwell, "Student Organizations and Activism," 139.

72. Blackwell, "Student Organizations and Activism," 136.

73. Morton Blackwell, interviewed by Peter Canellos and Peder Schaefer.

74. Antonin Scalia, "The Two Faces of Federalism," *Harvard Journal of Law and Public Policy* 6 (1982): 19–22, 19.

75. Scalia, "The Two Faces of Federalism," 22.

76. Noonan, "The Hatch Amendment and the New Federalism," 101.

77. Robert Bork, "Federalism and Gentrification," Presentation to Federalist Society, Yale Law School, April 24, 1982, https://www.reaganlibrary.gov/public/2023-10/40-219-6927378-005-003-2023.pdf, 4.

78. Bork, "Federalism and Gentrification," 5–6.

79. Morton Blackwell, interviewed by Peter Canellos and Peder Schaefer.

80. Bork, "Federalism and Gentrification," 8–9.

81. Bork, "Federalism and Gentrification," 8–9.

82. Bork, "Federalism and Gentrification," 9.

83. Ralph Winter, "Private Goals and Competition Among State Legal Systems," *Harvard Journal of Law and Public Policy* 6 (1982): 127.

84. William Glaberson, "A. Leon Higginbotham Jr., Federal Judge, Is Dead at 70," *New York Times*, December 15, 1998, https://www.nytimes.com/1998/12/15/us/a-leon-higginbotham-jr-federal-judge-is-dead-at-70.html.

85. Chambers, "Yale Is a Host to 2 Meetings About Politics."

86. Chambers, "Yale Is a Host to 2 Meetings About Politics."

CHAPTER SEVEN: ROBERT BORK'S AMERICA

1. Peggy Noonan, *What I Saw at the Revolution* (Random House, 1990), 53.

2. Noonan, *What I Saw at the Revolution*, 5.

3. Noonan, *What I Saw at the Revolution*.

4. Alito, "Questionnaire for US Senate Committee on the Judiciary."

5. "About Mike," Mike Lee US Senator for Utah, https://www.lee.senate.gov/about-mike; "About James Rex Lee," Gibson Dunn, https://www.gibsondunn.com/lawyer/lee-james-rex.

6. Charles J. Cooper, lawyer and assistant attorney general for Reagan Office of Legal Counsel from 1985 to 1988, interviewed by Peter Canellos and Peder Schaefer, September 29, 2025.

7. "Colleagues Recall Alito's Attention to Detail," Associated Press, November 2, 2005, https://www.nbcnews.com/id/wbna9901124.

8. "Judge Samuel A. Alito Nominated to US Supreme Court," October 31, 2005, https://www.pbs.org/newshour/show/judge-samuel-alito-nominated-to-u-s-supreme-court.

9. Samuel A. Alito Jr. "McDonald v. Smith" Memorandum, Washington, DC, US Justice Department, December 31, 1984, Record Group 60, Department of Justice, Files of Roger Clegg, 1984, accession #060-88-258, box 7, folder Solicitor General, https://www.archives.gov/files/news/samuel-alito/accession-060-88-258/Acc060-88-258-box7-Cleggnotes-1984.pdf.

10. Carolyn Kuhl, "McDonald v. Smith" Supplemental Memorandum, Washington, DC, US Justice Department, January 7, 1985, Record Group 60, Department of Justice, Files of Roger Clegg, 1984, accession #060-88-258, box 7, folder Solicitor General, https://www.archives.gov/files/news/samuel-alito/accession-060-88-258/Acc060-88-258-box7-Clegg-notes-1984.pdf.

11. McDonald v. Smith, 472 U.S. 479 (1985).

12. Janell Ross, "How Police Justify Shootings: The 1974 Killing of an Unarmed Teen Set a Standard," NBC News, January 23, 2020, https://www.nbcnews.com/news/nbcblk/officer-killed-unarmed-teen-1974-it-change-how-police-justify-n1120611.

13. Tennessee v. Garner, 471 U.S. 1 (1985).

14. Samuel A. Alito Jr. "Memphis Police Department v. Garner," Washington, DC, US Department of Justice, May 18, 1984, Record Group 60, Department of Justice, Files of the Deputy Assistant Attorney General, Charles Cooper, 1981–1985, accession #060-89-216, box 19, folder Memphis Police v. Garner, 1984, https://www.archives.gov/files/news/samuel-alito/accession-060-89-216/MemphisPol-v-Garner-1984-box19-memoAlitotoSolicitorGeneral.pdf.

15. Brian K. Landsberg, "Tennessee & Memphis Police Dept. v. Garner," Washington, DC, US Department of Justice, May 24, 1984, Record Group 60, Department of Justice, Files of the Deputy Assistant Attorney General, Charles Cooper, 1981–1985, accession #060-89-216, box 19, folder Memphis Police v. Garner, 1984, https://www.archives.gov/files/news/samuel-alito/accession-060-89-216/MemphisPol-v-Garner-1984-box19-memoLandsburgtoReynolds.pdf.

16. Tennessee v. Garner, 471 U.S. 1 (1985).

17. Thornburgh v. Amer. Coll. of Obstetricians, 476 U.S. 747 (1986); Diamond v. Charles, 476 U.S. 54 (1986).

18. Samuel A. Alito Jr. "Thornburgh v. American College of Obstetricians and Gynecologists; Diamond v. Charles," Memorandum, Washington, DC, US Justice Department, May 30 1985, Record Group 60, Department of Justice, Files of the Deputy Assistant Attorney General, Charles Cooper, 1981–1985, accession #060-89-216, box 20, folder Thornburgh v. American College of Obstetricians & Gynecologists, 8, 17, https://www.archives.gov /files/news/samuel-alito/accession-060-89-216/Thornburgh-v-ACOG-1985-box20 -memoAlitotoSolicitorGeneral-May30.pdf.

19. Charles J. Cooper, interviewed by Peter Canellos and Peder Schaefer.

20. David D. Kirkpatrick, "Alito File Shows Strategy to Curb Abortion Ruling," New York Times, December 1, 2005, https://www.nytimes.com/2005/12/01/politics/politics special1/alito-file-shows-strategy-to-curb-abortion-ruling.html.

21. Thornburgh v. Amer. Coll. of Obstetricians, 476 U.S. 747 (1986).

22. Kirkpatrick, "Alito File Shows Strategy to Curb Abortion Ruling."

23. Charles Fried, "Samuel Alito, In Context," New York Times, January 3, 2006, https://www .nytimes.com/2006/01/03/opinion/samuel-alito-in-context.html.

24. Martha-Ann Alito, "Carol Los Mansmann Award Ceremony," Pittsburgh, PA, April 28, 2007, https://www.c-span.org/program/public-affairs-event/carol-los-mansmann-award /173516.

25. Martha-Ann Alito, "Carol Los Mansmann Award Ceremony."

26. "Students to Study in New York," Lexington Herald, May 23, 1972; Josh Kegley, "Kentucky-Born Wife of Justice Alito Speaks to UK Audience," Lexington Herald-Leader, October 3, 2010, https://www.kentucky.com/latest-news/article44052267.html.

27. "Senior Girls Named Area 'Homemakers,'" Times of Trenton, February 15, 1971.

28. Martha-Ann Alito, "Carol Los Mansmann Award Ceremony."

29. Monsignor Thomas N. Gervasio, pastor at Our Lady of Sorrows Church in Mercerville, interviewed by Timmy Facciola and Peder Schaefer, January 27, 2024.

30. Martha-Ann Alito, "Letter from Martha-Ann Alito to Judge Ed Becker," February 10, 2006, Becker Papers, ser. III, folder II, Alito Confirmation Hearings, Yale Law School.

31. Person who observed the Alitos in social settings, interviewed by Peter Canellos, April 29, 2025.

32. Austin Lee Steelman, "Paper Gods: The Bible, the Constitution, and the Evangelical Revolt against Modernity, 1923–1986," PhD thesis, Stanford University, 2024, https://purl .stanford.edu/np775yg4479, 246-247.

33. Steelman, "Paper Gods," 267.

34. Lee Davidson, "Supreme Court Justices Pay Tribute to the Late Rex E. Lee," *BYU Magazine*, Fall 1996, https://magazine.byu.edu/article/supreme-court-justices-pay-tribute-to -the-late-rex-e-lee.

35. Evan Thomas, *First: Sandra Day O'Connor* (Random House, 2019), 5–7.

36. Thomas, *First*, 36.

37. Nina Totenberg, "O'Connor, Rehnquist and a Supreme Marriage Proposal," NPR, October 31, 2018, https://www.npr.org/2018/10/31/662293127/a-supreme-marriage-proposal.

38. Steelman, "Paper Gods," 264.

39. Steelman, "Paper Gods," 263, 267.

40. Steelman, "Paper Gods," 287.

41. Riehl, "The Federalist Society and Movement Conservatism," 105.

42. Margaret Talbot, "Justice Alito's Crusade Against Secular America Isn't Over," *New Yorker*, August 28, 2022.

43. Riehl, "The Federalist Society and Movement Conservatism," 89.

44. Riehl, "The Federalist Society and Movement Conservatism," 90

45. "Frank S. Meyer, Political Writer," *New York Times*, April 3, 1972.

46. Riehl, "The Federalist Society and Movement Conservatism," 92, 100–101.

47. Sherry Bebitch Jeffe and Douglas Jeffe, "From Big Tent to 'Pup Tent' GOP," *Politico*, July 20, 2011, https://www.politico.com/story/2011/07/from-big-tent-to-pup-tent-gop-059358.

48. Maurice Holland, "Prospects for Federalism," *Harvard Journal of Law and Public Policy* 6 (1982): 31–39, 31.

49. Edwin Meese, "American Bar Association Meeting Speech," Washington, DC, July 9, 1985, https://www.justice.gov/sites/default/files/ag/legacy/2011/08/23/07-09-1985.pdf.

50. Meese, "American Bar Association Meeting Speech."

51. Calabresi and Lawson, *The Meese Revolution*, 4.

52. Edwin Meese, "Christian Legal Society Breakfast Speech," San Diego, California, September 29, 1985, US Department of Justice, https://www.justice.gov/sites/default/files/ag /legacy/2011/08/23/09-29-1985.pdf.

53. Edwin Meese, "DC Chapter of the Federalist Society Lawyers Division Speech," Washington, DC, November 15, 1985, US Department of Justice, https://www.justice.gov/sites /default/files/ag/legacy/2011/08/23/11-15-1985.pdf.

54. Riehl, "The Federalist Society and Movement Conservatism," 92.

55. Edwin Meese, "The Law of the Constitution Speech at Tulane University," October 21, 1986, New Orleans, Louisiana, US Department of Justice, https://www.justice.gov/sites /default/files/ag/legacy/2011/08/23/10-21-1986.pdf.

56. Charles J. Cooper, interviewed by Peter Canellos and Peder Schaefer.

57. Charles J. Cooper, interviewed by Peter Canellos and Peder Schaefer.

58. Charles J. Cooper, interviewed by Peter Canellos and Peder Schaefer.

59. Charles J. Cooper, interviewed by Peter Canellos and Peder Schaefer.

60. Alito, "Samuel Alito Job Application 1985."

61. Memo from Carolyn Kuhl to the Litigation Strategy Working Group, Files of Galebach, Stephen, 1985–1987, accession #060-89-269, box 6, folder SG / Litigation Strategy Working Group, https://www.archives.gov/files/news/samuel-alito/accession-060-89-269 /Acc060-89-269-box6-SG-LSWG-memoKuhl-Jan311986.pdf; Memo from Edward Meese III to the Litigation Strategy Working Group, February 3, 1986, Files of Galebach, Stephen, 1985–1987 accession #060-89-1, box 9, folder SG / Litigation Strategy Working Group, https://www.archives.gov/files/news/samuel-alito/accession-060-89-1/Acc060-89 -1-box9-memoAyer-LSWG-Jul1986.pdf; Memo From Samuel A. Alito to the Litigation Strategy Working Group, February 5, 1986, Files of Galebach, Stephen, 1985–1987, accession #060-89-269, box 6, folder SG / Litigation Strategy Working Group, https:// www.archives.gov/files/news/samuel-alito/accession-060-89-269/Acc060-89-269-box6 -SG-LSWG-AlitotoLSWG-Feb1986.pdf; Memo from Donald B. Ayer to the Litigation Strategy Working Group Concerning Possible Separation of Powers Issue, September 2, 1986, Files of Galebach, Stephen, 1985–1987 accession #060-89-1, box 9, folder SG / Litigation Strategy Working Group, https://www.archives.gov/files/news/samuel -alito/accession-060-89-1/Acc060-89-1-box9-memoAyer-LSWG-Sep1986.pdf.

62. School Board of Nassau County Fla. v. Arline, 480 U.S. 273 (1987).

63. Elliot Pinsley, "New Face Joins War on the Mob," *Sunday Record*, March 22, 1987.

64. Samuel A. Alito Jr., "Administrative Law & Regulation: Presidential Oversight and the Administrative State," 2 *Engage* 12 (2001), in John Harrison, "The Unitary Executive and the Scope of Executive Power," *Yale Law Journal* 126 (2016), https://yalelawjournal.org /forum/the-unitary-executive-and-the-scope-of-executive-power.

65. Charles J. Cooper, interviewed by Peter Canellos and Peder Schaefer.

66. Grover J. Rees III, interviewed by Peter Canellos and Peder Schaefer.

67. Grover J. Rees III, interviewed by Peter Canellos and Peder Schaefer; Charles J. Cooper, interviewed by Peter Canellos and Peder Schaefer; John Bolton, interviewed by Peter Canellos and Peder Schaefer.

68. American Bar Association, "Standing Committee on the Federal Judiciary: What It Is and How It Works," 2025, https://www.americanbar.org/content/dam/aba/administrative /federal_judiciary/fjc-backgrounder-2025.pdf.

69. Joel K. Goldstein, "Choosing Justices: How Presidents Decide," *Journal of Law and Politics*, Stetson Law Review (2011), Saint Louis University Legal Studies Research Paper No. 2011-09, https://scholarship.law.slu.edu/cgi/viewcontent.cgi?article=1523&context =faculty; Roe v. Wade.

70. Calabresi and Lawson, *The Meese Revolution*, 268; Grover J. Rees III, interviewed by Peter Canellos and Peder Schaefer.

71. Charles J. Cooper, interviewed by Peter Canellos and Peder Schaefer.

72. Charles J. Cooper, interviewed by Peter Canellos and Peder Schaefer.

73. Calabresi and Lawson, *The Meese Revolution*, 267–68.

74. Federal Judicial Center, "Biographical Directory of Article III Federal Judges, 1789–present," https://www.fjc.gov/history/judges.

75. "Rehnquist, William Hubbs," Federal Judicial Center, https://www.fjc.gov/history/judges/rehnquist-william-hubbs; "Scalia, Antonin," Federal Judicial Center, https://www.fjc.gov/history/judges/scalia-antonin.

76. Ralph G. Neas, former Senate aide to Sen. Edward Brooke and Sen. David Durenberger, interviewed by Peter Canellos and Timmy Facciola, August 8, 2025.

77. Adam Liptak, "The Memo That Rehnquist Wrote and Had to Disown," *New York Times*, September 11, 2005, https://www.nytimes.com/2005/09/11/weekinreview/the-memo-that-rehnquist-wrote-and-had-to-disown.html.

78. Ralph G. Neas, interviewed by Peter Canellos and Timmy Facciola.

79. For Rehnquist debate, see "Cloture Motion," *Congressional Record*, December 10, 1971, pp. 46110–17 in "Supreme Court Appointment Process: Senate Debate and Confirmation Process," Congressional Research Service, https://www.congress.gov/crs-product/R44234.

80. "Antonin Scalia," 99th Congress, September 17, 1986, https://www.congress.gov/nomination/99th-congress/1193.

81. Ethan Bronner, *Battle for Justice: How the Bork Nomination Shook America* (W. W. Norton, 1989), 17.

82. Bronner, *Battle for Justice*, 208–40.

83. Sean Wilentz, *The Age of Reagan: A History, 1974–2008* (Harpers, 2008), 192.

84. Peter S. Canellos, ed., *Last Lion: The Fall and Rise of Ted Kennedy* (Simon & Schuster, 2009), 250–53.

85. Canellos, *Last Lion*, 252.

86. "News at a Glance," UPI, July 6, 1987, https://www.upi.com/Archives/1987/07/06/NEWS-AT-A-GLANCE/4309552542400.

87. Wilentz, *The Age of Reagan*, 127; John Bolton, interviewed by Peter Canellos and Peder Schaefer.

88. Bolling v. Sharpe, 347 U.S. 497 (1954).

89. Bronner, *Battle for Justice*, 238.

90. Bronner, *Battle for Justice*, 232–33.

91. John Bolton, interviewed by Peter Canellos and Peder Schaefer.

92. Wilentz, *The Age of Reagan*, 192.

93. "Text of Reagan's Statement on Bork," UPI, October 23, 1987, https://www.upi.com/Archives/1987/10/23/Text-of-Reagans-statement-on-Bork/3407561960000.

94. Ralph G. Neas, interviewed by Peter Canellos and Timmy Facciola.

95. John Bolton, interviewed by Peter Canellos and Peder Schaefer.

96. Tim Drake, "Judge Bork Converts to the Catholic Faith," Catholic Education Resource Center, 2003, https://catholiceducation.org/en/faith-and-character/judge-bork-converts -to-the-catholic-faith.html.

97. Robert H. Bork, *Slouching Towards Gomorrah: Modern Liberalism and Decline* (Harper-Collins, 1996).

CHAPTER EIGHT: ALITO RISING

1. *Confirmation Hearing on the Nomination of Samuel A. Alito, Jr. to Be an Associate Justice of the Supreme Court of the United States*, sec. Sen. Kohl Questioning.

2. Robert Cohen, "New US Attorney Appointed for Jersey," *Newark Star-Ledger*, March 20, 1987.

3. "New US Attorney Returning to His Home Turf," *Trenton Times*, March 21, 1987.

4. "Samuel A. Alito, 73, Pioneer in Legislature," *Trenton Times*, May 21, 1987.

5. Roberto Suro, "338 Guilty in Sicily in a Mafia Trial: 19 Get Life Terms," *New York Times*, December 17, 1987, https://www.nytimes.com/1987/12/17/world/338-guilty-in-sicily-in -a-mafia-trial-19-get-life-terms.html; M. A. Farber, "US-Italian Teamwork Bringing Organized-Crime Chiefs to Trial," *New York Times*, October 18, 1985, https://www.ny times.com/1985/10/18/world/us-italian-teamwork-bringing-organized-crime-chiefs-to -trial.html.

6. Alan Cowell, "Sicily Bomb Kills Anti-Mafia Fighter and 5 Others," *New York Times*, May 24, 1992, https://www.nytimes.com/1992/05/24/world/sicily-bomb-kills-anti -mafia-fighter-and-5-others.html.

7. Suro, "338 Guilty in Sicily in Mafia Trial."

8. Farber, "US-Italian Teamwork Bringing Organized-Crime Chiefs to Trial."

9. "Rudy in Leather and Lace," *Slate*, September 6, 2005, https://www.slate.com/articles /news_and_politics/politics/2005/09/rudy-in-leather-and-lace.html.

10. Arnold H. Lubasch, "17 Found Guilty in 'Pizza' Trial of a Drug Ring," *New York Times*, March 3, 1987, https://www.nytimes.com/1987/03/03/nyregion/17-found-guilty-in-pizza -trial-of-a-drug-ring.html.

11. Elliot Pinsley, "New Face Joins War on the Mob," *Sunday Record*, March 22, 1987.

12. Kathy Barrett Carter, "Expert Witness Rules Out 'Accident' in Attempted Murder of FBI Agent," *Newark Star-Ledger*, December 2, 1987.

13. Daniel J. Walkin, "A Prosecutor Known for His Common Sense and Straightforward Style," *New York Times*, November 2, 2005, https://www.nytimes.com/2005/11/02 /politics/politicsspecial1/a-prosecutor-known-for-his-common-sense-and.html.

14. Joseph F. Sullivan, "A New Breed of Crime Figure," *New York Times*, August 23, 1985, https://www.nytimes.com/1985/08/23/nyregion/a-new-breed-of-crime-figure.html.

15. Robert Rudolph, "Mob Trials Suffering from Illness-Induced Delays," *Newark Star-Ledger,* July 12, 1987.

16. "Prosecutor: Not Embarrassed by Mob Loss," UPI, August 26, 1988, https://www.upi .com/Archives/1988/08/26/Prosecutor-not-embarrassed-by-mob-loss/3191588571200.

17. Elliot Pinsley, "Judge Blamed for Lucchese Jury's Confusion," *Record,* August 30, 1988.

18. Charles Strum, "2 Top New Jersey Crime Figures Admit Jury Bribery in US Trials," *New York Times,* September 21, 1993.

19. Robert Rudolph, "Union Office, 14 Firms, Raided in Mob Probe," *Newark Star-Ledger,* July 23, 1987.

20. Ted Sherman, "John Riggi, Jersey Mob Boss Who Inspired 'The Sopranos,' Dead at 90," NJ.com, August 4, 2015, https://www.nj.com/news/2015/08/john_riggi_the_jersey _mob_boss_who_inspired_the_so.html.

21. Robert Rudolph, "Jury Hands Riggi a Split Decision," *Newark Star-Ledger,* July 21, 1990.

22. "Justice Alito Whacks 'The Sopranos,'" CBS News, February 14, 2008, https://www .cbsnews.com/news/justice-alito-whacks-the-sopranos.

23. Patricia Alex, "Alito Is No Fan of Tony Soprano," *Record,* February 14, 2008.

24. Cowell, "Sicily Bomb Kills Anti-Mafia Fighter and 5 Others."

25. Tony Mauro, "Justices, Law Enforcement Officials Pay Tribute to Assassinated Italian Judge," *Blog of Legal Times,* October 29, 2009, https://web.archive.org/web/20210 925162941/https://legaltimes.typepad.com/blt/2009/10/justices-law-enforcement-offi cials-pay-tribute-to-assassinated-italian-judge.html.

26. Philip Shenon, "Nominee Left College to Be Matchmaker," *New York Times,* October 30, 1987, https://www.nytimes.com/1987/10/30/us/nominee-left-college-to-be-matchmaker.html.

27. Steven V. Roberts, "Ginsburg Withdraws Name as Supreme Court Nominee, Citing Marijuana 'Clamor,'" *New York Times,* November 8, 1987, https://www.nytimes.com/1987/11/08 /us/ginsburg-withdraws-name-as-supreme-court-nominee-citing-marijuana-clamor.html.

28. Henry J. Reske, "Kennedy Could Be a Swing Vote Moderate Like Powell," UPI, November 12, 1987, https://www.upi.com/Archives/1987/11/12/Kennedy-could-be-a-swing -vote-moderate-like-Powell/4250563691600.

29. Steven Teles, *The Rise of the Conservative Legal Movement: The Battle for Control of the Law* (Princeton University Press, 2008), 169–70.

30. Teles, *The Rise of the Conservative Legal Movement.*

31. Teles, *The Rise of the Conservative Legal Movement,* 169.

32. Teles, *The Rise of the Conservative Legal Movement,* 148–49.

33. Charles J. Cooper, interviewed by Peter Canellos and Peder Schaefer; John Bolton, interviewed by Peter Canellos and Peder Schaefer.

34. Calvin Trillin, "A Reporter at Large: Harvard Law," *New Yorker,* March 19, 1984, 53–83, https://www.newyorker.com/magazine/1984/03/26/harvard-law.

35. Teles, *The Rise of the Conservative Legal Movement*, 193–94.
36. Teles, *The Rise of the Conservative Legal Movement*, 195.
37. Teles, *The Rise of the Conservative Legal Movement*, 196.
38. Judy Mann, "A Win for the 'Wrong Kind of Woman,'" *Washington Post*, September 29, 1993, https://www.washingtonpost.com/archive/sports/1993/09/29/a-win-for-the-wrong-kind -of-women/b01e5aec-c7bc-422d-b399-bb43a7c308d5.
39. Jelani Cobb, "The Man Behind Critical Race Theory," *New Yorker*, September 13, 2021, https://www.newyorker.com/magazine/2021/09/20/the-man-behind-critical-race-theory.
40. Mary Joe Frug, "A Postmodern Feminist Legal Manifesto (an Unfinished Draft)," *Harvard Law Review* 105, no. 5 (1992): 1045–75, https://doi.org/10.2307/1341520.
41. Stephen Frug, son of Mary Joe Frug and Gerald Frug and intellectual historian, interviewed by Peter Canellos and Peder Schaefer, September 25, 2025.
42. Matthew Brelis, "An Accomplished Life, a Brutal Death," *Boston Globe*, April 14, 1991.
43. Jennifer A. Kingson, "Harvard Tenure Battle Puts 'Critical Legal Studies' on Trial," *New York Times*, August 30, 1987, https://www.nytimes.com/1987/08/30/weekinreview /harvard-tenure-battle-puts-critical-legal-studies-on-trial.html.
44. Emily Bernstein, "Bok Rejects Dalton Tenure Appeal," *Harvard Crimson*, February 9, 2003, https://www.thecrimson.com/article/2003/2/9/bok-rejects-dalton-tenure-appeal-ppresident.
45. Anna D. Wilde, "Law School Settles Case of Sex Discrimination," September 21, 1993, https://www.thecrimson.com/article/1993/9/22/law-school-settles-case-of-sex.
46. Ronald Reagan, "Remarks to the Federalist Society for Law and Public Policy Studies," Washington, DC, September 9, 1988, https://www.reaganlibrary.gov/archives/speech /remarks-federalist-society-law-and-politics-studies.
47. "Robert C. Clark," Harvard Law School, https://hls.harvard.edu/faculty/robert-c-clark; Peter Collier, "Blood on the Charles," *Vanity Fair*, October 1992, https://archive.vanityfair .com/article/1992/10/blood-on-the-charles.
48. Matthew Brelis, "6 Months Shed Little Light on Frug Case," *Boston Globe*, October 20, 1991; "Murder Jolts Haven for Elite in Boston Area," *New York Times*, April 9, 1991; Collier, "Blood on the Charles"; Brelis, "An Accomplished Life, a Brutal Death."
49. Richard de Silva, "Reward Offered in Frug Case," *Harvard Crimson*, April 8, 1992, https:// www.thecrimson.com/article/1992/4/9/reward-offered-in-frug-case-pthe.
50. Brelis, "An Accomplished Life, a Brutal Death."
51. Frug, "A Postmodern Feminist Legal Manifesto (an Unfinished Draft)."
52. Collier, "Blood on the Charles."
53. Marion Gammill, "Law Review Apologizes for Parody of Frug Piece," *Harvard Crimson*, April 12, 1992, https://www.thecrimson.com/article/1992/4/13/law-review-apologizes -for-parody-of.
54. Collier, "Blood on the Charles."

55. Collier, "Blood on the Charles."

56. Stephen Frug, "Mary Joe Frug, 1941–1991," *Attempts*, April 4, 2011, https://stephenfrug .blogspot.com/2011/04/mary-joe-frug-1941-1991.html.

57. Stephen Frug, interviewed by Peter Canellos and Peder Schaefer.

58. Duncan Kennedy, interviewed by Peter Canellos.

59. Krever, Lisberger, and Utzschneider, "Law on the Left."

60. Philip Shenon, "Meese Says He'll Step Down, Contending He Is Vindicated by the Special Prosecutor," *New York Times*, July 6, 1988, https://www.nytimes.com/1988/07/06/us /meese-says-he-ll-step-down-contending-he-is-vindicated-by-the-special-prosecutor.html.

61. Richard L. Berke, "Senate Confirms Souter, 90 to 9, as Supreme Court's 105th Justice," *New York Times*, October 3, 1990, https://www.nytimes.com/1990/10/03/us/senate-con firms-souter-90-to-9-as-supreme-court-s-105th-justice.html.

62. Press Release from the Office of the White House Press Secretary, February 9, 1990, Lee S. Lieberman Files, Judicial Candidate Files, George H. W. Bush Presidential Records, White House Counsels Office, box 1, OA/ID 45297, stack G, row 17, sec. 15, shelf 6, position 1, George Bush Presidential Library, College Station, TX.

63. Memo from Samuel Alito Jr. to Lee Lieberman, November 17, 1989, Lee S. Lieberman Files, Judicial Candidate Files, George H. W. Bush Presidential Records, White House Counsels Office, box 1, OA/ID 45297, stack G, row 17, sec. 15, shelf 6, position 1, George Bush Presidential Library, College Station, TX.

64. Robert Cohen, "Alito Easily Clears Key Committee," *Newark Star-Ledger*, April 6, 1990.

65. Cohen, "Alito Easily Clears Key Committee."

66. Former Alito Third Circuit clerks, interviewed by Peter Canellos, April 2, 2025, and April 4, 2025.

67. Former Alito Third Circuit clerk, interviewed by Peter Canellos, April 4, 2025.

68. Former Alito Third Circuit clerk, interviewed by Peter Canellos, April 2, 2025.

69. Former Alito Third Circuit clerk, interviewed by Peter Canellos, April 2, 2025.

70. Former Alito Third Circuit clerk, interviewed by Peter Canellos, April 4, 2025.

71. *Confirmation Hearing on the Nomination of Samuel A. Alito*, sec. Judge Garth Statement; *Confirmation Hearing on the Nomination of Samuel A. Alito*, sec. Judge Trump Statement; *Confirmation Hearing on the Nomination of Samuel A. Alito*, sec. Judge Becker Statement; Former Alito Third Circuit clerk, interviewed by Peter Canellos and Peder Schaefer, October 14, 2025.

72. Planned Parenthood of Southeastern Pennsylvania et al. v. Casey, 947 F.2d 682 (1991).

73. Planned Parenthood of Southeastern Pennsylvania et al. v. Casey.

74. Planned Parenthood of Southeastern Pennsylvania et al. v. Casey.

75. United States of America v. Raymond Rybar, Jr., Appellant, 103 F.3d 273 (1996).

76. C.h., As Guardian Ad Litem of Z.h., a Minor, and C.h., Individually Appellant v. Grace Oliva; Gail Pratt; Patrick Johnson; Medford Township Board of Education; Leo Klag-

holtz, Commissioner of Education; the State of New Jersey Department of Education, 226 F.3d 198 (3d Cir. 2000).

77. Doe v. Groody, 361 F.3d 232 (2004).

CHAPTER NINE: A CONSERVATIVE REVOLT

1. Former Alito Third Circuit clerk, interviewed by Peter Canellos, April 2, 2025.

2. R. W. Apple Jr, "The Thomas Confirmation; Senate Confirms Thomas, 52–48, Ending Week of Bitter Battle; 'Time for Healing,' Judge Says," *New York Times*, October 16, 1991, https://www.nytimes.com/1991/10/16/us/thomas-confirmation-senate-confirms-thomas -52-48-ending-week-bitter-battle-time.html.

3. "Clarence Thomas," Federal Judicial Center, https://www.fjc.gov/history/judges/thomas -clarence ; "Samuel Alito," Federal Judicial Center, https://www.fjc.gov/history/judges /alito-samuel-jr.

4. Julia Jacobs, "Anita Hill's Testimony and Other Key Moments from the Clarence Thomas Hearings," *New York Times*, September 20, 2018, https://www.nytimes.com/2018/09/20 /us/politics/anita-hill-testimony-clarence-thomas.html.

5. Clarence Thomas, "Statement Before the Senate Judiciary Committee on Anita Hill Allegations," October 11, 1991, Senate Judiciary Committee, Washington, DC, https://www .americanrhetoric.com/speeches/clarencethomashightechlynching.htm.

6. Aaron Nielson and RonNell Andersen Jones, "Clarence Thomas the Questioner," *Northwestern University Law Review* 111, no. 4 (2017), https://scholarlycommons.law.north western.edu/nulr/vol111/iss4/8.

7. Jill Abramson and Jane Mayer, *Strange Justice: The Selling of Clarence Thomas* (Houghton Mifflin Harcourt, 1994).

8. David Brock, *The Real Anita Hill: The Untold Story* (Macmillan, 1993).

9. Nomination of Ruth Bader Ginsberg to the Supreme Court, US Senate, August 3, 1993, https://www.senate.gov/legislative/LIS/roll_call_votes/vote1031/vote_103_1_00232.htm; Nomination of Stephen Breyer to the Supreme Court, US Senate, July 29, 1994, https:// www.senate.gov/legislative/LIS/roll_call_votes/vote1032/vote_103_2_00242.htm.

10. Peter S. Canellos, "For Ex-Clinton Picks, Cold Comfort," *Boston Globe*, October 27, 1996.

11. "Federal Judges Nominated by Bill Clinton," Ballotpedia, https://ballotpedia.org /Federal_judges_nominated_by_Bill_Clinton.

12. Canellos, "For Ex-Clinton Picks, Cold Comfort."

13. "Strengthening The Judiciary," President George W. Bush Record of Achievement, White House, https://georgewbush-whitehouse.archives.gov/infocus/achievement/chap17.html.

14. "William Rehnquist Court (1986–2005)," Justia Law, https://supreme.justia.com /supreme-court-history/rehnquist-court.

15. Thomas, *First*, 82.

16. McCreary County v. American Civil Liberties Union, 545 U.S. 844 (2005).

17. David Daley, "'No More Souters,'" *Salon*, May 16, 2025, https://www.salon.com/2025/05
    /16/no-more-souters.

18. Alberto Gonzales, interviewed October 14–15, 2010, George W. Bush Oral History Proj-
    ect, University of Virginia Miller Center, https://millercenter.org/the-presidency/presi
    dential-oral-histories/alberto-r-gonzales.

19. Gonzales, George W. Bush Oral History Project.

20. Calabresi and Lawson, *The Meese Revolution*, 19.

21. Gonzales, George W. Bush Oral History Project.

22. Gonzales, George W. Bush Oral History Project.

23. Gonzales, George W. Bush Oral History Project.

24. Gonzales, George W. Bush Oral History Project.

25. Emily Bazelon, "The Front-Runners on Roe," *Slate*, July 5, 2005, https://slate.com
    /news-and-politics/2005/07/the-front-runners-on-roe.html.

26. Karl Rove, interviewed November 8–9, 2013, George W. Bush Oral History Project,
    University of Virginia Miller Center, https://millercenter.org/the-presidency/presiden
    tial-oral-histories/karl-rove-oral-history-part-ii.

27. Gonzales, George W. Bush Oral History Project.

28. Rove, George W. Bush Oral History Project.

29. Gonzales, George W. Bush Oral History Project.

30. Rove, George W. Bush Oral History Project.

31. Karl Rove, former George W. Bush advisor, interviewed by Peter Canellos, May 2, 2025.

32. Bush, *Decision Points*, 98.

33. Rove, George W. Bush Oral History Project.

34. Jeffrey Toobin, "Blowing Up the Senate," *New Yorker*, February 28, 2005, https://www
    .newyorker.com/magazine/2005/03/07/blowing-up-the-senate.

35. "Senators Compromise on Filibusters," CNN, May 24, 2005, https://www.cnn.com/2005
    /POLITICS/05/23/filibuster.fight/index.html.

36. Ralph Neas, interviewed by Peter Canellos and Timmy Facciola.

37. Todd S. Purdum, "Court Nominee's Life Is Rooted in Faith and Respect for Law," *New
    York Times*, July 21, 2005, https://www.nytimes.com/2005/07/21/politics/court-nomi
    nees-life-is-rooted-in-faith-and-respect-for-law.html.

38. Bush, *Decision Points*, 99.

39. *Confirmation Hearing on the Nomination of John G. Roberts, Jr. to Be Chief Justice of the United
    States*, US Senate (2005), https://www.judiciary.senate.gov/imo/media/doc/GPO-CHRG
    -ROBERTS.pdf; Gwyneth K. Shaw, "Roberts: Roe 'Settled as Precedent,'" *Chicago Tri-
    bune*, September 14, 2005, https://www.chicagotribune.com/2005/09/14/roberts-roe
    -settled-as-precedent.

40. Shaw, "Roberts: Roe 'Settled as Precedent.'"

41. Patrick Leahy, interviewed by Melissa Block, NPR, September 22, 2005, https://www.npr
.org/2005/09/22/4859802/leahy-backs-roberts-despite-initial-criticism.

42. Ralph Neas, interviewed by Peter Canellos and Timmy Facciola.

43. Nomination of John G. Roberts to the Supreme Court, US Senate, September 29, 2005,
https://www.senate.gov/legislative/LIS/roll_call_votes/vote1091/vote_109_1_00245.htm.

44. "Laura Bush Speaks Out on Abortion," ABC News, January 19, 2001, https://abcnews
.go.com/Politics/story?id=122008&page=1.

45. Bush, *Decision Points*, 99.

46. Bush, *Decision Points*, 100.

47. "Harriet Miers Fast Facts," CNN, September 19, 2013, https://www.cnn.com/us/harriet
-miers-fast-facts.

48. William McKinley appointed Joseph McKenna; Theodore Roosevelt appointed William
Henry Moody; Woodrow Wilson appointed James Clark McReynolds; Calvin Coolidge
appointed Harlan F. Stone; Franklin D. Roosevelt appointed Robert Jackson; Harry Truman appointed Tom Clark.

49. William Howard Taft is the former president; Charles Evans Hughes is the former Republican nominee for president; Earl Warren is the former California governor; Salmon Chase
is the former Ohio senator; Fred Vinson is the former Kentucky congressman.

50. Jan Crawford Greenberg, *Supreme Conflict: The Inside Story of the Struggle for Control of the
United States Supreme Court* (Penguin, 2008), 256.

51. Karl Rove, interviewed by Peter Canellos.

52. Richard Garnett, "The Miers Nomination," *National Review*, October 3, 2005.

53. John H. Fund, "Judgment Call," *Wall Street Journal*, October 17, 2005, https://www.wsj
.com/articles/SB112951254779770349.

54. John H. Fund, "Judgment Call."

55. Greenberg, *Supreme Conflict*, 269.

56. Randy E. Barnett, "Cronyism," *Wall Street Journal*, October 4, 2005, https://www.cato.org
/commentary/cronyism.

57. George F. Will, "Can This Nomination Be Justified?" *Washington Post*, October 4, 2005,
https://www.washingtonpost.com/archive/opinions/2005/10/05/can-this-nomination
-be-justified/f3dbdacd-734d-4625-abe0-500ced761b89.

58. David Stout, "Bush Seeks to Quell Criticism of Court Nominee from the Right," *New York
Times*, October 4, 2005, https://www.nytimes.com/2005/10/04/politics/politicsspecial1
/bush-seeks-to-quell-criticism-of-court-nominee.html.

59. *Advise & Dissent*, directed by David Van Taylor, 2012.

60. Editorial Board, "The President's Stealth Nominee," *New York Times*, October 4, 2005,
https://www.nytimes.com/2005/10/04/opinion/the-presidents-stealth-nominee.html.

61. "Cautious Reception for High Court Nominee," NPR, October 3, 2005, https://www.npr
.org/2005/10/03/4933993/cautious-reception-for-high-court-nominee.

62. Sheryl Gay Stolberg, "Court in Transition: Reaction; Some Liberals and Conservatives Find
Themselves in Awkward Spots," New York Times, October 4, 2005, https://www.nytimes.com
/2005/10/04/us/court-in-transition-reaction-some-liberals-and-conservatives-find.html.

63. Arlen Specter, Never Give In (Macmillan, 2008).

64. Karl Rove, interviewed by Peter Canellos.

65. Manu Raju, "Rove Bets Big against Reid," Politico, September 15, 2010, https://www
.politico.com/story/2010/09/rove-bets-big-against-reid-042180.

66. David D. Kirkpatrick, "Endorsement of Nominee Draws Committee's Interest," New
York Times, October 10, 2005, https://www.nytimes.com/2005/10/10/us/endorsement
-of-nominee-draws-committees-interest.html.

67. Jim Manley, former Reid spokesperson, interviewed by Peter Canellos, April 16, 2025.

68. "Republican Activists Slam Miers Nomination," Washington Times, October 6, 2005,
https://www.washingtontimes.com/news/2005/oct/6/20051006-120857-8475r.

69. John Podhoretz, "Harriet Miers—Yeesh," National Review, October 8, 2005, https://www
.nationalreview.com/corner/harriet-miers-writes-yeesh-john-podhoretz/

70. Charles Krauthammer, "Withdraw This Nominee," Washington Post, October 7, 2005,
https://www.washingtonpost.com/archive/opinions/2005/10/07/withdraw-this-nominee
/3b561dba-fbc3-4e73-b55e-9d07b5e81010.

71. Kirkpatrick, "Endorsement of Nominee Draws Committee's Interest."

72. Al Kamen, "Miers's Long-Ago Federalist Slap Still Stings," Washington Post, October 20,
2005, https://www.washingtonpost.com/archive/politics/2005/10/21/mierss-long-ago
-federalist-slap-still-stings/ab562d15-5018-4096-8eac-91ec447bd512.

73. Richard W. Stevenson, "White House Dismisses Idea of Withdrawal of Nominee," New
York Times, October 14, 2005, https://www.nytimes.com/2005/10/14/us/white-house
-dismisses-idea-of-withdrawal-by-nominee.html.

74. "More Info Demanded of Miers," Associated Press, October 19, 2005, https://www
.cbsnews.com/news/more-info-demanded-from-Miers.

75. Elisabeth Bumiller and David D. Kirkpatrick, "Bush Refuses to Release Nominee's Papers," New York Times, October 25, 2005, https://www.nytimes.com/2005/10/25/us
/bush-refuses-to-release-nominees-papers.html.

76. Greenberg, Supreme Conflict, 284.

77. Bush, Decision Points, 101.

78. Rove, George W. Bush Oral History Project.

79. Gonzales, George W. Bush Oral History Project.

80. Gonzales, George W. Bush Oral History Project.

81. Ed Whelan, "Harry Reid Botches Miers Nomination," *Confirmation Tales from Ed Whelan,* May 2, 2024, https://www.confirmationtales.come/p/harry-reid-botches-miers-confirmation.

82. Bush, *Decision Points,* 101.

83. Nathan Hecht, former chief justice of the Supreme Court of Texas, interviewed by Peter Canellos and Timmy Facciola, July 11, 2025.

CHAPTER TEN: "THE SOLEMN RESPONSIBILITY"

1. Alito, "Samuel Alito on the Supreme Court, Recent Court Decisions, and His Education."

2. Alito, "Samuel Alito on the Supreme Court, Recent Court Decisions, and His Education."

3. Report on Samuel A. Alito Jr., 97 pages released in whole on PRA re-review 05/20/2025 JLS, Counsel's Office, White House, Series Title: Brett Kavanaugh, Folder Title [Alito, Samuel A.] FRC ID 9799, George W. Bush Presidential Library.

4. Report on Samuel A. Alito Jr., 93.

5. Report on Samuel A. Alito Jr., Amendments to Alito memo.

6. Nancy Benac, "Alito Leaves Mark on Others," Associated Press, November 4, 2006, https://ocala.com/story/news/2006/01/04/alito-leaves-mark-on-others/31145908007.

7. Neil A. Lewis and Scott Shane, "Alito Is Seen as a Methodical Jurist with a Clear Record," *New York Times,* October 31, 2005, https://www.nytimes.com/2005/11/01/politics /politicsspecial1/alito-is-seen-as-a-methodicaljurist-with-a-clear.html.

8. Alito, "Samuel Alito on the Supreme Court, Recent Court Decisions, and His Education."

9. "Samuel Alito Nomination Remarks," NBC News, October 31, 2005, https://www.nbc news.com/id/wbna9875730.

10. Elisabeth Bumiller, "Back at Work After Battle, Prepping the Next in Line," *New York Times,* November 14, 2025, https://www.nytimes.com/2005/11/14/politics/back-at -work-after-battle-prepping-the-next-in-line.html.

11. Bill Agress, interviewed by Peter Canellos, Timmy Facciola, and Peder Schaefer.

12. "Former Law Clerks of Samuel A. Alito, Jr., Joint Letter," US Senate, November 9, 2006, https://www.govinfo.gov/content/pkg/GPO-CHRG-ALITO/pdf/GPO-CHRG -ALITO-4-3-40.pdf.

13. Judge Alito Briefing Binder, George W. Bush Presidential Library, Press Office, WH, Perino, Dana, 3.

14. David D. Kirkpatrick, "Liberal Coalition Is Making Plans to Take Fight Beyond Abortion," *New York Times,* November 13, 2005, https://www.nytimes.com/2005/11/14 /politics/politicsspecial1/liberal-coalition-is-making-plansto-take-fight.html.

15. Elisabeth Bumiller and Carl Hulse, "Bush Picks US Appeals Judge to Take O'Connor's Court Seat," *New York Times,* October 31, 2005, https://www.nytimes.com/2005/11/01 /us/front%20page/court-in-transition-the-overview-bush-picks-us-appeals-judge.html.

16. Ralph Neas, interviewed by Peter Canellos and Timmy Facciola.

17. Ralph Neas, interviewed by Peter Canellos and Timmy Facciola.

18. Tom Hester, "Mom: 'I Cannot Be Prouder of Him,'" *Newark Star-Ledger*, November 1, 2005.

19. Jamison Foser, "Matthews Falsely Claimed Democrats Accused Alito of Being 'Lenient on the Mob,'" *Media Matters*, November 1, 2005, https://www.mediamatters.org/chris-mat thews/matthews-falsely-claimed-democrats-accused-alito-being-lenient-mob.

20. Tim Chapman, "Matthews: Democrat Attacks 'Disgusting'" *Townhall*, October 31, 2005, https://web.archive.org/web/20051102031428/http://www.townhall.com/blogs/capitol report/TimChapman/story/2005/10/31/173672.html.

21. Charles Babington, "Alito Defends His Actions in Two Appeals Court Cases," *Washington Post*, November 11, 2005, https://www.washingtonpost.com/archive/politics/2005 /11/11/alito-defends-his-actions-in-two-appeals-court-cases/b8ac27db-01d0-4127-a666 -2772445d6a3c.

22. David D. Kirkpatrick, "Judge Said He Struggled on '91 Abortion Opinion," *New York Times*, November 3, 2005, https://www.nytimes.com/2005/11/03/politics/politics special1/judge-said-he-struggled-on-91-abortion-opinion.html.

23. John A. Farrell, "Alito Assured Ted Kennedy in 2005 of Respect for Roe v. Wade, Diary Says," *New York Times*, October 24, 2022, http://www.nytimes.com/2022/10/24/us /politics/alito-kennedy-abortion.html.

24. Lincoln Chafee, former US senator and governor of Rhode Island, interviewed by Peter Canellos and Peder Schaefer, July 15, 2025.

25. Samuel A. Alito Jr., "Letter from Judge Samuel Alito to Judge Ed Becker," February 6, 2003, Edward R. Becker Papers, ser. 1, box, folder IV, MS1929, Yale University.

26. Tim Weiner, "Edward R. Becker, 73, Judge on Federal Court of Appeals, Dies," *New York Times*, May 20, 2006, https://www.nytimes.com/2006/05/20/us/20becker.html.

27. Ruth Bader Ginsberg, "Letter from Justice Ruth Bader Ginsburg to Judge Samuel Alito," November 10, 2005, Edward R. Becker Papers, ser. III, box 29, folder III, MS1929, Yale University.

28. David D. Kirkpatrick, "Interlocking Friendships Connect a Chairman and a Nominee," *New York Times*, November 8, 2005, https://www.nytimes.com/2005/11/08/politics /interlocking-friendships-connect-a-chairman-and-a-nominee.html.

29. Ron Elving, "A Fighter to the End, Arlen Specter Seemed to Thrive on Controversy," NPR, October 15, 2012, https://www.npr.org/sections/itsallpolitics/2012/10/14/162907727 /a-fighter-to-the-end-arlen-specter-seemed-to-thrive-on-controversy.

30. Kirkpatrick, "Interlocking Friendships Connect a Chairman and a Nominee."

31. Arlen Specter, "Letter from Arlen Specter to Judge Samuel Alito," December 19, 2005, Edward R. Becker Papers, ser. III, box 29, folder III, MS1929, Yale University.

32. *Confirmation Hearing on the Nomination of Samuel A. Alito*, sec. Judge Becker Statement.

33. *Confirmation Hearing on the Nomination of Samuel A. Alito*, sec. Alito Statement.

34. *Confirmation Hearing on the Nomination of Samuel A. Alito, Jr. to Be an Associate Justice of the Supreme Court of the United States*, sec. Sen. Specter Statement.

35. *Confirmation Hearing on the Nomination of John G. Roberts, Jr. to be Chief Justice of the United States*, US Senate (2005), https://www.judiciary.senate.gov/imo/media/doc/GPO-CHRG-ROBERTS.pdf.

36. *Confirmation Hearing on the Nomination of Samuel A. Alito, Jr. to Be an Associate Justice of the Supreme Court of the United States*, sec. Sen. Specter Questioning.

37. *Confirmation Hearing on the Nomination of Samuel A. Alito*, sec. Sen. Durbin Questioning.

38. Alito, "Samuel Alito Job Application 1985."

39. Report on Samuel A. Alito Jr. [97 pages released in whole on PRA re-review 05/20/2025 JLS], Counsel's Office, White House, Series Title: Brett Kavanaugh, Folder Title [Alito, Samuel A.] FRC ID 9799, George W. Bush Presidential Library.

40. *Confirmation Hearing on the Nomination of Samuel A. Alito*, sec. Sen. Leahy Questioning.

41. *Confirmation Hearing on the Nomination of Samuel A. Alito*, sec. Sen. Leahy Questioning.

42. Jim Manley, interviewed by Peter Canellos.

43. *Confirmation Hearing on the Nomination of Samuel A. Alito, Jr. to Be an Associate Justice of the Supreme Court of the United States*, sec. Sen. Kennedy Questioning.

44. *Confirmation Hearing on the Nomination of Samuel A. Alito*, sec. Sen. Kennedy Questioning.

45. *Confirmation Hearing on the Nomination of Samuel A. Alito*, sec. Sen. Kennedy Questioning.

46. *Confirmation Hearing on the Nomination of Samuel A. Alito*, sec. Sen. Kennedy Questioning.

47. *Confirmation Hearing on the Nomination of Samuel A. Alito*, sec. Sen. Kennedy Questioning.

48. *Confirmation Hearing on the Nomination of Samuel A. Alito, Jr. to Be an Associate Justice of the Supreme Court of the United States*, sec. Sen. Graham Questioning.

49. *Confirmation Hearing on the Nomination of Samuel A. Alito*, sec. Sen. Graham Questioning.

50. Libby Copeland, "Debating the Tissues: What Makes a Good Cry?" *Washington Post*, January 13, 2006, https://www.washingtonpost.com/archive/lifestyle/2006/01/13/debating-the-tissues-what-makes-a-good-cry/e502d7f6-903e-4172-8c59-fe12f54d18a8.

51. Copeland, "Debating the Tissues."

52. Copeland, "Debating the Tissues."

53. Robin Givhan, "The Alitos: Well Suited, and Dressed for Duress," *Washington Post*, January 13, 2006, https://www.washingtonpost.com/archive/lifestyle/2006/01/13/the-alitos-well-suited-and-dressed-for-duress/745cecef-5541-4a57-8694-68843710ff5f.

54. Givhan, "The Alitos: Well Suited, and Dressed for Duress."

55. Andrea Gonzalez-Ramirez, "Martha-Ann Alito Is Beefing," *New York Magazine*, June 11, 2024, https://www.thecut.com/article/martha-ann-alito-beefs-robin-givhan.html.

56. *Confirmation Hearing on the Nomination of Samuel A. Alito*, sec. Sen. Kennedy Questioning.

57. *Confirmation Hearing on the Nomination of Samuel A. Alito*, sec. Sen. Specter Questioning; William A. Rusher, "William A. Rusher Papers, 1940–2010," Manuscript Division, Library of Congress, Washington, DC.

58. Adam Nagourney, "Rove Attack Signals Strategy for Election," *New York Times*, January 22, 2006, https://www.nytimes.com/2006/01/22/world/americas/rove-attack-signals -strategy-for-election.html.

59. Michael Janofsky, "At March on the Mall, Abortion Foes Rally Behind a New Theme: Alito," *New York Times*, January 23, 2006, https://www.nytimes.com/2006/01/24 /politics/at-march-on-the-mall-abortion-foes-rally-behind-a-new-theme-alito.html.

60. David D. Kirkpatrick, "Kerry Gets Cool Response to Call to Filibuster Alito," *New York Times*, January 27, 2006, https://www.nytimes.com/2006/01/27/politics/politicsspecial1 /kerry-gets-cool-response-to-call-to-filibuster.html.

61. "On the Nomination of Samuel Alito to the Supreme Court," US Senate, January 31, 2006, https://www.senate.gov/legislative/LIS/roll_call_votes/vote1092/vote_109_2_00002 .htm; "On the Cloture Motion On the Nomination of Samuel Alito to the Supreme Court," US Senate, January 30, 2006, https://www.senate.gov/legislative/LIS/roll_call_votes /vote1092/vote_109_2_00001.htm#position.

62. "On the Cloture Motion On the Nomination of Samuel Alito to the Supreme Court."

63. Martha-Ann Alito, "Letter from Martha-Ann Alito to Judge Ed Becker."

64. Martha-Ann Alito, "Letter from Martha-Ann Alito to Judge Ed Becker."

65. Bill Agress, interviewed by Peter Canellos, Timmy Facciola, and Peder Schaefer.

66. D. Michael Fisher, "Letter from Judge D. Michael Fisher to Judge Ed Becker et al.," January 31, 2006, Edward R. Becker Papers, ser. III, box 29, folder II, MS1929, Yale University.

67. William T. Coleman Jr., "Letter from William T. Coleman to Judge Ed Becker," February 3, 2006, Edward R. Becker Papers, ser. III, box 29, folder II, Yale University.

68. Adam Nagourney, Richard W. Stevenson, and Neil A. Lewis, "Glum Democrats Can't See Halting Bush on Courts," *New York Times*, January 15, 2006, https://www.nytimes.com/2006 /01/15/politics/politicsspecial1/glum-democrats-cant-see-halting-bush-on-courts.html.

69. Lincoln Chafee, interviewed by Peter Canellos and Peder Schaefer.

70. Stuart Taylor, Jr., "Borking Alito: He Is Neither Far Right Nor Activist," *Atlantic*, November 8, 2005, https://www.theatlantic.com/magazine/archive/2005/11/borking-alito -he-is-neither-far-right-nor-activist/304436.

71. *Confirmation Hearing on the Nomination of Samuel A. Alito*, sec. Sen. Kohl Questioning.

72. Riehl, "The Federalist Society and Movement Conservatism."

CHAPTER ELEVEN: STEPPING UP, TAKING COMMAND

1. Former Alito Supreme Court clerk, interviewed by Peter Canellos and Peder Schaefer, October 14, 2025.

2. Alexander Volokh, professor of law at Emory University and former Alito Supreme Court clerk, interviewed by Peter Canellos and Peder Schaefer, November 5, 2025.

3. Riehl, "The Federalist Society and Movement Conservatism," 124; Jeffrey Toobin, "The Conservative Pipeline to the Supreme Court," *New Yorker*, April 10, 2017, https://www.newyorker.com/magazine/2017/04/17/the-conservative-pipeline-to-the-supreme-court.

4. Richard Epstein, interviewed by Peter Canellos and Peder Schaefer.

5. Robert O'Harrow Jr. and Shawn Boburg, "A Conservative Activist's Behind-the-Scenes Campaign to Remake the Nation's Courts," *Washington Post*, May 21, 2019, https://www.washingtonpost.com/graphics/2019/investigations/leonard-leo-federalists-society-courts.

6. Robin Cook, "Confirmation of High Court Justices Akin to a Political Campaign, Leo Says," *UVA Lawyer*, Fall 2006, https://www.law.virginia.edu/static/uvalawyer/html/alumni/uvalawyer/f06/leo.htm.

7. Cook, "Confirmation of High Court Justices Akin to a Political Campaign."

8. O'Harrow Jr. and Boburg, "A Conservative Activist's Behind-the-Scenes Campaign."

9. Toobin, "The Conservative Pipeline to the Supreme Court."

10. Kenneth P. Vogel and Shane Goldmacher, "An Unusual $1.6 Billion Donation Bolsters Conservatives," *New York Times*, August 22, 2022, https://www.nytimes.com/2022/08/22/us/politics/republican-dark-money.html.

11. Heidi Przybyla, "Leonard Leo Used Federalist Society Contact to Obtain $1.6 Billion Donation," *Politico*, May 2, 2023, https://www.politico.com/news/2023/05/02/leonard-leo-federalist-society-00094761.

12. Heidi Przybyla, "Dark Money and Special Deals: How Leonard Leo and His Friends Benefited from His Judicial Activism," *Politico*, March 1, 2023, https://www.politico.com/news/2023/03/01/dark-money-leonard-leo-judicial-activism-00084864; O'Harrow Jr. and Boburg, "A Conservative Activist's Behind-the-Scenes Campaign."

13. Classical Liberal Institute at NYU School of Law, Mission Statement, classicalliberalinstitute.org.

14. Richard Epstein, interviewed by Peter Canellos and Peder Schaefer.

15. Przybyla, "Dark Money and Special Deals."

16. Cook, "Confirmation of High Court Justices Akin to a Political Campaign."

17. Andy Kroll, Andrea Bernstein, Ilya Marritz, "We Don't Talk About Leonard: The Man Behind the Right's Supreme Court Supermajority," ProPublica, October 11, 2023, https://www.propublica.org/article/we-dont-talk-about-leonard-leo-supreme-court-supermajority.

18. Alexander Volokh, interviewed by Peter Canellos and Peder Schaefer.

19. American Constitution Society, Mission Statement, https://www.acslaw.org/about-us.

20. "2023: A Year in Review," American Constitution Society, www.acslaw.org/about-us/annual-reports; "Sheldon Gilbert to Become Next Federalist Society President and CEO,"

Federalist Society, December 14, 2024, https://fedsoc.org/commentary/fedsoc-blog/sheldon-gilbert-to-become-next-federalist-society-president-and-ceo.

21. Jed Glickstein, "After Midnight: The Circuit Judges and the Repeal of the Judiciary Act of 1801," *Yale Journal of Law & the Humanities* 24 (2012), 544, http://dx.doi.org/10.2139/ssrn.1809207.

22. David McCullough, *John Adams* (Simon & Schuster, 2001), 563.

23. Glickstein, "After Midnight," 547.

24. Glickstein, "After Midnight," 544.

25. Marbury v. Madison, 5 U.S. 137 (1803).

26. Dred Scott v. Sandford, 60 U.S. 393 (1857).

27. Rachel A. Shelden, "Anatomy of a Presidential Campaign from the Supreme Court Bench: John McLean, Levi Woodbury, and the Election of 1848," *Journal of Supreme Court History* 47, no. 3 (2022): 241–64, https://doi.org/10.1111/jsch.12305, 242.

28. 1980s-era Supreme Court clerk, interviewed by Peter Canellos, November 7, 2025.

29. Alexander Volokh, interviewed by Peter Canellos and Peder Schaefer; Former Alito Supreme Court clerk, interviewed by Peter Canellos and Peder Schaefer, October 14, 2025.

30. Adam Liptak, "New Clerk for Alito Has a Long Paper Trail," *New York Times*, February 19, 2006, https://www.nytimes.com/2006/02/19/weekinreview/new-clerk-for-alito-has-a-long-paper-trail.html.

31. Liptak, "New Clerk for Alito Has a Long Paper Trail."

32. "The National Italian American Foundation Reacts to Ethnic Stereotyping of Judge Alito," National Italian American Foundation, November 15, 2005, https://www.niaf.org/niaf_event/the-national-italian-american-foundation-reacts-to-ethnic-stereotyping-of-judge-alito-with-open-letter-in-the-new-york-times.

33. "Hannah Clayson Smith," International Center for Law and Religion Studies at BYU Law, https://www.iclrs.org/blurb/hannah-clayson-smith-2.

34. Hamdan v. Rumsfeld, U.S. 548 U.S. 577 (2006).

35. Hamdan v. Rumsfeld.

36. Gonzales v. Carhart, 550 U.S. 124 (2007).

37. "President Bush Signs Partial Birth Abortion Ban Act," White House Archives, November 5, 2003, https://georgewbush-whitehouse.archives.gov/news/releases/2003/11/20031105-1.html.

38. "Poll: Abortion Support Conditional," ABC News, November 21, 2003, https://abcnews.go.com/US/story?id=90413&page=1.

39. Julie Rovner, "'Partial-Birth Abortion': Separating Fact from Spin," NPR, February 21, 2006, https://www.npr.org/2006/02/21/5168163/partial-birth-abortion-separating-fact-from-spin.

40. Rovner, "'Partial-Birth Abortion.'"

41. Stenberg v. Carhart, 530 U.S. 914 (2000).

42. Gonzales v. Carhart.

43. Gonzales v. Carhart.

44. Ledbetter v. Goodyear Tire and Rubber Company, 550 U.S. 618 (2007).

45. Ledbetter v. Goodyear Tire and Rubber Company.

46. The Lilly Ledbetter Fair Pay Act, US Congress, 111th Congress, 2009–11, https://www
.congress.gov/bill/111th-congress/senate-bill/181.

47. US Constitution, Second Amendment.

48. United States v. Miller, 307 U.S. 174 (1939).

49. Lewis v. United States, 445 U.S. 55 (1980).

50. District of Columbia v. Heller, 554 U.S. 570 (2008).

51. District of Columbia v. Heller.

52. District of Columbia v. Heller.

53. McDonald v. City of Chicago, 561 U.S. 742 (2010).

54. "How the Court Works—The Justices' Conference," Supreme Court Historical Society,
https://supremecourthistory.org/how-the-court-works/the-justices-conference/.

55. United States v. Stevens, 559 U.S. 460 (2010).

56. David H. Gans, "Justices Scalia, Alito Square Off on Originalism," Constitutional Ac-
countability Center, November 4, 2010, https://www.theusconstitution.org/blog
/justices-scalia-alito-square-off-on-originalism.

57. Brown v. Entertainment Merchants Association, 564 U.S. 786 (2011).

58. Brown v. Entertainment Merchants Association.

59. Brown v. Entertainment Merchants Association.

60. Snyder v. Phelps, 562 U.S. 443 (2011).

61. Snyder v. Phelps.

62. Associated Press, "Guam Becomes First US Territory to Recognise Same-Sex Marriage," Guardian, June 5, 2015, https://www.theguardian.com/us-news/2015/jun/05
/guam-us-territory-recognise-same-sex-marriage.

63. Obergefell v. Hodges, 576 U.S. 644 (2015).

64. Anthony M. Kennedy, Life, Law, & Liberty (Simon & Schuster 2025), 222–23.

65. Obergefell v. Hodges.

66. Obergefell v. Hodges.

67. Obergefell v. Hodges.

68. Kennedy, Life, Law, & Liberty, 227.

69. Obergefell v. Hodges.

70. Obergefell v. Hodges.

71. Obergefell v. Hodges.

CHAPTER TWELVE: FREE EXERCISE

1. "Remarks by the President in State of the Union Address," White House, November 27, 2010, https://obamawhitehouse.archives.gov/the-press-office/remarks-president-state-union-address.

2. Citizens United v. FEC, 558 U.S. 310 (2010).

3. Austin v. Michigan Chamber of Commerce, 494 U.S. 652 (1990).

4. Citizens United v. FEC.

5. Kennedy, *Life, Law & Liberty*, 209; "Justice Alito, Citizens United, and the Press," Editorial, *New York Times*, November 20, 2012, https://www.nytimes.com/2012/11/20/opinion/justice-alito-citizens-united-and-the-press.html.

6. Citizens United v. FEC.

7. "Remarks by the President in State of the Union Address," White House.

8. Martin Kady II, "Justice Alito Mouths 'Not True,'" *Politico*, November 27, 2010, https://www.politico.com/blogs/politico-now/2010/01/justice-alito-mouths-not-true-024608.

9. Walther, "Sam Alito: A Civil Man."

10. Walther, "Sam Alito: A Civil Man."

11. Walther, "Sam Alito: A Civil Man."

12. Gonzalez-Ramirez, "Martha-Ann Alito Is Beefing."

13. Karl Rove, interviewed by Peter Canellos.

14. Lewis and Shane, "Alito Is Seen as a Methodical Jurist with a Clear Record."

15. Thomas, *First*, 394–95.

16. Thomas, *First*, 388.

17. Linda Greenhouse, "Sandra Day O'Connor, First Woman on the Supreme Court, Is Dead at 93," *New York Times*, December 1, 2023, https://www.nytimes.com/2023/12/01/us/sandra-day-oconnor-dead.html.

18. Amita Kelly, "McConnell: Blocking Supreme Court Nomination 'About a Principle, Not a Person,'" NPR, March 16, 2016, https://www.npr.org/2016/03/16/470664561/mcconnell-blocking-supreme-court-nomination-about-a-principle-not-a-person.

19. O'Harrow Jr. and Boburg, "A Conservative Activist's Behind-the-Scenes Campaign."

20. Bob Woodward and Robert Costa, "In a Revealing Interview, Trump Predicts a 'Massive Recession' but Intends to Eliminate the National Debt in 8 Years," *Washington Post*, April 2, 2016, https://www.washingtonpost.com/politics/in-turmoil-or-triumph-donald-trump-stands-alone/2016/04/02/8c0619b6-f8d6-11e5-a3ce-f06b5ba21f33_story.html.

21. Nick Gass, "Trump Unveils 11 Possible Supreme Court Nominees," *Politico*, May 18, 2016, https://www.politico.com/story/2016/05/trumps-supreme-court-nominees-223331.

22. Elana Schor, "Senate Confirms Gorsuch to Supreme Court," *Politico*, April 7, 2017, https://www.politico.com/story/2017/04/senate-confirms-gorsuch-to-supreme-court-237005.

23. John Bresnahan and Burgess Everett, "Kavanaugh Wins Confirmation to Supreme Court," *Politico*, October 6, 2018, https://www.politico.com/story/2018/10/06/kavanaugh-confir mation-vote-877357.

24. Greenhouse, "Ruth Bader Ginsburg, Supreme Court's Feminist Icon, Is Dead at 87."

25. Amy Howe, "Profile of a Potential Nominee: Amy Coney Barrett," *SCOTUSBlog*, September 21, 2020, https://www.scotusblog.com/2020/09/profile-of-a-potential-nominee -amy-coney-barrett.

26. Andrew Desiderio, "Senate Confirms Barrett to Supreme Court, Sealing a Conservative Majority for Decades," *Politico*, October 26, 2020, https://www.politico.com/news/2020 /10/26/senate-confirmation-barrett-supreme-court-432520.

27. Reynolds v. United States, 98 U.S. 145 (1878).

28. Sherbert v. Verner, 374 U.S. 398 (1963).

29. Employment Division v. Smith, 494 U.S. 872 (1990).

30. Fraternal Order of Police, Newark Lodge No. 12 v. City of Newark, 170 F.3d 359 (3d Cir. 1999).

31. Charles J. Cooper, interviewed by Peter Canellos and Peder Schaefer; "Becket Fund History," Becket Fund, https://becketfund.org/about-us/history; "Fraternal Order of Police v. City of Newark," Becket Fund, https://becketfund.org/case/fraternal-order-police-v-city -newark.

32. Burwell v. Hobby Lobby, 573 U.S. 682 (2014).

33. Hosanna-Tabor Evangelical Lutheran Church and School v. Equal Employment Opportunity Commission, 565 U.S. 171 (2012).

34. Our Lady of Guadalupe School v. Morrissey-Berru, 591 U.S. 732 (2020).

35. Our Lady of Guadalupe School v. Morrissey-Berru.

36. Our Lady of Guadalupe School v. Morrissey-Berru.

37. Fulton v. City of Philadelphia, 593 U.S. 522 (2021).

38. Linda Greenhouse, *Justice on the Brink: A Requiem for the Supreme Court* (Random House, 2021), 78–79.

39. Fulton v. City of Philadelphia.

40. Fulton v. City of Philadelphia.

41. Victor Phillip Muñoz, "The Original Meaning of the Free Exercise Clause: The Evidence from the First Congress," *Harvard Journal of Law and Social Policy* 31, no. 3, 1083–120, 1086, https://papers.ssrn.com/sol3/papers.cfm?abstract_id=1150780.

42. Andrew Koppelman, "Justice Alito, Originalism, and the Aztecs," *Loyola University Chicago Law Journal* 54, 445, 455, https://lawecommons.luc.edu/cgi/viewcontent.cgi?article =2812&context=luclj.

43. Mahmoud v. Taylor, 606 U.S., ____ (2025).

44. Mahmoud v. Taylor.

45. James C. Duff, "Update Regarding Exposure Draft—Advisory Opinion No. 117," July 30, 2020, Administrative Office of the United States Courts, https://fixthecourt.com/wp-con tent/uploads/2020/07/Duff-update-on-draft-of-op.-117.pdf.

46. "Ethics Policies," US Courts, https://www.uscourts.gov/administration-policies/judiciary -policies/ethics-policies.

47. Sen. Sheldon Whitehouse et al., "Letter on Advisory Opinion 117 from US Senators," May 11, 2020, https://www.whitehouse.senate.gov/wp-content/uploads/imo/media/doc /201511_Judicial%20Conference%20Letter.pdf.

48. Federal Judges, "Letter from Federal Judges in Opposition to Advisory Opinion 117," Personal communication, March 18, 2020.

49. Sen. Sheldon Whitehouse et al., "Letter on Advisory Opinion 117."

50. Duff, "Update Regarding Exposure Draft—Advisory Opinion No. 117."

51. Samuel A. Alito Jr., "Remarks to the 2020 Federalist Society National Lawyers Convention," *Harvard Journal of Law & Public Policy* 45, 84–101, https://journals.law.harvard.edu /jlpp/wp-content/uploads/sites/90/2022/02/ALITO_VOL45_ISS1.pdf, 85–86.

52. Alito, "Remarks to the 2020 Federalist Society National Lawyers Convention," 87.

53. Alito, "Remarks to the 2020 Federalist Society National Lawyers Convention," 89.

54. Alito, "Remarks to the 2020 Federalist Society National Lawyers Convention," 86.

55. Calvary Chapel Dayton Valley v. Sisolak, 140 S. Ct. 2604 (2020).

56. Alito, "Remarks to the 2020 Federalist Society National Lawyers Convention," 93.

57. Alito, "Remarks to the 2020 Federalist Society National Lawyers Convention," 94.

58. Masterpiece Cakeshop v. Colorado, 138 S. Ct. 1719 (2018).

59. Alito, "Remarks to the 2020 Federalist Society National Lawyers Convention," 96.

60. Alito, "Remarks to the 2020 Federalist Society National Lawyers Convention," 98–99.

61. Alito, "Remarks to the 2020 Federalist Society National Lawyers Convention," 99.

62. Federalist Society member, interviewed by Peter Canellos, January 10, 2025.

CHAPTER THIRTEEN: THE BACKLASH

1. Nate Raymond, "US Supreme Court's Alito Cancels Conference Appearance After Abortion Ruling Leak," Reuters, May 5, 2022, https://www.reuters.com/legal/gov ernment/us-supreme-courts-alito-cancels-conference-appearance-after-abortion-ruling -leak-2022-05-04.

2. Kevin Wolf, "Demonstrators Show Their Support for Supreme Court Justice Samuel A. Alito Outside His Home in Alexandria on May 5," Associated Press photo published in *Washington Post*, May 12, 2022, https://www.washingtonpost.com/opinions/2022/05/12 /alito-draft-opinion-myths.

3. Ford Fischer, "Protestors March to Home of Justice Alito," X.com, May 9, 2022, https://x .com/FordFischer/status/1523810337601949696.

4. Bill McCarthy, "How a Rumor about Justice Alito in 'Hiding' Jumped to Primetime TV," *PolitiFact*, May 11, 2022, https://www.politifact.com/article/2022/may/11/how-rumor -about-alito-hiding-moved-primetime-tv.

5. Nina Totenberg, "An Attacker Killed a Judge's Son. Now She Wants to Protect Other Families," NPR, November 20, 2020, https://www.npr.org/2020/11/20/936717194 /a-judge-watched-her-son-die-now-she-wants-to-protect-other-judicial-families.

6. Alito and Malcolm, "A Conversation with Justice Samuel Alito."

7. Suzanne Monyak and Jacqueline Thomsen, "Would-be Kavanaugh Assassin Gets Just Over 8 Years in Prison," *Bloomberg News*, October 3, 2025, https://news.bloomberglaw .com/us-law-week/would-be-kavanaugh-assassin-gets-more-than-eight-years-in-prison; Suzanne Monyak, "Federal Judges Got Over 500 Threats Since October, Marshals Say," *Bloomberg News*, September 10, 2025, https://news.bloomberglaw.com/us-law-week /federal-judges-got-over-500-threats-since-october-marshals-say.

8. Alito and Malcolm, "A Conversation with Justice Samuel Alito."

9. Alito acquaintance, interviewed by Peter Canellos, November 17, 2025.

10. Hailey Fuchs, Josh Gerstein, and Peter S. Canellos, "Justices Shield Spouses' Work from Potential Conflict-of-Interest Disclosures," *Politico*, September 29, 2022, https:// www.politico.com/news/2022/09/29/justices-spouses-conflict-of-interest-disclosures -00059549.

11. "Read the Financial Disclosures from Justices Clarence Thomas and Samuel Alito," *Politico*, August 31, 2023, https://www.politico.com/news/2023/08/31/financial-disclosures -clarence-thomas-samuel-alito-scotus-00113595.

12. Justin Elliott, Joshua Kaplan, and Alex Mierjeski, "Clarence Thomas and the Billionaire," ProPublica, April 6, 2023, https://www.propublica.org/article/clarence-thomas-scotus -undisclosed-luxury-travel-gifts-crow.

13. Justin Elliott, Joshua Kaplan, and Alex Mierjeski, "Justice Samuel Alito Took Luxury Fishing Vacation with GOP Billionaire Who Later Had Cases Before the Court," ProPublica, June 20, 2023, https://www.propublica.org/article/samuel-alito-luxury-fishing -trip-paul-singer-scotus-supreme-court.

14. Paul Fahri and Robert Barnes, "ProPublica Asked About Alito's travel. He Responded in the Wall Street Journal," *Washington Post*, June 21, 2023, https://www.washington post.com/media/2023/06/21/alito-wsj-propublica-fishing-trip; Samuel A. Alito Jr. "Justice Samuel Alito: ProPublica Misleads Its Readers," *Wall Street Journal*, June 20, 2023, https://www.wsj.com/opinion/propublica-misleads-its-readers-alito-gifts-disclosure -alaska-singer-23b51eda.

15. "ProPublica's Fishing Expedition for Justice Alito," *Wall Street Journal*, June 21, 2023, https://www.wsj.com/opinion/justice-samuel-alito-propublica-fishing-trip-alaska-paul -singer-supreme-court-5f4bd925.

16. See Alito's interview with John Malcolm at the Heritage Foundation (2022); interview with *Weekly Standard* founder William Kristol (2015); interview with *American Spectator* writer Matthew Walther (2014); Federalist Society speech (2020); commencement address to Catholic University of America (2008); speech to Notre Dame Religious Liberty Summit (2022); keynote address to "Making Moral Men 30th Anniversary Conference, Catholic University (2023); commencement address at Franciscan University (2024); interview with *Wall Street Journal* editorial page (2023); interview with Hoover Institution (2025).

17. David B. Rivkin and James Taranto, "Samuel Alito, the Court's Plain-Spoken Defender," *Wall Street Journal,* July 28, 2023, https://www.wsj.com/opinion/samuel-alito-the -supreme-courts-plain-spoken-defender-precedent-ethics-originalism-5e3e9a7.

18. Elliott, Kaplan, and Mierjeski, "Justice Samuel Alito Took Luxury Fishing Vacation."

19. Republic of Argentina v. NML Capital Ltd., 573 U.S. 134 (2014).

20. "Testimony of Rev. Robert Schenck," US House of Representatives Committee on the Judiciary, Congress, December 8, 2022, https://www.congress.gov/117/meeting/house /115220/witnesses/HHRG-117-JU00-Wstate-SchenckR-20221208.pdf.

21. Rev. Robert Schenck, interviewed by Peter Canellos, November 17, 2025.

22. Peter Canellos and Josh Gerstein, "'Operation Higher Court': Inside the Religious Right's Efforts to Wine and Dine Supreme Court Justices," *Politico,* July 8, 2022, https://www .politico.com/news/2022/07/08/religious-right-supreme-court-00044739.

23. Rev. Robert Schenck, interviewed by Peter Canellos.

24. "Judicial Salaries: Supreme Court Justices," Federal Judicial Center, https://www.fjc.gov /history/judges/judicial-salaries-supreme-court-justices.

25. Rev. Robert Schenck, interviewed by Peter Canellos.

26. Jodi Kantor and Jo Becker, "Former Anti-Abortion Leader Alleges Another Supreme Court Breach," *New York Times,* November 19, 2022, https://www.nytimes.com/2022/11 /19/us/supreme-court-leak-abortion-roe-wade.html.

27. Canellos and Gerstein, "'Operation Higher Court.'"

28. Rev. Rob Schenck, interviewed by Peter Canellos.

29. Rev. Rob Schenck, interviewed by Peter Canellos.

30. Rev. Rob Schenck, interviewed by Peter Canellos.

31. "Testimony of Rev. Robert Schenck," US House of Representatives Committee on the Judiciary.

32. Kantor and Becker, "Former Anti-Abortion Leader Alleges Another Supreme Court Breach."

33. Rev. Robert Schenck, interviewed by Peter Canellos.

34. Kennedy, *Life, Law & Liberty,* 224.

35. Tracey E. George, Mitu Gulati, and Albert Yoon, "Beyond Merit: The Hidden Gatekeepers to Supreme Court Clerkships," Vanderbilt Law Research Paper No. 5375406, Virginia

Public Law and Legal Theory Research Paper No. 2025-61, Virginia Law and Economics Research Paper No. 2025-17, August 1, 2025, 38, https://doi.org/10.2139/ssrn.5375406.

36. George, Gulati, and Yoon, "Beyond Merit"; twenty-five Alito clerks attended Yale Law School, sixteen attended Harvard Law School, and four attended Stanford Law School— that amounts to forty-five clerks, or 51.7 percent of all eighty-seven Alito clerks. Data compiled from publicly available clerkship sources.

37. Twenty-five Alito clerks attended Yale Law School, or 28.7 percent of all eighty-seven Alito clerks. Data compiled from publicly available clerkship sources.

38. Adam Feldman, "Supreme Court Clerks and Networks of Power," *SCOTUSblog*, October 20, 2025, https://www.scotusblog.com/2025/10/supreme-court-clerks-and-networks -of-power; Adam Feldman, "Clerks, Chambers, and Power: The Networks Behind the Court," *Legalytics*, September 19, 2025, https://legalytics.substack.com/p/clerks -chambers-and-power-the-networks.

39. Feldman, "Clerks, Chambers, and Power."

40. George, Gulati, and Yoon, "Beyond Merit," 42–45; Feldman, "Supreme Court Clerks and Networks of Power."

41. The eleven former Alito Third Circuit clerks who also clerked with Alito on the Supreme Court are Hannah Clayson Smith, Mike Lee, Matthew A. Schwartz, Adam G. Ciongoli, Christopher J. Paolella, David H. Moore, James A. Hunter, Geoffrey J. Michael, Jack L. White, Michael Hun Park, and John W. Cerreta.

42. Alito selected seven clerks from Griffith, seven from Thapar, six from Pryor, five from Hardiman, five from Kavanaugh, and five from Sutton. Including Alito's own eleven clerks selected from his Third Circuit chambers, that amounts to forty-six clerks, or 52.8 percent of his eighty-seven Supreme Court clerks. Data compiled from publicly available clerkship sources.

43. Former Alito clerks, including Trump administration officials from both terms, are David H. Moore (USAID), Tara Morrissey (DOJ), Steven Menashi (White House), Ryan Dean Newman (DOJ and DoD), William Ranney Levi (White House and DOJ), Claire McCusker Murray (White House and DOJ), Paul J. Ray (White House), Michael McGinley (White House), Jonathan Berry (DOL, White House and Trump transition), Sopan Joshi (DOJ), Alex Potapov (FTC), Sean Mirski (State), Aimee Brown (DOJ), Taylor C. Hoogendoorn (FTC), T. Elliot Gaiser (OLC), Joshua Hanley (DOGE); US senator is Mike Lee, federal judges are Whitney Downs Hermandorfer, Andy Oldham, Steven Menashi, and Michael Hun Park, law school professors are Alexander Volokh, Jose J. Alicea, Sherif Girgis, and Edward Garrett West Jr., Ron DeSantis aide is Ryan Dean Newman, former Ken Paxton aides are Zina Bash and Aaron Lloyd Nielson, DOGE member is Joshua Hanley.

44. "Adam G. Ciongoli," Fox Corporation, https://www.foxcorporation.com/management /executive-team/adam-ciongoli.

45. "Hannah Clayson Smith," BYU International Center for Law and Religious Studies, https://www.iclrs.org/blurb/hannah-clayson-smith.

46. Former Alito clerks include Biden administration officials and campaign staffers Dana Ann Remus (Biden White House counsel) and Amit Agarwal (Biden reelection campaign senior counsel).

47. Former Alito clerks who have donated to Democrats include Alexander Volokh, Ben Horwich, and Amit Agarwal. See donation records at www.fec.gov/data.

48. Former Alito clerk, interviewed by Peter Canellos, April 2, 2025; former Alito clerk, interviewed by Peter Canellos, April 4, 2025.

49. Former Alito clerk, interviewed by Peter Canellos, April 2, 2025.

50. Judge Richard Clifton, interviewed by Peter Canellos and Peder Schaefer; Arthur Aidala, lawyer and Alito friend, interviewed by Peter Canellos and Timmy Facciola, August 15, 2025; former Alito clerk, interviewed by Peter Canellos, April 2, 2025; Alito acquaintance, interviewed by Peter Canellos, October 17, 2025.

51. Emily Baden, Alito neighbor, interviewed by Timmy Facciola, February 6, 2025.

52. Emily Baden, interviewed by Timmy Facciola.

53. Jodi Kantor, "At Justice Alito's House, a 'Stop the Steal' Symbol on Display," *New York Times*, May 16, 2024, https://www.nytimes.com/2024/05/16/us/justice-alito-upside-down-flag.html.

54. Jodi Kantor, "The Alitos, the Neighborhood Clash, and the Upside-Down Flag," *New York Times*, May 28, 2024, https://www.nytimes.com/2024/05/28/us/justice-alito-neighbors-stop-steal-flag.html.

55. Kantor, "The Alitos, the Neighborhood Clash, and the Upside-Down Flag."

56. Emily Baden, interviewed by Timmy Facciola.

57. Jodi Kantor, Julie Tate, and Aric Toler, "Another Provocative Flag Was Flown at Another Alito Home," *New York Times*, May 22, 2024, https://www.nytimes.com/2024/05/22/us/justice-alito-flag-appeal-to-heaven.html.

58. AJ Willingham, "The History Behind the Controversial 'Appeal to Heaven' Flag," CNN, May 31, 2024, https://www.cnn.com/2024/05/31/us/appeal-to-heaven-flag-meaning-cec.

59. Noah Rothman, "The *New York Times'* Specious Crusade Against Justice Alito," *National Review*, May 29, 2024, https://www.nationalreview.com/2024/05/the-new-york-times-specious-crusade-against-justice-alito.

60. Emily Baden, interviewed by Timmy Facciola.

61. "Justice Alito Questions Possibility of Political Compromise in Secret Recording," June 11, 2024, Associated Press, https://www.nbcwashington.com/news/national-international/justice-alito-questions-possibility-of-political-compromise-in-secret-recording/3638218.

62. Lauren Windsor, audiotape of conservation with Martha-Ann Alito, X.com, June 20, 2024, https://x.com/lawindsor/status/1800201783945683120.

63. Andrew Kitchenman, "Diocese Honors Alito," *Trenton Times*, June 25, 2006.

64. Steve Lash, "Alito Wins Award from Catholic Law Group in Maryland," *Daily Record*, October 30, 2014, https://thedailyrecord.com/2014/10/30/alito-wins-award-from-catho lic-law-group-in-maryland.

65. Kate Quinones, "Justice Samuel Alito to Address Record-Breaking 2024 Class at Franciscan University," Catholic News Agency, May 7, 2024, https://www.catholicnewsagency.com /amp/news/257599/justice-samuel-alito-to-address-record-breaking-2024-class-at-fran ciscan-university-of-steubenville.

66. Nina Burleigh, "Justice Alito's Royalist Cosplay," *New York Magazine*, October 31, 2024, https://nymag.com/intelligencer/article/justice-alitos-royalist-cosplay.html.

67. Peter S. Canellos, "Why We Should Worry About the Cult of RBG," *Politico*, December 25, 2018, https://www.politico.com/magazine/story/2018/12/25/on-the-basis-of-sex -review-rbg-223557.

68. Rivkin and Taranto, "Samuel Alito, the Court's Plain-Spoken Defender."

69. Robert P. George, "Introduction: The Jurisprudence of Justice Samuel Alito," *Harvard Journal of Law & Public Policy Per Curiam*, no. 12 (Spring 2023), 1, https://journals.law .harvard.edu/jlpp/wp-content/uploads/sites/90/2023/04/George-Robert-vFF-1.pdf.

70. George, "Introduction: The Jurisprudence of Justice Samuel Alito," 3.

71. Bostock v. Clayton County, 590 U.S. 644 (2020).

72. Jones v. United States, 565 U.S. 400 (2012), see also United States v. Stevens, Brown v. Entertainment Merchants Association, and Snyder v. Phelps.

73. Steven G. Calabresi and Todd W. Shaw, "The Jurisprudence of Samuel Alito," *George Washington Law Review* 87, no. 3 (May 2019), 508, https://www.gwlr.org/wp-content/up loads/2019/06/87-Geo.-Wash.-L.-Rev.-507.pdf.

74. "U.S. Supreme Court Justice Samuel Alito Says Pragmatism, Stability Should Guide Court," Columbia Law School, April 24, 2012, https://www.law.columbia.edu/news /archive/us-supreme-court-justice-samuel-alito-says-pragmatism-stability-should -guide-court.

75. Adam J. White, "Samuel Alito's Conservatism—Burkean and American," *Harvard Journal of Law & Public Policy Per Curiam*, no. 22 (Spring 2023), 14, https://journals.law.harvard .edu/jlpp/wp-content/uploads/sites/90/2023/04/White-Adam-vFF.pdf.

76. White, "Samuel Alito's Conservatism—Burkean and American," 14.

77. Peter S. Canellos, "'A Moment of Truth for the Federalist Society': Politics or Principle?" *Politico*, November 10, 2022, https://www.politico.com/news/magazine/2022/11/10/fed eralist-society-dobbs-abortion-00066067.

78. Students for Fair Admissions v. Harvard, 600 U.S. 181 (2023).

79. Amy Howe, "Supreme Court Strikes Down *Chevron*, Curtailing Power of Federal Agencies," *SCOTUSBlog*, June 28, 2024, https://www.scotusblog.com/2024/06/supreme-court -strikes-down-chevron-curtailing-power-of-federal-agencies.

80. Loper Bright Enterprises v. Raimondo, 603 U.S. 369 (2024).

81. Loper Bright Enterprises v. Raimondo.

82. John Kruzel and Andrew Chung, "US Supreme Court Rules Trump Has Broad Immunity from Prosecution," Reuters, July 1, 2024, https://www.reuters.com/legal/us-supreme-court-due-rule-trumps-immunity-bid-blockbuster-case-2024-07-01.

83. Trump v. United States, 603 U.S. 593 (2024).

84. Nixon v. Fitzgerald, 457 U.S. 731 (1982).

85. Trump v. United States.

86. Trump v. United States.

EPILOGUE: "THINGS HAVE UNFORTUNATELY CHANGED A LOT"

1. Josh Gerstein, "The Tariff Case Puts the Supreme Court's Conservatives in a Bind," *Politico*, November 5, 2025, https://www.politico.com/news/2025/11/05/donald-trump-tariffs-case-supreme-court-arguments-00635882; Amy Howe, "The Other Arguments in Trump's Tariffs Case," *SCOTUSblog*, November 4, 2025, https://www.scotusblog.com/2025/11/the-other-arguments-in-trumps-tariffs-case.

2. James Romoser, Kara Dapena, and Noah Higgins-Dunn, "A Justice-by-Justice Breakdown on Trump's Tariffs," *Wall Street Journal*, November 5, 2025, https://www.wsj.com/politics/policy/a-justice-by-justice-breakdown-on-trumps-tariffs-bb3b5cab.

3. Learning Resources v. Trump, Supreme Court of the United States, No. 24-1287 and No. 25-250, Oral argument, November 5, 2025, 124, https://www.supremecourt.gov/oral_arguments/argument_transcripts/2025/24-1287_097c.pdf.

4. "Trump's Taxing Supreme Court Argument," *National Review*, unsigned editorial, November 6, 2025, https://www.nationalreview.com/2025/11/trumps-taxing-supreme-court-argument.

5. Jill Colvin and Bill Barrow, "Trump's Vow to Only Be a Dictator on 'Day One' Follows Growing Worry Over Violent and Authoritarian Rhetoric," Associated Press, December 7, 2023, https://apnews.com/article/trump-hannity-dictator-authoritarian-presidential-election-f27e7e9d7c13fabbe3ae7dd7f1235c72.

6. Trump Tariff Tracker, *Atlantic Council*, https://www.atlanticcouncil.org/programs/geoeconomics-center/trump-tariff-tracker; Trump v. J.G.G., 04 U. S. ____ (2025); Executive Order 14160, "Protecting the Meaning and Value of American Citizenship," January 20, 2025, Federal Register, https://www.federalregister.gov/documents/2025/01/29/2025-02007/protecting-the-meaning-and-value-of-american-citizenship; Chris Hippensteel and Pooja Salhotra, "How Courts Have Ruled in Challenges to Trump's National Guard Deployments," *New York Times*, October 10, 2025, https://www.nytimes.com/2025/10/10/us/federal-courts-national-guard-trump.html; Adam Liptak, "The Fate of the Fed May Turn on Two Words: 'For Cause,'" *New York Times*, August 27, 2025, https://www

.nytimes.com/2025/08/27/us/politics/supreme-court-fed-trump.html; Alice Masquelier-Page, "USAID Workers Clear Their Desks in Trump's Final Push to Dismantle the Agency," Associated Press, February 28, 2025, https://www.ap.org/news-highlights/spotlights/2025/usaid-workers-clear-their-desks-in-trumps-final-push-to-dismantle-the-agency; Peter Stone, "How Trump Is Weaponizing the DoJ to 'Bully, Prosecute, Punish and Silence' His Foes," *Guardian*, November 4, 2025, https://www.theguardian.com/us-news/2025/nov/04/trump-department-of-justice-weaponization-enemies; Geoffrey Corn and Ken Watkin, "Attacking Drug Boats: Bending or Breaking the Law?," *War on the Rocks*, December 3, 2025, https://warontherocks.com/2025/12/attacking-drug-boats-bending-or-breaking-the-law.

7. "Emergency Docket 2025-26," *SCOTUSblog*, https://www.scotusblog.com/case-files/emergency/emergency-docket-2025.

8. State v. AIDS Vaccine Advocacy Coalition, 604 U.S. ___ (2025).

9. Mattathias Schwartz, "The Federalist Society Is Torn Between Its Legal Philosophy and Trump's Demands," *New York Times*, November 22, 2025, https://www.nytimes.com/2025/11/22/us/trump-federalist-society.html.

10. Federalist Society member, interviewed by Peter Canellos, November 13, 2025.

11. Josh Gerstein, "Todd Blanche on Defending Trump Policies Before 'Rogue Activist Judges': 'It's a War, Man,'" *Politico*, November 7, 2025, https://www.politico.com/news/2025/11/07/todd-blanche-justice-department-trump-policies-00643602; Robert Draper, "America First Legal, a Trump-Aligned Group, Is Spoiling for a Fight," *New York Times*, March 20, 2024, https://www.nytimes.com/2024/03/21/us/politics/stephen-miller-america-first-legal.html.

12. "AFL President Gene Hamilton Moderates a Federalist Society Fireside Chat with Deputy AG Todd Blanche," November 14, 2025, YouTube, https://www.youtube.com/watch?v=guXmBF1a3ro.

13. Alanna Durkin Richer and Eric Tucker, "US Attorney Under Pressure to Charge Letitia James in Mortgage Fraud Case Has Resigned," Associated Press, September 19, 2025, https://apnews.com/article/justice-department-letitia-james-siebert-trump-9ec1a96c05fa77d8acc558bd803622a2.

14. Casey Gannon, Holmes Lybrand, and Katelyn Polantz, "Uncertainty Grips US Attorney's Office in Virginia After Judge Tosses James Comey and Letitia James Cases," CNN, November 25, 2025, https://www.cnn.com/2025/11/25/politics/lindsey-halligan-justice-department-prosecutors-dont-know-whos-in-charge.

15. "AFL President Gene Hamilton Moderates a Federalist Society Fireside Chat with Deputy AG Todd Blanche."

16. Schwartz, "The Federalist Society Is Torn Between Its Legal Philosophy and Trump's Demands."

17. Paige Sutherland and Megna Chakrabarti, "The State of America's Judiciary with Judge J. Michael Luttig," *WBUR*, August 5, 2025, https://www.wbur.org/onpoint/2025/08/05/judiciary-judge-j-michael-luttig-trump.

18. United States v. Texas, 599 U.S. 670 (2023).

19. John Harrison, interviewed by Peter Canellos, June 13, 2025; Harrison, "The Unitary Executive and the Scope of Executive Power."

20. Samuel A. Alito Jr., "Samuel Alito Nomination Remarks," NBC News, October 31, 2005, https://www.nbcnews.com/id/wbna9875730.

21. Elaine Tarr, interviewed by Peder Schaefer.

22. Elaine Tarr, interviewed by Peder Schaefer.

23. Alito circuit court clerk, interviewed by Peter Canellos, April 4, 2025.

24. "Former law clerks of Samuel A. Alito, Jr., Joint Letter," US Senate, November 9, 2005, https://www.govinfo.gov/content/pkg/GPO-CHRG-ALITO/pdf/GPO-CHRG-ALITO-4-3-40.pdf.

25. "President Meets with Former Law Clerks of Judge Samuel Alito," White House, January 25, 2006, https://georgewbush-whitehouse.archives.gov/news/releases/2006/01/20060125-4.html. Bush said, "In fact, he has the strong support of all 54 of his former clerks, regardless of their political beliefs."

26. "President Meets with Former Law Clerks of Judge Samuel Alito."

27. Ellis Hanson, response to emailed questions from Peter Canellos, May 16, 2025.

28. Andrew Napolitano, interviewed by Peter Canellos and Peder Schaefer.

29. Alito friend and classmate at Princeton, interviewed by Peter Canellos and Peder Schaefer, May 14, 2025.

30. George Carpinello, interviewed by Peder Schaefer.

31. Dennis Grzezinski, interviewed by Peder Schaefer.

32. Emily Aronson, "Princeton Dedicates Building, Unveils Portrait in Honor of US Supreme Court Justice Sotomayor '76," Princeton University, April 18, 2025, https://www.princeton.edu/news/2025/04/18/princeton-dedicates-building-unveils-portrait-honor-us-supreme-court-justice.

33. Aronson, "Princeton Dedicates Building, Unveils Portrait."

34. Aronson, "Princeton Dedicates Building, Unveils Portrait."

35. *Confirmation Hearing on the Nomination of Samuel A. Alito*, sec. Alito Statement.

36. Damien Cave, "At Princeton, the Hearings Cause Unease," *New York Times*, January 13, 2006, https://www.nytimes.com/2006/01/13/politics/politicsspecial1/at-princeton-the-hearings-cause-unease.html.

37. "Robert P. George," Princeton University, https://politics.princeton.edu/people/robert-p-george.

38. "In Response to Alito '72, A Defense of Women's Rights," *Princeton Alumni Weekly*, https://paw.princeton.edu/inbox/response-alito-72-defense-womens-rights.

39. "Standing with the Women of '72," *Princeton Alumni Weekly*, https://paw.princeton.edu /inbox/standing-women-72.

40. Susan Squier, "Letter to President Eisgruber," *Princeton Alumni Weekly*, April 1, 2025, https://paw.princeton.edu/inbox/letter-president-eisgruber; Susan Squier, interviewed by Peter Canellos and Peder Schaefer; Helena Novakova, class of 1972 at Princeton, interviewed by Peter Canellos and Peder Schaefer, October 27, 2025.

41. Helena Novakova, interviewed by Peter Canellos and Peder Schaefer.

42. "I-Italy Interviews Justice Samuel A. Alito," *I-Italy*.

43. "Leadership," NJ Italian Heritage Commission, https://www.njitalianheritage.org/leadership.

44. Gilda Rorro, chairwoman emerita of the NJ Italian Heritage Commission, interviewed by Peder Schaefer, August 7, 2025.

45. The Black Ivy League and Key, "The Renaming Christopher Columbus Park after David Dinkins & Statue Removal," Change.org, June 25, 2020, https://www.change.org/p/statue -removal-and-renaming-park-of-christopher-columbus-the-renaming-christopher-colum bus-park-after-david-dinkins-statue-removal.

46. Parker, "Goodbye, Columbus: It Was Time for You to Go."

47. "Samuel Alito (Supreme Court Justice)," *We the Italians*.

48. Gilda Rorro, interviewed by Peder Schaefer.

49. Jeffrey Laurenti, interviewed by Peter Canellos and Peder Schaefer.

50. Gilda Rorro, email communication with Peder Schaefer, November 21, 2025.

51. David Karas, "Documentary by TCNJ Professor Chronicles Transformation of Trenton's Chambersburg Neighborhood," *Trenton Times*, February 18, 2013, https://www.nj.com /mercer/2013/02/new_documentary_chronicles_a_t.html.

52. "La Sirena Menu," La Sirena, Trenton, NJ, accessed February 26, 2025, https://web .archive.org/web/20250327131748/https://www.lasirenamenu.com.

53. Walther, "Sam Alito: A Civil Man."

Bibliography

Abramson, Jill, and Jane Mayer. *Strange Justice: The Selling of Clarence Thomas*. Houghton Mifflin Harcourt, 1994.

Breyer, Stephen. *Reading the Constitution: Why I Chose Pragmatism, Not Textualism*. Simon & Schuster, 2024.

Bork, Robert H. *Slouching Towards Gomorrah: Modern Liberalism and Decline*. HarperCollins, 1996.

Brock, David. *The Real Anita Hill: The Untold Story*. Macmillan, 1993.

Bronner, Ethan. *Battle for Justice: How the Bork Nomination Shook America*. W. W. Norton Company, 1989.

Bush, George W. *Decision Points*. Crown, 2010.

Calabresi, Steven Gow, and Gary Lawson. *The Meese Revolution: The Making of a Constitutional Moment*. Encounter Books, 2024.

Canellos, Peter S., ed. *Last Lion: The Fall and Rise of Ted Kennedy*. Simon & Schuster, 2009.

Ciccolella, Erasmo S. *Vibrant Life, 1886–1942: Trenton's Italian Americans*. Center for Migration Studies, 1986.

Confirmation Hearing on the Nomination of Samuel A. Alito, Jr. to Be an Associate Justice of the Supreme Court of the United States: Hearing at Committee on the Judiciary. US Senate, 2006, https://www.congress.gov/109/chrg/shrg25429/CHRG-109shrg25429.htm.

Fitzgerald, F. Scott. *This Side of Paradise*. Charles Scribner's Sons, 1920.

Gerstle, Gary. *The Rise and Fall of the Neoliberal Order: America and the World in the Free Market Era*. Oxford University Press, 2022.

Greenberg, Jan Crawford. *Supreme Conflict: The Inside Story of the Struggle for Control of the United States Supreme Court*. Penguin, 2008.

Greenhouse, Linda. *Becoming Justice Blackmun: Harry Blackmun's Supreme Court Journey*. Times Books, 2005.

Greenhouse, Linda. *Justice on the Brink: A Requiem for the Supreme Court*. Random House, 2021.

Kalman, Laura. *Yale Law School and the Sixties: Revolt and Reverberations*. University of North Carolina Press, 2010.

Kennedy, Anthony M. *Life, Law & Liberty*. Simon & Schuster 2025.

Kennedy, Duncan. *Legal Education and the Reproduction of Hierarchy: A Polemic Against the System*. New York University Press, 2007.

Langguth, A. J. *Our Vietnam*. Simon & Schuster, 2002.

McCullough, David. *John Adams*. Simon & Schuster, 2001.

Noonan, Peggy. *What I Saw at the Revolution*. Random House, 1990.

Posner, Richard. *Economic Analysis of Law*. Little Brown and Company, 1986.

Reich, Charles. *The Greening of America*. Random House, 1970.

Rove, Karl. *Courage and Consequences: My Life as a Conservative in the Fight*. Simon & Schuster, 2010.

Savage, Charlie. *Takeover: The Return of the Imperial President and the Subversion of American Democracy*. Little, Brown, 2007.

Scalia, Antonin. *Scalia Speaks: Reflections on Law, Faith, and Life Well Lived*. Crown Forum, 2017.

Specter, Arlen. *Never Give In*. Macmillan, 2008.

Starr, Dennis J. *The Italians of New Jersey*. Collections of the New Jersey Historical Society, 1985.

Teles, Steven. *The Rise of the Conservative Legal Movement: The Battle for Control of the Law*. Princeton University Press.

Thomas, Evan. *First: Sandra Day O'Connor*. Random House, 2019.

Trump, Mary L. *Too Much and Never Enough: How My Family Created the World's Most Dangerous Man*. Simon & Schuster, 2020.

Wilentz, Sean. *The Age of Reagan: A History, 1974–2008*. Harper, 2008.

Zink, Clifford W., and Dorothy White Hartman. *Spanning the Industrial Age: The John A. Roebling's Sons Company*. Trenton Roebling Community Development Corporation, 1992.

Zinn, Howard. *A People's History of the United States*. HarperCollins Publishers, 2015.

Image Credits

Plate 1. Trentoniana Local History Archive, Trenton Free Public Library, Trenton, New Jersey

Plate 2. Jerome Fritz / *Trenton Times*

Plate 3. Mel Evans / Associated Press·

Plate 4. *Trenton Times*

Plate 5. *The Cresset* / Steinert High School

Plate 6. © 1970 The Daily Princetonian Publishing Co., republished with permission

Plate 7. © 1970 The Daily Princetonian Publishing Co., republished with permission

Plate 8. © 1971 The Daily Princetonian Publishing Co., republished with permission

Plate 9. Princeton University Publications Collection, Princeton University Archives, Department of Special Collections, Princeton University Library

Plate 10. Princeton University Publications Collection, Princeton University Archives, Department of Special Collections, Princeton University Library

Plate 11. *Doonesbury* © 1971 G. B. Trudeau, reprinted with permission of Andrews McMeel Syndication. All rights reserved.

Plate 12. Used with permission of Harvard University / Law School, from *Unbound: Harvard Journal of the Legal Left*, vol. 10, 2015, permission conveyed through Copyright Clearance Center, Inc.

Plate 13. Bettmann/Getty

Plate 14. Mike Benedetti / Wikimedia Commons

Plate 15. Mel Evans / Associated Press via the Alito family

Plate 16. Mandel Ngan / Getty

Plate 17. George W. Bush White House Photo Office

Plate 18. Joe Raedle / Getty

Plate 19. *The Washington Post* / Getty

Plate 20. Tasos Katopodis / Getty

Plate 21. *The Washington Post* / Getty

Plate 22. Rich Hundley III

Index

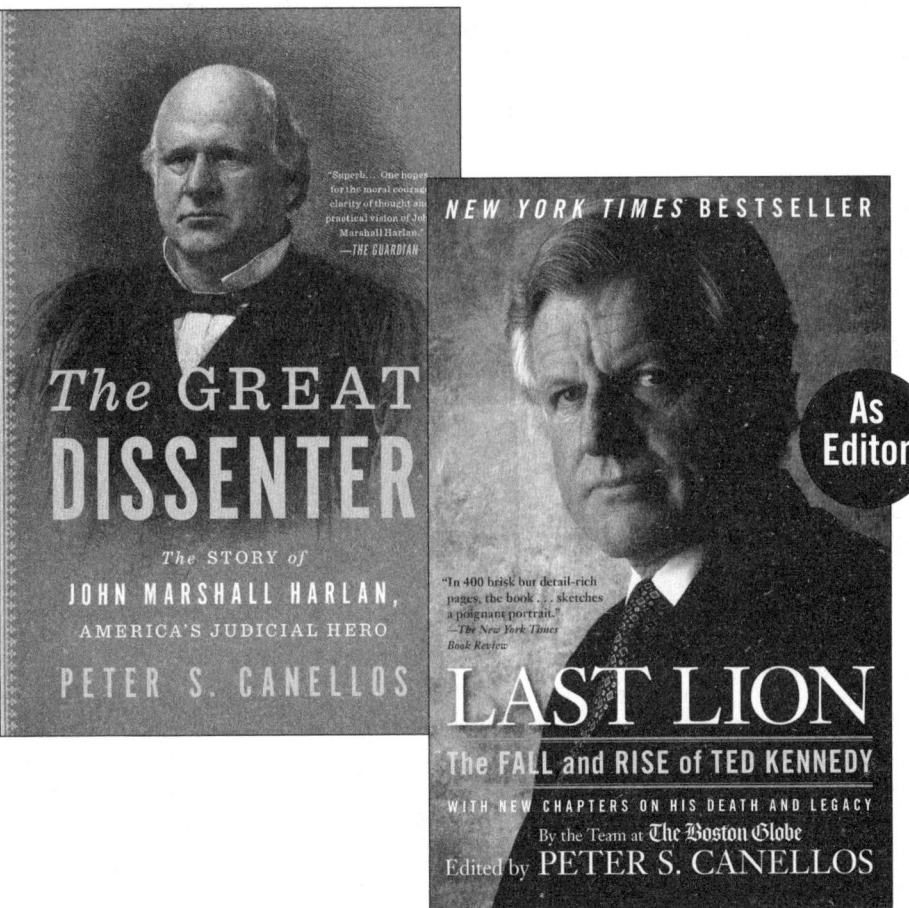